CW00926257

Advertising Works 24

Proving the payback on marketing investment

Case studies from the IPA Effectiveness Awards 2018

Edited and introduced by
Neil Godber
Convenor of Judges

First published 2018 by WARC
85 Newman Street, London W1T 3EU
Telephone: 0207 467 8100
Email: enquiries@warc.com
www.warc.com

A CIP catalogue record for this book is available from the British Library

ISBN: 978-1-84116-229-4

Typeset by HWA Text and Data Management, London
Printed and bound by CPI Group (UK) Ltd, Croydon, CR0 4YY

Contents

SECTION 3 SILVER WINNERS

Sponsors

The success of the 2018 IPA Effectiveness Awards is in no small part down to its sponsors, and the IPA would like to thank the companies listed here for their continuing support.

System1

WARC

Acknowledgements

Many people worked hard to make the Awards a success, especially the following: Neil Godber, Convenor of Judges, and Sue Unerman, Deputy Convenor of Judges

At the IPA, the team were: Lewis Coe, Robin Forrester, Ava Gill, Carlos Grande, Maria Grey, Tessa Gooding, Kay Heenan, Janet Hull, Roger Ingham, Rachael Lynch, Kathryn Patten, Kirsty Walker, Sylvia Wood, and Charlie Young.

We also owe a debt of gratitude to:

The IPA Awards Board Members

1980/82 Convenor of Judges, Simon Broadbent (d)	
1984/86 Convenor of Judges, Charles Channon (d)	
1988/90 Convenor of Judges, Paul Feldwick	
1992/94 Convenor of Judges, Chris Baker	Bacon Strategy and Research
1996 Convenor of Judges, Gary Duckworth	Paths with Heart
1998 Convenor of Judges, Nick Kendall	Bro-Ken
2000 Convenor of Judges, Tim Broadbent (d)	
2002 Convenor of Judges, Marco Rimini	Mindshare
2004 Convenor of Judges, Alison Hoad	BBH
2005 Convenor of Judges, Les Binet	adam&eveDDB
2006 Convenor of Judges, Laurence Green	MullenLowe
2007 Convenor of Judges, Richard Storey	M&C Saatchi
2008 Convenor of Judges, Neil Dawson	SapientRazorfish
2009 Convenor of Judges, Andy Nairn	Lucky Generals
2010 Convenor of Judges, David Golding	adam&eveDDB
2011 Convenor of Judges, Charlie Snow	Consultant
2012 Convenor of Judges, Marie Oldham	VCCP Media
2014 Convenor of Judges, Lorna Hawtin	TBWA\Manchester
2016 Convenor of Judges, Bridget Angear	AMV BBDO
2018 Convenor of Judges, Neil Godber	J. Walter Thompson
IPA Director General, Paul Bainsfair	
IPA Director of Marketing Strategy, Janet Hull	
IPA Head of Marketing Strategy, Kathryn Patten	

The Judges

Neil Godber
Head of Planning, J. Walter Thompson
Convenor of Judges

Sue Unerman
Chief Transformation Officer, MediaCom
Deputy Convenor of Judges

INDUSTRY JUDGING PANEL

Lucy Banister
Founder
The Nursery Research and Planning

Kate Cox
VP, CMO
GoDaddy EMEA

Nikki Crumpton
Consultant
The Active Strategist

Jane Cunningham
Co-Founder
PrettyLittleHead

Andy Davidson
CSO
Flamingo Group

Russell Davies
Strategy Director
ustwo

Andy Davies
Founder
Davies+McKerr

Dr Carl Driesener
Senior Marketing Scientist
Ehrenberg-Bass Institute

Paul Edwards
Non-Executive Director

Helen Edwards
Partner
PASSIONBRAND

John Griffiths
CEO Founder
Planning Above and Beyond

Caroline Hayter
Owner
Acacia Avenue

Lucy Jameson
Founder
Uncommon London

Tom Morton
US Head of Strategy
R/GA

Ray Poynter
Founder
NewMR, The Future Place

Alex Steer
Chief Product Officer
Wavemaker

Mark Stockdale
Strategic Partner
The Effectiveness Partnership

Amelia Torode
Founder
The Fawnbrake Collective

CLIENT JUDGING PANEL

Dame Carolyn McCall, DBE
CEO, ITV
Chair of Judges

Zaid Al-Qassab
Chief Brand & Marketing Officer
BT

Helen Carroll
Director of Co-op Brand
The Co-operative Group

Steve Coghlan
Marketing Director, EMEA
Kimberly-Clark

Barnaby Dawe
Global Chief Marketing Officer
Just Eat

Mark Evans
Marketing Director
Direct Line Group

Margaret Jobling
Group Chief Marketing Officer
Centrica

Chris Pitt
UK Head of Marketing
HSBC

Alexander Schlaubitz
VP, Marketing
Lufthansa

Lisa Thomas
Chief Brand Officer
Virgin

Anuraag Trikha
Global Brand Director
Heineken

TECHNICAL JUDGING PANEL

Alan Bloodworth
CEO EMEA, Gain Theory
Chair of Technical Judges

Sam Dias
Director
Data Sciences Group, Publicis Media

Vasileios Kourakis
Global Director, Marketing ROI
L'Oréal

Matthew Taylor
Econometrics Program Lead
Google

Jon Webb
Managing Partner
Gain Theory

Introduction

By Neil Godber
Head of Planning, J. Walter Thompson

'If you want to go down deep you do not need to travel far.'
Wittgenstein

Before we embarked on the 2018 IPA Effectiveness Awards, we were conscious of the turbulence, stress and exciting possibilities arising from the debates taking place within business, marketing and creativity.

In trying to engage consumers, the ultimate arbiters of our efforts, marketers can feel pulled in opposite directions. On the one hand, brands are seen as mental shortcuts simplifying choice, and on the other as beacons of meaningful purpose. The established view that communications should generate desire can seem irrelevant if demand is always-on. Mass marketing may appear wasteful when technology has the potential to hyper-personalise offerings; craft and consideration could be downgraded in favour of speed and disposability, and so on.

Given how strongly proponents assert their different creeds, this can feel like a conflicted era defined by neophilia, dogma, opposition, and either/or perspectives. Sitting on the fence is rarely a comfortable position to take.

So for people working within this world, we wanted the Awards to fulfil at least two purposes. First, they should give better than best-in-class, citable examples of what can be said to be regularly working. Second, they should unearth cases of what is working at the fringes, to give us confident footholds in what may be possible, from communications serving different business models to snapshots of the future of technology or new uses and ways of combining existing media and methods.

Reflecting our ambitions, we pushed to invite a wider range of agencies and clients to enter the Awards, suggested papers use co-authors to combine talents, and encouraged different-shaped solutions incorporating a more pluralist approach to creative thinking.

What we've seen in the 2018 entries are gems of technologically enabled communications – using AI in the case of cough remedy Prospan; practical applications of mass personalisation in L'Oréal Paris's True Match; sponsorship that worked in similar ways to TV shows, and intelligent business uses of advertising to defend brand territory.

We also saw a range of timely returns to effective first principles through analysis of brand fundamentals for Audi, the triumph of emotion over short-term response for The AA and deep empathetic understanding of the sense of belonging that the British Army could offer new recruits.

From what we've seen, we believe that this should be an age of curiosity, openness and experimentation, of eagerly anticipated test cases exploring new ways to apply technology, data, experience, imagination and rigour – all in service of building businesses. It should be characterised by versatility, fluidity, craft, and appreciation. Just as the greatest sportspeople, artists, inventors, and businesspeople don't stop their existing practices when new opportunities arise, but enthusiastically incorporate them into their armoury of options, so should we.

So please read and re-read, cite, steal, quote, copy, and download the cases in this book to propel your own success. When you win, we all win.

SPECIAL PRIZES

Grand Prix
Audi UK

Best New Learning (The Channon Prize)
Direct Line Group

Best International (The Tim Broadbent Prize)
Heineken

Best Multi-Market
Heineken

Best Small Budget
Ella's Kitchen

Best Use of Social Media (The #IPASocialWorks Prize)
L'Oréal Paris True Match

Best Use of Tech-Led Data (The President's Prize)
Prospan

Best Dedication to Effectiveness (The Simon Broadbent Prize)
Diageo

Effectiveness Company of the Year
BBH

Effectiveness Network of the Year
McCann

SECTION 1

New learning

Forward to basics

By Helen Edwards
Partner, PASSIONBRAND

Some ten years ago, struggling to steer a small business through the recession, I found myself one Sunday evening putting the final touches to an RFP for a global marketing-training assignment. Due the next day, obviously.

I was happy with my answers to most of the questions on the form, but one had bugged me from the off and I'd dodged it since. It asked: 'In what ways will marketing have changed a decade from now?'

The answer I wanted to give – 'How the hell should I know?' – would earn me zero points for smarts even if I picked up the odd one for honesty. I had to do better than that.

With time running out, bemusement turned to irritation. What did the procurement team hope to gain from such an open-ended question? Would it really reveal the one potential partner whose prescience and insight would be obvious long before the event? Or was it there to give them a bit of light relief on a Tuesday afternoon as they reviewed the ever-more fanciful predictions from the competing agencies, none of which would ever materialise?

In the end I opted for a two-pronged answer, and it's one I can recommend if you are ever asked a similarly daft question. Not because it won the contract – it didn't – but because, over any ten-year period, it is guaranteed to be true:

1. Marketing will be completely different.
2. Marketing will be exactly the same.

From memory I extemporised a bit from there, but that was the gist of it. And look – it turns out to be spot on. Point 1 is self-evidently accurate. These are just some of the changes that have swept in on the ecology of our discipline since 2008: Instagram, Snapchat, Siri, chatbots, the burgeoning possibilities of AI and the Internet of Things, the intensifying tech 'duopoly', GDPR, the inexorable rise of adtech and programmatic buying – not to mention Brexit and Trump.

It is also obvious – if you are prepared to dig a bit deeper – that nothing has changed at the level of fundamentals. How could it? We are dealing with ancient neurological circuitry known as human nature, first wired sometime around 10,000 years ago and modified at only the ponderous pace of evolution since. The advertiser's task of drawing people in through appeal to primitive emotions, ensuring that any rational hurdle is easily cleared, and carving out positive memory structures for the brand is neither new nor mutable.

General, particular. Particular, general. One shifts, the other stays put.

Working in marketing over the last ten years has been like gazing at one of those time-lapse cityscape scenes, where the heavens are constantly hurtling, while the edifices beneath solidly stand their ground. It's a strange ride: the feeling of both constant, swirling, dizzying momentum, and, at the same time, steadfast, calming implacability.

Marketers, to survive, need to keep their eyes on the sky and their feet on the ground. Those who ignore the weather are quickly marked down as Luddites and find themselves justly missing out on the corporate prizes.

Curiously, though, the industry is more forgiving of those who preach the 'change' mantra at the expense of the underlying basics, and can even accord them a certain star status. Just a couple of years ago, PepsiCo's Brad Jakeman informed a rapt audience at the ANA Masters of Marketing conference in Orlando that 'best practice is dead'. His counsel for the agency people in the crowd was 'not to expect what worked last year to work today'.

At a tactical level – channel choice, perhaps – that might be fair advice. At the level of fundamentals, and especially at the interface between consumption practice and human emotions, it is way off the mark. Approaches that worked not just a year ago but in, say, 1957 might well still apply.

It was clear from some of the winning entries at the IPA Effectiveness judging this year that agencies are not giving mindless credence to the protestations of the everything-has-changed brigade. But it's not that they have assumed a blinkered, 'back-to-basics' approach either. Rather, they have fused contemporary technological and data-harnessing possibilities with classical marketing theory: forward to basics.

The most elegant example of that was the paper from the British Army, via agencies Karmarama and MediaCom. Facing the pincer problem of ambitious recruitment targets and dwindling numbers in the key 16–24 demographic group, the team knew it had to widen the appeal of this life choice beyond the typical 'army types' – because there were no longer enough of them.

Sophisticated data mining revealed 12 'drivers' that could motivate young people in the next attitudinal tier down. Many modern strategists would stop right there and use smart digital targeting to best match individual driver to individual candidate. Instead, the team first took a step back and recognised that precision ordnance would be ineffective without a 'powerful, surprising and universally appealing' emotional benefit that could make people consider the Army in the first place.

How did they find it? By going out to where today's army people were and talking to them: the agency's foot soldiers among the military professionals doing face-to-face exchanges in the field.

The result was an emotionally charged, yet non-obvious, benefit of army life – brotherhood, camaraderie – initially dramatised in TV ads culminating in the line 'This is belonging'. A variant of that line – 'Find where you belong' – could now be used to pick off and give emotional unity to the 12 'drivers' in precision-targeted social and online media.

As the paper's authors concluded, the strategists had succeeded by 'embracing new tools alongside classical techniques'. It's a combination that helped achieve a 38% upsurge in regular solider applications. Taxpayers will be thankful for that.

Another brand with recruitment issues was the AA – once the UK's most trusted brand, but in recent years suffering serious erosion in brand perceptions. It wasn't hard to see the reason for that: for a decade the brand had piled almost all marketing expenditure into direct-response promotions to existing members. But neither was it easy to stop it, since it brought in short-term revenue.

By 2015, with AA membership in a spiral of decline, agency adam&eveDDB found itself arguing for the most elemental marketing principle of all: brand building. But, as the agency observed, it would take a courageous board to sanction this 'imprecise' activity in place of one that at least paid the bills.

Courageous they were. The resulting strategy aimed at moving the communications target from 'members to masses', and giving new people reasons to connect. It didn't ditch DR – a balance needed to be struck between long- and short-term returns – but reduced it to 40% of total expenditure. The bulk was diverted to television, with a campaign that lionised the AA's roadside heroics. Print and online executions were better linked through strong yellow-and-black colour coding.

So far, so basic. The added sophistication came in 2017 with an attitudinal segmentation created by partnering with a data strategist 'better known for his work understanding voter behaviour'. By focusing on the most promising segment, and up-weighting both the emotional content of the new ads and the category share of voice, the campaign achieved hikes across the board: brand awareness, quality perceptions, purchase intention, website visits and customer acquisition.

The overall impression of this modestly argued case is of seemingly obvious steps taken remarkably well, combined with an imaginative, data-enabled 'kicker' to take results to the next level. As an example of the intelligent fusion of the classic and the contemporary, it is an instructive read.

Another take on that classic/contemporary motif, and the subject of several papers, was the discipline of reinterpreting foundational roots for today's consumers. The aim – aside from fostering an unmistakable authenticity – is to reawaken memory structures already latent in the brand. 'Fresh familiarity' is the ideal outcome, to give the brand a, literal, head start in the quest for the prize of 'mental availability'.

As agency BBH observed in its paper for Weetabix, 'the brand looks back in order to go forward'. In this case, there was a forward-facing technique even to the process of retrospection: the agency worked with neuroscientists, commissioned a pioneering analysis from Ebiquity into which kinds of asset had the most effect, and recruited the specialists at Decode to explore the latent value in over 30 existing Weetabix assets – from pack colour to historical advertising characters.

The result was the discovery of 'a Rembrandt in the attic' – an asset that the professionals on the brand had all but forgotten, though consumers hadn't. The old slogan 'Have you had your Weetabix?' still resonated strongly, despite almost a decade in the dark.

Reinterpretation came in the form of the retelling of the fable 'Jack and the Beanstalk'. The rewards, in a declining market that was increasingly threatened by own-label brands, were a 2% sales increase, and a 0.2% market share gain. A brand that had been in stasis was moving forward again.

BBH was also behind the paper for Audi, and this time, let's start with the results. Between 2015 and 2018 its advertising helped sell more cars at a higher specification, grow three times faster than the UK market and 2.5 times faster than Audi globally, increase lifetime customer value, and create £1.7bn of incremental sales. How had the brand achieved this, from its position in 2014 where it lagged in the higher-specification models and seriously underperformed on price?

The answer comes back to Audi's 36-year-old slogan, 'Vorsprung durch Technik', which it did not merely retain, nor merely reinterpret, but navigated by: a north star to guide its new strategy of 'progressive premium'.

'Progressive data tools' used in the analytical phase included factor analysis from Kantar Millward Brown, which identified 'intelligent tech, performance and excitement' as the three movers of desire in the premium category. Further work on how luxury codes were changing led to a distinctively 'Audi-progressive' creative brief: 'Beautiful cars with amazing brains'.

In a pattern any agency with a car account will recognise, Audi's historic adspend had been split between 'product' and 'brand' – in this case, 89%/11% in favour of the former. That now changed to a 50/50 balance, which gave superbly crafted commercials, including the Cannes Lions Gold winner 'Clowns', enviable scope.

In its summary, BBH offers up this case as 'a study in how magic can move metal and margins'. It isn't, and it doesn't, because 'magic' has nothing to do with it. Progressive data tools, yes; stunning creative, yes; the enduring influence of a three-word fragment that isn't just a slogan but an ethos: certainly. There is no magic, or there'd be no need for the brilliance of BBH; we'd all simply reach for our wands.

Two more effectiveness fragments before I summarise.

Covonia and Yorkshire Tea both turned to rational or factual elements of their history and reinterpreted them by shining them through a cultural lens.

Covonia saw off the challenge from an upstart cough medicine by using its somewhat severe packaging, and its even more off-putting taste, to persuade users to self-identify as fighters with 'bottle', rather than wimps who fade at the merest hint of a tickly throat. Agency: Bray Leino.

Yorkshire Tea rounded on its suite of minor product virtues, and its historical ethos of doing every small thing to exacting standards, to bring 'cultural fame' to the brand. Its 'Where everything's done proper' campaign, to a track from Yorkshire band the Kaiser Chiefs, helped elevate the brand to its long-coveted No. 2 spot, finally muscling out Tetley. All the more impressive in an FMCG market where brand-switching was uncharacteristically rare; the agencies involved were Lucky Generals, and Goodstuff Communications.

For both these cases, as with the others above, modern data analytics helped unveil potential areas of strength, while mass-market TV helped drive penetration and recruit new customers.

In summary

If recent years in marketing have been characterised by an uncritical genuflection to the new, the social, the user-generated, the hyper-targeted – and to anything whatsoever with an 'e' in front of it – perhaps 2018 will go down as the year when first principles got a second chance and came through with flying colours. Long-term brand building. Emotional connection. Respect for roots. Consistency of brand assets. An open mind to all media channels, not just the fashionable few.

Best practice is not dead. It is alive and well and cohabiting with big data and precision technology – for the most part harmoniously, although you do get the occasional argument over who should take the bins out.

If that collaboration of the classic and the contemporary can power advertising effectiveness, and if that newly-supercharged efficiency can make itself felt in the wider economy, then it is as good a way as any to keep the next recession at bay.

Social grows up

By Alex Steer
Chief Product Officer, Wavemaker

Watching Mark Zuckerberg sip his water, blinking in the spotlight of the Senate hearing committee, fending off the awkward questions that his company, Facebook, had danced past for more than a decade, I wonder how many of us of a certain age shared the same thought. That this was the year in which social media grew up – and that, as for any of us coming of age, growing up has turned out to be harder and more full of compromise than we might have imagined.

The scrutiny of social media has come from shareholders as well as senators – and, of course, from advertisers and agencies, asking tougher questions about everything from viewability to the credibility of influencers. This is, we sense, as it should be. Businesses invest in their brands, and in advertising, because it is the last source of unfair advantage, building presence and perceptions that drive profit by changing minds. These Awards remain an eloquent testimony to the credible, measurable, proven impact of brand building on business results. Any medium, new or established, needs to deliver quality impacts that stick in the mind and perform in the marketplace. Our business is commerically driven, after all, and we expect high standards of our partners. The best of the new media (Facebook included) have applied themselves to measuring impacts and effectiveness with the same tenacity as the old. We expect all media to be grown-up.

And yet ... is this how we thought it would play out? Back when the authors of the Cluetrain Manifesto[1] wrote that markets are conversations; back when Facebook and Twitter were a student hangout and a meme factory untroubled by fake news and echo-chamber electioneering; back when it looked for a moment like brands online might be able to speak with an intimacy and authenticity impossible in broadcast media. Wasn't it supposed to be different? How many of us who lived through that springtime of enthusiasm look at the social media landscape today and think, *this is what we wanted to be when we grew up?*

At its worst, 'grown-up' social advertising is indistinguishable from any other broadcast medium, delivering its payload with little regard to context, feeling broadcast except for the nagging doubt that different versions of it are being seen by different people in ways we can't easily account for. Grown-up, yes, but in the way that a friend who used to play guitar and is now an accountant is grown-up: respectable, rather than respected. As several high-profile CMOs have said, playtime is over, and in the backs of our minds how many of us wish that it weren't? Social, once wildly experimental, risks being a safe bet.

And so several of this year's papers, that make heavy use of social media, give me confidence for two reasons. First, because they prove beyond doubt that social media pays back for businesses and builds brands. But second, and just as important, because they show how it does so in a way that is true to the founding spirit of social media: collaborative, plural, experimental, contentious and noisy, but ultimately humane. They are studies where social media works *because* it is social media – not grown up into something else, but into a better version of its original self. They are a reminder of what we, quite literally, signed up for.

One from many

The authors of L'Oréal Paris's True Match paper demonstrate eloquently how a problem can be turned into the source of its own solution. The foundation range, with its 23 shades to match almost any skin tone, was losing traction in a crowded market, hampered by its own complexity. The strategic solution was to see a strength in that weakness, and to put diversity at the heart of the brand's promise to its customers. The right foundation is the foundation that is right for *you*, and the '23 Shades, 23 stories' campaign brought vividly to life the truth that True Match has a foundation for every face – every shade, age and gender. This ethos – that diversity is a source of strength, not a weakness – was carried through to every part of the campaign, and most of all to its use of social media and influencer marketing to talk to very specific audiences, and highly targeted dynamic creative to maintain that sense of closeness right through to sales-driving media. The True Match campaign built the scale that a mass-market beauty brand needs, reaching 19 million people through the social activity, but building that reach layer by layer. To paraphrase Steven Spielberg, this campaign used social to talk to an audience of millions, but to talk to them one at a time. The results – a 26% increase in value share, 332,000 new customers, and a move from fifth to first place in the market – show the power of defying the average.

Breaking the rules

You would think the laws of charity advertising were enshrined in a charter somewhere deep in the UN. Conservation campaigns follow a pattern: the slow-motion shot, the serious voiceover, the painstaking appeal for help. The David Sheldrick Wildlife Trust campaign shows that you can break all these rules and succeed. In fact, the challenge the charity faced was a false sense of understanding of the causes of elephant endangerment: people were so sure that poaching was the biggest threat, that the crackdown on the ivory trade had also driven donations down by 17%. But the biggest killer of elephants is, appropriately, social: human conflict encroaching on elephant territory. Playing by the rules would have meant being one serious voice among the noise. The 'Hello in Elephant' campaign used technology and social media to bring elephants' complex body language signalling to life, encouraging people to 'translate' English into elephant.

This was an intelligent, focused use of social media to turn one voice into many, dominating activity around World Elephant Day, and increasing donations to the trust by 34%.

From shamed to shared

At its worst, social media creates an environment that magnifies our insecurities by encouraging constant comparison with the curated lives of others; and many people find themselves being shamed or abused by strangers. At its best, though, social media shows us that we are not alone and can turn an individual insecurity into a source of shared pride and strength. Sport England's paper shows insightful communications planning at work: while three-quarters of women want to exercise more, many feel ashamed to be seen doing it. The 'This girl can' campaign was social by design, using broadcast and social media together to show millions of women that breaking a sweat is nothing to be ashamed of. While broadcast media built the sense of a shared behaviour, social media was used to create hundreds of statements of individual defiance against the rule that exercise is not for girls, and delivering (in the campaign's own words) 'a kick right in the stereotypes' that led to two million women becoming more active, reducing the exercise gender gap by 13%.

Taking down walls

As marketers and advertisers we like to think a lot about the power of social media to drive sharing – but this is only possible in the first place because of the impact it has had on publishing and discovery. Part of the appeal (and, in these grown-up times, the challenge) of social media is that it lets us find ideas and creative expressions that would never normally have made their way into our lives.

The Art Institute of Chicago used social's ability to drive discovery to its advantage. It knew that its galleries and exhibitions were rich, accessible and inspiring ... but seen outside its walls, the art world can look austere and unapproachable, 'art for art people'. The 'Van Gogh's Bedroom' campaign showed that art appreciation is about exploration as much as expertise. By faithfully recreating the artist's bedroom in the style of Van Gogh's painting of it, and listing the room on Airbnb with a well-coordinated PR, influence and social media campaign around it, the institute found a new way to bring the experience of art into people's lives, and a record number of visitors to its Van Gogh exhibition, increasing revenue by $1.8 million.

Failing better

Social media's Silicon Valley founders have a famously high tolerance for learning through failure. 'Move fast and break things', originally one of Facebook's engineering principles, has become a guiding principle for a type of business that prides itself on agility and disruption. For many businesses – especially those, like food and drink retail, that have big capital investments to consider – the cost of failure can be a little higher.

The Starbucks case is, on one level, the story of how one of the world's most valuable brands used social media to sell over 11 million drinks and drive £14.9 million in additional profit back to its business. Told in that way, it might be impressive but not inspiring. But the paper tells the whole story of the Starbucks journey to understand and make the most of social media over many years. It is told with a refreshing honesty, taking a sharp look at the strategic twists and turns, both the disappointing failures and the surprise successes. If effectiveness papers can sometimes draw too straight a line between intimidating challenge, inspired solution and inevitable brilliant results, Starbucks take some delight in the unpredictability of progress. It is, for me, a model of media innovation – starting with a conviction that a brand that brings people together for coffee *should* be in social media, Starbucks set about working out how to do it in a way that is consistent with its brand, while checking in regularly to understand the impact on its business. In a world where media tend to be either well-established or here-today, gone-tomorrow, it is rare to see a case study of a brand learning to use a new medium, and bringing it to scale as an established part of the marketing mix.

Forward

The difference between growing old and growing up, as they say, is what you learn along the way. Those of us in communications and media over the last decade have had the chance to watch a mass medium growing up, a chance we may not get for another generation. For most brands, 'social' in its various guises is now an intrinsic part of their marketing efforts. The days of the 'social account' being run by the interns is, mercifully, largely over.

What does social learn next? It feels like it's in an awkward adolescence, perhaps an intern itself – the suit a bit too shiny, worn with too little self-assurance. And yet, like many teenagers, it has grown fantastically fast, even ahead of its ability to coordinate itself. In our industry, we have a tendency to talk about the growth of social and digital spend – especially the 'duopoly' of Google and Facebook – as some sort of extraordinary accident or by-product of these platforms' popularity with the public, giving too little credit to the ingenuity of the engineers and product managers who have made viable, buyable advertising products out of these wayward environments. There are going to be tough, adult conversations to come – about the ethics of echo chambers, about measurement standards, about the balance of broad and targeted delivery, and ultimately about effectiveness. But social media, while pursuing quality and impact, should avoid the temptation to file off too many of the rough edges that make it distinctive.

These papers point the way forward. Social media works best when it attaches shared meaning to brands. This is not the same as a lofty discussion about brand purpose, or the over-stated claims that people want to have conversations with brands. But brands play a role in people's lives – as badges of achievement or pride, as markers of shared interest or belief, as little units of currency for the communities we want to be part of or the lives we want to lead. Great social communication helps brands find those roles better, and play them with more humility and humanity in environments where everyone has the right to speak – against you, over you, or on your behalf. We're not asking people to talk to brands – we're asking brands to talk to people, and to listen, a little better.

Yes, social delivers reach and precision, but it also forms a proving ground for understanding a brand's relationship with its customers. Losing sight of this means we treat social media as a pure delivery and response mechanism, and focus all our efforts on the cleanest impacts and the leanest performance. This year's winners are effective because they understand that to be social is to listen, to start conversations that you allow others to finish, and to accept responsibility for the things you say and do.

Growing up should not just mean becoming outwardly respectable, though it should mean that. It should mean a commitment to retaining your enthusiasm, and balancing it with learning, so that when you fail you fail better, and when you grow you grow faster. If social media can do that, it will live up to its youthful promise, and be the better environment for brands to grow in that we first suspected it might be.

Note

1. Rick Levine, Christopher Locke, Doc Searls and David Weinberger (2000) *The Cluetrain Manifesto: The End of Business as Usual*. New York: Perseus Publishing.

Making robots do the work

By Kate Cox
VP, CMO, GoDaddy EMEA

The film *Minority Report* was released in 2002. For those of us working in advertising and media it was at the time perhaps a first glimpse of the future potential of mass personalised advertising.

Set in 2054, the film features Tom Cruise's character, John Anderton, strolling through a shopping centre in which he is targeted by numerous brands calling for his attention.

In 2018, arguably, it's the concept of a shopping mall that feels more old-fashioned than the idea of mass personalisation in advertising. Such personalisation has been much discussed recently, particularly in relation to the use of hyper-targeting and messaging on social media platforms by political parties, terrorist organisations, and pressure groups.

There has clearly been a shift in both marketing tech and media investment towards greater use of data and targeting. As an indication, according to estimates from WARC and the Internet Advertising Bureau, UK spend on programmatic advertising – defined as automated media buying of channels using data-based criteria – has increased more than fourfold since 2013 to reach £2.7bn in 2016.

However, scrolling through the 2018 IPA Effectiveness Awards papers, it tends to be Byron Sharp's tenet of building '*mass-marketing campaigns through distinctive and continuous advertising in low cost-per-thousand media*' that is more often treated as a principle of twenty-first-century marketing best practice rather than building a case entirely on mass personalisation.

It is notable that those 2018 cases that significantly incorporated targeting techniques at scale used them to build engagement or activation layers on top of mass-marketing campaigns, and not as a brand's sole activity.

We saw great cases from L'Oréal Paris True Match, Heineken and IKEA that added personalisation engagement layers to mass-marketing campaigns and from Prospan and 32Red that used data-mining techniques to make small marketing budgets punch above their weight.

L'Oréal Paris's True Match campaign delivered great success, helping the foundation brand move from fifth in the category to first in a year.

The team focused its communications on True Match's competitive advantage of having the widest range of foundation shades (23 versus the average of 12 amongst competitor brands) to fuel this dramatic turnaround.

It partnered with 23 different social media influencers across the ethnic, age and gender spectrum to highlight its 23 shades and used communications not to target a mass audience with one message, but gain a mass audience with 23 appeals started through influencer-driven social media activity.

Make no mistake, this was a mass-marketing approach but with more precision in the messaging. The campaign launched with the influencers telling their stories to their 19m social media followers in one single roadblock. These stories were then launched on TV, cinema, YouTube, Instagram and Facebook to gain mass reach, followed by a segmented programmatic display campaign using creative that contained a select number of these 23 stories, either in long form or scroller formats.

The campaign clearly achieved its goals with a short-term campaign ROI of £2.90 for every £1 invested and a long-term ROI of £5.20.

It also heralded a more inclusive approach for L'Oréal, became the launch pad for an international roll-out of this marketing strategy, and the platform for L'Oréal's first CSR activity with the Prince's Trust in 2017. It helped the team turn up the dial on engagement levels in social media whilst also utilising social media as a mass-market medium.

IKEA's 'Improve the everyday' campaign used a similar 'engagement layer' technique on top of a mass-marketing campaign. This engagement activity generated 117 different pieces of copy against 31 core audiences.

The IKEA case is interesting as it explores the interplay between this 'engagement' messaging and both the 'inspire' brand activity at the top of the funnel and 'offer' driving campaigns at the bottom to greater depth.

The engagement layer was built on insights derived from IKEA designers' product insight research about everyday problems inside people's homes. The team turned this into a messaging concept and developed audience targeting through in-depth data mining to turn conceptual audiences into buyable media targets. The team then activated these campaigns in Facebook, Instagram and Pinterest, turning the creative inspiration into a story, and then precisely targeting this versus the relevant audience.

This approach enabled the IKEA team to increase steadily the amount of budget set aside for top-of-the-funnel brand communications and reduce the amount spent on promotions and sales-driving activity. Building on the success of the top-of-the-funnel approach to grow penetration amongst new audiences, the team planned a slow decline in investment for activation spend from FY2014 to its lowest investment level ever for IKEA UK in FY2017. This shift in investment helped fund the larger-scale brand campaign, culminating with an 87%/13% split in investment between brand and activation respectively. The team also cite a 100% increase in the ROI from engagement communications from the introduction of the mass personalisation activity and a 400% increase in spend for this activity.

The authors write: '*Our campaign shows that the marriage between data, algorithms and human creativity can provide targeted relevance, delivered at scale to a collective mass audience.*'

Finally, we turn to another great example of mass personalisation being built into a mass marketing campaign as an activation layer with Heineken's sponsorship of UEFA Champions League (UCL) football. This case study used the power of machines to deliver more personalised messages to UCL fans across the globe and encourage them to make a special occasion of watching the match in large groups and to buy the right premium beer for the occasion.

The team developed a 'Personal at scale' campaign using José Mourinho, the coach of two UCL-winning sides, to encourage fans to make the next match a special occasion. This activation work was localised across 81 countries. As with other case studies discussed here, Heineken kicked off the campaign with mass-marketing messaging in the form of a 'Pep talk' seen across TV and online video to act as a rallying cry to football fans.

The campaign was then split into modular content, with 1,000 different messages in social media content platforms. To maximise peer pressure, the team created content and match reminders that could be easily shared between friends. A chatbot bearing Mourinho's likeness and character was also used to deliver custom 'excuse busters' amongst social groups. Content was customised across 81 markets with 15 key markets selected for additional brand activations.

The 81 markets with UCL activations increased sales by 13.7% over non-activated markets, which acted as a control group for the purposes of comparison. The team estimated that this brand activation campaign drove an 8.6% increase in penetration for Heineken in 2016–17.

These cases from L'Oréal Paris True Match, IKEA and Heineken provide three great examples of letting the robots do the work on top of mass-marketing activity. Within the 2018 Awards entries, there were also some fantastic examples of employing digital data-mining to drive meaningful insights into behaviours, which were then used to enable small brands to outperform in marketing terms.

The team at Prospan Australia did just that and made an extraordinary impact for its natural children's cough medicine product on very low marketing budgets. It came up with an ingenious method of analysing Google search queries and social listening data to pinpoint the exact time mums will typically start to worry about their children's winter coughs and sniffles – namely, three days after symptoms first appear.

It then harnessed the predictability of the common cold virus to propagate amongst human populations to come up with a 'cough predictor algorithm'. The algorithm was developed by overlaying temperature data, pollution stats and national health information to identify the precise window for mums to consider buying cough mixtures, suburb-by-suburb, throughout the Australian winter. Once the 'cough predictor algorithm' suggested an opportunity was imminent, digital programmatic activity was turned on in the right locations. This solution was so effective it enabled the team to reduce media costs by 67% and increase sales by 27%.

In a similar vein, the entry submitted by 32Red, the online casino gambling brand, provides some great new learning in how to apply sophisticated new data-mining and targeting techniques – in this instance, to double revenue and triple profits in just four years.

The team overhauled its online targeting systems to segment 32Red customers based on their potential future lifetime value by monitoring players' initial deposit values and periodically rechecking these deposits at different intervals after acquisition.

The case authors write that: '*Over and above Day 1, we also made reports available for each cohort of acquired players at Days 7, 14, 30, 60, 90, 180, 365 and lifetime, giving us a clear understanding which combinations of creative, media and offer drove volume into the business, but also which ultimately delivered profit.*'

This exercise enabled the team to mark out potential high-value customers at the point of acquisition and then prioritise the online journeys that led to these high-spending players' initial purchases, so they could target 'look-alikes' from within the general population.

The analysis encouraged the team to overhaul its pay-per-click (PPC) strategy, change the foundations of its SEO strategy, and rapidly expand the brand's affiliates programme. It also led to a revamp of 32Red's TV buying approach by appending this analysis to its TV planning and buying systems, and enabled the team to identify and implement more effective sponsorships with which to grow the business.

The team report that, following these changes, new customer acquisition volumes increased by 141% between 2014 and 2017. Year 1 revenues from these acquired players increased by 281%, driving a 58% increase in the average Year 1 value across 32Red's customer base. Simultaneously, the brand also reduced player churn.

In conclusion, in 2018, we are not yet delivering the future predicted in *Minority Report* in which the robots do all the work. All the case studies discussed here still required smart people to mine data to develop hypotheses, creative thinkers to turn these into insights and to develop engaging new ways of connecting with audiences, and creativity in the delivery of channels in order to turn insights into buyable media opportunities.

However, we are seeing a fabulous flourishing of creativity through a close working relationship between data, insights and algorithms, which is leading to extremely effective activity for brands and great results for businesses.

Paying performance the respect it deserves

By Chris Pitt
UK Head of Marketing, HSBC

You do not need a large marketing budget to read this chapter and you will struggle to find any awareness or brand-equity charts. Instead, you will find four stories of businesses that have understood what matters to their customers at a human level and then driven growth through relatively small investments in direct, measurable media.

Do not infer from this that brand investment is never needed or that direct marketing is either always 'the answer' or always the 'poor relation' to brand-building activities. Today's direct-media infrastructure allows better measurement and flexibility, and the ability to amend media plans and marketing investment on the fly. If your budget is small and your options to grow your business limited, then reading these cases studies could be time well spent.

All the case studies that made it through to the 2018 Effectiveness Awards client judges were impressive in their results and the quality of the evidence than underpin them.

What unites the cases highlighted in this chapter is not a common focus on digital and social channels, or a shared interest in the targeting of existing customers for the purposes of cross-selling – both of which you might have expected to feature in a chapter on performance. Instead, the connecting theme is that all of the selected cases make prominent use of data, either to understand the performance of media, to measure results, or to respond to developments in the moment.

In addition, they all operate nearly exclusively at the 'action' end of the AIDA (attention, interest, desire, action) model. However, in these cases, data-driven direct marketing techniques are not used to the exclusion of gaining an understanding of customers at a personal level. They demonstrate very clear understanding of how to motivate the chosen audiences to engage with their brands, whether the customers in question are parents attempting to wean their child or sales agents persuading a freight forwarder about the best way to transport cargo. These brands have understood not just how to get to their audience efficiently and how to measure and optimise results, but they have also shown they can deliver compelling messages built on powerful insights.

I detail below the key highlights from my perspective from these case studies. I hope you enjoy reading them as much as I have.

Ella's Kitchen

The second sentence of the Ella's Kitchen case study lays out very clearly the challenge the business was facing, one that may be familiar to many:

> *'With an ambitious growth target, yet a declining market and small budget, we needed to find a smarter way to reach parents.'*

The case goes on to show that the baby-foods brand did this very successfully, by engaging with and recruiting 40% of all new UK parents to its weaning service.

Beyond the excellent performance-marketing techniques it deployed, Ella's Kitchen also went on a voyage of self-discovery prior to the implementation of its strategy. The purpose of the organisation was reframed from making weaning products to supporting parents through their child's weaning phase. At its heart, this case has a content delivery strategy, which shifted the brand from 'sporadic content creation' to 'always-on recruitment driving'.

Rather than overtly selling to parents, the brand aimed to identify new parents and support them through the weaning process by building an online service which acknowledged that for many parents, weaning was a new and unfamiliar experience, and provided them with the tools and content to cope. The approach resulted in £12.5m of incremental sales and 28.3% growth over a three-year period. Based on the brand's £345k marketing investment, this represents a return on marketing investment (ROMI) of £12 for every £1 invested.

In this regard, Ella's Kitchen takes an approach characteristic of performance campaigns in demonstrating its impact by quantifying incremental gains to sales and revenue. What marks this case as contemporary, however, is the way in which it relied on the ability to get helpful and usable content to specific customer segments efficiently via online channels.

IAG Cargo

The subtitle of this case is 'Putting the Relationship Back into Customer Relationship Management'. And if you were in any doubt, the opening sentence of the case is:

> *'This is a story of customer relationship management done right.'*

I agree with this assertion, but it is also the story of the implementation of a very simple loyalty programme, with an added dash of personalisation in both the programme's elements and their delivery.

If, like me, you know very little about the world of international air cargo, do not let this put you off. Read this case for the lessons it can teach in how to reimagine a loyalty programme.

IAG Cargo's marketing function did not just scatter out incentives in the hope that reward alone would drive sales. Such an approach might have generated a seeming rise in sales, without leading to truly incremental growth and this shortcoming might not have been evident to the wider business outside the marketing team.

Instead, IAG's marketers took on the challenge posed by the fact that a tiny number of big IAG clients were responsible for a large chunk of its revenues. To change this dependency, the business would need to understand the needs of the small and medium-sized enterprises (SME) segment in order to provide a rewards programme that appealed to them, and persuaded them to put more of their business with IAG. In the words of the case, smaller companies comprised a prospect pool that:

> *'Offered much less value individually, but collectively offered significant revenue headroom if it could be persuaded to buy more capacity.'*

IAG Cargo expected 200 SMEs to take up the loyalty scheme. In reality, 788 signed up (+394% above target). An entire quarter's target was delivered in 28 days. Between March 2017 and February 2018, an estimated €14m of revenue was generated an additional 10,500 orders created that would have filled 65 jumbo jets. The sustainability of the programme's success was highlighted by the fact that SMEs that enrolled onto the scheme spent 18% more year-on-year with IAG Cargo.

For me, the most interesting and compelling element of this case is the attention paid to detail in the insight and delivery components. IAG Cargo identified that SMEs did not think that the cargo operator was interested in them as a customer group. The brand was not getting onto the consideration lists of SMEs since they thought that IAG Cargo was only after larger corporate accounts.

Starting with an ethnographic study that uncovered insights into the mindset of a freight forwarding agent called "Little Vinnie" (not his real name) in a warehouse in Jamaica NY, the brand's team identified and analysed the strong relationships between sales agents and freight forwarders, and between the owners of SMEs and key employees such as clerks who carried out much of the day to day business of shipping goods. It used its understanding of these dynamics to design the features of the loyalty programme.

For instance, the programme allowed sales agents the authority to implement the loyalty programme and it gave the SME owners a key say in who to say thank you to in their teams. These were excellent business decisions that turned a loyalty programme built on strong insight from good to great in a commercial sense.

Wonderbly

This case study did not make it on to the shortlist for the client judges panel. However, the case of digital children's publisher Wonderbly has its merits. Its failure to make the shortlist may be more of a reflection of the strength of the other cases that were shortlisted.

In some ways, Wonderbly is a more straightforward performance case study than IAG or Ella's Kitchen. It exemplifies direct marketing reimagined for the digital age by a digital-only business developing personalised content for a highly defined audience, with this content communicated when it is most relevant. It uses efficient and effective always-on media to drive sales and business momentum, optimised through continuous test and learn.

The authors themselves put it very well:

'The advertising is not about a big creative idea, the BIG idea here is that the product and marketing is used to connect that idea with customers at the perfect moment.'

The central sales-generating medium in the case is Facebook where the brand puts 60–70% of its investment. This investment is increased and supplemented at the Q4 seasonal peak, when 60% of sales are generated, by DRTV and out of home (OOH). This is an example of combining new with the old in a direct-marketing sense. Facebook investment was optimised through the use of custom audiences and 'look-alike' models, as well as a test-and-learn approach to Facebook creative formats.

The result of all this activity has been strong: sales of 3,000,000 personalised books and revenue of £70m. The case estimates a return on marketing investment (ROMI) of £1.77 for every £1 spent as a result of the activity delivered over a two-year period.

This ROMI figure is not as high as those in some of the case studies that reached the eyes of the client judges, but it is nonetheless impressive and evidence that a 'simple song well sung' can still deliver results. The lesson for other businesses is the value in understanding what media works for them and why it works, and in optimising activity on an ongoing basis.

32Red

This case study is not a pure example of performance in terms of media, since sports and TV programme sponsorship is also part of the mix used to drive over £100m in annual revenue and an EBITDA of £15m at the end of the period assessed. But it is in essence a tale of how to maximise the efficiency and effectiveness of classic direct media, in this case organic and paid search, affiliate marketing, and DRTV.

The tale is a very common one in highly competitive, commoditised transactional markets. 32Red is an online gambling and casino business that faced stiff business targets and competition, a challenging new tax regime in its core UK market, and high player churn. It took on these challenges head on, and won.

The strategy was simple. Rather than shifting its attention away from the UK, or away from its core casino business or its emphasis on new customer acquisition, 32Red renewed its focus in these three areas.

The business was very clear on the metrics it wanted to prioritize in its marketing, elevating return on investment (ROI) and downplaying cost per acquisition (CPA) as metrics against which its activities could be measured and optimised. This clarity seems to have pervaded the whole organisation as shown in the business strategy, marketing metrics, and direction from the very top. If you have ever wondered what connects Britney Spears, Alan Shearer and a £2 coin, then I will not spoil the surprise, except to say that you may be using more exciting and interesting language to bring to life your business objectives in 2019. It may have been called the 'Accelerated Growth Plan' by the 32Red's chief commercial officer, but that is not how I have remembered it.

According to the case results, new customer acquisition volumes increased by 141% between 2014 and 2017, at the same time as Year 1 revenue increased by 281%. Acquired customers stayed with the site for longer: with 23% of customers acquired in 2017 still playing in Month 4 compared to 15% in 2013.

This turnaround was achieved at the same time as the upfront incentives to players were being managed down. The case also offers interesting insights into how pay-per-click (PPC) investment was optimised to focus on generating customers who would drive the highest revenue, as well as how revised reporting allowed these customers to be identified and the brand's media planning to be amended live. Reporting took into account not only the profile of the customer and how much they initially deposited, but also the region they lived in, the media through which they engaged with 32Red, and the keywords which drew them to the brand.

Overall, a thought-provoking case that impressed the judges.

Congratulations to all four brands discussed here for their business success and on being published in *Advertising Works 24*.

You deserve your success and thank you for taking the time to enter the awards to share your experiences and insights with others.

Does purpose pay?

By Sue Unerman
Chief Transformation Officer, MediaCom

What is the point of 'purpose' for marcoms? It seems to be the thing that divides a room faster than whether Bob Dylan was a worthy recipient of the Nobel Prize (that is if you're sitting in the kind of room where people have an opinion about the Nobel Prize for Literature, which I am sure IPA *Advertising Works* readers are).

When it comes to 'purpose' very often the cynics dominate. Cynics will say: 'They're only doing it to make money, they don't mean it'. Or they will state 'They're just doing it because they haven't got anything else differentiating to say about their product'. On the other hand, there are the idealists, those who think every brand should be doing work that is making the world a better place, even if there's no evidence that doing so delivers business results.

This chapter doesn't argue one way or another about the motives of a business in delivering campaigns with purpose. (In fact, of course, there is no requirement for the papers to show evidence about the intent, just about its effect on business outcomes.) Within a large organisation there are probably some who truly believe in the purpose and others who primarily see it as a useful marketing tool. The point is that both sides can win. It is possible and here proven that you can do good for the world and do good for the business.

Purpose does pay. A couple of this year's papers have given an object lesson in how to deliver purpose for their business.

There are two ways in which this is demonstrated in this body of work.

- *Purpose motivates employees:* having a higher purpose to the communications helps employees feel positive about the day job and creates opportunities for the business to get more from them.
- *Purpose boosts brand saliency:* it's one way of standing out from a crowd of similar work and therefore driving return on marketing investment.

Let's start here: purpose motivates employees.

Positivity at work can be boosted by communications with purpose

This is crucial because so many people hate their jobs and regret their choice of career. Research from the BBC in summer 2018 claims that two out of every three British workers would change jobs if they could.[1] It is no wonder that so many people do change jobs. Half the workforce plans to change jobs either now or within three years.[2]

This costs firms money. The impact of this churn to British business is estimated at £4bn.[3] New employees take eight months to become productive which means you really only get a couple of years of great productivity out of them if you're lucky, after that they're on the hunt for a different job again. If you can improve loyalty even marginally, this can have significant effect on the company's fortunes.

This is particularly true in today's climate. As business deals with the staggering changes that technology and Brexit are imposing, continuity of staff can help with transition. With inflation at a low, pay rises are unlikely to be a reason that anyone will stay long term at their business.

Pay rises aren't even always the best way to motivate employees

Purpose can be seen as a way to get more from the workforce than a financial incentive alone will deliver.

Pay alone isn't the key motivator. A fair wage for fair work is important to people. But it is a long way from being the only reason that people enjoy work. As Daniel Pink relates eloquently in his book, *Drive,* people want more than money from work.[4]

Pink's analysis explains that there are three key ways to improve employee happiness at work.

The first two ways to drive happiness are *autonomy* — the desire to be self-directed, which increases engagement over compliance, and *mastery* — the urge to get better skills. The third is fulfilling people's desire for *purpose* — to do something that has meaning and is important.

The first two are key criteria for training and development. The third is as critical and this is the one that falls into the scope of the marketing community to play a key role.

Businesses that only focus on profits without valuing purpose may end up with poor customer service and unhappy employees.

When considering whether to stay in their current job, with their current employer, even if pay rises and promotions are not on the cards, purpose will help retain talent.

If an employer can give its workforce real pride in what the company does, this can help reduce churn and drive job satisfaction.

At its best, then, this is when employers create campaigns that give employees pride because there is a cause beyond the immediate job role that their employer supports. A cause with meaning for them beyond the production of whatever product or service is created normally. A cause that they can relate to.

If a business can give employees a purpose, then the business can get more out of employees in at least two ways. First, they will put more effort into the day job. Second, they are likely to have a reason to stay with their employer beyond the standard two year turn-around.

Campaigns with purpose are good for business

They make employees happy. This can also help with grassroots marketing, as happy employees are likely to tell their friends and family. For big businesses who count their employees in the thousands, this has a multiplier effect. If 30,000 employees tell 10 people each, and if those 10 tell another 10 friends, well, you can do the math.

A look at the decline in trust in the annual Edelman Trust survey of business, media and government provides more evidence for why this is important, and creates hard evidence for the second role for campaigns with purpose, that is to restore trust in brands.[5] A trusted brand is more salient (according to BrandZ) and will stand out.

Let's turn now to the second point: purpose boosts brand saliency.

Trust is in crisis worldwide

With levels of trust, not just in brands, but in government, institutions and media at all-time lows, a brand that acts for a higher purpose can restore trust and create salience and cut through.

It's worth dwelling on just how bad levels of trust are. The Edelman Trust Barometer has been tracking trust for over 15 years, and its latest survey paints a stark picture.

Over half the countries surveyed (including the UK) have fallen into the 'distruster' category. This means that less than half the respondents trust anything or anyone. This used not to be true, but the culmination of fake news, stock-market downturns, FIFA bribery scandals, emissions scandals, banking scandals and refugee crises not to mention Brexit, have meant trust throughout many nations has taken a tumble.

According to Edelman, with such a trust vacuum people expect businesses to be agents of change. Its survey asserts that people turn to businesses for safe governance, and most people believe that business can deliver profits and simultaneously improve social and economic conditions in society. One of the few metrics where trust has grown is in company CEOs. Nearly two-thirds of respondents to the Trust Barometer say they want CEOs to take the lead on policy change instead of waiting for government, which now ranks significantly below business in trust in 20 markets. Edelman state that:

> *'this show of faith comes with new expectations; building trust is now the* No. *1 job for CEOs, surpassing producing high-quality products and services.'*

It really isn't this black and white in my view. There is no return yet to the paternalistic requirements of the Industrial Revolution where employers took a role in the community with a positive social contract. But what is clear from the papers the IPA reviewed is that there is a established case that acting with purpose pays off in two ways: in terms of employees and in terms of brand reputation overall.

Broadcasting what a business does in terms of acting with purpose for society is still not the mainstream however, and only a minority of 2018's IPA papers even mentioned it.

The two that stand out in this respect do so for very different reasons.

The first campaign shows how a bank reinstigated trust by advertising the actions it had put in place to drive purpose amongst its own employees. The change happened first in the workplace, and was then broadcast to the nation.

The IPA Effectiveness Award entry from Barclays sets out to justify the necessity of acting with purpose. The paper points out that the issue does divide a room. For some, it is a powerful business tool for the reasons outlined above. For others, it is dismissed as 'green- or purpose-washing', frivolous, even a joke.

The paper sets out powerful evidence that acting with purpose does matter, that consumers care, and makes a good case for the positive impact on the bank's employees.

Barclays had a need to take action to restore trust after the 2008 global financial crisis. An internal transformation programme put brand purpose at the heart of the plan. Barclays UK colleagues were empowered by the stated purpose of 'Helping people achieve their ambitions in the right way' to create initiatives. One of these, the 'Digital Eagles' began as a group of 12 colleagues and grew into an army of thousands with the objective of ensuring that other colleagues and customers don't get left behind because they don't have digital skills to cope with advances in technology. Dozens of initiatives were started to help to deliver a culture change in the bank.

To begin with, these initiatives purely existed in the bank's branches and workplaces. In 2014 the decision was taken to communicate four of them to the wider public. Rather than talk about how the bank was changing in terms of an emotional ad saying the bank was putting the customer first, Barclays chose to use advertising to demonstrate some of the initiatives in action.

It is impossible to dismiss these efforts as green- or purpose-washing. Barclays acted first and talked about it afterwards. The effect is evidenced amongst millions of people in its target audience. Its CEO, Ashok Vaswani, mentioned the impact of two schemes: LifeSkills and the Digital Safety campaign in his foreword to the 2017 annual report. £153m income was delivered and thousands of colleagues volunteered to help with the schemes thus giving them a reason to be proud of their employer.

The campaigns worked on a number of levels from improvements in employee satisfaction to cut through to the consumer. The campaigns were different from category norms, cutting through in a low-interest category to drive brand consideration. In such a tough category, they drove trust in and consideration for the brand throughout the UK.

The second paper that proves purpose pays is from the other side of the world, and is about a very different type of purpose. SK-II, a brand originating in Japan and owned now by Procter & Gamble, decided in its own words 'to give a voice to the "leftover women" of China'.

In this instance, most (but not all) of the proof points of effectiveness are consumer-related.

Winning in China is crucial to winning in Asia, especially in luxury skin care. The market favoured European heritage, and was dominated by luxury French brands. The product was good, but the category was awash with similar images and messages. The existing communication platform for the brand was called 'Change destiny'. Its meaning was intended to apply to delaying the aging process. The team decided to rethink the meaning and inject emotional purpose into the comms. They wanted to reimagine it to mean changing your destiny in life.

There's lots of pressure in China to marry. In fact, if you're not married by 27 you're labelled 'sheng nu': 'leftover woman'.

Pressure is predominantly from parents to marry early. SK-II decided to give daughters a voice to reach out to their parents and give them a chance to express a different point of view.

A hero film, 'The marriage market takeover', was produced and premiered on video hosting sites, Tencent and Youku, and with influencers and on social in a change from SK-II's usual TV channels.

The story generated its own news coverage in 54 countries. Thousands of women in China and around the world shared personal stories and created their own statements on the issue.

The campaign's effectiveness is evidenced through sales, brand equity, and search metrics. Like Barclays, however, it also had an effect on a workforce, this time at the brand's retail partners. People involved in distribution at retailers remarked on the power of the campaign and wanted to be involved in it. The campaign led to a new level of dialogue with retailers and opened up the possibility of a step change in distribution and display. SK-II was offered 16 department store takeovers in 2016 versus two in 2015.

Following its 'Marriage market takeover' the brand, which a decade earlier had had to undertake a high profile recall of its products in China and other markets, had its most successful year in its history in China and became the number one brand across Asia. The brand equity that was delivered has performed in terms of pricing and distribution. Without purpose, the brand would not have had the cut through to achieve such stellar success. There is little doubt that there is no other way in which the brand could have received such positive PR and word of mouth.

There is a third paper in this set of effectiveness awards that also used purpose to drive product sales. The paper for confectionery brand, Skittles, describes its support of Pride and the LBGT+ community as 'an unconventional activation strategy'. At its heart this campaign had a tie up with Tesco to create buzz and differentiation by launching a limited edition of the product, without its trademark rainbow-coloured flag in order to show support for the LGBT+ community during the Pride in London festival season.

The brand enjoyed some of the same benefits SK-II reported from its strategy. As a result of its rainbow-less range, Skittles became more talked about, and improved both distribution and its ongoing relationship with a key retail partner. As in the examples of Barclays and SK-II, the impact of the Skittles campaign on the people involved in the work (in this instance at the retail partner) is clear.

Unlike Barclays and SK-II, Skittles hasn't included evidence that it elevated its chosen cause into an organising principle which could be used to motivate its employees or make its product communications stand out long term. Who knows? On the basis of its self-proclaimed 'bold little experiment' and its clear success the brand may yet decide to do this.

So in summary Barclays and SK-II are two papers that prove the role of purpose in effectiveness.

Why wouldn't you want a campaign with purpose? It makes your employees feel better about working for you, it gets you talked about in the right way, and it delivers. Cynicism is abundant. Neither of these campaigns would have reaped such success without the most important ingredient of all. Authenticity.

Notes

1. Emma Kennedy (2018), 'The Wrong Job', BBC Radio 4.
2. Indeed blog (2015) 'Half of UK employees will change jobs in 3 years – and that's a good thing', 10 December, available online at: http://blog.indeed.co.uk/2015/12/10/change-jobs-in-3-years/
3. Simon Campbell (2014) 'Replacing staff costs British businesses £4bn each year', *The Telegraph*, 24 February, available online at: https://www.telegraph.co.uk/finance/jobs/10657008/Replacing-staff-costs-British-businesses-4bn-each-year.html
4. Daniel H. Pink, (2010) *Drive: The Surprising Truth about What Motivates Us*, Edinburgh: Canongate.
5. Edelman (2018) 'Edelman Trust Barometer' available online at https://www.edelman.com/trust-barometer.

Sponsorship comes of age

By Paul Edwards
Non-Executive Director

Sponsorship has certainly come a long way since decisions were taken on the basis of the chairman's love of showjumping or women's golf. Big sums of money are still changing hands in support of various sports or programmes, but the thinking and the process behind it have developed significantly; and the realities of the modern marketing world have meant that sponsorship has had to evolve.

Today's marketing world requires a much higher level of accountability to ensure that every marketing pound spent is making a difference. This means demonstrating both efficiency (return on investment) and effectiveness (achievement of business goals). Historically this might have been challenging for sponsorship with assessment focusing on what are now seen as 'softer' measures such as awareness or association with the activity being sponsored.

Additionally we see a much greater focus on ever-tighter targeting with large-scale datasets and computing power being used to narrow down the audience in a behavioural/geographic/temporal matrix. The wider reach of sponsorship and the necessity of following the sponsored activity might traditionally have put it into the 'higher wastage' category.

And the work of Binet and Field in their analysis of IPA Effectiveness cases has demonstrated the power of emotion in communications.[1] Putting your name alongside a sport or programme might allow you to 'borrow' some emotion from the activity, but it has not always been easy to generate emotion specifically through sponsorship and therefore own it for your brand.

To be considered for an IPA Effectiveness Award, sponsorship cannot be seen to be given any favours. The same high and rigorous standards of proof and argument must apply if sponsorship is to walk tall with the other forms of advertising. Sponsorship has to demonstrate that it has gone beyond general awareness-raising and is delivering specific communication and business objectives.

We are fortunate this year to have three cases which meet these criteria. Each demonstrates a command of targeting and objective setting which when combined with critical measurement and evaluation goes on to show how the chosen sponsorship delivered what was being asked of it.

Suzuki knew from their research and social media analysis that their route to differentiation was through the 'fun' of driving their cars. They teamed up with the ITV property 'Ant & Dec's Saturday Night Takeaway'. However, they were conscious that this was not just an association – they were not simply borrowing 'fun' but had to generate it themselves if their sponsorship activity was to rise above their competition.

Suzuki chose not just to appear as break bumpers but created their own content using the stars and the format from the show. Short films and longer formats using typical Ant & Dec pranks enabled them to create a Saturday night event. The content was also repurposed into a highly targeted and supported YouTube campaign. It was further used as the basis for a road show and a dealer programme. This was an integrated campaign not just a layer of sponsorship; it actually used the format it was sponsoring rather than just sitting passively alongside it.

This activity was given specific and demanding sales objectives and the paper shows how these were met, allowing Suzuki to outperform a difficult market.

32Red is an online casino with big growth ambitions in a frantically competitive market. They set clear sales targets and were determined to get beyond cost per acquisition (CPA) in their evaluation. CPA was leading to poor short-term decision-making with the resultant problems that come with high churn rates. The data-rich nature of their business allowed then to disaggregate their sales goals in terms of acquisition, retention and average spend. It also allowed them to do significant segmentation work to identify the most lucrative targets. They knew that TV would be a powerful medium for them as they had observed the multi-screen behaviour of their audience who were viewing TV and playing online simultaneously.

Their segmentation analysis was used to identify football, horse racing, and boxing as key sponsorship vehicles. These were deployed in combination to deliver volume, propensity to play and at the most relevant times of day (and night!). 32Red were another partner for Ant & Dec and included within their negotiation the rights to make online games based on elements of 'Saturday Night Takeaway' and 'I'm a Celebrity Get Me Out Of Here'.

To demonstrate they were having an effect they measured their share of branded Google search queries versus competitor brands which was a very simple way of looking at their progress at the expense of their competitors. However, the key measures were hard sales numbers showing the financial success of the campaign and the delivery of the business objectives.

Heineken are no strangers to sponsorship and have been sponsoring the UEFA Champions League (UCL) around the world since 2005. Here is a case not only with solid business goals, but a clear and well-thought-through behavioural plan to achieve them.

Their goal was to increase sales through higher penetration. But as a responsible drinks company, Heineken wanted to do more than just promote drinking. Brand choice was therefore key to their success. They identified that watching UCL on the TV at home on your own was not a significant enough occasion to warrant selecting Heineken as the lager of choice. Their solution was to make UCL matches into more of a special occasion such that you would want to experience them with friends and therefore upgrade the lager to Heineken. This overall approach was supplemented with a highly targeted digital campaign to overcome specific local or personal barriers to making it a more special occasion. Shareable match reminders added to the social pressure to get together for the match. They even organised apps to help you to get your chores done or to deliver the beer and pizzas. There were truly no excuses.

Demonstration of business success was thorough and even employed a form of A/B testing, comparing markets that activated the sponsorship with those that did not. They achieved the behavioural change they were aiming for and were thus able to demonstrate the required growth in penetration leading to increased sales.

Three cases, each with a fascinating and individual story and a well argued case. And each collecting and displaying the high quality of evidence which thoroughly qualifies them for inclusion amongst the IPA Effectiveness Awards.

Can we draw any themes from these sponsorship stories?

Each of them in different ways was a brand operating in a fiercely competitive market. This is another coming-of-age for sponsorship: it is not just the light duties of lifting familiarity or creating warm feelings by association but hard-nosed business contexts where sponsorship was made into the right vehicle for tough financial objectives.

There is no need to compromise on the rigour and quality of evidence. Putting up individual posts from Twitter or Facebook is no better than adding in one or two quotes from qualitative research; useful for colour and illustration but certainly not evidence. However, diligent analysis of social media or search data really can yield solid results whether in demonstrating effectiveness or in developing a robust strategy. It is easy to quote big numbers but requires more skill to interpret their meaning; there is still value in expertise (despite the denigration of experts that we hear so glibly parroted).

Get with the format

In each of these cases, marketers did not just attach the brand to the sponsored vehicle, but used its content and style to create the messages for the brand and guide the sponsorship activity. Again, we are well past the days of looking for a sponsorship with a 'good creative fit'. These cases show a real understanding of the relationship between brand and sponsorship so that there is true synergy in the communication and the brand is able to feed off that relationship. There may also be a case to argue that this also benefits the sponsored activity beyond the money paid for the deal. If the UCL feels like more of a special occasion, then surely this is good news to both parties.

As with any other marketing activity, it is important to set specific targets and have in place sensible metrics for determining whether these targets have been achieved. As part of this, it is good practice to have a hypothesis about how this activity will deliver its objectives. Even if this is only a 'back of the envelope' approach it creates a discipline of thinking that helps to link goals and results. If objective setting and measurement are done thoughtfully, then you already have the skeleton for an IPA Effectiveness Awards submission.

Integrate the sponsorship campaign. Sponsorship should not float above or be in the background. The more it works with other media and is supplemented with digital and social media, the harder it will work.

For an integrated example, we could look at the case of DFS, the sofa retailer. Although the brand's repositioning away from being perceived as almost constantly offering sales was driven by advertising, sponsorship had a key role in supporting this strategy.

DFS sponsored Team GB as part of its long-term strategy to emphasise the brand's UK roots and make it more likeable, which also included adverts about its products' quality and testing using characters from the leading animation company, Aardman.

A series of ads featuring Team GB stars, such as gymnast Max Whitlock and cyclist Laura Kenny (née Trott), featured in DFS campaigns using the line 'Quality made in Britain'. As the case details:

> *'After some early modest reputational gains associated with the new advertising, the real uplift in DFS' improved reputation occurred when the Team GB partnership was communicated in advertising.'*

It should hardly need saying that sponsorship ought to follow the rules that have been around other media for decades.

Targeting is both possible and necessary with sponsorship. It has been shown to be able to deliver excellent reach, but also be targeted rather precisely in combination with other, particularly digital, media.

There is absolutely no excuse for being bland and vanilla. Suzuki took on the prankish fun of Ant & Dec and Heineken made excellent use of José Mourinho and his quirky character. Clearly it is not possible to go against the grain of the sponsored activity, but using it and pushing it further enhances the involvement and effectiveness of the deal.

It can be a long-term game. It is definitely possible to persist with a particular sponsorship and there was early evidence in these cases to suggest that long-term use of a property could yield increasing benefits. It will be interesting to see if long-term effects of sponsorship crop up in future IPA Effectiveness Awards rounds.

There is nothing perhaps in these themes that seems dramatically different to other forms of marketing promotion. But maybe that is the point: sponsorship now looks more like the mainstream and therefore is subject to similar rules and opportunities.

In this context of carefully planned and specifically executed sponsorships, it is interesting to speculate on the future of the really big global sponsorship events. The behemoths of the sponsorship world are the Olympics and the FIFA World Cup. In both of these events, sponsors spend a small fortune to be one of several brands associated with a global phenomenon. Certainly these events will continue to give coverage and scale and it may well be something that brands will fear missing out on. On the other hand, using budgets of that size to create a sponsorship that is bespoke to the brand's strategy and targeted more specifically might just lead to stronger business effects. Perhaps the way Heineken has shaped its interaction with UCL will provide more of a hybrid model for the future.

These papers certainly demonstrate a call for more creativity in thinking about sponsorship. In terms of media, they have shown how careful and creative thinking about segmentation, targeting and timing can deliver spectacular payback. And in terms of the sponsorship content there is a clear message that you no longer need to sit back and borrow the values of the sponsored vehicle, but you should lean into it and interact with it to create a tailored and effective set of communications for your brand. If this is an appropriate sponsorship, then both the sponsor and the sponsored should emerge stronger as a result.

The IPA Effectiveness Awards exist to prove beyond doubt that communication ideas deliver positive financial value. At their best, they provide learning on how communication ideas work. These sponsorship cases are worthy of inclusion as they demonstrate a rigour of measurement without compromise. They also provide some useful themes to guide others in their future use of sponsorship. Sponsorship has the potential to provide significant reach yet also be efficiently targeted in today's data rich world. This newly strategic form of sponsorship can look forward to a bright future.

Note

1. Les Binet and Peter Field (2015) *The Long and the Short of It*. London: IPA.

Remember this: Make your brand available

By Dr Carl Driesener
Senior Marketing Scientist, Ehrenberg-Bass Institute

There is a market narrative that a great product or service will sell itself, seemingly without the need for marketing communications. This is not a new view; American poet and essayist Ralph Waldo Emerson reportedly said in the late 1800s 'If a man can ... make a better mousetrap ... the world will make a beaten path to his door.'

Some have, unfortunately, taken this advice to heart and repeat it to anyone foolish enough to listen. Regrettably, it is advice that could not be further from the truth. A good, great, or even the best product or service will not sell itself. Otherwise, functionally superior products that present great value for money would be the biggest brands in every category.

Assuming you have a reasonable product, two additional things are needed for any sale to occur. In no particular order: first, the brand has to come to mind at the right time; second, the brand needs to be present where a consumer is looking to buy (which might be online or offline). Coming to mind at the right time effectively means that the product is recalled from memory when someone has a need, situation, or reason for buying from the category. Being present also requires that the prospective buyer can locate the brand amongst the typically cluttered environment where it is present. Byron Sharp, Jenni Romaniuk and others at the Ehrenberg-Bass Institute for Marketing Science refer to these things as mental and physical availability.

This chapter focuses on the role of marketing communications in developing both mental and physical availability, and uses three very interesting case studies submitted for the 2018 IPA Effectiveness Awards that demonstrate the exact opposite of the 'just build a better mouse trap' philosophy. But before commencing the cases, a consumer framework encompassing memory, decision-making and buying will help to uncover the problems with the mousetrap approach and why business needs well-branded, high-reach (amongst other things) marketing communications.

A framework that looks to describe consumers should first consider how memory works. One of the most widely accepted models of human memory is Anderson and Bower's Associative Network Theory. This theory suggests that an individual's collective memory is associative; where one memory is linked with another, and through spreading activation, these links help bring other relevant memories to mind. Importantly, memory is not deterministic, but rather probabilistic; just because two memories are linked does not mean one being stimulated will result in the recall of the other. The chances of retrieval can be improved by recent activation and reinforcement, and are lowered by the presence of alternative links (competitive interference for want of a better term), neglect, or a good enough alternative already being recalled. And of course, if the link is not created, one cannot lead to the recall of the other. Links can be created through direct personal experience or by being told about something.

Anything encountered in the same context as a brand can be linked to that brand in memory, building a brand memory structure. Marketing-relevant memory structures include consumption situations, brand identifiers, and locations of purchase. Product usage and marketing communications can refresh memories and sometimes create new ones. Similarly, recent activation of relevant memories (again by usage or marketing communications) increases the chance of the brand being thought of and located in the purchasing environment at the next relevant opportunity.

The theory of mental availability refers to the potential of the brand to be recalled from memory when a consumer experiences a stimulus that can result in a buying situation (e.g. 'I think I need a *pick-me-up* after reading all this stuff'). Hence mental availability is the sum of the links between a brand and reasons that might conceivably result in the use of that brand.

And in terms of the theory of physical availability, memory plays a critical role if only because of the need to know where to find something and how to locate it in the actual purchasing environment. Marketers must refresh and build links to the cues that consumers encounter in buying situations (e.g. packaging) to give their brand a greater chance of being chosen.

Traditional marketing theory supposes that consumers undertake a multi-stage decision process when choosing brands; one that involves comprehensive information search and careful evaluation of alternatives on critical attributes. This information search represents the opportunity to 'discover' a brand. Such decision processes can happen, but are atypical.

The alternative viewpoint of bounded rationality and 'satisficing' (developed by Nobel prize-winner Herbert A. Simon) accepts that consumers select an option that is good enough given the particular choice situation. Bounded rationality and satisficing are consistent with recent findings in behavioural economics where people tend to use simple and efficient rules (i.e. heuristics). This is certainly the case in many, if not most, buying situations. Go on, tell me how many banks did you consider for your home loan?

Because consumers are busy and spend very little time thinking about brands, it is critical for a brand to be easy to think of, easy to find, and quickly recognised or located. And this does not happen by itself. If a business does not actively undertake marketing communications then it relies on someone else to do that hard work. The business might get lucky, and be picked up as an interesting story by the media, but to be honest, it almost certainly won't. And the exceptions to this rule, as we shall see, are telling.

Selling on a mass scale requires the sophisticated use of marketing communications. The following IPA cases did just that; these brands used marketing communications in an effective manner to gain an unfair advantage over their competitors with wonderful results.

No sea of red here

In 2014 32Red contemplated an intimidating set of problems in the UK market. Facing high rates of customer churn, strict legislative requirements (including a new 15% tax on all bets) and fierce competition, 32Red set ambitious goals to increase revenue, share price, and EBITDA. The business clearly identified the need for customer acquisition; partly to address high customer churn but also as the key source of growth. It also sought increased loyalty (both spend and retention) by those customers.

The strategy to achieve its ambitions was built on SEO, PPC and affiliate marketing combined with the effective use of TV as a mass-reach media. While TV remained a critical element of the media mix for its ability to deliver a 'consistent base of demand', the brand moved away from prime time shows, developed a partnership with ITV and some of its properties, and made clever use of football sponsorship. These shifts helped deliver eyeballs (and their attached brains) at key gaming times, as in-home dual screening is an important occasion for gambling. Furthermore, these strategic decisions increased reach amongst important category user demographics (not just the stereotypical younger male). Marketing communications helped to deliver a memory-refreshing nudge at a time when viewers may be looking for a little distraction (perhaps during ad breaks). The use of the logo and brand throughout the ad builds brand assets that help to locate the service online.

Pretty much every online casino uses the same game developers and with this use the same game descriptions supplied by those developers. One very interesting aspect of 32Red's approach was to make its game descriptions distinct by rewriting them. While this is expensive, it distinctiveness paid off in terms of improved returns from search marketing. Aside from meeting its ambitious targets, 32Red grew its UK business by 205% on the back of these activities.

In terms of behavioural metrics, 32Red massively grew its acquisition rates, from 36,000 customers acquired during 2013 to nearly 90,000 during 2017, a growth of approximately 140%, and in that same period improved its four-month retention by about 55%. So while both played a role in its success, the growth of the customer base was greater, as we would anticipate given patterns observed in consumer behaviour, such as Double Jeopardy.

It should also be noted that the business significantly reworked its internal reporting to improve its understanding of the (online) channels through which the 'better' customers were acquired. The results of this quite likely showed through in its improved loyalty. However, the customers of bigger brands normally display higher loyalty to those brands; so the growth in 32Red's loyalty is expected given the growth in the total customer base, and shouldn't be (largely) attributed to these activities.

Keeping it real – the exception proving the rule

Meanwhile on the other side of the pond, the Art Institute of Chicago (AIC) faced the problem of famous attractions everywhere; the AIC tends to attract a lot more out-of-towners than locals. And while in one sense this is not a problem, in another, especially as the AIC was founded to benefit the people of Chicago, it is. Only 5% of Chicagoans visited AIC in any given year, representing only 25% of visitor numbers. While there are many reasons that someone might choose not to visit, by far the most important reason is most likely that they just didn't think about it in the first place. And while special exhibits might counteract the 'been there, done that' syndrome, locals are still under-represented at these events. The AIC's 'Van Gogh's Bedrooms' exhibition was given the dual challenge of a) reaching the highest number of visitors for any special exhibition in the last three years and b) ensuring at least 50% of attendees were locals. Perhaps what makes this especially ambitious was the 'product' itself; it did not consist of a gallery full of paintings but rather only three. Three views of the artist's bedroom, painted over the span of about 18 months. Not much to it at all really.

The marketing of this exhibition, though, was inspired by a great idea and skilfully executed. Rather than just observing a painting on the wall, people were invited into Van Gogh's bedroom in an act inspired by the voyeuristic nature of social media itself. A replica of the depicted bedroom was constructed, announced on AIC's Facebook page, and rented out on Airbnb. Supporting this great idea was a local campaign connected by the tagline 'let yourself in', a campaign that utilised outdoor in the form of posters, billboards, and Chicago bus advertising.

By itself, this campaign in all likelihood would not have been enough to achieve its objectives. However the creative idea, linking so wonderfully with the paintings, and combined with the fame of Van Gogh himself, resulted in a little bit of magic. USA and international media noticed the campaign, which consequently received additional coverage worth an estimated $8.6m, significantly magnifying the total initial $500,000 spend. So they achieved higher mental availability through earned rather than paid reach – the building of which can occur through any number of touch points delivered with scale.

So what was the outcome of this little bit of magic? Total visitor numbers were significantly increased – up by about 50% on the recent exhibits. Local visitors, however, almost doubled, representing three-quarters of the lift in total visitor numbers. While it is hard to unpick the effects of the sustained media coverage from the local campaigns, there can be little doubt that the links between AIC, Van Gogh and an activity we all secretly like so much were created in the brains of a very wide audience.

Et tu, Brute?

Like many business categories, real estate agents have experienced the disruption caused by the internet. To some extent, this has benefited the traditional agents, making it easier to show properties and providing alternatives for advertising. Unlike other sectors, disruption had not particularly affected the industry's fee structure, nor had online agencies come to dominate.

The experience of Purplebricks, a UK online estate agent, presents a classic case of the application of marketing communications principles, with outstanding outcomes. While not particularly lifting ad spend or rebalancing its use of media, it successfully drove growth nationwide by building on the memory structures created by prior campaigns and presenting the brand as a solution to a specific problem. The problem, of course, is the pain of paying an agent commission on the property's sales price. This was combined with a campaign to recruit more local property experts (increasing the brand's physical availability).

The key objective of this campaign was to grow the number of paying customers (instructions to sell) by over 50%. A critical decision was to focus on the mass market, not just those that were comfortable with the idea of hybrid agencies, or those that had previously used one. The big idea driving the campaign and this decision was 'commisery' – the misery experienced when paying exorbitant commissions to agents who don't seem to do much. While TV had always been at the heart of the Purplebricks media plan, its humour-led execution resulted in a campaign that captured attention, delivered the key message, and successfully linked it to the brand.

Aside from creating success across a wide range of metrics including by lowering barriers to use, increasing product understanding and growing consideration, the campaign resulted in a near doubling of valuations and instructions to sell, and a doubling of revenue. All of this helped the business bounce back from a £4.4m loss in 2015–16 to a profit of £3.7m in 2016–17.

There are of course many other great examples in the IPA case studies that highlight the importance of great marketing campaigns in achieving great results that are well worth considering. And to return to the past, it turns out that Emerson most likely did not make the comment about the mousetrap in that form. It was rather a journalist of the time that tidied it up, perhaps, ironically, demonstrating the importance of good marketing to making something truly great.

SECTION 2

Gold winners

GOLD AWARD
GRAND PRIX

Audi UK

Beauty and brains: How we supercharged the Audi premium, 2015–2018

By Will Lion, BBH
Contributing author: Thomas Gwin, BBH
Credited companies: BBH; DBG; Kantar Millward Brown; MediaCom; Nepa; Neustar MarketShare; Northstar; Northstar Research; PHD; Salmon; Somo; The Sound; We Are Social

Summary

Audi's UK growth had come from its less expensive cars. It aspired to sell more cars to higher-value customers. Using a strategic idea of the 'progressive premium', Audi launched a programme to communicate the desirability and technical innovation of its cars to higher-spending users across various channels. Following the activity, Audi became top for desirability among the prestige audience. Sales volumes grew three times faster than the UK market. Between 2015 and 2017, an estimated £1.78bn of incremental revenue was generated and the profit ROMI was £2.07 for every £1 invested.

Editor's comment

The judges especially admired the impressively detailed analysis of the fundamentals of the Audi brand, with the resulting strategy beautifully executed through creative and media principles.

Client comment

Benjamin Braun, Marketing Director, Audi UK

Once upon a time, in a kingdom far, far away, there was to be a frog race. The goal was to reach the top of a high castle tower. Many villagers gathered at the foot of the tower to see and support the frogs. The race began. But in reality, the villagers didn't believe the frogs would succeed in reaching the top of the tower. The people started to say, 'They'll never make it!'. The frogs began to doubt themselves. 'They'll never make it!'. And the frogs, one-by-one, admitted defeat and dropped off the tower. Except for one little frog that continued to climb. At the end he, alone, and with and enormous effort, reached the top of the tower. One of the quitters approached him to ask him how he had done it, to finish the race. And discovered that he ... was deaf.

So what have I learnt? Dare to be different. Be true to the aspirations of your heart and be deaf. Don't let the nay-sayers interrupt you. With 'Beautiful cars with amazing brains' we went a different way, we dared to be simpler and more emotional in our communications. And it worked.

Executive summary

Audi had been on an impressive winning streak since 2000 in the UK, coming from half the sales of leader BMW to leading in 2014. Despite the gains made, the brand's growth was within the lower specification and less profitable cars in its portfolio. It also lagged competitors on price and being seen as desirable and innovative, a core part of the brand's identity and with a proven link to future sales.

A new strategy was needed.

This is the story of how we supercharged an already premium brand between 2015 and 2018 by defining the feeling of 'progressive premium' and telling the story of 'beautiful cars with amazing brains'.

The result was a new chapter to the 'Vorsprung durch Technik' journey, a creative high point for Audi and a return to dominance in perceptions around innovation and brand desire. This helped sell more cars at higher specification, grow three times faster than the UK market and two and a half times faster than Audi globally, close the price gap to competitors, increase lifetime customer value, create £1.7bn of incremental sales, a revenue ROMI of £27: £1 and a profit ROMI of £2.07, the highest Audi has ever recorded.

Introduction

In Lewis Carroll's *Through the Looking-Glass* Alice meets the Red Queen who is constantly running but remains in the same spot.

> *"Well, in our country," said Alice, still panting a little, "you'd generally get to somewhere else if you run very fast for a long time, as we've been doing." "A slow sort of country!" said the Queen. "Now, here, you see, it takes all the running you can do, to keep in the same place. If you want to get somewhere else, you must run at least twice as fast as that!"*

In the world of cars, everyone is moving fast. New competitors, new cars, new innovations and new models of ownership are accelerating change in the market.

To stay put, you need to be running. To get ahead, you need to listen to the Red Queen.

This is the story of how we supercharged an already premium brand so it could run faster.

It's about how we were guided by the progressive spirit of 'Vorsprung durch Technik' to understand what modern premium needed to feel like and brought this to life famously, emotionally and distinctly with stories about 'beautiful cars with amazing brains'.

But let's back up to 2014.

The objectives

Audi had experienced remarkable growth since the 2000s, moving from third place in premium car market sales (with half the sales of the leader BMW) to first place at the end of 2014.[1]

Despite this growth there were three challenges.

1. The overall market was slowing

In 2015, total market growth had halved in just two years (Figure 1). We needed to prepare for a future where value would have to come from other places than just volume.

Figure 1: The slowing growth of the car market, as seen from 2015

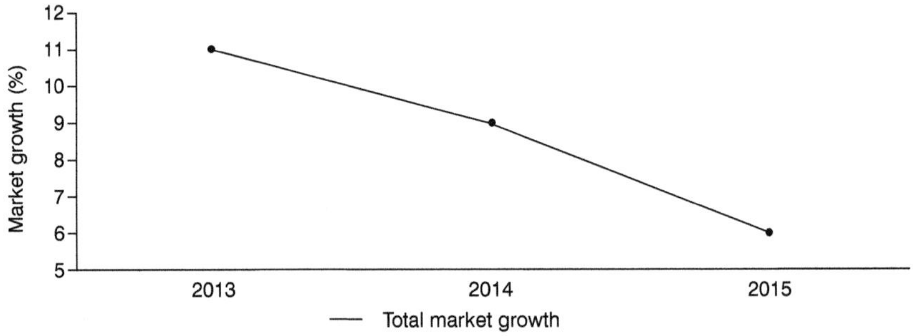

Market growth (%)
12
11
10
9
8
7
6
5
2013
2014
2015
Total market growth

Source: Audi UK data – 2010–2015

2. Audi lagged competitors on average selling price

Audi had a disproportionate amount of sales coming from the smaller and lower-specification cars in its portfolio versus the larger, higher-specification cars[2] and lagged competitors on the metric 'brand worth'.[3] BMW and Mercedes were considered worth more and sold for more (Figure 2, Table 1).

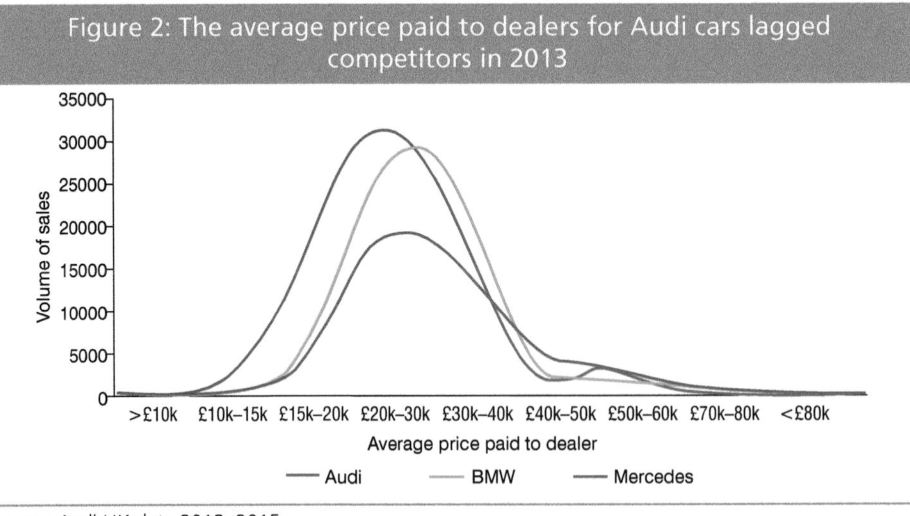

Figure 2: The average price paid to dealers for Audi cars lagged competitors in 2013

Source: Audi UK data 2013–2015

Table 1: Audi vs. most expensive main competitor on average model price 2014–2017

	Audi price	Mercedes price	Difference to Mercedes
2014	£30,078	£34,407	–14%

Source: Audi UK (2014) Competitor Pricing Data

3. Brand desire, linked with future sales, and distinctiveness was dipping

For a brand whose promise was 'Vorsprung durch Technik' or 'Progress through technology' declining perceptions were concerning. While attractive, powerful cars were being produced with exciting new innovations, the brand's desirability and distinctiveness were falling – especially among the 'Prestige' audience, made up of those with higher incomes and aspirations to own higher-specification cars.[4] This mattered as econometrics showed that a 10% desirability shift had a 3.7% sales impact (Figure 3).[5]

Figure 3: Audi's desirability and distinctiveness metrics between 2013 and 2014

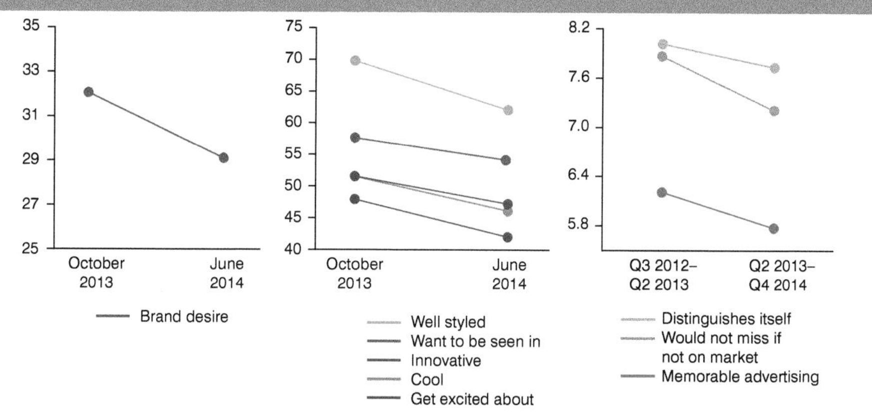

Source: Kantar Millward Brown data for KPIs – Brand desire, Well styled, Want to be seen in, Innovative, Cool, Get excited about.
UK Marketing Performance Monitor Data (Q1 2014 data release) for KPIs – Distinguishes itself, Would miss if not on the market, Memorable advertising (mean scores out of 10)

In short, Audi faced a slowing market and was behind competitors on both price and the metrics that mattered. Therefore, the following objectives were created to unlock further growth.

The commercial objectives

→ Increase profit

→ Increase share of car market, selling 'more cars' and 'more car'

→ Increase of higher-specification cars, supporting more competitive pricing and increasing customer lifetime value

The marketing objectives

→ Get more drivers into the Audi brand having bought higher-specification models

→ Drive more visits to the brand on and offline and more exploration of high-specification features

→ Make Audi appear i) highly desirable, ii) distinctive and iii) worth more, especially among the prestige audience

The strategy

To unlock these challenges we asked four strategic questions:

1. What made a brand feel desirable, distinctive and worth more in the modern world?
2. How should Audi be positioned to feel desirable, distinctive and worth more?
3. What type of stories should we tell to feel desirable, distinctive and worth more?
4. Where should we be telling these stories to feel desirable, distinctive and worth more?

Here's how we got to the answers.

1. What made a brand feel desirable, distinctive and worth more in the modern world?

We turned to the maths and the market for inspiration.

The maths showed us through factor analysis that the following would build brand desire most strongly (Figure 4).

Figure 4: Factor analysis by Kantar Millward Brown showing the relative contributions of different factors to building brand desire

Source: Kantar Millward Brown, 2013, Contributions to Brand Desire – A Factor Analysis

Other work showed a 0.7 correlation between distinctiveness and desirability, suggesting we couldn't just roll out that formula without making it distinctly Audi. So, guided by the progressive spirit of 'Vorsprung durch Technik', we undertook research to define the *Codes of Progressive Premium* by analysing luxury brands, interviewing their leaders and going deep on the changing desires of their audiences.

This revealed that there's an expected core to luxury[6] but it also showed that new codes were emerging[7]:

- *Exciting* – luxury was getting more emotional and thrilling
- *Creative* – luxury was becoming more unexpected and imaginative
- *Playful* – luxury was relaxing and having fun

These brands achieved this by overcommitting to halo stories and emotional storytelling.

It was clear Audi needed to behave more like them but also strengthen its distinct tone of voice to win over new customers (Figure 5).

Figure 5: A selection of the progressive luxury brands from food, fashion, fragrance and beauty that were analysed

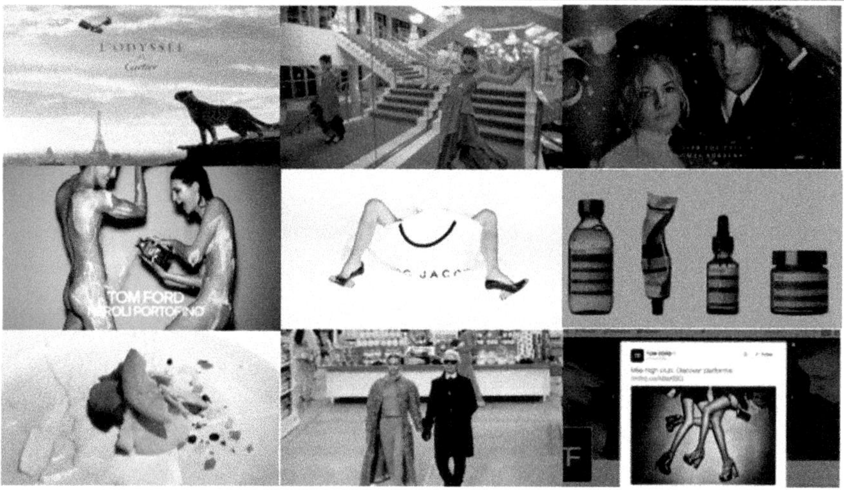

Top row, Exciting, creative playful communications: Left: Cartier's epic and emotional storytelling. Middle: Kenzo fragrance ad where a young woman rebels against stuffy luxury with a crazed dance, a great metaphor for the shift in luxury. Right: Burberry's Christmas film, showing the power of a halo product and emotional storytelling.
Middle row, Exciting, creative playful products: Tom Ford, Marc Jacobs, Aesop.
Bottom row, Exciting, creative playful behaviours: "Oops! I've dropped the lemon tart!" by Massimo Bottura, chef patron of Osteria Francescana, a three-Michelin-star restaurant based in Modena, Italy; Karl Lagerfeld and Cara Delevingne for Chanel's 'Supermarket' show and a tweet from Tom Ford, 'Mile high club. Discover platforms'.
Source: BBH (2014) The Codes of Progressive Premium

2. How should Audi be positioned to feel desirable, distinctive and worth more?

The task: remix Audi's voice with the new codes of 'progressive premium'.

To keep: 'progressiveness' and 'charm'. Research had shown people wanted to feel ahead on technology and taste, they wanted the brand to be an understated and modern symbol of their success without showing off – and the brand's charm and playfulness helped achieve this.[8]

To turn up: the progressive premium codes of 'playfulness', 'excitement' and 'creativity', which implicit research had shown were in the brand already but were buried.[9] So we decided the new Audi brand must feel:

- Progressive
- Exciting
- Creative
- Charming

We then swept these values through the whole brand, including ...

How we look

BBH created the 'World of white' look and feel in 2007 to modernise the brand with a clean, understated approach. We moved this on to the 'World of excitement', with more vibrant colour, more visceral photography and further simplicity and impact applied to branding devices (Figures 6 and 7).

Figure 6: The 'World of white' (left, 2007–2014) through to the 'World of excitement' (right, 2014–present)

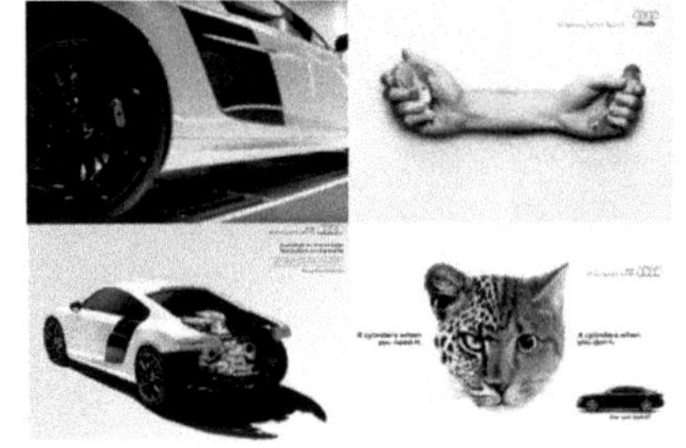

How we sound

We developed a new musical signature. Research had shown the power of nostalgic, emotional music but also had shown a white space for Audi in the area of progressive and cool.[10] We simply combined these into an approach we called 'Radio 2 song, Radio 6 execution': iconic songs with a progressive twist. We picked music from charming sources like *The Wizard of Oz* and *Charlie and the Chocolate Factory* and then had exciting new talent like Rou Reynolds and Lisa Hannigan cover them.

How we behave

We created a new set of 'progressive premium' behaviours for automotive storytelling, detailed in Table 2.

Figure 7: Simplifying and emboldening the branding in endframes and stills through bigger, simpler logos and fewer words

Table 2: Progressive premium behaviours we adapted for automotive

Behaviour	Descriptions
Car as characters, at the heart	We found the shared characteristics of drivers and cars and then did emotional product demonstrations of these with cars at the heart. For example, we made the RS 3 a restless little tearaway, the R8 poised and elegant, and the RS 4 a calm and powerful stallion.
Adding magic to the metal	We looked to warm up all the cold metal with unexpected, playful and charming ideas, locations, writing and music that undercut the seriousness.
Progressive, confident techniques	We wanted to signal progressiveness, so we pushed for CGI firsts, novel uses of new cameras, assured use of negative space in layouts and macro visceral photography. Just as with our cars, we wanted to delight people with the beauty and technical wonder of our communications.
Emotional body language across the customer journey	Across the whole journey we made sure people *felt* Audi before we hit them with the tech specs, the reverse of Audi communications before 2015

3. What type of stories should we tell to feel desirable, distinctive and worth more?

In 2013, 89% of Audi communications were 'product' and 11% were 'brand' by media weight.[11] We flipped this to a 'progressive premium' comms model, with 50% 'brand' stories and 50% 'product' stories between 2015 and 2017.[12]

But which brand stories to focus on? They needed to build brand desire most effectively but also contribute incremental revenue – 'performance' and 'intelligent tech' delivered on both (Tables 3 and 4).

Table 3: The relative prices of several Audi cars with different levels of Sport options, as retrieved from audi.co.uk in March 2018

Model	Base price	S Model base price	RS base price	% Price increase
A3	£20,365	S3 £33,505	RS 3 £45,725	+65–125%
TT	£28,850	TTS £41,190	TT RS £52,450	+43–82%
A5	£31,940	S5 £48,850	RS 5 £63,575	+53–99%
A6	£33,160	S6 £58,565	RS 6 £81,430	+77–146%

Sport option reflects lowest variant price to ensure we benchmark correctly to non-sport option same model base price. S Model is an option to add sportier trim whereas RS models are re-engineered high-performance versions of the standard cars.

Table 4: The relative prices of several Audi cars with and without the 'Technology Pack', an assortment of 'brains' features that customers could add to their car, as retrieved from audi.co.uk in January 2018

Model	Base price	Price + 'Technology Pack'	% Price Increase
Mid range			
Q5	£38,760	£44,600*	+15%
A4	£27,810	£39,995 **	+44%
Top end			
A8	£69,100	£76,750 ***	+11%
Q7	£51,110	£62,470 ****	+22%

* Audi website Q5 Technology configuration – 2.0 TDI quattro 190 PS S tronic/Technology Pack/ LED headlights with LED rear lights and dynamic rear indicators/Adaptive Cruise Control Plus with Audi Pre-Sense Basic

** Audi Website A4 Technology configuration – ultra 2.0 TDI 190 PS S tronic/Technology Pack/Comfort and Sound Pack/Driver Assistance Pack – Tour

*** Audi Website A8 Technology configuration – 55 TFSI quattro 340 PS tiptronic/HD Matrix LED headlights and dynamic rear indicators/OLED rear lights/Dynamic all-wheel steering

****Audi Website A8 Technology configuration – 55 TFSI quattro 340 PS tiptronic/HD Matrix LED headlights and dynamic rear indicators/OLED rear lights/Dynamic all-wheel steering

Therefore, from 2015 we focused on Audi Sport, the performance car sub-brand. This would be the story of beautiful, powerful cars. Then, when new innovation arrived in 2017, we would focus on intelligent Audi technologies. This would be the story of the amazing brains in every Audi.

During this of course we still supported other car launches and short-term sales but the creative energy and media weight was directed at these big stories to drive long-term growth and build the brand.

We called this the 'beautiful cars with amazing brains' strategy.

4. Where should we be telling these stories to deliver maximum desire and growth?

We created a 'progressive premium' media model[13] to make this new Audi as famous as possible. We combined media to build emotion at massive reach with behaviours that would signal progressiveness, mixing iconic film and out of home with media firsts in new channels (see Table 5 for detail; Figures 8 and 9).

Figure 8: The desire quadrant – a simplified way of approaching the many Audi communication tasks

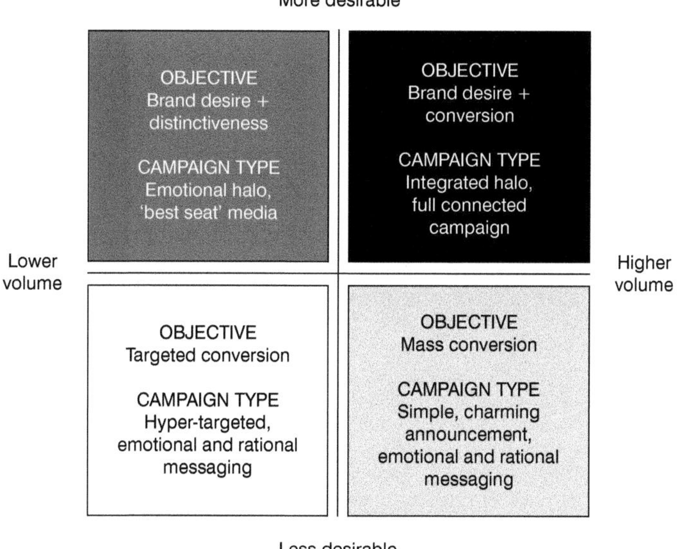

Source: BBH (2014) Moving to a Progressive Premium Comms Model

The strategy in a nutshell

To unlock maximum brand desirability, distinctiveness and brand worth we needed to blend stories of performance and intelligent technology with a progressive Audi take on premium. That created a new set of tonal, media and communication guidelines that moved the brand on without moving it off – and created the story we needed to tell: beautiful cars with amazing brains.

Table 5: The Audi 'progressive premium' media model

Progressive premium media behaviour	Implications	Example
'The desire quadrant'	We organised activity into four categories (Figure 8) with specific media implications. This was designed to maximise desirability while satisfying all business communication tasks.	R8 and RS 3 were 'top left' tasks that required entertaining, emotional halo stories. A5 – a desirable volume model – got the 'top right' treatment with a full campaign. A3 – a relatively less desirable volume model – got 'bottom right', a simple announcement campaign.
'Most exciting seat'	We wanted people's hearts racing already so our stories felt even more emotional. So we placed in blockbusters, TV finales and massive sporting events, combined with premium locations like front covers, bold double-page spreads, iconic out of home, Gold Spots and solo spots in cinema.	The film 'Spin' aired in the last break of the French Open, a moment of calm and beauty amid incredible tension.
'Programmatic desire loops'	We built a new engagement model (Figure 9), which connected all the activity. We used programmatic innovatively to hold people not in market to buy in our 'desire loop', keeping them interested from campaign to campaign. For those who were interested in buying, the depth was there to dive into and then the data-driven, programmatic CRM machine would hold their hand to digital and physical stores for conversion, on-boarding and, much later down the line, to be kept in the Audi brand.	For our RS 3 'Born restless' and 'Birth' campaigns, once people had engaged with the campaign we served them more entertainment programmatically, eventually creating a pool of hot leads to move into the rest of the purchase funnel.
Progressive media firsts	We aimed to signal progressiveness with media firsts and innovation.	We designed 'Clowns' to be chopped down into YouTube's new 6-second Unskippable stings. We partnered with Shazam and road charity Brake to donate money every time the song from 'Clowns' was Shazammed. We created out of home that could react to the weather and read number plates for more engaging creative.

Figure 9: The Audi connected engagement model, skimming people along the top or diving them down towards purchase

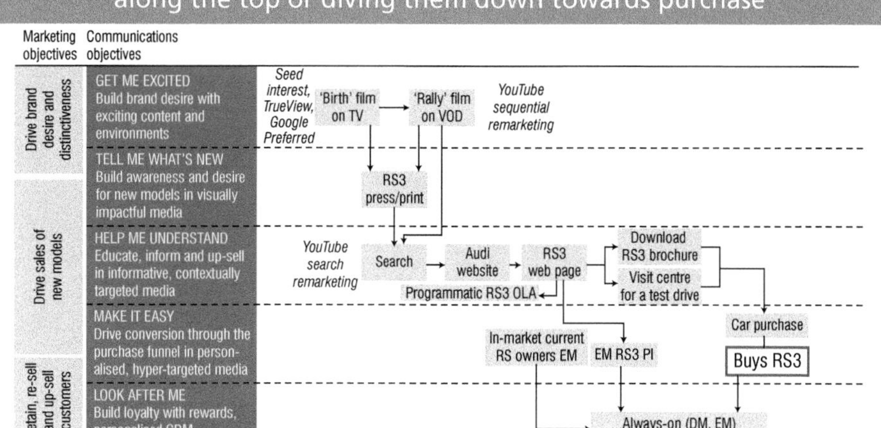

Source: BBH (2014) Moving to a Progressive Premium Comms Model

This created the following communications objectives:

→ Make Audi number one for brand desire and brand worth and increase distinctiveness

→ By becoming famous for 'beautiful cars with amazing brains', told in progressive, exciting, creative and playful ways across the journey

The work

This all came to life in two distinct chapters of work.

The first was around 'beautiful cars' to flex some performance muscle.

The second was around the 'amazing brains' in every Audi to show off the intelligent technology.

Other work announced models and converted people but still adhered to the progressive premium codes and tight Audi tonality.

Chapter 1: Beautiful cars

The easy solution would be to show Audi Sport models travelling at breakneck speed. But speed was generic to the category and difficult with the Advertising Standards Authority, which prohibited any glorification of speed.

Again, 'Vorsprung durch Technik' guided us to a progressive version of performance. Digging into drivers' attitudes showed that they valued control, anticipation, composure, precision and skill – just like Audi engineers. This was what we had been looking for. We called it 'Speed isn't everything' – dramatising the poetry of performance, not brute force. So we searched for the deeper, subtler characteristics in Audi Sport that would appeal to drivers, creating the following work around these themes (Figures 10 and 11).

Figure 10

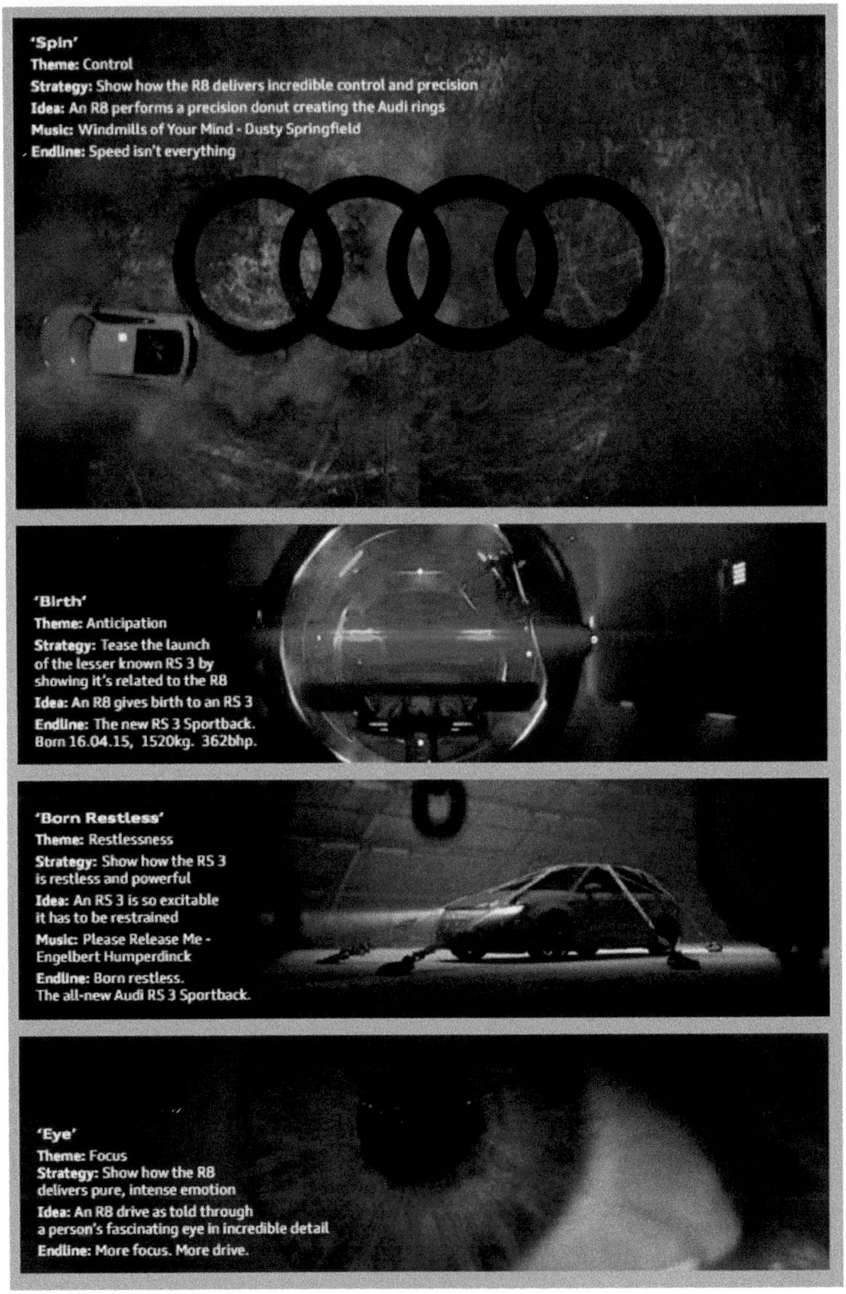

'Spin'
Theme: Control
Strategy: Show how the R8 delivers incredible control and precision
Idea: An R8 performs a precision donut creating the Audi rings
Music: Windmills of Your Mind - Dusty Springfield
Endline: Speed isn't everything

'Birth'
Theme: Anticipation
Strategy: Tease the launch of the lesser known RS 3 by showing it's related to the R8
Idea: An R8 gives birth to an RS 3
Endline: The new RS 3 Sportback. Born 16.04.15, 1520kg. 362bhp.

'Born Restless'
Theme: Restlessness
Strategy: Show how the RS 3 is restless and powerful
Idea: An RS 3 is so excitable it has to be restrained
Music: Please Release Me - Engelbert Humperdinck
Endline: Born restless. The all-new Audi RS 3 Sportback.

'Eye'
Theme: Focus
Strategy: Show how the R8 delivers pure, intense emotion
Idea: An R8 drive as told through a person's fascinating eye in incredible detail
Endline: More focus. More drive.

Figure 11

Figure 12 is a selection of the other activity, including print, programmatic content (entertainment that we linked people to from ads to go deeper), website layouts, activations at key Audi events, direct mail and other customer assets, showing how we'd shifted to much more emotional body language elsewhere in the journey.

Figure 12

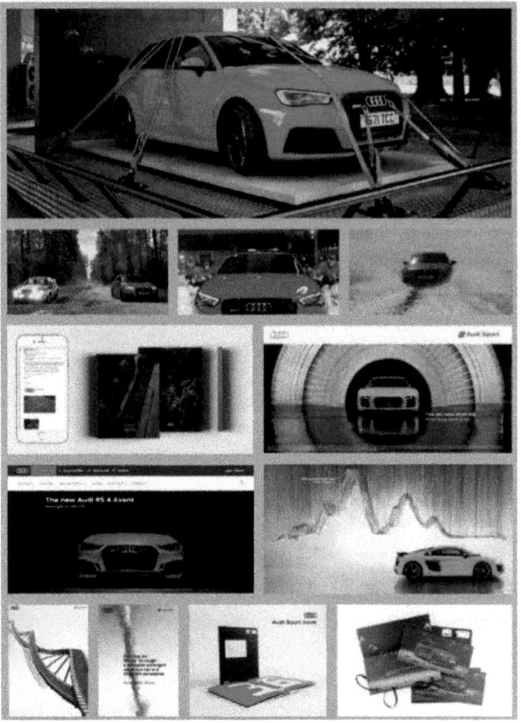

Chapter 2: Amazing brains

By 2017, in addition to talking about beautiful, powerful cars, we could now talk about their amazing brains too. In particular the brains had the major benefits of making life safer and slicker. For example:

- A new, more intelligent version of the legendary Audi four-wheel drive, quattro, was available. This could read the road and redirect power to the wheels that needed it most, improving grip and safety.
- All of the car's cockpit information was collapsed into a single new screen called Virtual Cockpit for easier control of the car's systems and fewer distractions.
- The car's many sensors and on-board intelligence could spot danger and protect the driver from it, like if a vehicle was approaching it would warn passengers opening the door. Or it would spot pedestrians crossing the road, jolt the car to get the driver's attention and, if that failed, bring the car to a safe halt itself.

The evidence was showing that features such as these were improving road safety and reducing deaths. We liked the idea of democratising the technology, just like the introduction of seatbelts in the 1960s and airbags in the 1980s. More uptake of these features could be life-saving.

The following work represents the first five campaigns to bring that to life (Figures 13 and 14).

Figure 13

Figure 14

React

Strategy: Show the sheer volume of thinking Audi does that you might not know to keep you safe

Idea: A second of a Q5 driving is slowed down to show all the thinking going on behind the scenes

Music: If I Only Had A Brain - Faultline feat. Rou Reynolds

Endline: It doesn't just drive. It thinks.

UNEVEN SURFACE DETECTED

Virtual Cockpit

Strategy: Show how the new Virtual Cockpit improves driving confidence

Idea: A pilot uses all of Audi's cockpit technology to prepare for a rescue on his drive to his helicopter

Endline: Information is everything. Virtual Cockpit.

Brains stills and animated world for digital outdoor and online

Strategy: Make the brains features feel magical and charming

Idea: A brains world of benefits

Endline: Your sixth sense

The benefits of 'Brains' were then explained across the whole customer journey, including emails to customers, social films (by We Are Social) dramatising 'No drama, just intelligence' and on the website (Figure 15).

Figure 15

The results

We'll look at the effects through three lenses:

- *Minds:* did people think differently about Audi?
- *Movements:* were people moved to action?
- *Money:* did this have a positive effect on the brand's fortunes?

Minds

Did people think differently about Audi as a result?

Yes. The objective of building brand desirability, distinctiveness, brand worth and associations with intelligent tech, especially among the prestige audience was achieved. In many cases Audi is now ahead of its competitors on these metrics in 2018.

1. The communications were heard: Audi consistently stayed ahead of competitors on media visibility despite having overall less spend

Audi leads on media visibility despite trailing BMW on overall media spend, suggesting that communications punched above their media weight (Figure 16).

Figure 16: Audi and competitors media visibility until March 2018

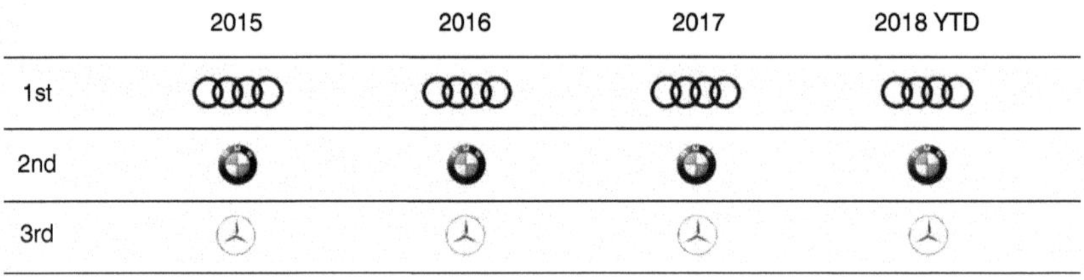

	2015	2016	2017	2018 YTD
1st				
2nd				
3rd				

Source: Kantar Millward Brown. KPI Dashboard March 2018

During the 'amazing brains' chapter of work in 2017 the brand successfully pulled away from the competition despite share of voice remaining consistent and BMW significantly increasing it in 2016 (Figure 17 and Table 6).

Table 6: Audi, BMW and Mercedes Benz share of voice 2015–2017

	2015	**2016**	**2017**
Audi	21%	21%	22%
BMW	24%	30%	25%
Mercedes-Benz	22%	18%	16%

Source: Nielsen Ad Dynamix – BMW includes Mini

2. The communications sparked creative and automotive industry buzz and won awards

'Birth', for example, won a Cannes Gold Lion in 2015 and 'Clowns' won *Campaign's* Creative Grand Prix, Thinkbox Academy's award for TV Ad Creativity and The Drum's TV/Radio Campaign of The Year 2017 (Figure 18).

Figure 17: Media visibility in H2 2017 versus key competitors

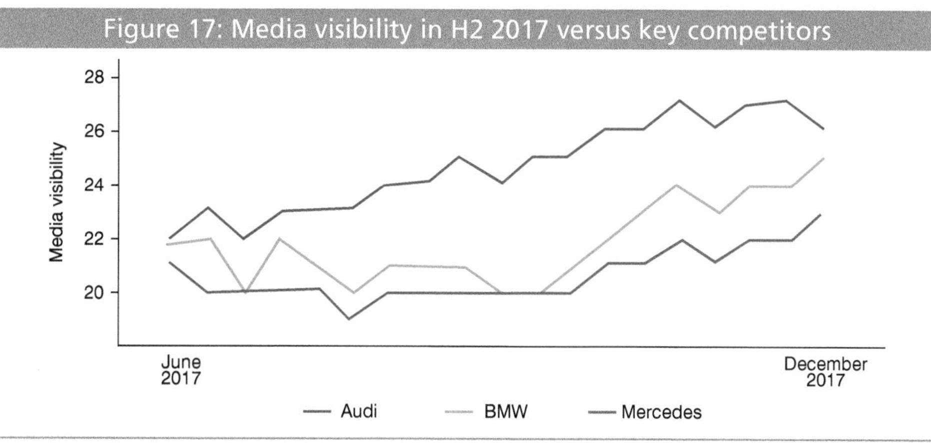

Source: Kantar Media Millward Brown, Total Audience

Figure 18: Press reaction to 'Clowns' and 'Spin'

3. The communications were highly engaging

Campaign films were watched with up to three times the average industry view-through rate (Table 7).

Table 7: Audi Campaigns view through rates on YouTube TrueView versus the industry average of 16%

Campaign	YouTube TrueView view-through rate %
Industry average	16%
'Virtual cockpit'	28%
'Going home'	30%
'Drag race'	31%
'Snow'	49%
'Cooling down'	43%
'React'	33%
'Clowns'	36%

Source: PHD (2018) TrueView data

4. The communications drove appeal for the total and prestige market

Campaigns between 2015 and 2018 consistently outperformed the historical baseline of Audi communications on brand appeal (Figure 19).

Figure 19: Audi Advertising Performance Summary – appeal index for the total market with new campaigns highlighted

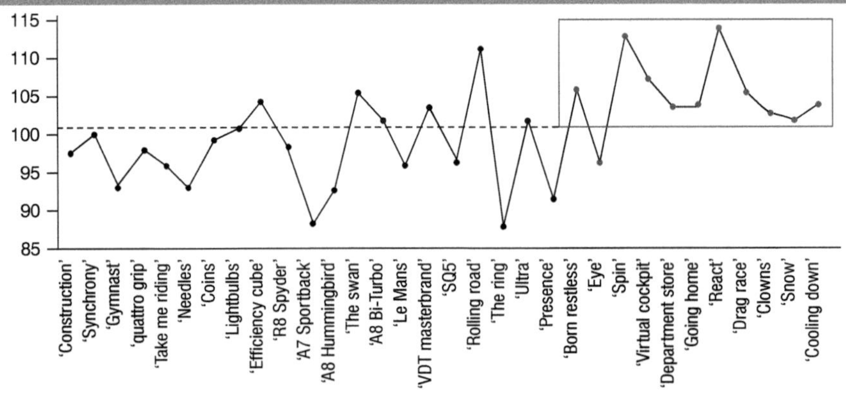

Source: Kantar Millward Brown

This holds true for both total and prestige audiences, with the same campaigns having the some of the highest brand appeal and impact scores ever recorded on Audi (Figure 20).

Figure 20: Audi communications by indexed brand appeal and impact for the total market (top) and prestige market (bottom)

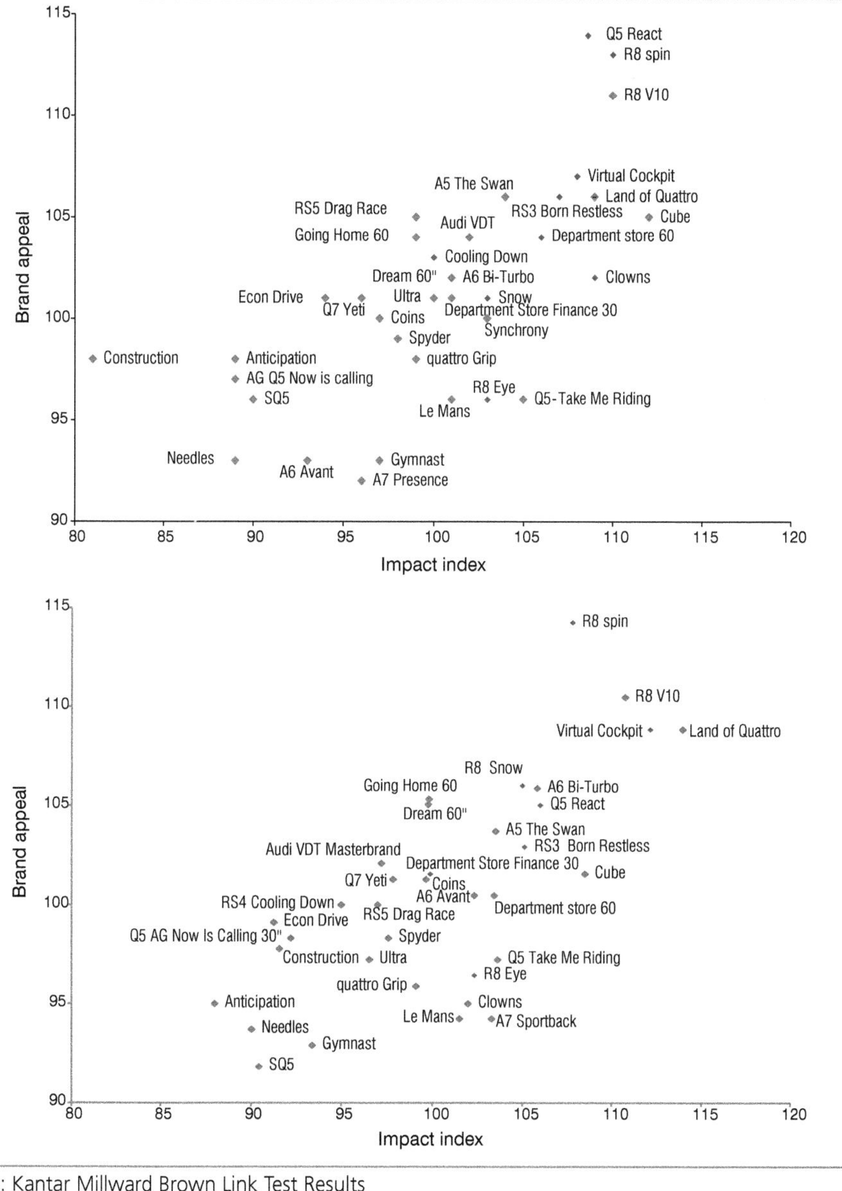

Source: Kantar Millward Brown Link Test Results

5. The communications were considered distinctive and well-branded

The campaigns successfully lifted perceptions of brand difference versus work before 2015 and 'Clowns' and 'Spin' tested in the top 1% of all ads for distinctiveness and top 2% of all ads for 'well-branded'[14] against Kantar Millward Brown's entire database (Figure 21).

Figure 21: Audi Advertising Performance Summary – brand difference index for the total audience

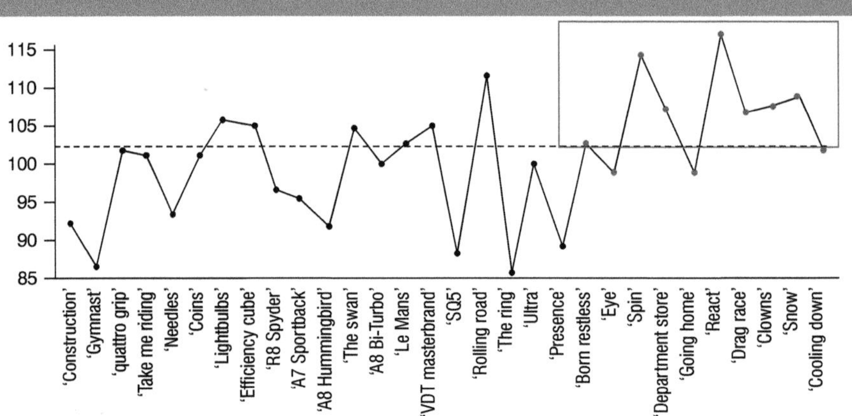

Source: Kantar Millward Brown Link Test Results

6. The communications played to new codes of progressive premium, being highly exciting, emotional, playful and creative

'Spin', for example, was found to be in the top 1% of all ads for 'creative viral potential' and was called 'captivating' and 'premium' in pre-testing and 'very, very classy', 'imaginative', 'sublime' and 'genius' on top upvoted YouTube comments,[15] with industry commentators calling it 'stunning', 'poetic' and 'innovative'.[16]

Clowns registered in the top 2% of all ads for 'emotional engagement' and top 5% for 'exciting'. YouTubers called it 'The best Audi TV ad I've ever seen', 'a great concept', 'light-hearted', 'clever' and 'understated'. The industry said: 'Next time someone is bemoaning the lack of creativity in advertising, stick this under their noses' (David Reviews), '"Clown Proof" is about as perfect an endline as you'll see' (*Adweek*), 'a delightful fantasia' (*Campaign*) and 'I hate clowns but this is too beautiful to watch' (*Creativity*).

Both *Campaign* and WARC ran articles celebrating the 'progressive premium' thinking in campaigns.[17]

7. The communications made Audi more distinctive on its core 'progressive' attribute

Audi was considered more 'progressive' and 'ahead'. For example, after seeing 'Clowns' 64% of people see Audi 'leading the way' (+11% above norm) and 58% see Audi as 'better than other premium cars' (+11% above norm). Similarly, for 'React', 75% see Audi 'leading the way' (+22% above norm) and 61% see Audi as 'better than other premium cars', (+14% above norm).

8. The communications drove the key desire-building metrics of 'performance' and 'excitement'

Across a range of campaigns, lifts were observed in the main desire-building metrics (Figure 22).

Figure 22: Increases to key desire-building performance and excitement metrics during campaigns

Campaign	Performance (start)	Performance (end)	Excitement (start)	Excitement (end)
'Eye' Dec. 2015–Apr. 2016	67	75	53	60
'Spin' Mar. 2016–Apr. 2016	71	76	59	62
'Going home' Nov. 2016–Apr. 2017	69	73	57	57
'React' Mar. 2017–Aug 2017	69	73	56	57

Source: Kantar Millward Brown (2018) UK Brand Tracking Data

9. Audi is now number one against competitors for associations with 'intelligent technology'

Shifting from advertising tracking to brand tracking, by February 2018 for the total market, Audi had overtaken BMW to become the number one on associations with intelligent technology having been in last place (Figure 23).

Figure 23: Responses to 'makes cars with intelligent technology' for total and prestige audience

	Total sample: Make cars with intelligent technology	Total sample: –/+ vs. previous time period	Prestige sample: Make cars with intelligent technology	Prestige sample: –/+ vs. previous time period
Audi	42	+4	50	=
BMW	41	–1	46	+2
Mercedes	38	=	42	–4

Source: Kantar Millward Brown (2018) UK Brand Tracking Data

Among the more difficult-to-please prestige audience, perceptions increased over the course of 2017 by 10%, getting to number two in the market and successfully closing the gap to leader BMW (Figure 24).

10. Audi is now the most desirable brand among its main competitors

For the major performance indicator of brand desire Audi closed 2017 with a five-point lead against competitors with an increasing lead over 2017[18] and in March 2018 Audi became number one on brand desire for the prestige audience (Figure 25).[19]

Figure 24: Responses to 'makes cars with intelligent technology' for prestige audience versus BMW over time

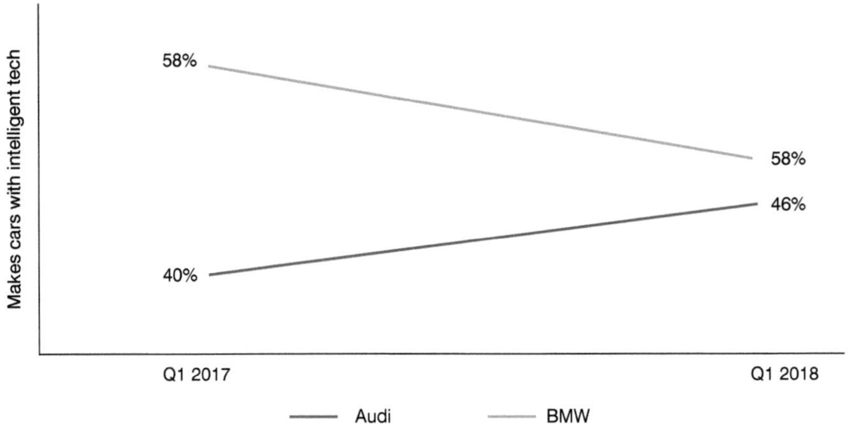

Makes cars with intelligent tech
58%
58%
46%
40%
Q1 2017
Q1 2018
Audi
BMW

Source: Kantar Millward Brown (2018) UK Brand Tracking Data

Figure 25: Brand desire for total market between 2015–2017

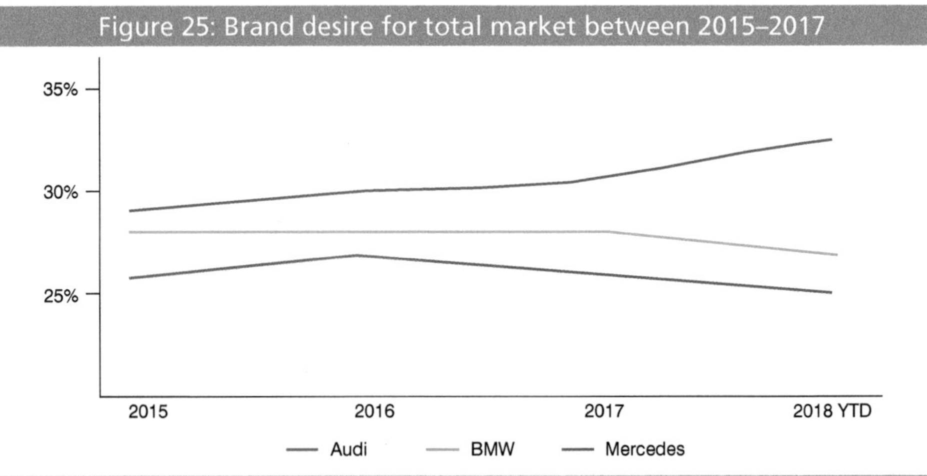

Source: Kantar Millward Brown (2018) UK Brand Tracking Data

11. Among the prestige audience, Audi now has the highest brand worth

The prestige audience also now considers Audi to have the highest brand worth, climbing considerably in 2017 to first place from last (Figure 26).

Figure 26: Mean brand worth (out of three) for Audi versus competitors among the prestige audience

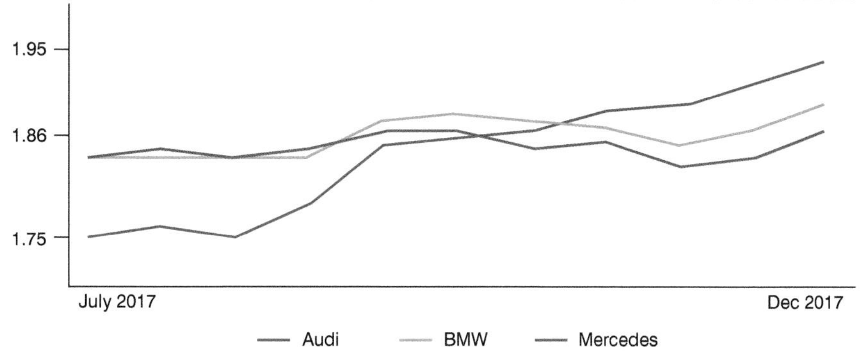

1.95
1.86
1.75
July 2017
Dec 2017
Audi
BMW
Mercedes

Source: Kantar Millward Brown (2018) UK Brand Tracking Data

Movements

Were people moved to action?

Yes. The objective of driving more visits to the brand physically and online, and for those visits to explore higher-specification models, was achieved. Using pockets of the database that were not exposed to the campaigns we can be confident communications activity drove this. Communications brought more people into the brand and converted them through it more strongly.

1. More and more people visited the Audi website

Monthly unique visitors have increased by 74% over the period 2015–2017. This rate of increase is above and beyond the UK public's online media take-up over a similar period.[20] As more and more people choose not to test drive (around 40% in 2018) and with the website as the biggest 'showroom' for Audi, this channel is increasingly vital (Figure 27).

Figure 27: Audi.co.uk monthly unique visitors, indexed relative to 2015

2013 index
100
113
137
155
2015
2016
2017
2018 YTD

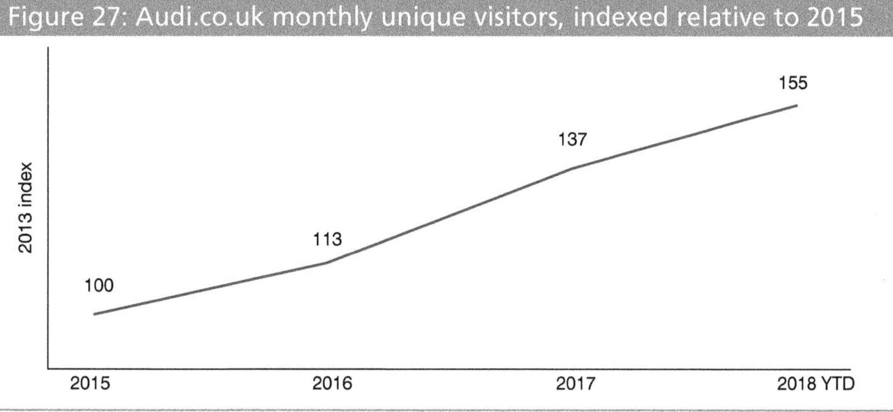

Source: Audi UK data

2. More and more people visited Audi Centres

In 2017 we also saw 16% more store visits vs. 2016.[21] This increase in footfall compares favourably to recorded industry statistics and fits into a longer-term increase in footfall of 10% compared to 2015 (Figure 28).[22]

Figure 28: Visits to Audi Centres between 2015 and 2017, indexed relative to 2015

2015 index
110
100
2015
2017

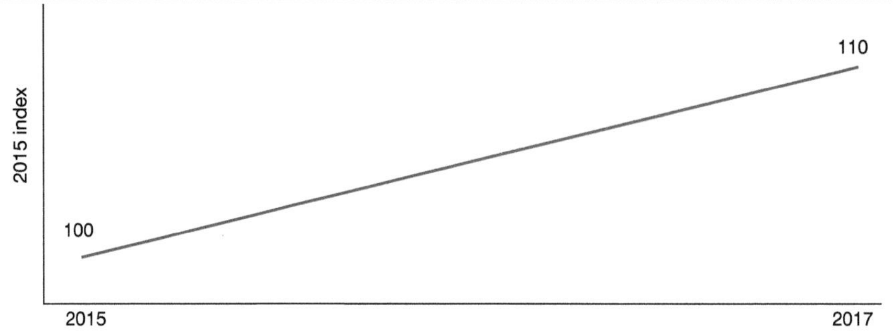

3. More and more people became named leads

In 2017 we also recorded double the number of email captures into the database from the website, phones and centres versus 2016,[23] suggesting communications was fuelling the funnel with more and higher quality prospects.

4. Exploration of higher specification models and features increased

Over the period of 2015 to 2017 there were increased visits to the higher specification model pages on the Audi website, as demonstrated by a sample of higher-end cars across the range in Figure 29.

Figure 29: Visits to Audi.co.uk key high-specification model pages between 2015 and 2017, indexed relative to 2015

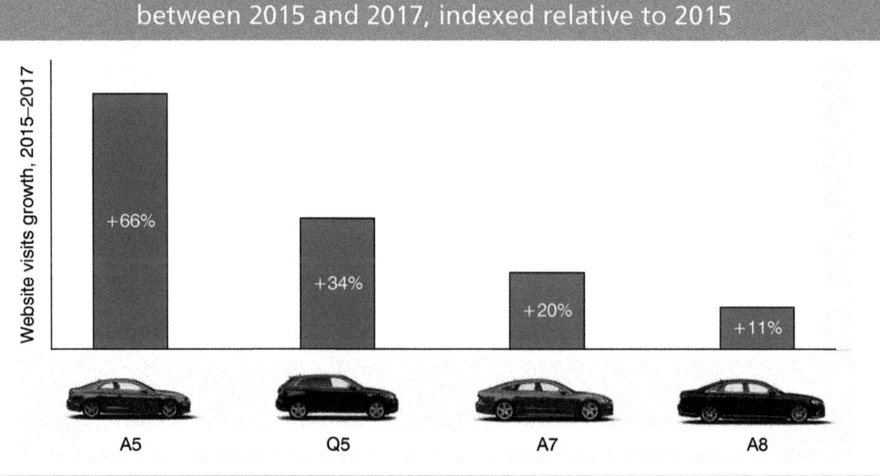

Source: Audi UK data

5. More people exposed to the campaigns converted to orders versus those unexposed

Within the Audi ecosystem there is a pool of customers who receive no campaign communication through emails or direct mail. Comparing this unexposed group with others can give us insights about campaign effectiveness. For example, between 2015 to 2017 there was a 14% prospect-to-order conversion rate versus a 0.2% rate for 'the unexposed' and a 36% order-to-service conversion versus 14% for the unexposed group.[25] This strongly suggests communications improved the conversion rate in the funnel, as well as bringing more people into it.

Money

Did this have a positive effect on Audi fortunes?

Yes. The objective of selling 'more cars' and 'more car' was achieved. More models were sold, especially those of a higher specification and for an increased average price, closing the gap to competitors and driving lifetime customer value up, especially amongst the highest value segments. The brand's growth exceeded that of the overall market by three times and by Audi globally by two and a half times.

1. Audi increased its volume sales and overall market share

From 2014 to 2017 Audi sold 10.1% more cars from 159,000 to 175,000 and went from 6.4% market share to 6.9%. This growth is over three times that of the overall UK new car sales market[25] and is two and half times that of Audi globally over the same period of time.[26] Given the same products exist globally but different communications are in play, it strongly suggests UK communications had a powerful role in driving growth (Figure 30).

Figure 30: Audi units sold and market share 2014–2017

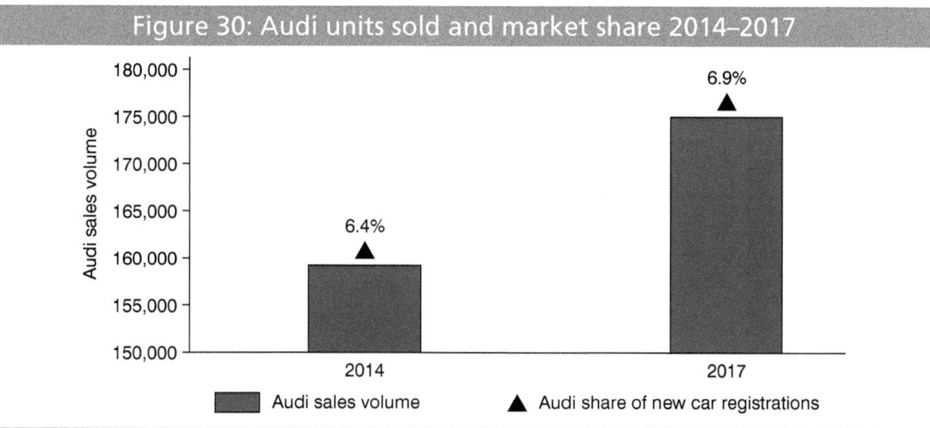

Source: Audi UK data

2. Audi increased its average selling price, closing the gap to highest priced competitor

In 2014 the Audi average price was 14% below the Mercedes average price. In 2018 it was 5% below.

Table 8: Audi and Mercedes average model price 2014–2017 (Mercedes picked as highest priced major competitor)

	Audi Price	Mercedes	Difference to Mercedes
2014	£30,078	£34,407	–14%
2017	£33,705	£35,460	–5%

3. Audi sold more models at a higher average price across the range between 2015 and 2017

If we compare the sales distribution of 2015 to 2017 the curve moves right, selling more models for a higher price (Figure 31).

Figure 31: Comparing Audi value sales distribution 2015–2017

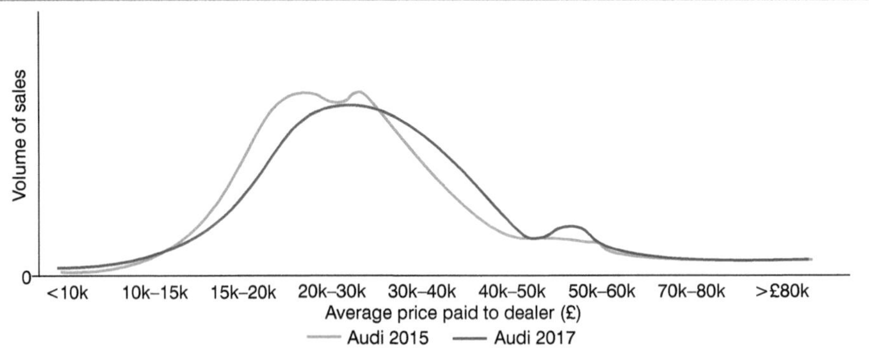

Source: Audi UK data

4. Audi sold more higher specification models like Audi Sport and S cars

Across the 2015–2017 timeframe, Audi increased Sport and S order take penetration by 33% (Table 9).

Table 9: RS and S line model sales as % of total orders

2015	8.1%
2017	10.8%

Source: Audi UK data

5. Brand messaging drove a greater proportion of sales in 2017 vs. 2015

Detailed econometric analysis of media-driven order take reveals how the change to communicate more brand halo stories and fewer product ones created more orders

overall. As we'll see shortly, together with the best profit and revenue ROMIs Audi has ever recorded, this strongly suggests the refreshed communications strategy was responsible (Figure 32).

Figure 32: Media-driven order take by marketing type 2015 vs. 2017

	2015	2017
Brand	9%	13%
Product	9%	3%
Halo	5%	7%

Source: Neustar MarketShare (2018) Annual Econometrics Report 2015–2017.

6. Higher specification models cast halos across the range selling incremental models

The econometric data shows the campaigns had an impact beyond the model featured, showing that models which spoke volumes could also sell volumes.

For example, 'React' featured a Q5 model and sold 136 Q5 models. But it also generated 1,254 incremental sales of other models, including A1, A3, A4, A5, Q2 and Q3 (Figure 33).

Figure 33: Q5 'React' incremental order take from econometrics in 2017

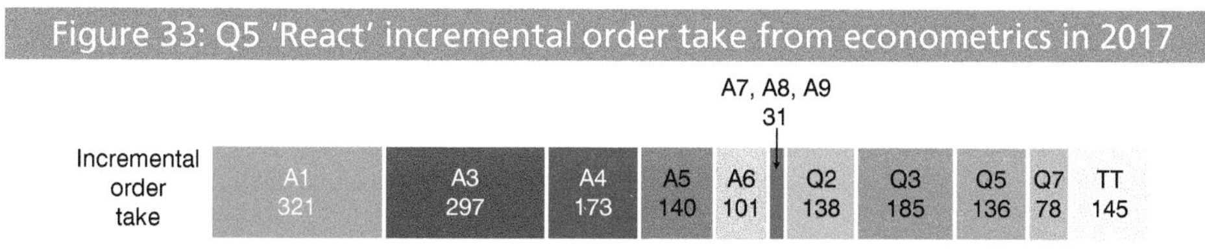

Source: Neustar MarketShare (2018) 'React' Campaign Report.

Similarly 'Spin' sold 11 of the featured R8s. But also created 1,526 incremental sales of other models in the range (Figure 34).

Figure 34: R8 'Spin' incremental order take from econometrics in 2016

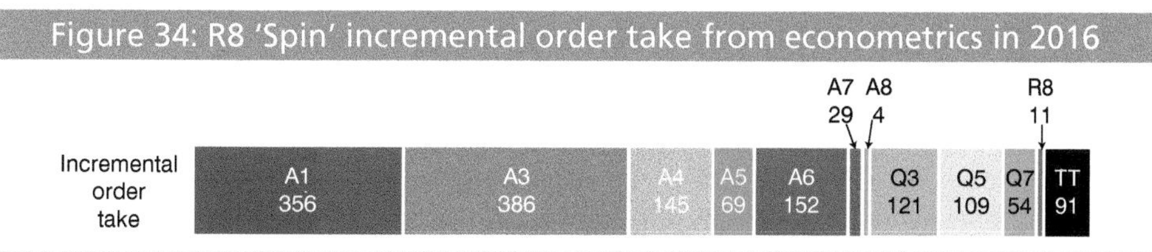

Source: Neustar MarketShare (2017) 'Spin' Campaign Report.

7. Audi was able to sell more added options through quattro and technology add-ons

From 2015 to 2017, Audi increased total option sales relating to safety, parking and driver assistance by 36% (Table 10) and improved the sales mix of quattro, the safety enhancing four-wheel drive feature, from 31.5% of all Audis in 2015 to 34% in 2017 (Table 11).

Table 10: How many additional options customers added from 2015 to 2017, indexed at 2015 levels

	Total options sales for safety, parking and driver assistance
2015	100
2017	136

Source: Audi UK Data (2018).

Table 11: Percentage of Audi cars sold with quattro, from 2015 to 2017

	Quattro sale mix
2015	31.5%
2017	34%

Source: Audi UK Data (2018)

8. The broader Audi ecosystem of used cars saw positive growth

While communications was primarily aimed at stimulating the sales of new cars, the Audi used cars business also saw strong growth (Table 12).

Table 12: Unit sales for the Audi used car network

	Used Audi sales Audi network	Estimated Audi used sales – total	Used car sales total market
2015	73,264	168,422	7,640,015
2017	83,031	190,876	8,113,020

Source: Audi UK Data (2018)

9. Audi increased its average customer value, especially among the most valuable customers

The average customer value increased by 6% from 2017 to 2018 YTD.[27] Average customer value includes revenue from model sales, but also from aftersales and finance/leasing products, making it a much more complete measure of commercial success than total vehicle sales or vehicle segment mix.

Best of all, the average annual contribution coming from the highest value customers also increased by 8%.[28] This shows that Audi is generating more revenue from its higher value customers in addition to generating pure values sales.[29]

Isolating activity

Econometrics shows that communications delivered £1.7bn of incremental revenue between 2015 and 2017, increasing in amount across the years.

Table 13: Econometric results by year 2015–2017

2015	2016	2017
£500,081,400	£623,493,273	£628,666,935

Source: Neustar MarketShare (2018) Annual Econometrics Report 2015–2017.

This is, however, likely to be a large underestimate as it only accounts for new retail car sales and excludes 53% of Audi's volume business, including fleet sales (20.5% of overall Audi 2017 volume[30]) and network used car sales (32.4% of overall Audi 2017 volume[31]).

Given that fleet customers are like retail customers but are given a choice of brands from their CFO or equivalent to choose from, it is reasonable to assume that marketing will have had similar effects on them. However, the dynamics of used car sales may differ somewhat.

So while the econometrics may only be accounting for 47% of total volume, we are reporting on the retail returns only.

Measuring a return on investment

1. Communications delivered £27 revenue for every £1 of investment by between 2015 and 2017

For revenues, this strategy returned nearly four times the amount to Audi than the average for previous IPA-winning papers in the automotive category.

Table 14: Audi 2017 revenue ROMI versus IPA winning papers in automotive category since 2008

Year	Revenue ROMI
IPA winning papers in automotive category *	£7.43
Audi 2015–2017	£27
Audi multiplier	3.7x

* Previous IPA winners with revenue ROMI: Nissan 'What is the most efficient path between two points?' 2012: 1.80; Renault Dacia 'Making frugality pay' 2014: 4.00; Audi 'Firing up the Quattro: how Audi accelerated into the 21st century' 2008: 7.50; Volvo '"Or by": how two little words made Volvo's safety matter again' 2016: 10.00; Mercedes-Benz 'How a change in body language transformed the fortunes of Mercedes-Benz': 13.87.

2. 27% of all order take was driven by media directly in 2017, up every year since 2015

By way of comparison, the Audi 2010 IPA paper recorded a contribution to order take of 15.3%,[32] showing the doubled power of this strategy.

Table 15: Audi media-driven order take as percentage of overall order take	
Year	**%**
2015	25%
2016	26%
2017	27%

3. The profit ROMI was £2.07 for every £1 invested

We cannot disclose a UK specific profit return on marketing investment since Audi UK profit margins are understandably confidential. However, if we were to assume that the global profit margin disclosed publicly by Audi AG in the company report roughly applies to the UK market then the campaigns where we have econometrics have generated a profit of £2.07 for every £1 invested in marketing[33] contributing 27% to overall order take. Given this strategy was designed to sell 'more car' and drive up margin this is likely an underestimate. By way of comparison, the Audi 2010 IPA paper recorded a profit ROMI of £1.70,[34] illustrating the 21% improved power of this strategy.

4. The return to morale was very high

Beyond the return on investment there are the returns to morale to consider. From across the Audi organisation – marketing, engineering, senior to centre staff – the communications returned more than just money, see Table 16 for a summary.

Summary

When everyone is moving at pace, you need to move faster to keep growing.

By 2014 Audi needed to supercharge its premium to grow.

By taking the spirit of progress of 'Vorsprung durch Technik' to the world of premium and telling the story of 'beautiful cars with amazing brains', Audi was able to:

- become number one on 'brand desire' and 'brand worth' for total and prestige audiences;
- become number one on 'intelligent tech';
- grow three times faster than the UK car market and two-and-a half times faster than Audi globally;
- close the price gap to the highest-priced competitors by 10%;
- increase lifetime customer value by 6% and by 8% among the highest-value customers;
- generate £1.7bn of incremental revenue;
- create £2.07 of profit for every £1 invested, the highest Audi has ever recorded;
- give a sense of pride and excitement to staff in the UK, Germany and around the world.

Table 16: Quotes and data from Audi staff about the broader effects of communications

Area	Quote/Data
Audi Global Audi engineers Audi designers	"We at Audi love to celebrate new things. When we showed the UK work to our international marketing and management community, they simply loved it! Also our Audi designers and engineers admire work like 'Birth', 'Spin', 'React', 'A5 Imagination' and 'Clowns'. They capture the spirit and feeling of what Audi's about and make us all a lot prouder to work here! Grazie!" *Giovanni Perosino, Vice President Marketing Communication, Audi AG*
Audi UK	"BBH has lovingly crafted the Audi brand for 36 years. They get Audi. They are Audi. Their work is a great source of pride from the marketing team right through the organisation. We are proud to work at Audi because of our cars and our communications." *Benjamin Braun, Audi UK Marketing Director*
Audi Fleet	"It's easy to assume Fleet is a different thing to retail when it comes to marketing but ultimately it's the same people choosing a brand just by slightly different means, so the comms matters to us too. Beyond that though it has an important effect on our staff. The stories from the brand give us all a deep feeling of pride and energy to be working on Audi." *Tom Brennan, Audi UK, Head of Fleet*
Audi Retail	Advertising from Audi in the UK overall rating – 8/10 Audi's advertising better than Mercedes and BMW – 9/10 Audi communications driving pride to work for Audi – 9/10 Adverts from Audi making the brand feel exciting – 8/10 Advertising making Audi feel ahead of other brands – 8.5/10 *In-centre questionnaires with staff, March 2018*
Audi Retail	"Audi's marketing is a real source of pride for so many of us in the Audi Centres. They get us excited about work and very proud to talk about the brand with customers." *Laura Ayers, Audi UK Retail and Brand Experience Marketing Manager*

It gives the marketing community:

- a rare case study in how to premiumise in automotive, how magic can move metal and margins;
- a lesson in how a 36-year old line can still inspire difference and still make a difference;
- a glimpse into how progressive tools, research and data can unlock progressive thinking, making the whole of a brand's experience more progressive and exciting;
- a reminder that the very complex business of keeping it simple can move mountains;
- inspiration to keep running at the future.

We hope the Red Queen is pleased.

Appendix

1. Discounting other factors

- *Prices:* Audi, Mercedes-Benz and BMW have all been applying similar levels of discounts to their product lines. Therefore a change in price in favour of Audi cannot explain the success of its communications.
- *PCP Offers:* The PCP offers from Audi were less attractive than those of BMW and Mercedes over the last two years. Therefore a change in PCP offers in favour of Audi cannot explain the success of its communications. In fact, these less competitive trading conditions are likely to have counted against us.
- *Distribution:* Audi only created one additional dealership in the last three years. This number is significantly lower than that of BMW and Mercedes. Therefore, a stronger presence of dealerships in favour of Audi cannot explain the success of the communications.
- *Share of voice:* Share of voice is already accounted for within the econometric modelling and can therefore be discounted.
- *Product:* The econometrics models takes account of product lifecycle, removing this factor from consideration. Another way to discount product is by looking at the global Audi market, where the same products exist but there is different marketing. If we do this we find Audi UK is growing at two-and-a-half times the rate of Audi Global, suggesting that UK market dynamics and communications must be driving the difference.

2. Other creative work

In the body of this paper we share the main brand stories. However, there were many campaigns to drive awareness and conversion – but which still adhered to progressive premium codes and the new Audi tonality.

3. Naming

Kantar and Millward Brown joined forces in 2016. We refer to Kantar Millward Brown through this paper however pre-2016 data technically was provided by Millward Brown.

Notes

1. Audi UK data – 1996–2014.
2. Audi UK data – *Winners & Losers Report,* September 2014.
3. Kantar Millward Brown, UK brand tracking data.
4. Kantar Millward Brown, 2016.
5. Neustar MarketShare, 2014.
6. Superior quality, craftsmanship, design, customer service, heritage, exceptionalism and status.
7. New codes around creativity, adventure, fun, leisure, thrill, curiosity, simplicity and well-being were emerging. Luxury was getting less stuffy and serious. It was more colourful, more emotional, more creative, more playful, more essential and more confident about using a few key products to define itself versus using all of its products. This was how progressive premium brands built desire and distinction.
8. The Sound (2014).
9. Millward Brown (2016) *Deeper Understanding of Audi Brand Perceptions through Implicit Measures.*
10. Kantar Millward Brown (2015).

11. MediaCom, 2013.
12. Neustar MarketShare, 2018 average media investment by media type.
13. With MediaCom until 2016 and then PHD afterwards.
14. Kantar Millward Brown (2015) 'Spin' pre-testing, Kantar Millward Brown (2017) 'Clowns' pre-testing.
15. https://www.youtube.com/watch?v=ELKDYJMWOGo
16. https://lbbonline.com/news/bbh-london-rogue-put-a-poetic-new-spin-on-the-audi-r8/
17. https://www.warc.com/content/paywall/article/warc-exclusive/send_in_the_clowns_audi_shows_off_its_intelligent_cars/118185 and https://www.campaignlive.co.uk/article/audi-adopted-bbhs-progressive-thinking-accelerate-growth/1450285
18. Kantar Millward Brown (2018) UK brand tracking data.
19. Kantar Millward Brown (2018) UK brand tracking data.
20. Ofcom data: volume of internet use per week – 2013 = 16.9 hours, 2016 (latest data point) = 22.9 hours, increase of 36%.
21. Audi UK data.
22. ICDP data: average number of visits for customers buying a car increased from 2.61 in 2016 to 2.66 in 2017 (+2%), number of car dealers visited increased from 2.6 in 2016 to 2.7 in 2017 (+4%) and total number of dealers visits increased from 3.4 in 2016 to 3.8 in 2017 (+12%).
23. Audi UK data.
24. DBG Merkle Group data – CRM asset performance measured in comparison to fallow group – exact timeframe 15 October–17 August.
25. Audi UK data – Audi volume sales increased 10.1% 2014–2017, total UK volume sales increased 2.59%.
26. Between 2014 and 2017 Audi Global reported growth of 4% from 1,804,624 to 1,879,840 models sold.
27. Audi customer value segmentation – comparing customer average annual contribution 2018. (January–March) vs. 2017 (FY) where contribution is calculated from estimated customer revenue across vehicle sales, aftersales events and finance products.
28. Audi customer segmentation organises customers in value deciles using an average annual contribution figure based on vehicle sale, aftersale event and financial product (i.e. leasing) data – the top 2 deciles of this customer value segmentation contributed +30% to the brand in value in 2018 (January–March) vs. 2017 (FY).
29. Audi 2017 volume sales decline vs. 2016 equates to –1.3%.
30. Audi 2017 data.
31. Audi 2017 data.
32. Audi IPA Paper (2010) 'Audi – The new more fuel efficient Audi communications model'.
33. In the appendix we have discounted the other factors that may have driven growth.
34. Audi IPA Paper (2010) 'Audi – The new more fuel efficient Audi communications model'.

British Army

Helping a new generation find where they belong in the British Army

By Matthew Waksman, Karmarama;
Rob Fullerton-Batten, MediaCom
Contributing authors: Nick Terry, Capita; Niall McEvoy, MediaCom
Credited companies: Karmarama; MediaCom; Capita

Summary

Applications to join the British Army were plateauing. With social, political and demographic factors diminishing the recruitment pool, it needed to broaden its pool of potential applicants. Through insight, bespoke research and data analysis, it uncovered a new and surprising benefit with universal appeal – the sense of belonging. Storytelling channels, such as TV, cinema and VOD, showcased moments of authentic camaraderie and strong bonds, while using targeted media and executions helped exhibit a range of individual motivating factors for different audience segments. Social content invited potential applicants to engage individually with real soldiers and influencers. Regular soldier applicants rose by 38%, reserve soldier applicants grew by 48%, and the cost per application was significantly less than projected with increased media spend.

Editor's comment

The judges particularly appreciated the depth of data and insight into understanding the potential recruitment audience, which led to a strong strategic shift in emphasis from individualism to group belonging. This shift was matched with a brilliant analysis of the drivers of financial payback, which is all the more impressive in a non-commercial category.

Client comment

Nick Terry, Marketing Director, Defence Recruiting Services, Capita, for the British Army

The importance of meeting Army recruitment objectives cannot be understated. With young people having more options than ever before, and social, economic, and geo-political factors working against us, our recruitment environment had become highly competitive. We couldn't just rely on a traditional pool of recruits to provide the sufficient number of applicants needed to keep the Army at full strength. We had to make the Army a more relevant career choice to more young people, and to do that we couldn't continue doing what we had always done.

At its core the 'This is belonging' campaign has allowed us to appeal to a new generation in a much more human and authentic way. But more than that, it's a campaign that appreciates not every young person is the same, and that different aspects will appeal to different candidates in different media contexts. It uses data and technology to make the campaign persuasively tailored in social and digital channels where candidates spend time making their decision.

'This is belonging' has given us a clear point of difference and a consistent emotional benefit that we have applied to all our internal and external communications. The data-driven insight from the campaign around individual drivers has allowed us to create a variety of targeted messaging across our campaigns and optimise them to get the most effective results. The complex and nuanced media mix, backed up with econometric modelling, has allowed us to reach our audience who have a more fragmented media consumption than ever before in the most efficient way possible.

Ultimately, it has given us a long-term platform that we can continue to develop and build on so that a new generation can truly understand what it means to belong in the British Army.

Introduction

A new way of working, for a decision that really mattered.

Joining the Army isn't like other consumer decisions.

It's a decision to change your life.

Over the decades, Army advertising has acquired a set way of doing things. But now, faced with declining applications, and an increasing number of roles left to fill, it was time to do things differently.

Our 'This is belonging' campaign used traditional planning methods alongside embracing data and technology to find a new path for Army communications that broke with conventions in three ways:

1. we broadened out the target audience;
2. we identified a new, overarching, human benefit to joining;
3. on top of attention-grabbing TV and above the line media, we added a layer of tailored digital communications that drove conversion.

Doing things differently paid off.

We transformed how a new generation saw the British Army, with immediate impact:

- regular soldier applications increased 38% YOY;
- reserve soldier applications increased 48% YOY.

This was achieved when economic, geopolitical and demographic factors were working against us more than ever.

Crucially, in a period of public sector cuts, where every pound spent is scrutinised, we increased these application volumes in a more efficient way.

Context

Failure was not an option

The impact of missing Army recruitment objectives is severe.

Even in austerity, the government is still increasing targets for Army applications as a priority.

From taking a leading role in combatting Daesh, to strengthening security in Estonia, Latvia, Lithuania and Poland, we rely on the Army to protect the UK in a very unstable world.

Having unfilled roles has wide-reaching consequences:

- soldiers do not have proper time to rest between tours;
- less choice and talent for special forces units;
- less ability for recruits to rise through ranks;
- not enough soldiers to maintain complex pieces of equipment, so they must be stored, making them harder to mobilise.

All this results in a lowering of morale, which, in turn, lowers advocacy, escalating the negative cycle of understaffing.

Macro factors were against us

Many factors impact applications beyond advertising. The three biggest were working against us.

First, there was no major conflict in the headlines. This makes recruitment harder. In one soldier's words, 'you wouldn't apply to be a fireman if you never got to run into a burning building'. Front-line action seekers are less motivated in peacetime and without war patriotic candidates have less reason to defend their country.

It's true that the recruiting age group had lived through two high-profile wars, but their attitudes towards these wars were negative, especially the Iraq war (Figures 1 and 2).

Figure 1: This audience had lived through two wars

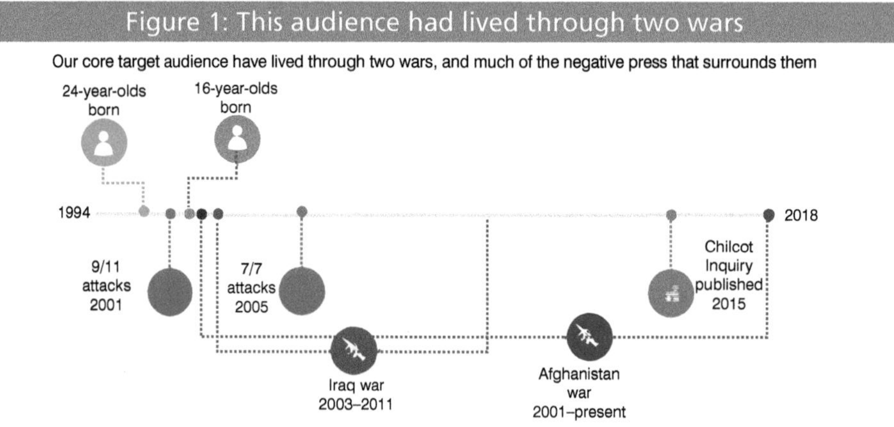

Source: MediaCom, Army Accelerator Research, 2018

Figure 2: Negative attitudes towards Iraq war

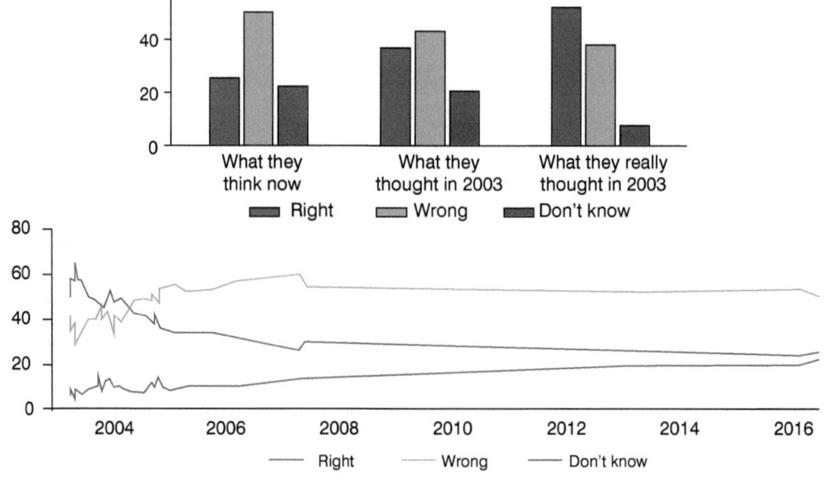

Source: YouGov, 2018. 'Were Britain and the US right to take military action against Iraq?'

Second, levels of young people not in employment, education or training (NEET) were low. Historically, the higher these levels, the higher Army applications. So there were fewer recruits turning to the Army for a job per se (Figure 3).

Figure 3: Levels of 16- to 24-year-olds NEET declining

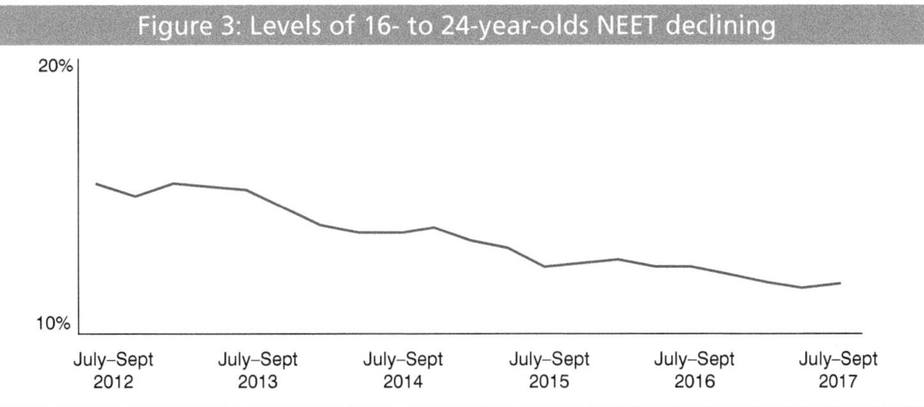

Source: Labour Force Survey, ONS

Unemployment levels were declining further in the North East, North West and Scotland, areas which traditionally the Army had relied on (Figure 4).

Figure 4: Unemployment levels in key army recruiting areas

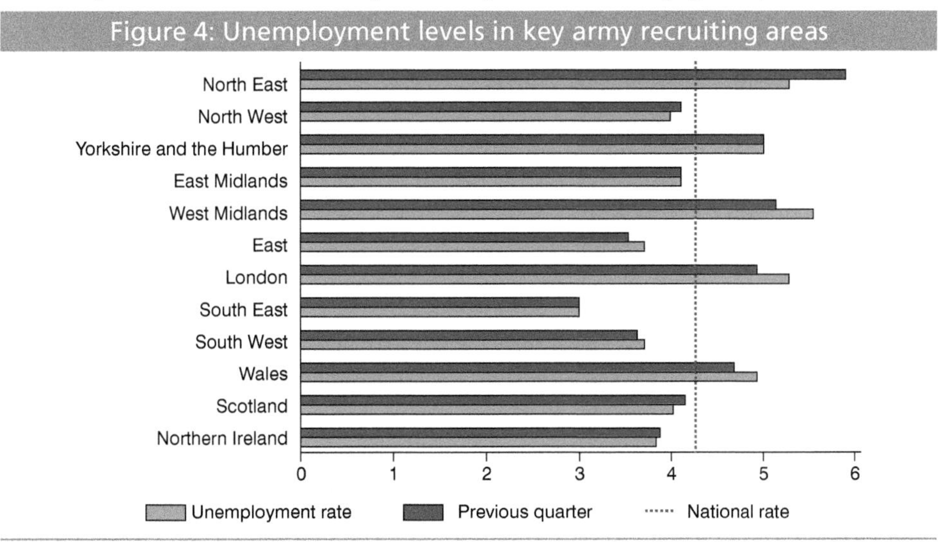

Source: BBC, ONS. September–November 2017

Third, the Army had been shrinking significantly since 1982. Having a family member or knowing someone in the Army is a big driver of applications.

This, coupled with steady population increase, means someone today is much less likely to be inspired to join by a parent or someone they know (Figures 5 and 6).

Figure 5: Shrinking size of UK army since 1982

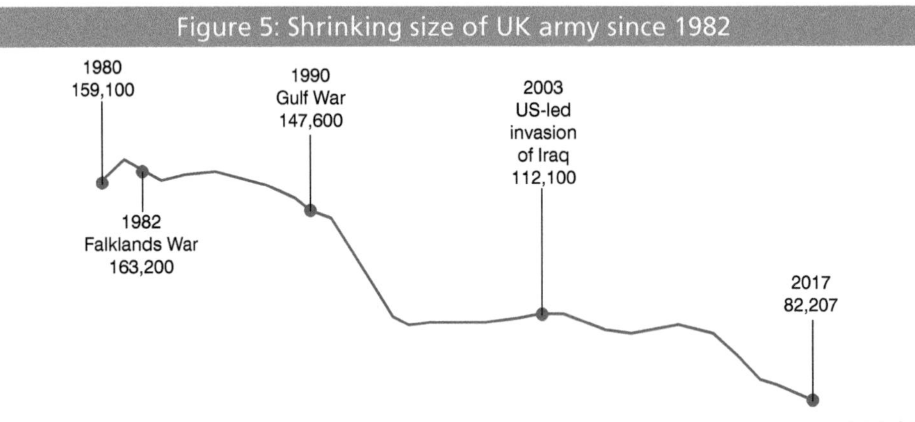

Source: Belfast Telegraph article, MOD Figures

Figure 6: Shrinking size of Army influence

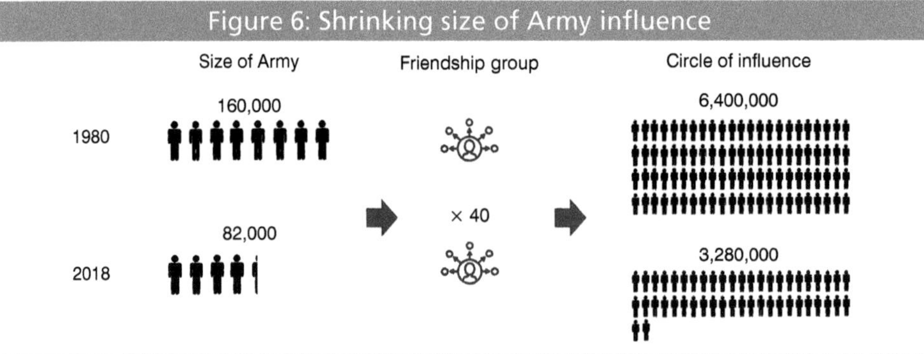

Source: MediaCom, Army Accelerator Research, 2018

In addition, the total recruitment pool itself had shrunk. Demographically, there was a significant reduction in the number of 16–17 year olds in the population (Figure 7).

Figure 7: ONS 16–17-year-old population

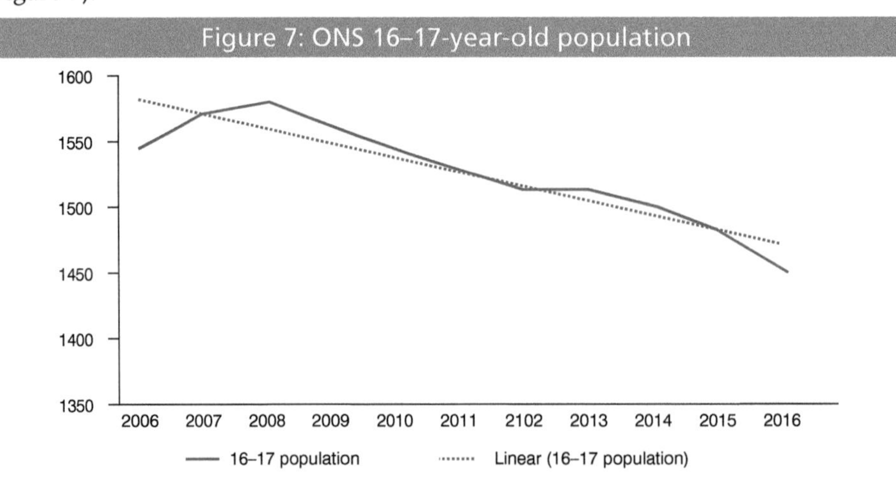

Source: Office for National Statistics, 2018

These trends combined meant the Army could not rely on classic Army types as a sustainable source of applications especially in the face of ambitious recruitment targets.

Furthermore, reaching our audience in media had become a much more complex task. Their channel and device habits had become more fragmented, meaning getting a message out to a broad group wasn't a case of a simple big TV buy anymore (Figure 8).

Figure 8: UK Commercial TVRs, falling amongst younger audiences

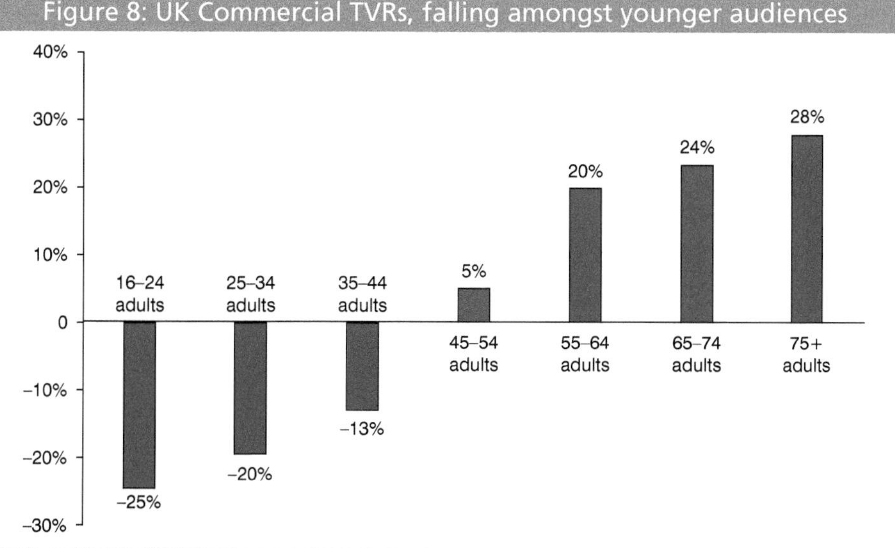

Source: BARB, 2018

Their world is digital, social, and private. Penetrating the target audience's domain would require a big change in channel implementation; we would have to build a media plan that went beyond TV and placed as much focus on digital and content.

In short, our campaign had to motivate a harder-to-reach, broader group of young people who neither felt the Army was their immediate calling, nor saw it as a financial necessity.

Role for communications

Years of Forces advertising meant there was a general sense of knowing it all. There were no new strategies or ideas to be had.

Army communications had become expected and ignored. There was even a term for this specific apathy: 'khaki blindness'.

But given the context outlined, new ideas and strategies were exactly what we needed.

First, we had to identify who the right 'broader audience' was.

The Army had identified three main tiers of recruits with multiple segments in each (Figure 9).

Figure 9: Army recruitment segments

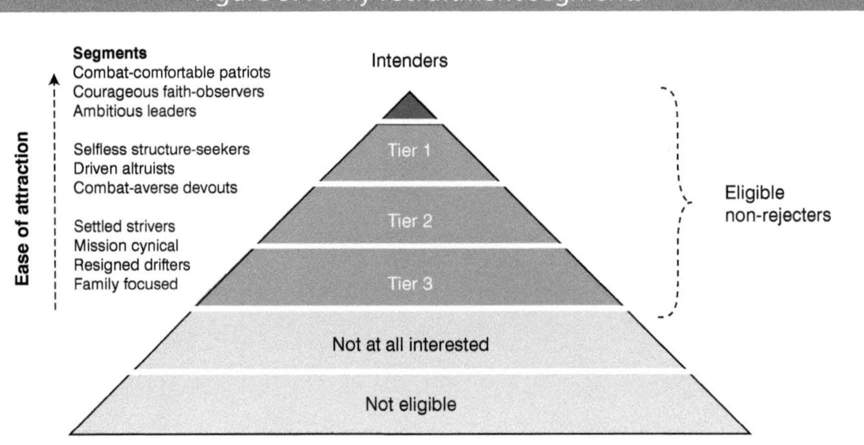

Source: Army Briefing Document, 2016

Previous campaigns focussed on those classified as Tier 1 or 'core intenders' at the top of the pyramid. This group over-indexed on drivers like 'desire to defend country' and wanting 'front-line action'.

We wanted to broaden our focus beyond this group for two reasons:

1. as laid out in the context section, this pool was getting smaller;
2. we believed focusing the advertising on people most likely to join off their own back wasn't the most effective plan – this group still had to overhear our message and be nudged, but didn't need to be the primary target.

We went one tier down and identified an additional three segments in Tier 2 who were open, but wouldn't join instinctively (Figure 10).

Now we had to motivate this new broader audience

Our decision to target a broader audience who were less inherently and selflessly drawn to the Army had two key implications:

1. At an overarching level, we had to find a new and surprising way to reframe the Army as something that would benefit them personally and stand out.
2. A broad range of factors would come into their decision-making. As a result, a one-size-fits-all approach wouldn't work. We would have to tailor our messaging to be persuasive at the right point in their journey.

We set out to tackle the above with a new way of working.

First, our team of data planners were briefed to identify the full range of drivers that our broader audience could be motivated by.

Through social listening they analysed previously successful candidates' online interests and activity in the run up to applying; revealing twelve diverse drivers that motivate applications which vary from individual to individual (Figure 11).

Figure 10: Strategy slide stating focus for comms would be Tier 2 segments

We identified that the role for communications is strongest for Tier 2 segments

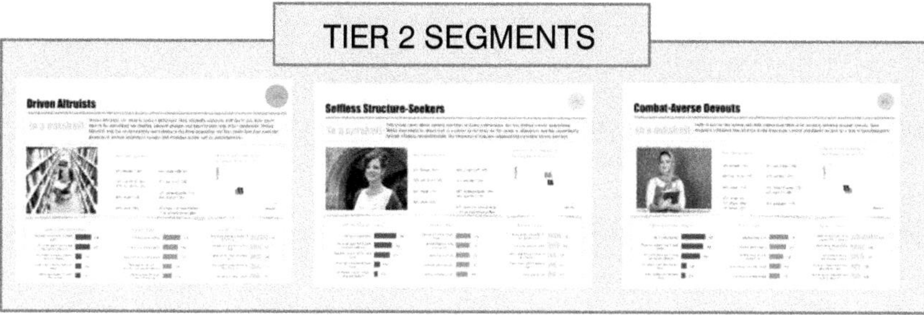

Tier 1 are core intenders. They are most likely to join off their own bat. Comms need to be present to nudge them, not persuade them.

Tier 3 are least likely to be persuaded to join by comms as they are tied into work life/ family life and habit.

Source: Karmarama strategy presentation, 2016

Figure 11: Twelve drivers that motivate applications

SKILLS	FRIENDSHIPS	MAKE A DIFFERENCE
MAKE PEOPLE PROUD	REALISE POTENTIAL	**TRAVEL**
BE A LEADER	**SALARY AND BENEFITS**	BE INDEPENDENT
ADVENTURE	CHALLENGE MYSELF	FITNESS

Source: Personal drivers from Karmarama data research

The data revealed twelve drivers that would play a key part in rationalising different candidates' decisions. To persuade them in a relevant way, we would need to create tailored messaging around each of these once candidates were seriously considering applying.

But we knew that was not enough.

Whilst creating these tailored messages would be helpful at an individual level, we still needed something powerful, surprising, and universally appealing, that could make our audience consider the Army in the first place.

So we set out to uncover a new positioning that could:

- inspire our audience to see the Army in a totally new light;
- ultimately encompass the twelve drivers that our data insight had identified.

We knew what we needed.

It was a tall order.

Now we had to find it.

Creative strategy

Strong bonds were the key

Motivating life-changing decisions is a big responsibility. Authenticity is non-negotiable. So we spent a lot of time on base.

We started by talking to recruits mid-way through basic training.

We ran in-depth interviews and focus groups. And we got on the ground with soldiers, grabbing ten minutes here and there, on breaks.

Informal conversations, one-on-one, helped people open up. And they revealed to us time and time again the biggest benefit they felt vs. civilian life.

Crucially, it wasn't a benefit they had expected, or been motivated by.

It wasn't a benefit they'd seen in communications.

The benefit was *each other*.

Brotherhood, some called it.

Others, family.

Even love, once.

We explored the notion of strong bonds as an overarching benefit with long-serving soldiers. Its importance was even stronger from the challenges they'd dealt with.

Bonds were the lifeblood of the Army. They created a sense of belonging that meant all could be relied on and trusted in the face of adversity.

Strong bonds were also the key to the personal benefits of the Army. Because strong bonds created this sense of belonging, soldiers felt supported and motivated to achieve things they wouldn't have imagined.

We summed up our proposition in this way:

Belong to something bigger than you

> *Join a brotherhood/sisterhood that will support you and help you grow beyond anything you thought possible.*

We validated the power of *belonging* as a universal benefit through relevant psychological literature.[1] We found support in a seminal paper by Baumeister and Leary (1995) 'The Fundamental Human Need to Belong', where *belonging* is shown to be one of the most powerful drivers in human nature.

When we spoke to soldiers about our twelve functional drivers from our data analysis, we learned that *belonging* had a meaningful part to play in each of them.

Take the skills driver:

> *In the Army, you learn and retain skills you might have failed at before because you now have the support of strong bonds around you.*

Or take the most functional driver like salary:

> *In the Army, salary is made more meaningful by bonds* because you can spend it with people who are such a close-knit group of friends.

We summarised how belonging connected/elevated all 12 drivers (Figure 12)

Figure 12: Strategy chart how belonging encompasses/elevates key drivers

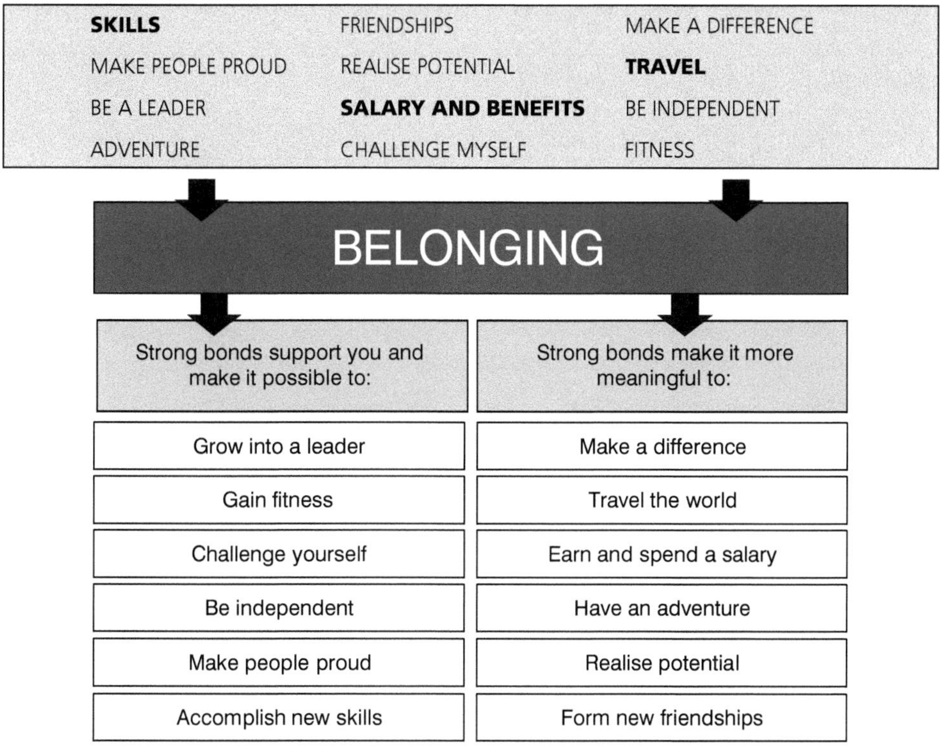

SKILLS	FRIENDSHIPS	MAKE A DIFFERENCE
MAKE PEOPLE PROUD	REALISE POTENTIAL	**TRAVEL**
BE A LEADER	**SALARY AND BENEFITS**	BE INDEPENDENT
ADVENTURE	CHALLENGE MYSELF	FITNESS

BELONGING

Strong bonds support you and make it possible to:	Strong bonds make it more meaningful to:
Grow into a leader	Make a difference
Gain fitness	Travel the world
Challenge yourself	Earn and spend a salary
Be independent	Have an adventure
Make people proud	Realise potential
Accomplish new skills	Form new friendships

Source: Karmarama, creative strategy chart

The creative idea

'This is belonging'

The creative team were tasked to bring the sense of *belonging* to life in the most unexpected, yet authentic way.

The obvious way would be the no-man-left-behind moment from action army films. To avoid the trap of 'khaki blindness', we stressed the importance of presenting a different face of the Army.

So, the creative team did the opposite of the action-packed no-man-left-behind moment. Through conversations with soldiers, they recorded moments of *belonging* outside, or in-between the action.

They unearthed touching moments, funny moments, inappropriate-for-advertising moments, but always human and surprising moments that would cast the Army in a different light.

With every story, they were struck by how the sense of *belonging* you have in the Army is unlike anything you can experience in civilian life.

Their idea 'This is belonging' would highlight unique moments of belonging you don't get in civilian jobs, ending with a new emotional call to action – *find where you belong*.

The campaign would use real soldiers who worked together and had natural bonds, using directors who would let them riff off-script (Figures 13 and 14).

Figure 13: Creative manifesto

A sense of belonging may sound like a small thing. Yet it fuels us as much as food and water. Because it doesn't just feed our bodies, it feeds our minds and souls.

And the stronger the sense of belonging – the stronger we become.

Sure, you could look for belonging in a football team or club. But the sense of belonging you'll find in the Army – well, that's the next level.

When you've trained together side-by-side. Learnt things no classroon can teach you. Fought with each other, for each other.

That creates a bond like no other. A bond that lasts a lifetime.

And sees you through whatever life – on and off the battlefield – may throw at you.

This is belonging.

Source: Karmarama, creative idea presentation

Figure 14: OOH featuring real soldiers shot by a reportage photographer

In TV, we created six moments of belonging that we rotated and optimised throughout the year (Figure 15).

Figure 15: Key frames from two out of the six TV ads

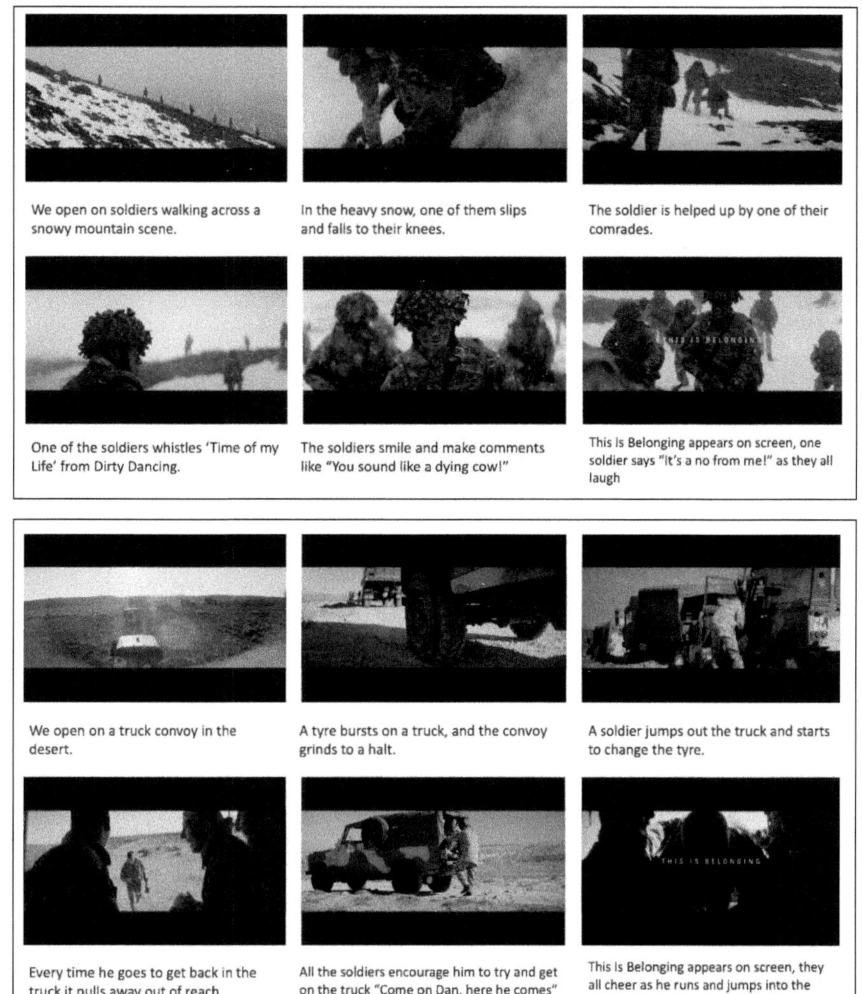

In digital channels, we tailored our belonging message to the twelve drivers identified through data analysis. We created digital messaging that tied each of the drivers to the core belonging message. For example. a message about travel had the line, 'Travel the world with 130 of your closest friends. This is belonging'

Publishing all of these rather than just one brand execution in digital channels meant our audience could see a side of *belonging* most relevant to their interests, especially where we were able to directly target them with a message based on their online profile, media context, and behaviour – (for example someone interested in learning new skills would be targeted with the message "Gain new skills and old friends. This is belonging") (Figure 16).

Figure 16: Digital creative tailored to drivers – here: pay, skills, travel

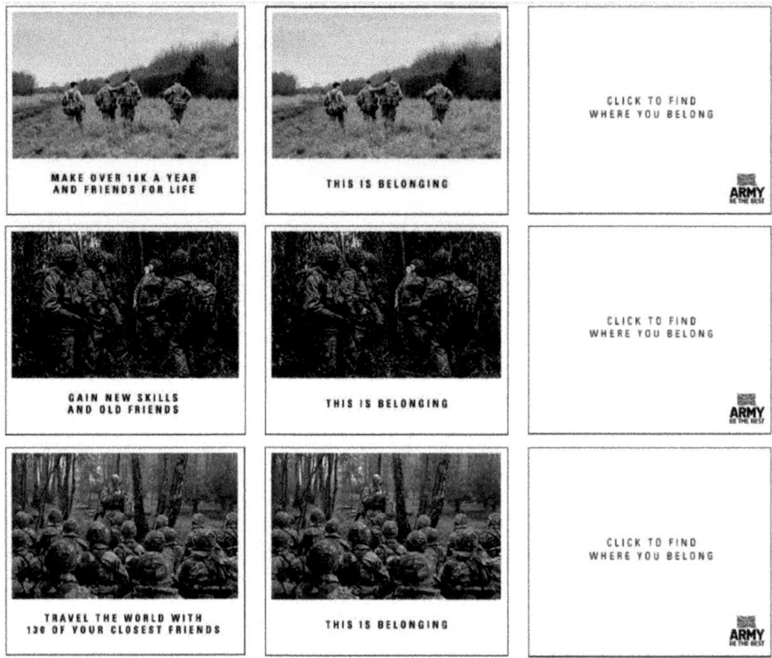

Our campaign did more than deliver targeted messaging, it ensured targeted messaging was part of the bigger, more emotional idea, making it more persuasive and cohesive as a result.

Digital messaging drove candidates through to the application website where we created simpler user journeys based on how far down the consideration journey applicants were from just wanting to explore, to being ready to apply (Figure 17).

Figure 17: Screenshot from 'This is belonging' website

Ultimately, when everyone expected more guns and tanks in TV ads, we shone a light on the unique sense of belonging that only the Army can deliver, when you stand shoulder-to-shoulder, and totally depend on each other.

And we used data to make each aspect of *belonging* more persuasive and relevant to each candidate the closer they got to applying.

Media strategy

Making belonging feel universal, and personal

We knew the category was shrinking amongst our core recruitment pool, so our media approach needed to reach out to a wider candidate set.

For our broader audience, who felt less natural affinity with the Army, the media approach was two-fold.

Drive consideration at a universal level

To do this, we needed storytelling channels that could showcase the emotional benefit of *belonging* to get candidates to see the Army in a new way.

We recommended a powerful combination of AV channels including TV, cinema, video on demand, and AdSmart making up over 60% of our media buy.

In contrast to traditional Army advertising, which was predominantly composed of broad brushstrokes, we made better use of VOD and AdSmart to target our AV and select which *belonging* moment we served to each audience (Figure 18).

Figure 18: Media spend by channel

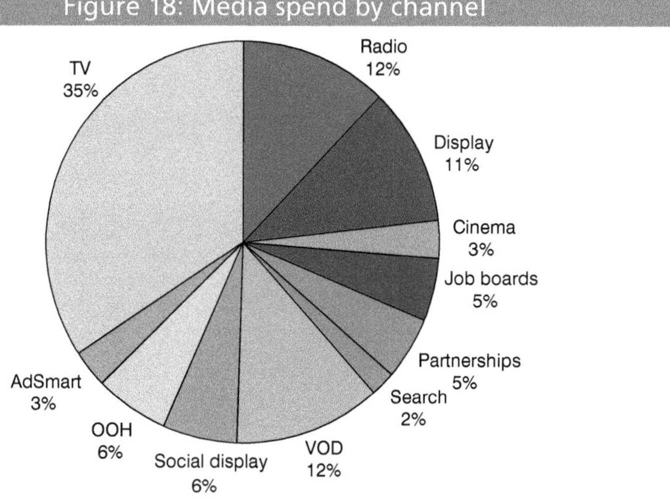

Source: MediaCom channel report, 2017

Help candidates evaluate and decide at a personal level

To drive applications, we needed to make sure our communications were as relevant as possible in the decision-making stage.

We used digital and social channels to allow us to serve candidates a *belonging* message tailored to their interests rather than just reiterating the above the line message.

To reassure candidates in the decision-making stage, we also needed to make sure our campaign felt real and genuine.

So we added an innovative content layer, allowing us to speak to our audience where they spent much of their time – social media.

We created a content partnership with the world's most viewed and engaged online video publisher: UNILAD.

The media partnership used real soldiers alongside two influencers to create a six-part content series highlighting the real life skills, diverse experiences, and bonds of brotherhood and sisterhood that are entrenched in Army life in an entertaining way.

The combination of actual soldiers, influencers, and the UNILAD platform meant we reached a large and engaged audience in an authentic way, helping people feel like they knew what they were applying for.

Results

Applications dramatically increased, showing people wanted to belong.

Here we compare the nine-month campaign period so far to the same campaign period during three previous years.

We look at completed applications for regular soldiers and reserve soldiers to show how communications delivered against the brief.

Compared to the same period the year before, regular soldier applications increased by 38% (Figure 19).

Figure 19: Regular soldier applications during the 'This is belonging' campaign period vs. previous years' campaigns

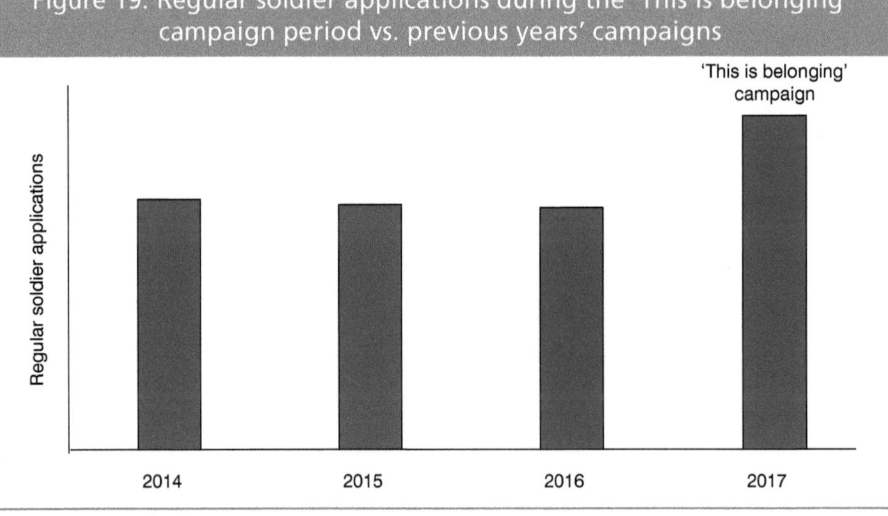

Source: Capita Application Data

This step change is also seen in reserve soldier applications.

Compared to the same period the year before, Reserve Soldier applications increased by 48% (Figure 20).

Figure 20: Reserve soldier applications during the 'This is belonging' campaign period vs. previous years' campaigns

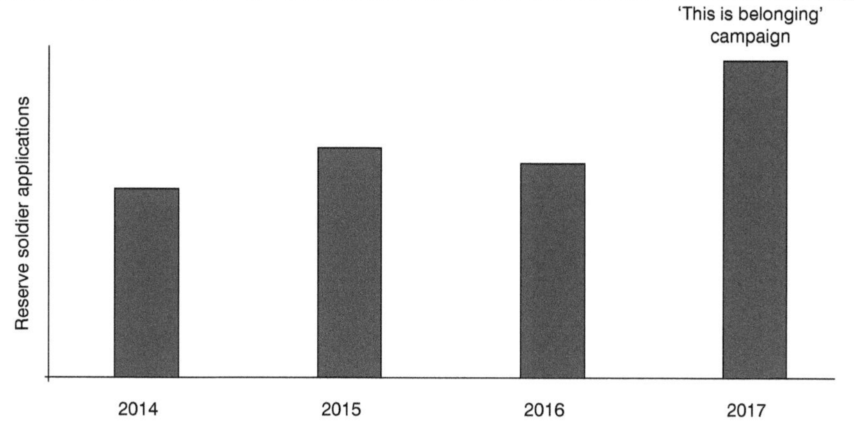

Source: Capita Application Data

Even though messaging didn't focus on officers, we see the halo effect of the campaign.

Compared to the same period the year before, regular officer applications increased by 38% (Figure 21).

Figure 21: Regular officer applications during the 'This is belonging' campaign period vs. previous years' campaigns

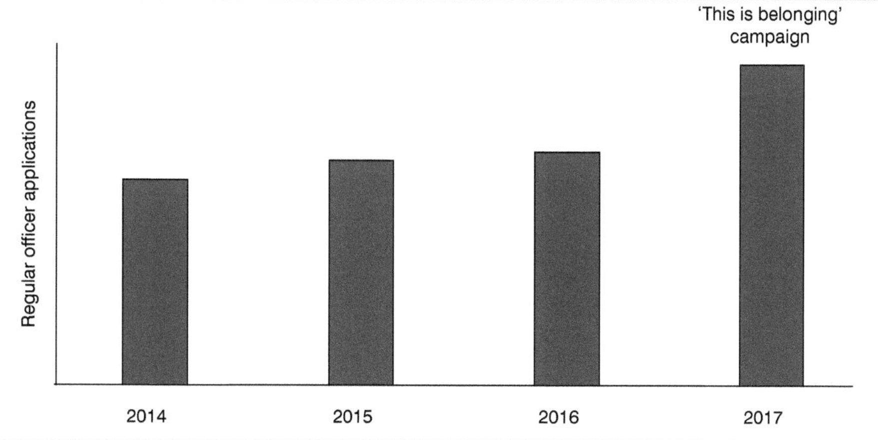

Source: Capita Application Data

Positive impact on brand/campaign measures

Since campaign launch in January 2017, the key message of *belonging*, tracked as 'camaraderie' has continued to land strongly (Figure 22).

Figure 22: The key message of camaraderie landed strongly and clearly

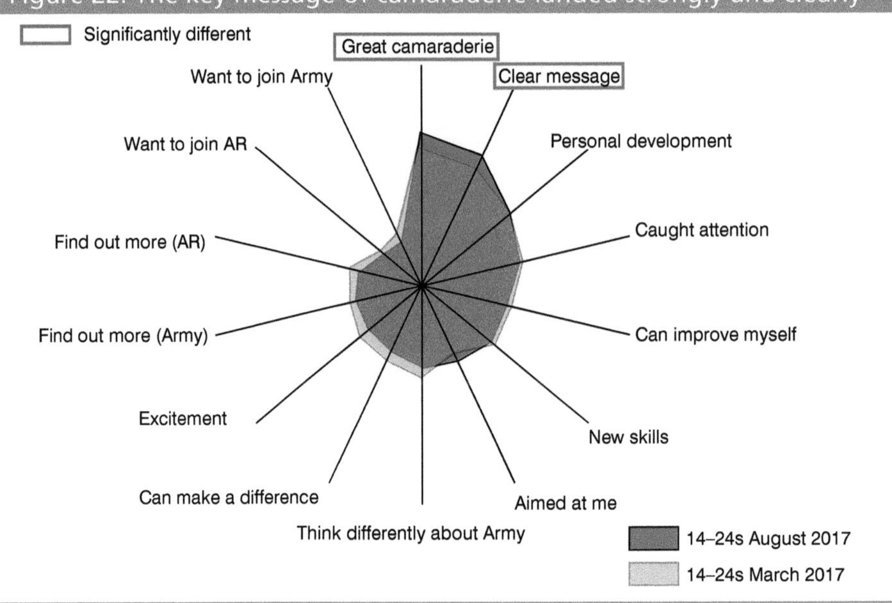

Source: Jigsaw Army Campaign evaluation Tracker, Wave 60

The new, human, angle drove a more emotional connection with the audience than any other Defence communications that had been previously tracked. This is tested through facial coding that analyses emotional response (Figure 23).

Figure 23: Emotional engagement of 'This is belonging' vs. other campaigns

Overall position	Armed Force	Creative	Rank (%)	Emotion score
1	Army	'Pick up'	89%	9
2	Army	'Birthday boy'	73%	7
3	Army	'Shooting the breeze'	33%	4
4	Army	'Jungle'	27%	4
5	RAF	RAF creative 1	23%	4
6	Royal Navy	Royal Navy creative 1	21%	3
7	RAF	RAF creative 2	17%	3
8	Royal Navy	Royal Navy creative 2	15%	3
9	Royal Navy	Royal Navy creative 3	15%	3
10	Royal Navy	Royal Navy creative 4	10%	2
11	Royal Navy	Royal Navy creative 5	3%	1

Source: Jigsaw Army Campaign evaluation Tracker, Wave 60

All key attitudes that affect recruitment have improved since campaign launch both for those already interested in the Army and amongst all nationally representative 14–24 year olds (Figure 24).

Figure 24: Key attitudes towards the Army during 'This is belonging' and the same period the previous year

Before 'This is belonging' – Percentage agreeing

Statement	All 14–24-year-olds	Army interested
Train for one of many roles	69	76
More to Army career than just military combat	65	75
Army career gives you skills highly valued in civilian life	52	66
Army is modern and up-to-date	42	61
Army has something to offer someone like me	35	59
Once you join, you're in the Army for life	29	34
People only join the Army when can't find other job	23	23

After 'This is belonging' – Percentage agreeing

Statement	All 14–24-year-olds	Army interested
Can train from one of many different roles	79	83
More to an Army career than just military combat	72	81
Army career gives you skills highly valued in civilian life	64	80
The Army is modern and up-to-date	47	65
The Army has something to offer people like me/my child	41	75
Once you join, you're in the Army for life	35	40
People only join the Army when they can't find another job	23	25

Source: Jigsaw Army Campaign evaluation Tracker, Wave 57 and Wave 60

Positive attitudes from parents increased. This is important when appealing to a broader audience where parents are less likely be encouraging (Figure 25).

Figure 25: Parents' attitudes towards the Army during 'This is belonging' and the same period the previous year

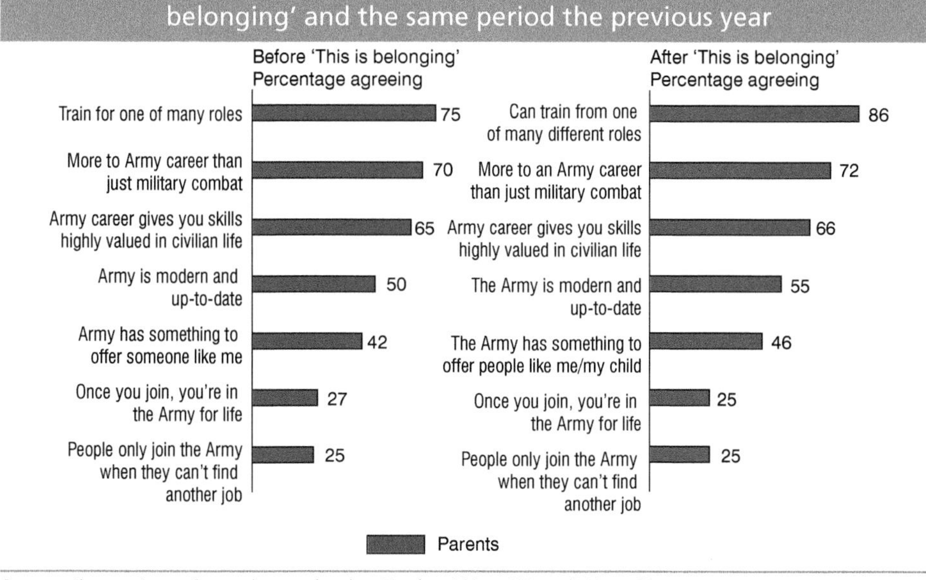

Source: Jigsaw Army Campaign evaluation Tracker, Wave 57 and Wave 60

Ruling out other factors

One major factor helped us.

Prior to making a major investment in the new campaign, Capita refined the application process making it smoother, in a project called QuickApp.

Improving the application process and making a big marketing investment together makes perfect sense, but to demonstrate the effect of *communications* in this paper, we will isolate the impact of QuickApp, and of the 'This is belonging' campaign separately, over and above non-campaign factors.

First, we'll isolate the non-campaign factors that affect applications.

Non-campaign factors in our econometric model are made up of two things.

1. *Non-media factors:* these are a combination of everything that affects recruitment outside of advertising media from the economy to PR. (This will be broken down later on).
2. *Long-term factors*: these are applications driven by long-term campaign interest from before the current 'This is belonging' campaign.

Figures 26 and 27 show that the amount of applications driven by the both the 'non-media' factors and 'long-term' campaign interest was less during 'This is belonging' (January–September 2017) than the previous year (January–September 2016).

This is the case for both regular soldier applications and total applications (which includes all streams).

Figure 26: Regular soldier applications driven by non-media and long-term were lower during the 'This is belonging' campaign vs. previous year

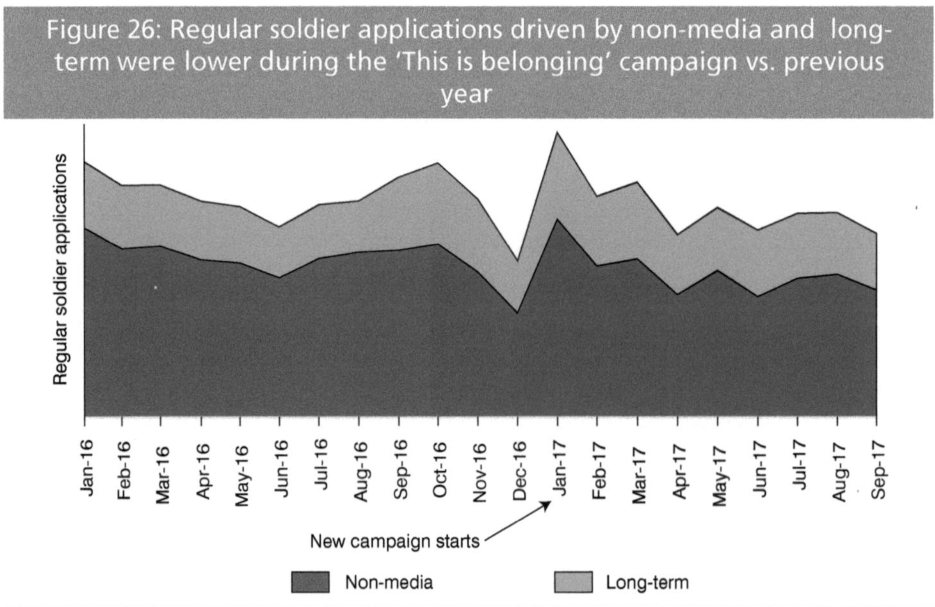

Source: MediaCom Business Science, Econometrics Data, January 2018

Figure 27: Total applications (all streams) driven by non-media and long-term were lower during the 'This is belonging' campaign vs. previous year

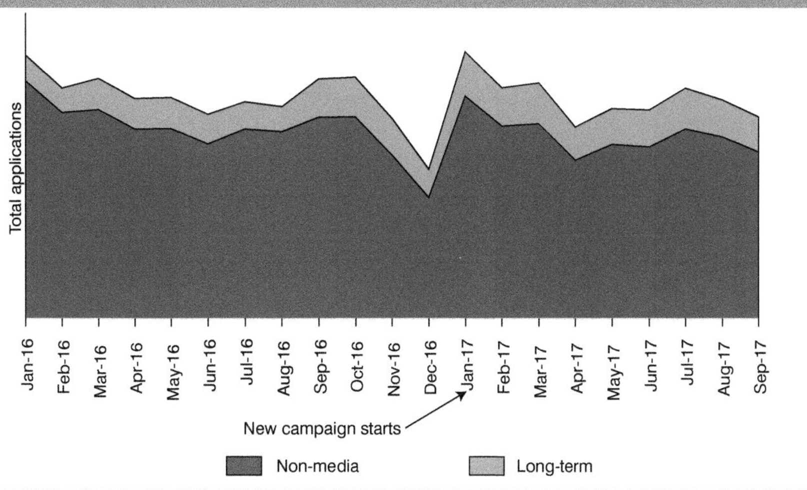

Source: MediaCom Business Science, Econometrics Data, January 2018

Now we'll isolate the QuickApp effect.

QuickApp created an initial application spike formed from quickly processing a lag of incomplete applications.

Once this lag was complete, QuickApp uplift stabilised but still had an ongoing positive effect on applications, that was not there throughout the previous year (Figure 28 and 29).

Figure 28: Uplift on regular soldier applications driven by the new QuickApp

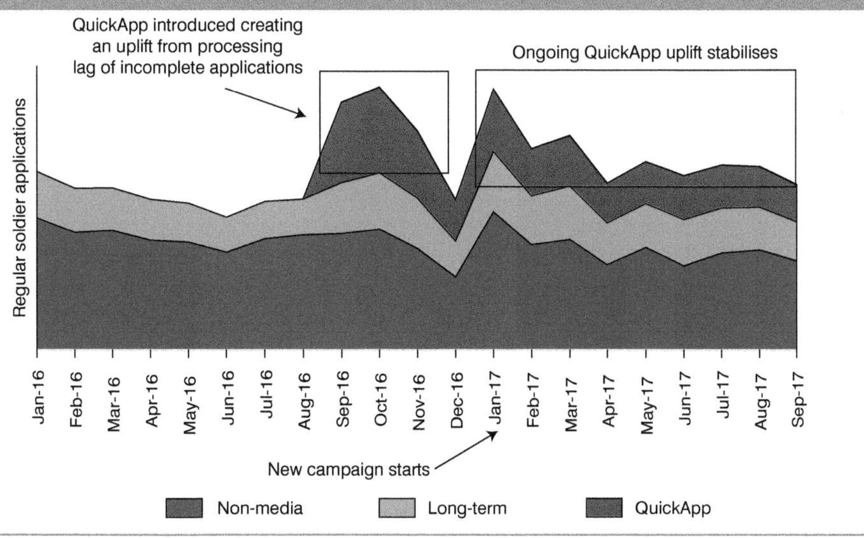

Source: MediaCom Business Science, Econometrics Data, January 2018

Figure 29: Uplift on total applications driven by the new QuickApp

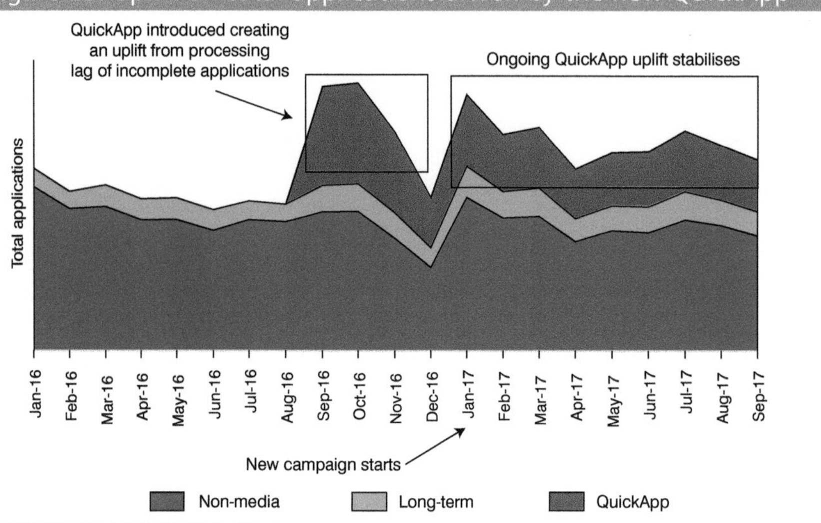

Source: MediaCom Business Science, Econometrics Data, January 2018

Crucially however, our model has isolated the impact of *campaign driven* applications (Figures 30 and 31).

1. *Despite* the declining base and long-term interest.
2. *Over and above* the positive effect of QuickApp.

Figure 30: Regular soldier applications driven by campaign increased during the 'This is belonging' campaign vs. previous year

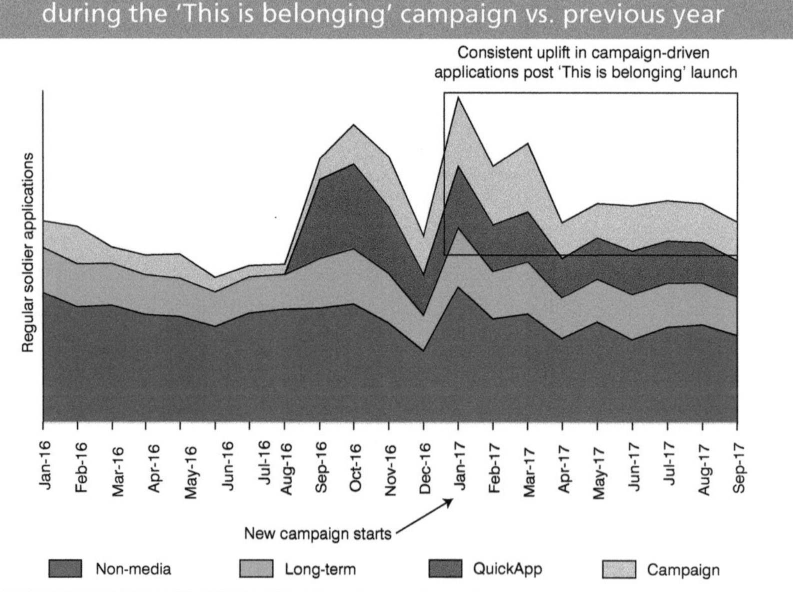

Source: MediaCom Business Science, Econometrics Data, January 2018

Figure 31: Total applications driven by campaign increased during the 'This is belonging' campaign vs. previous year

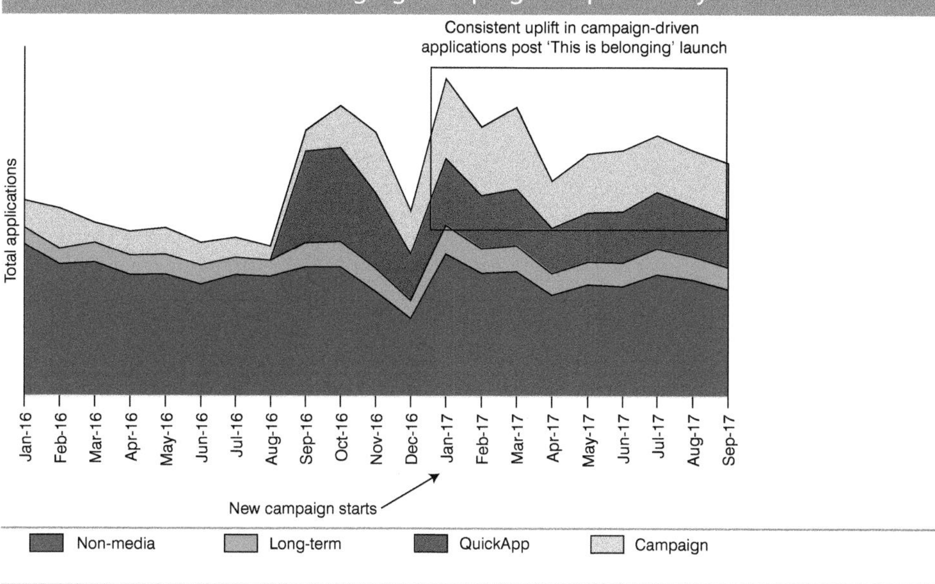

Source: MediaCom Business Science, Econometrics Data, January 2018

Once all factors are taken into account, the final econometrics report showed a significant increase in campaign-driven applications during the 'This is belonging' period vs. the previous year. Campaign-driven short-term impact during 'This is belonging' was 26% vs. 15% the previous year (Figure 32).

Figure 32: Increased campaign contribution to applications during 'This is belonging' vs. previous year

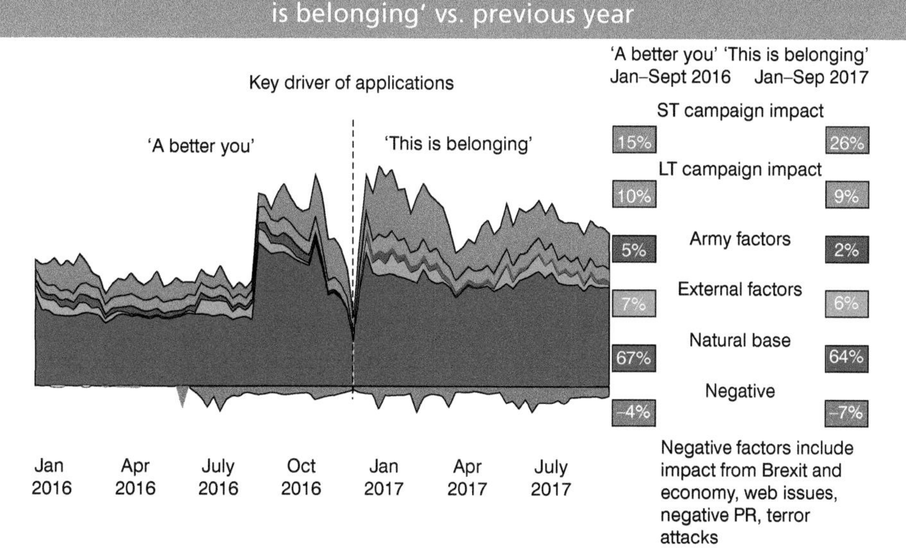

Source: MediaCom Business Science, The Army Final Econometrics Debrief, January 2018.

The waterfall chart also isolates the significant impact that the new campaign alone had on increasing the overall applications (Figure 33).

Figure 33: Waterfall chart showing drivers behind increased applications

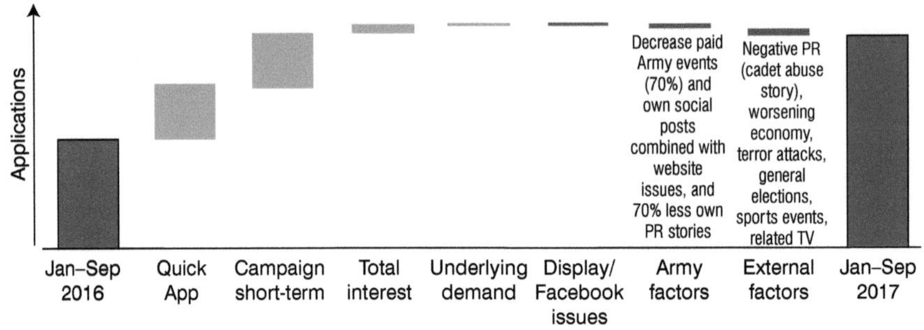

Source: MediaCom Business Science, The Army Final Econometrics Debrief, January 2018

We'll now turn to individual factors that make up the non-media factors in the econometric model and rule them out one by one.

Paid for Army recruitment events reduced in number

Paid for recruitment events reduced by 70% vs. the previous year. Events have always been one of the most powerful recruitment tools as candidates are able to speak with actual soldiers and start the application process (Figure 34).

Figure 34: Positive impact of paid events was reduced during our campaign

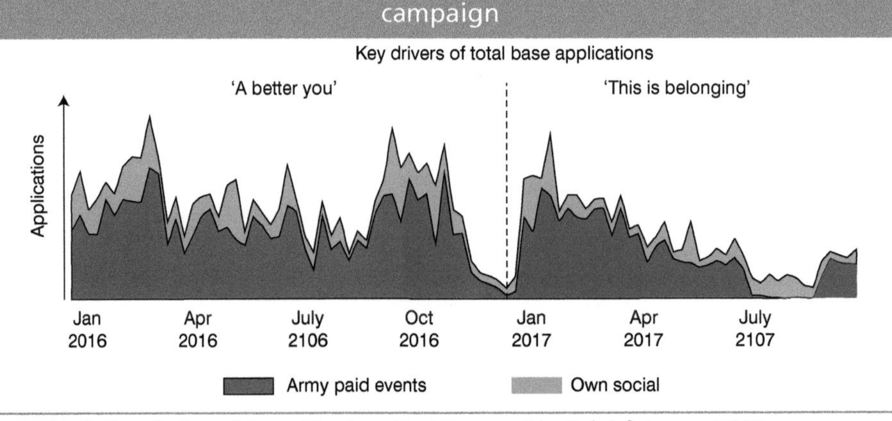

Source: MediaCom Business Science, The Army Final Econometrics Debrief, January 2018

Events matter because speaking to an actual soldier helps you realise they are normal people, just like you. To some extent, the human side of our campaign has helped to take on this role.

The economy had a negative impact on recruitment

NEET levels for young people during the campaign were lower than previous years (Figure 35).

Figure 35: NEET levels of 16–24 during the campaign

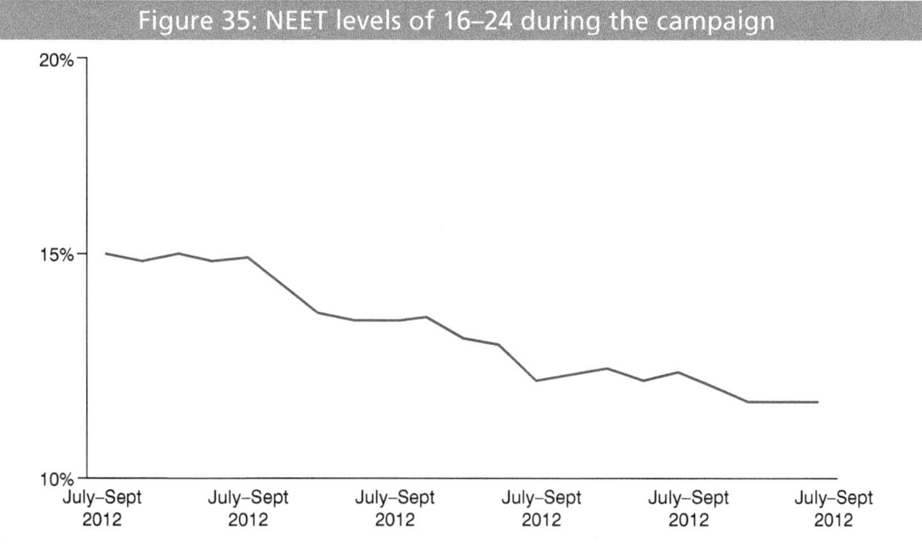

Source: Labour Force Survey ONS

Economic uncertainty from Brexit didn't help.

In theory, Brexit would only positively impact recruitment if employment levels worsened. In fact, within this period both unemployment levels and NEET levels declined.

However, the lack of consumer confidence did have a negative impact on applications as people delayed big decisions (Figure 36).

Figure 36: Economic uncertainty stemming from Brexit had a more negative impact on our new campaign period vs. the previous year

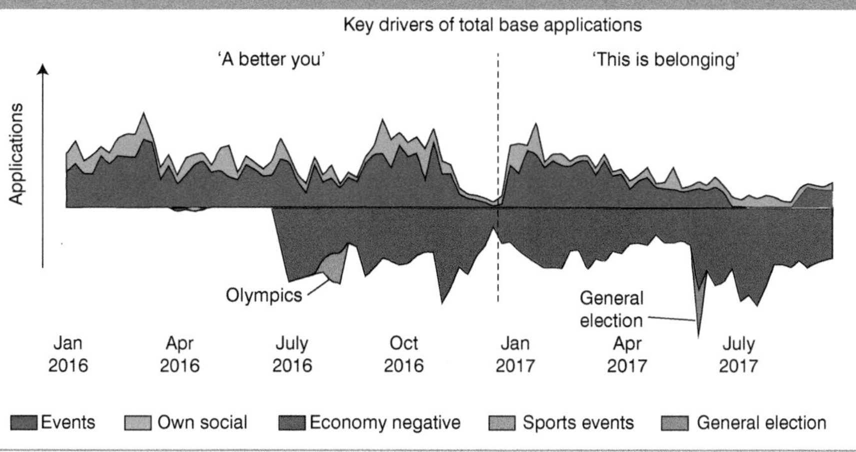

Source: MediaCom Business Science, The Army Final Econometrics Debrief, January 2018

Competitor spend didn't change significantly

Our competitors' spend had a positive effect, as many candidates who are motivated to join one defence force are naturally motivated to apply to all. However, competitor spend was not significantly higher than the previous year (Figure 37).

Figure 37: Stable competitor spend before and during the campaign

Key drivers of total base applications
'A better you'
'This is belonging'
Applications
Olympics
General election
Jan 2016
Apr 2016
July 2016
Oct 2016
Jan 2017
Apr 2017
July 2017
Competitors
Economy negative
Events
Sports events
Own social
General election

Source: MediaCom Business Science, The Army Final Econometrics Debrief, January 2018

Negative PR had a damaging impact on recruitment

Cadet abuse coverage had a negative impact on applications vs. the previous year (Figure 38).

Figure 38: Increased impact of negative PR on applications during our new campaign period vs. the year before

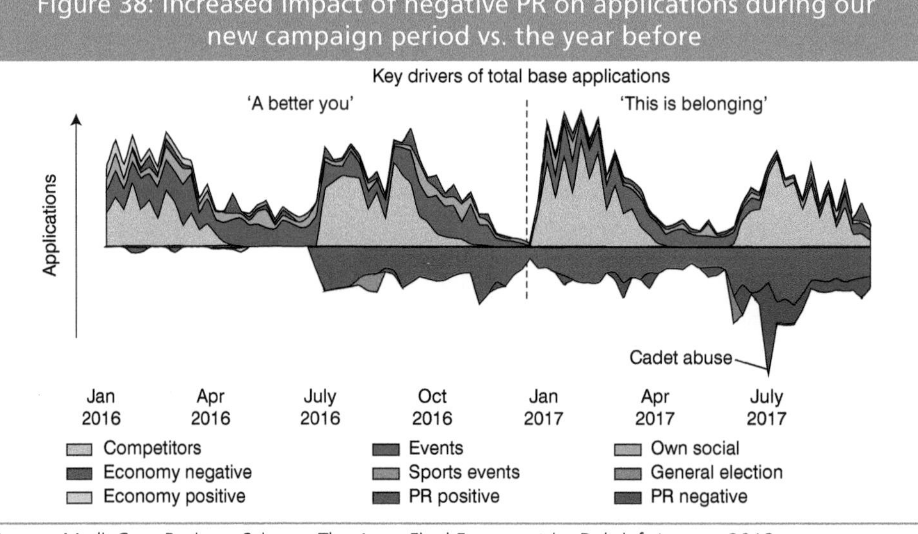

Source: MediaCom Business Science, The Army Final Econometrics Debrief, January 2018

Terror attacks meant we had to turn off media due to government policy, causing an overall negative effect on recruitment

Although higher levels of terror attacks motivated some applications, the Army was obliged to turn off communications during these periods meaning the positive effect was counterbalanced (Figure 39).

Figure 39: Negative impact of terror attacks during new campaign

Key drivers of total base applications

'A better you'
'This is belonging'
Applications
Brussels, NIce, Orlando, Berlin
Paris, Stockholm
Finsbury
Jan 2016
Apr 2016
July 2016
Oct 2016
Jan 2017
Apr 2017
July 2017
Competitors
Economy negative
Economy positive
Events
Sports events
PR positive
Own social
General election
PR negative
Terror attacks
Impacts of conflicts

Source: MediaCom Business Science, The Army Final Econometrics Debrief, January 2018

Lack of inspiring TV shows had a negative impact

Inspiring TV shows like *Our Girl* in 2016 made becoming a soldier feel attainable and drove applications in the previous year but did not air again during the new campaign (Figure 40).

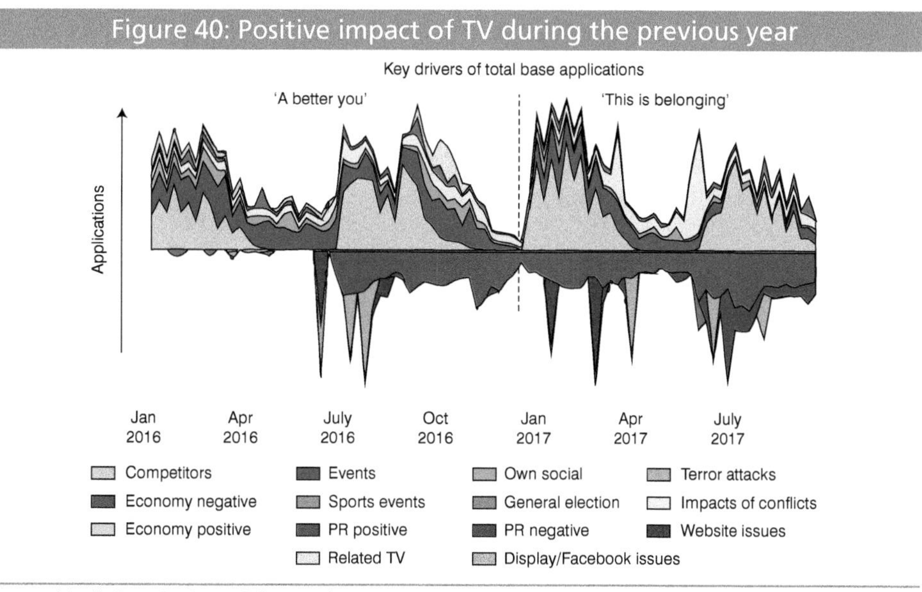

Figure 40: Positive impact of TV during the previous year

Source: MediaCom Business Science, The Army Final Econometrics Debrief, January 2018

Applications driven by seasonality and underlying demand remained stable YOY

Figure 41: Impact of seasonality/underlying remained unchanged

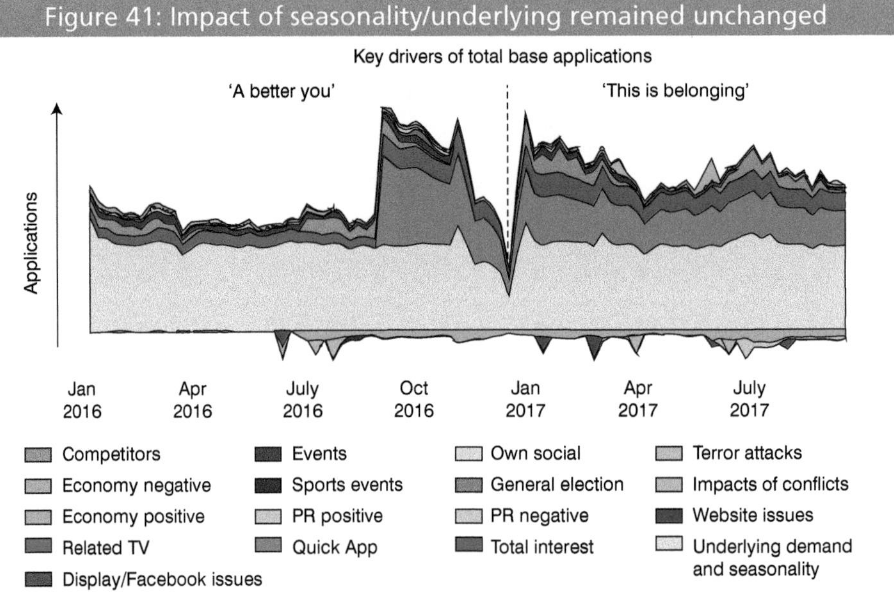

Source: MediaCom Business Science, The Army Final Econometrics Debrief, January 2018

The campaign didn't just increase applications, it increased them more efficiently.

To increase applications to the desired level, our econometric model showed the Army would have to spend significantly more, past the point of diminishing returns, causing a rising cost per application.

This was accepted as increasing applications was critically important.

Our model shows that if we had just increased spend without switching the campaign to 'This is belonging', our campaign-driven cost per application would have gone up by 22%.

What we actually see is that the whole response curve during 'This is belonging in 2017' is lifted, meaning that for every pound spent we received more applications (Figure 42).

Rather than the projected 22% increase per application, our cost per application increased by 16%, creating a significant efficiency saving for every application.

Payback

The primary payback is that after years of flatlining applications, we generated a huge increase in application volumes. We can now start to narrow the gap of the recruitment shortfall and ultimately help protect the UK at home and abroad.

Figure 42: Improved return on media for 'This is belonging'

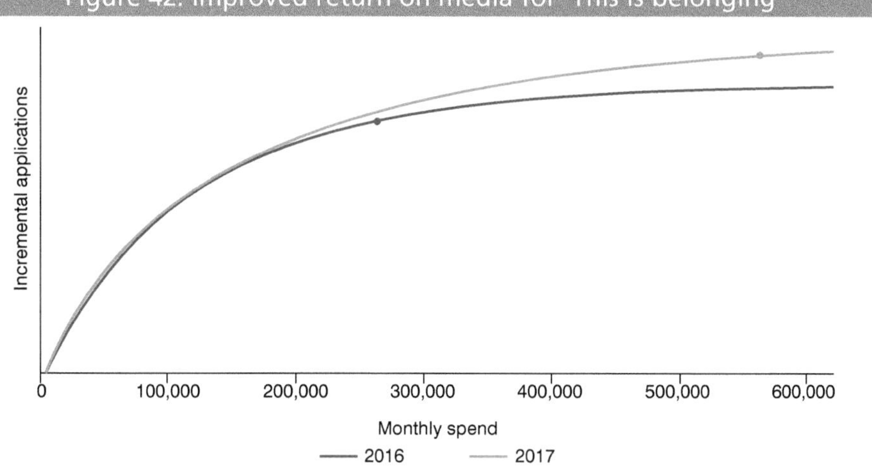

Source: MediaCom Business Science, The Army Final Econometrics Debrief, January 2018

Compared to the same campaign period the previous year:

- regular soldier applications increased 38% YOY;
- reserve soldier applications increased 48% YOY.

To demonstrate a further ROI, we have calculated the cost saving achieved by employing this specific campaign strategy and creative.

As explained, during 'This is belonging', the media spend increased 140% year on year. According to laws of diminishing returns from our econometric model our cost per application should have increased by 22%. However with 'This is belonging' our cost per application increased by only 16%.[2]

Conclusion and learnings

Our role as strategists in 'the new era of data and technology'

As creative strategists, we simply embraced the new tools that technology and data gave us alongside classic techniques, to do what we do best – find fresh insights that help us to reach our clients' objectives.

Even when it felt like every avenue had already been exhausted:

- we identified a new broader audience for the Army;
- we discovered a new benefit in *belonging*;
- we delivered it in a more relevant and targeted way.

This 'new era of data and technology' doesn't make traditional creative strategy redundant – rather, it gives us yet another tool to re-examine what we think we know in our categories to get to new thinking.

This paper shows how a powerful creative insight in the traditional sense will always be necessary to stand a chance of reframing something meaningful, like the Army.

But this paper also shows that when you are trying to motivate a significant life decision, data and technology are crucial in allowing you to make your core idea more relevant to individuals' needs.

It was through a combination of the two that 'This is belonging' could inspire someone to first consider a totally new possibility, and ultimately persuade them to change their life. For categories where we are asking people to make major choices, creativity needs data, as much as data needs creativity.

In addition, the lessons of the long and short of it have been much embraced for long-term brand-building campaigns. This direct response campaign shows the value of seeking out an emotional proposition to drive decision-making in the short term, especially when that decision is a big one.

Finally, although the effects of this campaign have been significant in the short-term, 'This is belonging' has just begun its second year and is in planning for its third. This is important because the job of any Army campaign is not just to recruit the best candidates of today, but also of tomorrow.

Notes

1. R. F. Baumeister and M. R. Leary (1995) 'The Need to Belong: Desire for Interpersonal Attachments as a Fundamental Human Motivation', *Journal of Research in Personality*, 32, 222–235.
2. MediaCom Business Science, The Army Final Econometrics Debrief, January 2018.

DFS

Turning DFS from a value brand into a brand that people value

By Aileen Ross, krow communications
Contributing author: Joy Talbot, MediaCom
Credited companies: krow communications; MediaCom

Summary

To hit growth targets, DFS needed to attract a more affluent sofa shopper by broadening its appeal. It was critical, however, to address the balance between the competing needs of short-term sales driving activity and long-term brand health goals of increasing brand consideration and love. A multi-year strategy positioned DFS as a more realistic, revealing, popular, and likeable brand without downplaying the price offers it was famous for. Advertising campaigns featuring animated characters celebrated the production and quality testing of its sofas, with British Heart Foundation and Team GB partnerships used to build affinity. Following the activity, there was a 28% increase in consideration and penetration amongst the more affluent sofa shopper rose by 32%. The approach delivered an estimated £109m of incremental sales over six years and a 64% increase in profit ROI.

Editor's comment

The judges especially admired the way that communications responded to the business reality of a new private-equity owner targeting for the brand to become a £1bn business. This was done by taking on the challenging task of broadening appeal by building the brand 'without dropping as sale'. An especially tough ask, which was brilliantly met.

Client comment

Toni Wood, CMO, DFS

Over the last six years, we have been evolving our approach to marketing. With a clear strategy of broadening our brand appeal with a key growth customer segment ('quality seekers'), whilst maintaining our core customer segment ('value seekers'), we have continuously learnt our way towards a communication model that is less reliant on short-term sales-activation tactics and that is better equipped for long-term growth.

During this period we have learnt that key consumer segments are more likely to consider the DFS brand, when they are made aware of our vertical business model (especially that all our sofas are handmade to order with many crafted in our own UK factories), as opposed to our historical one-dimensional promotional-based communications. Value will always be important to our customers, but what our communication evolution and strategic brand manoeuvres have taught us is that price is just one part of the value equation. We have been building value by growing the nation's trust, affection, and belief in the purpose of our brand – that DFS exists to deliver what consumers really need and want from their sofa – the joy of comfort (physical, emotional, aesthetic and, of course, financial comfort).

We are committed to a future where we develop a deeper understanding of our customer and what role comfort (and therefore DFS) will play in this ever-changing sofa-buying landscape. Looking to the future, we have more confidence than ever before in the strength of our brand to drive sales and we will continue to review the balance of our communications investment.

Introduction

This is the story of how six years ago we embarked on a patient, evolutionary journey that has dramatically improved the effectiveness, efficiency, and most importantly the profitability of DFS' advertising, resulting in a 64% increase in profit ROI.

Moreover this is the story of how we helped DFS to walk a creative tightrope and strike a balance between the competing needs of short-term sales-driving activity and long-term brand health. With a full appreciation of the business critical nature of advertising, we did all of this by not fundamentally changing the main message of DFS' infamously direct advertising.

Background

DFS began life in the swinging sixties when 24-year-old Graham Kirkham had an idea: make what you sell, cut out the middleman and you can do it cheaper for the customer. He rented a room above a snooker hall in Carcroft, South Yorkshire, and started making furniture upstairs and retailing it downstairs. Over the next 40 years the DFS business successfully expanded its retail footprint, TV region by TV region and, by investing heavily in advertising, made its brand famous for offering great-value sofas.

DFS floated on the Stock Exchange in 1993 valued at £271m, was taken private again in 2004 by its original founder and then sold to private equity giants, Advent International, for £500m in 2010. Today, DFS is the largest retailer in the living room furniture market by some distance with a share by value of 18.3%.[1]

DFS' success was built on many things: vertical integration, cost control of the supply chain, a broad range of products to suit all tastes and a response-driven approach to pricing and promotion. But a significant factor distinguished DFS from the competition: an unwavering dedication to the power of advertising, one specific type of advertising (Figure 1).

Figure 1: Screenshots of DFS advertising – ads aired in the early 2000s

In the five years to 2010, DFS invested £491m on short-term sales activation advertising.[2] It had become famous (perhaps synonymous) with 'act now' advertising; sales starting, sales ending, limited availability of low prices and finance deals to facilitate purchase.

A new plan

Like all private equity owners, Advent Internationals' sights were set on accelerating growth and making a healthy return on their investment, and they had the ambitious target of growing DFS into a £1bn business. Ian Filby, the new CEO, devised a clear business plan focused on five key levers of growth.[3] The most important of these for marketing was to broaden DFS' appeal to a wider group of people than those whose main focus was on price and discount, and to improve the efficiency of DFS' advertising spend.

Broadening appeal

Analysis conducted in 2011 identified that DFS was under-indexing with an audience that had great potential for future growth (Figure 2).

Figure 2: DFS Share of segments versus the category

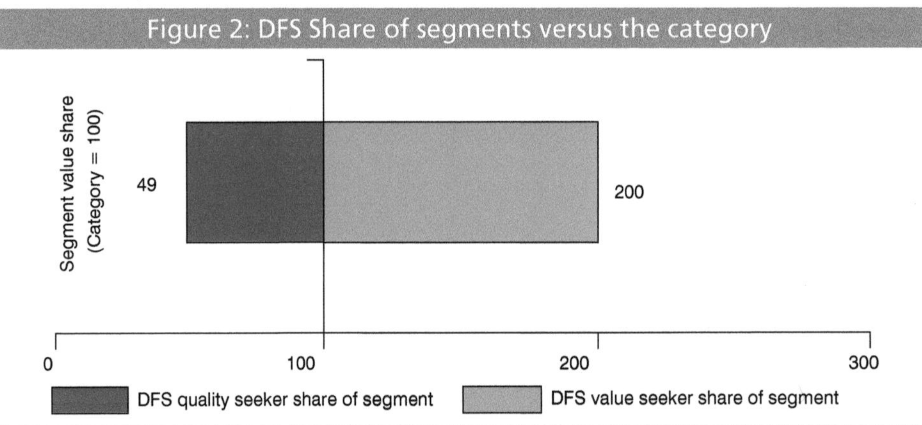

Source: Bain and Company 2012

This audience, whom we now call 'quality seekers' was a more affluent, aspirational group of consumers than the core DFS customer called 'value seekers' amongst whom DFS over-indexed to a very considerable degree (+200%). Increasing penetration of the 'quality seekers' segment to 25% by the end of financial year (FY) 2018 was a key business objective.[4]

Driving efficiencies

Improving the efficiency and effectiveness of the DFS advertising spend was another area of focus. Every £1 invested in advertising would need to work harder to drive immediate sales. Advertising had to increase consideration to build base sales. Crucially, for the first time for DFS, every £1 spent had to also strengthen the long-term position of the brand.

New objectives

This business-growth plan spawned a new set of challenging marketing objectives (Figure 3).

Figure 3: DFS Marketing objectives, as set out in 2011

These objectives formed the basis of the advertising pitch brief in 2011, neatly summarised in Figure 4.

Figure 4: Marketing vision as in 2011 pitch brief

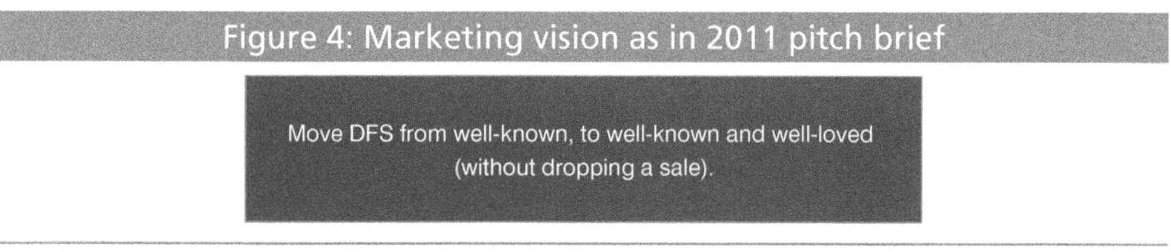

The first task for us was to understand the barriers to love and consideration.

The barriers

DFS was a value brand that people didn't value

Being famous for its promotional mechanics had restricted DFS' emotional brand equity, as can be seen in Figure 5.[5]

Figure 5: DFS brand image February 2012

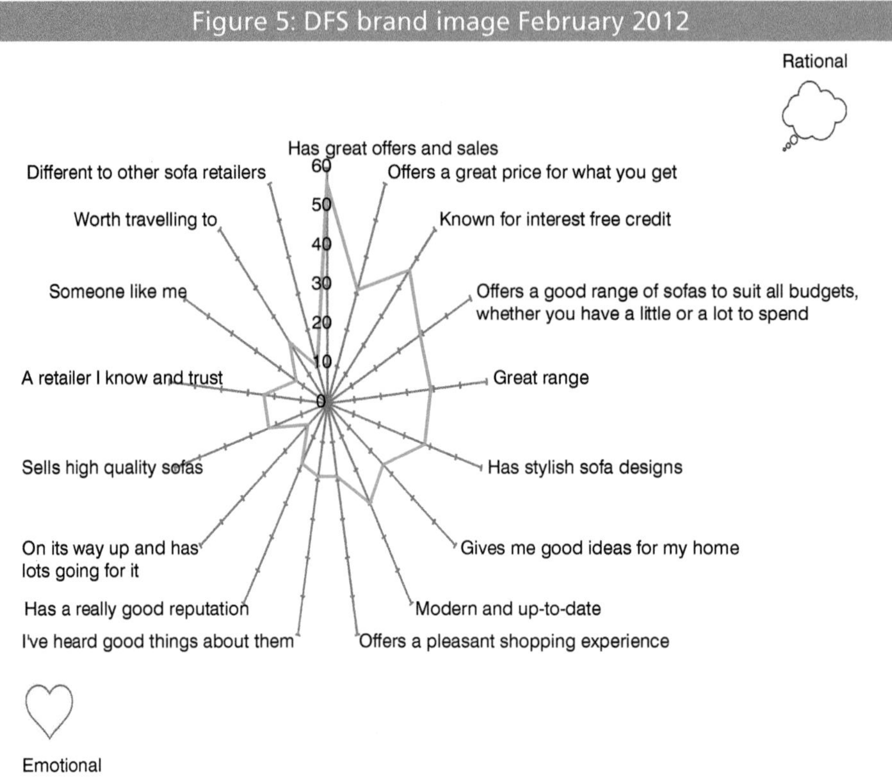

Source: Monkey See Brand and Communications Tracker, February 2012. Base: total sample of 'in-market' shoppers

1 in 4 people didn't like DFS (Figure 6)[6]

Figure 6: DFS brand impressions

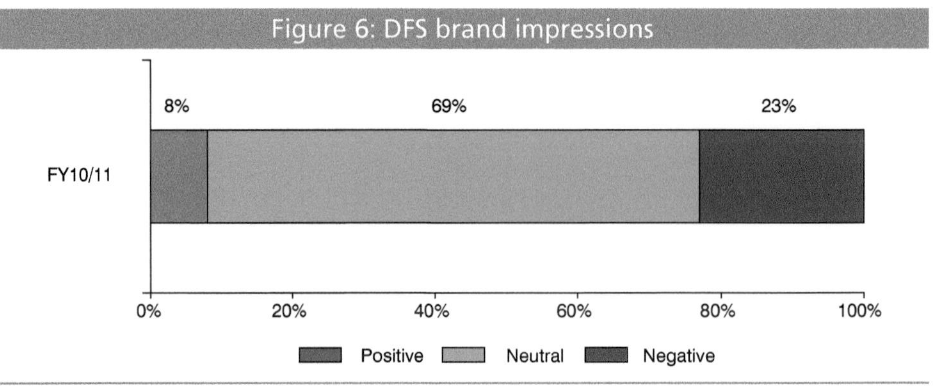

Source: YouGov BrandIndex 2011

Although people responded to the sale, they derided DFS for it 'never-ending'

Figure 7: The DFS Sale became the butt of many a joke

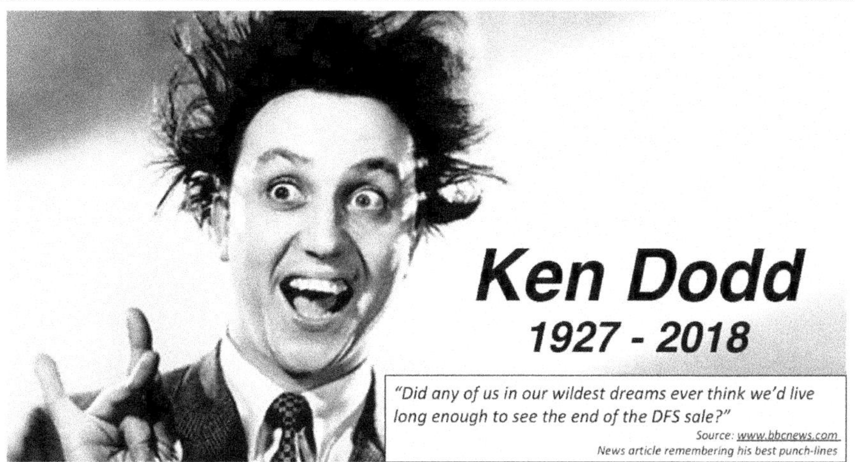

People found DFS' advertising annoying

In 2011, 25% of sofa shoppers claimed they did not consider DFS because they were 'put off by their advertising' (Figure 8).[7]

Figure 8: DFS TV ad 'Rockstar' 2008 shortlisted in a public poll of the most annoying adverts ever

M TV › TV News › Danny Baker

Most annoying TV adverts EVER: From Daz's Doorstep Challenge to Webuyanycardotcom to Go Compare

There have been a fair few cringeworthy ads over the years but none more so than some of these rotters

DFS - Rockstar

Yes, you knew everyone's favourite perma-sale sofa experts would be in here somewhere didn't you? To be fair, most of their adverts are a bit ropey, but get the job done; however, this was a step too far, combining the aural atrocity that was Nickelback's *Rockstar* with some actors who were only too willing to surrender their dignity for a free leather 3-piece suite. How and why was this song ever popular? But then people thought it was OK to burn witches once too, we suppose.

Source: *The Mirror* July 2015

And because there was so much of it, the advertising dominated perceptions of the DFS brand. During the summer of 2010, 93.4% of UK housewives had the opportunity to see a DFS advert 27.9 times.[8]

Switch off the sale!

Our objective was to persuade more people to love and consider DFS. Given the barriers identified, the answer should have been really simple shouldn't it?

Switch off the sale! Change the message! Change the model! But for the huge influence of four words in the original brief 'without dropping a sale' it might have been.

More likely, it would have been business suicide because, over the years, the DFS' vertically integrated operation and the DR advertising model had become intertwined (Figure 9).

Figure 9: The DFS machine

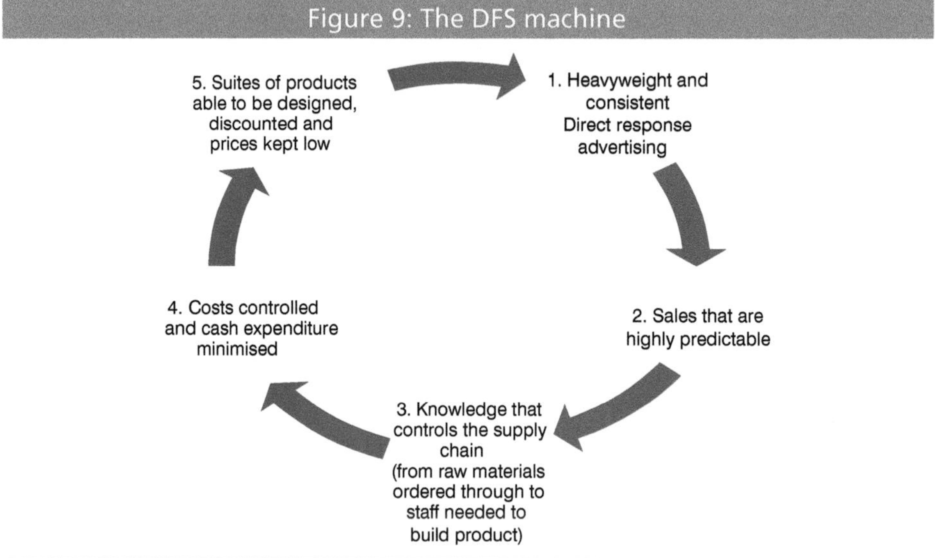

While conventional marketing wisdom would say that to make the kind of big changes we wanted to make you have to make big communications changes, the business realities of DFS prevented us from taking such actions. The risk of switching off what made the business successful in the first place was just too great. What, on earth could we do?

A surprising solution: It's not what you say but how you say it

We couldn't switch off the sale and we couldn't turn off the direct-response model, but we could turn DFS' persistent advertising presence to our advantage and emotionally prime people to see DFS as more than just well known for sale.

And so, from 2012, we embarked on a skilful courtship of both 'quality seekers' and 'value seekers' through lots of changes, not to the message of the advertising, but to the detail of how we communicated sales and offers. In so doing, we rewired consumers' mental and emotional associations with the value offered by DFS in its sales.

The last six years of DFS communications activity can be summarised by four key themes, underpinned by a constant drive to increase media efficiencies (Figure 10).

Figure 10: The themes that drove DFS advertising effectiveness and efficiency improvements

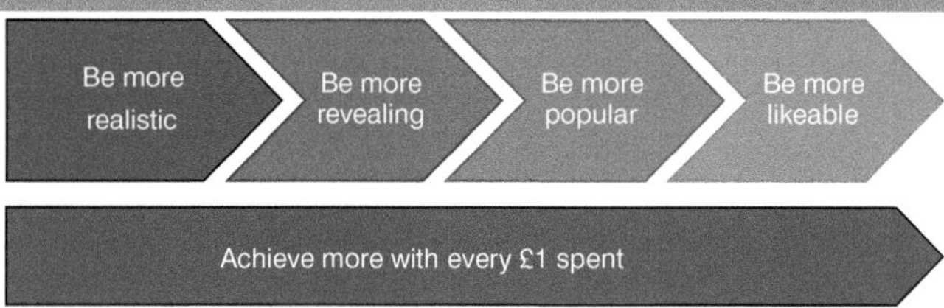

Be more realistic

Historically, DFS advertising tended to 'model' impossibly large sofas in implausibly glamorous houses: more 'footballers' wives' homes' than real homes. Now, although the core promotional message remained the same, the sets, the sofas, the casting, the action and the tone of voice were all changed to be presented and rendered in an everyday aspirational way, in both TV and press, that people could emotionally relate to rather than reject (Figures 11–14).

Figure 11: 30-second TV ad February 2012: '£400 off never felt so good'

V/O: With at least £400 off Koko collection sofas and 4 years interest free credit, sleeping, diving, brum-bruming and walking the plank on a dfs sofa has never felt more comfortable. DFS. Making everyday more comfortable

Figure 12: 30-second TV ad May 2012: '50% off family play zones'

V/O: Right now our planets, dance floors and spaceships are half price. And, as always, there's 4 years interest free credit. Dfs. Making everyday more comfortable

Figure 13: 30-second TV ad June 2012: 'No kidding, half price sofas to make your home even happier'

V/O: No kidding, our Moda Collection sofas are half price and as always, come with 4 years interest free credit. DFS. making everyday more comfortable.

Figure 14: Typical example of the direct-response press ads running from 2012

Be more revealing

Proprietary krow research identified that there were a number of 'truths' about DFS that many people did not know and which, when tested, were surprising and motivating to our key audiences, especially 'quality seekers' (Table 1).[9]

Table 1: DFS hidden truths 'quality seekers' response

	Aware of...	Gives a more positive impression ...	% point shift in positive impression from awareness	Would make me likely to consider...	% point shift in consideration from awareness
Free 10 year guarantee as standard for all sofas made in our UK factories	14%	38%	+23%	40%	+26%
There is a qualified upholsterer in every DFS store who you can call out if you have a sofa mishap	4%	28%	+24%	26%	+22%
Every sofa is individually hand made to order for you	12%	27%	+15%	23%	+11%
DFS is a British company with over 40 years experience	19%	34%	+15%	29%	+10%

Source: YouGov form krow 2012. Ranked in order of consideration shift.

Because the sales-activation model had to be retained we had to find a way to skilfully and persistently weave these truths into our communications. Our hypothesis was that these truths would make the promotional messaging work harder and would improve perceptions of DFS' 'value for money' (VFM). In order to achieve standout however, we needed to give the messaging a bit of room to breathe and be noticed from the 'act now' encouragements. Figure 15 illustrates how we achieved (and continue to achieve) this.

Figure 15: Average DFS advertising spend ratio from September 2012 onwards

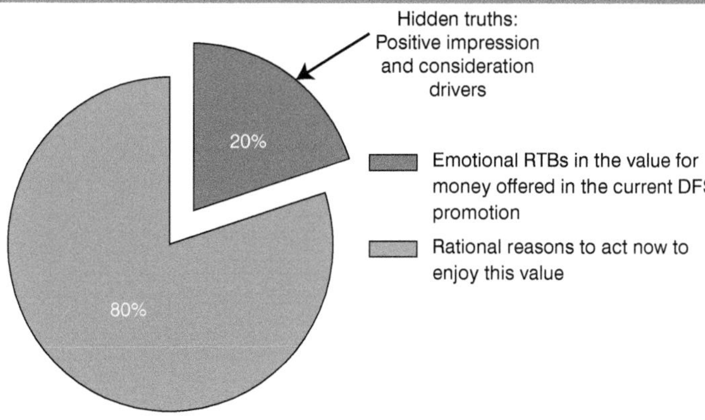

For consistency, all executions within each promotional period carried the same music and contained the same 'Hidden Truth' thematic link to announce and support the value offered in the current promotion (Figures 16 and 17).

Figure 16: 30-second TV September 2012: 'The benefit of experience' (typical of September 2012 September 2015) integrated hidden truths into 'more realistic' homes based promotional announcement advertising

V.O: Some things get better with experience. We've been hand making sofas for 43 years and our new Style Collection sofas come with at least £500 off as well as 4 years interest free credit.
Dfs. making everyday more comfortable

Figure 17: September 2012 screenshots from short-time length ads that focus on hard-working, sofa display, pricing and act now messaging (typical of all future campaigns following the 20:80 model)

In the advertising in October 2015, we ventured outside of the home and into our UK factories to further emphasise the value for money consumers can enjoy during DFS by linking the standard 'act now' message to the pre-preparedness of DFS expert craftspeople (Figures 18–20).

Figure 18: 40-second TV ad spotlighting DFS craftspeople as reasons to believe in VFM offered during the 'Guaranteed Christmas Delivery' campaign period of October 2015

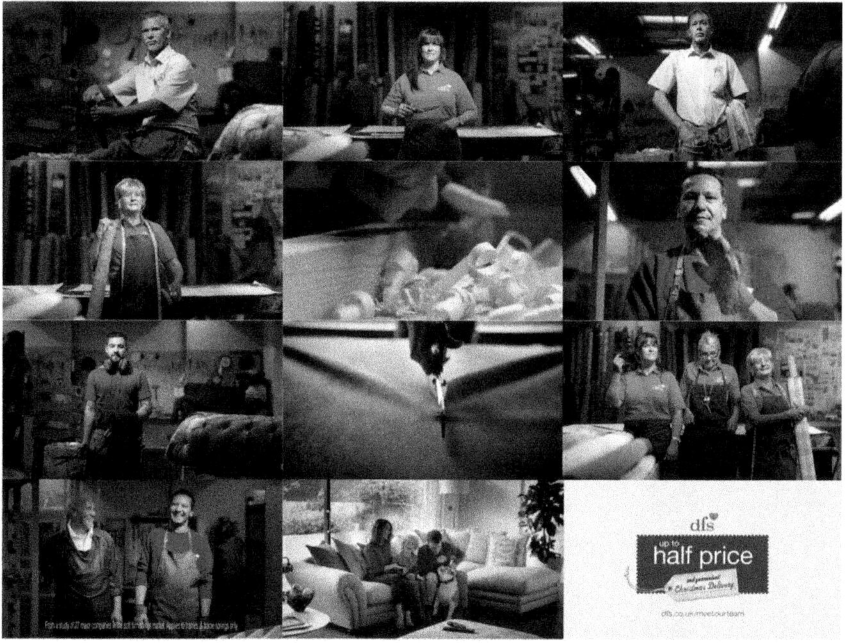

VO: We're ready... So when you order a half price new season collection sofa it's guaranteed to be handmade and delivered in time for Christmas. DFS – making every day more comfortable

Figure 19: One of a selection of product, price and 'act now' short time length adverts during the 'Guaranteed Christmas Delivery' campaign period of October 2015

VO: All DFS sofas are handmade to order. And now, New Season Collection sofas are half price. Like the EVOLUTION double recliner, now £699. And the PIZZAZZ sofa, now £299...with guaranteed Christmas Delivery

Figure 20: Typical suite of press ads

Reasons to believe in the brand *Reasons to believe in the value* *Act now value*

Be more popular

DFS entered into a number of partnerships with popular lifestyle brands such as the magazine *Country Living* and the retailer French Connection. The intention was to develop and advertise branded sofas exclusively available at DFS. As well as driving sales, the objective was to catch the eye and turn the heads of 'quality seekers' and create new associations in their minds about DFS (Figure 21).[10]

Figure 21: Typical example of a short time length 'Exclusive brand' ad that featured in normal campaign rotations

VO: At DFS our Exclusive Brand sofas are all handmade to order.. like the House Beautiful Freya sofa, or the Gower sofa from our Country Living collection and the French Connection Zinc sofa just £899... and they can be delivered before Christmas. See more at dfs.co.uk

DFS also partnered with The British Heart Foundation's (BHF) sofa collection initiative. This was a CSR partnership that helped to remove one of the biggest pain points for sofa buyers whilst at the same time raising money for an extremely worthy cause (Figure 22).[11]

Figure 22: 2013, 20-second TV, digital video and press ad used to build awareness of the service

Krow also devised the surprising partnership with Britain's most loved sporting brand, Team GB, to help to amplify appreciation for, and improve DFS' reputation as, a credible, quality British brand (Figures 23 and 24).

Figure 23: Summary of some of the elements that formed a year's worth of integrated communications to raise awareness of the 'Quality made in Britain' DFS and Team GB partnership

Figure 24: 30-second TV campaign to celebrate DFS partnership with Team GB and our latest award for quality manufacturing

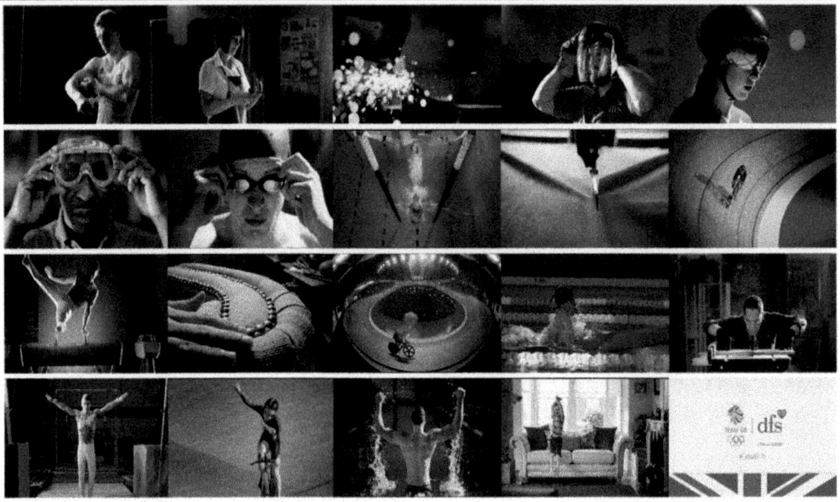

VO: We're proud to be official Team GB partners and to have our sofas awarded a British Standard for strength and durability. DFS – Proud Team GB Partners

Be more likeable

In 2016, under the leadership of DFS' new CMO Toni Wood, we worked with Aardman Animations to develop a new style of advertising that had at its heart the idea to showcase the expertise, enthusiasm and infectious likeability of the DFS workforce through the medium of upholstered people (Figure 25).

Figure 25: A selection of key-frames since the 16 November launch of the DFS 'Upholstered people' campaign

We were aiming for a new type of fame for DFS: a feel-good and meaningful fame. We had created a brand vehicle to literally 'soften' the image of DFS (Figure 26).

Figure 26: Selection of 'Upholstered DFS people' bringing a new 'feel good' equity to 'sales' messaging

The vehicle allowed us to implicitly turn consumers attention to what we wanted to make popular and valuable to them, without changing our message or model:

> *DFS is a team of hard-working people who care about the quality of the products they hand make and the comfort they bring to your home.*

Previously the equity that held the brand together was the sale; today it's the DFS people (Figure 27).

Figure 27: Every 'Upholstered' character is based on a real DFS employee: here are some meeting their characters

This relationship was later strengthened when we partnered with the launch of Nick Park's Early Man film in cinemas in February 2018 (Figure 28).

Figure 28: Keyframes from the 2017/18 'Mammoth winter sale' campaign

The media strategy

A rigorous approach to finding DFS' optimum balance

On the one hand, the key role for media was to maximise awareness of these brand perception-changing steps (especially amongst 'quality seekers'). On the other, for an advertising responsive brand like DFS, every £ spent in both existing and new channels had to continue to be profitable, accounted for and deliver an instant return in terms of incremental sales.

The reach of response driving activity has always been critical to DFS' success. This had to be maintained at all costs, but we had to find new ways to help the evolved DFS communications approach achieve its maximum effect. Year-on-year, by applying a rigorous test and learn approach (and using econometrics and brand tracking to monitor performance), we made incremental improvements to the quality of this reach and consequently the relevance, consideration-driving power and conversion potential of every interaction (Figure 29).

Figure 29: The incremental improvements made to the planning and buying of DFS media to help deliver greater efficiency

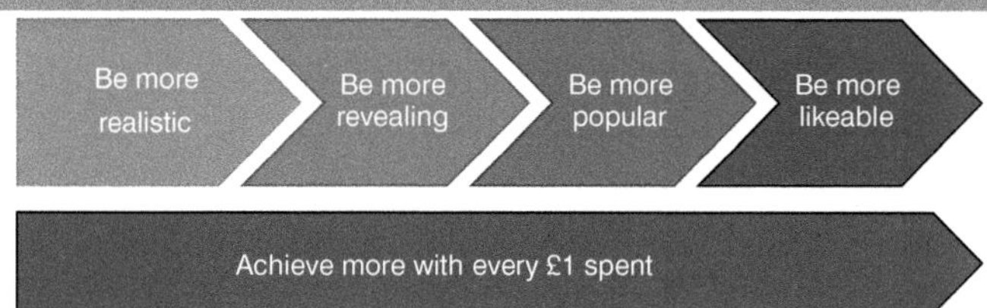

2011	2012	2013	2014	2015	2016	2017
More cost-effective TV channel mix with no reduction of reach Switch from mono to colour national press Removal of local print investment Broadening of the national press to reach 'quality Seekers' but not at the expense of 'value seekers'	TV time lengths change, introduction of 40-second, 20-second and 10-second ITV product placement on 'This Morning' National press Boxing Day takeover blitzes Introduction of digital newsbrands Exclusive brands launched onto TV and quality newsbrands	C5 channel ident sponsorship AV neutral planning and introduction of VOD Introduction of national OOH Print content partnerships with *The Telegraph* and *Daily Mail's You* magazine.	Connected online and offline syncing TV spots Re-targeting 'quality seekers' and 'value seekers' exposed to OOH with mobile Telegraph partnership themed around British quality program-matically	SKY IQ Panel and DFS customer data fusion to improve channel selection Introduction of digital audio brands	Team GB partnership with the *Evening Standard*, Ocean outdoor, specific Team GB TV ads Supercharg-ing TV ads through synced	TVR and SOV TV planning by day for Christmas, Easter and Bank Holidays Amplifica-tion of film tie-in with Aardman's *Early Man* in winter through TV, printbrands, outdoor and digital

Source: MediaCom

Achieving more with every £1 spent

In order to ensure that we met the business growth challenge of making every pound invested work harder than ever before, marginal spend curve modelling was employed to optimise spend for maximal results.

The result of all this work was that DFS was able to spend not one penny more than was necessary to maintain an all-year round, always-on and heavyweight presence and remain the biggest-spending furniture retailer by some distance, while still delivering a highly profitable return (Figure 30).

Figure 30: The average spend FY 2015/16 to 2016/17 was 32% lower than FY 2010/11 while the profit generated was +11%

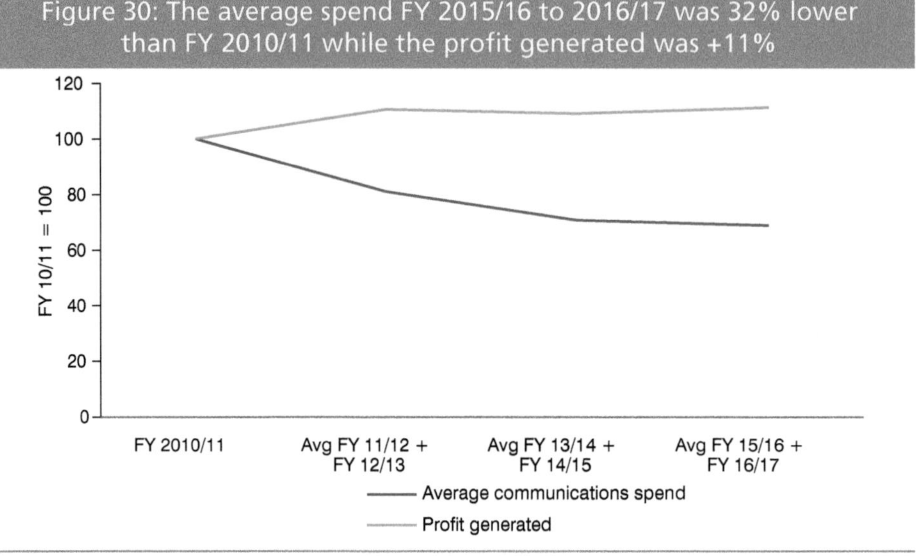

Source: MediaCom and DFS

The objective of focusing on continuous efficiency gains throughout the DFS operation has had the added benefit of allowing DFS to reinvest and redeploy these savings back into the business to ensure we continue to strengthen the long-term position of the brand and enhance our ability to deliver future growth.

What has been achieved since 2011?

Despite economic storm clouds, fragile consumer confidence and huge pressures on the retail category over the last six years, the DFS brand is in its strongest position in its 50-year history, and DFS successfully returned to the London Stock Exchange in 2015.

More people bought from DFS

DFS' sales have grown dramatically since 2011/12, and the DFS Group sales broke through the through £1 billion pounds mark in March 2017 in sales in the current financial year (Figure 31).[12]

Every year of our journey, up until FY 2015/16, we have seen steady sales volume increases. Despite a slight YOY –3.6% decline in orders between 2015/16 and 2016/17, our latest volume sales still equate to 21% more sofa shoppers having bought their new sofa from DFS in 2016/17, versus 2011 (Figure 32).

Figure 31: 17% increase in DFS value sales since FY 2011/12

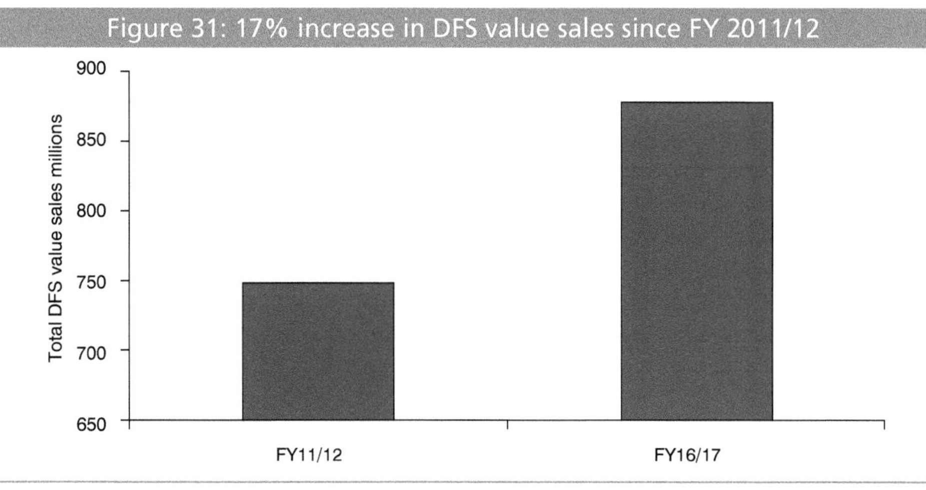

Figure 32: Total DFS volume orders indexed vs. FY 2011/12

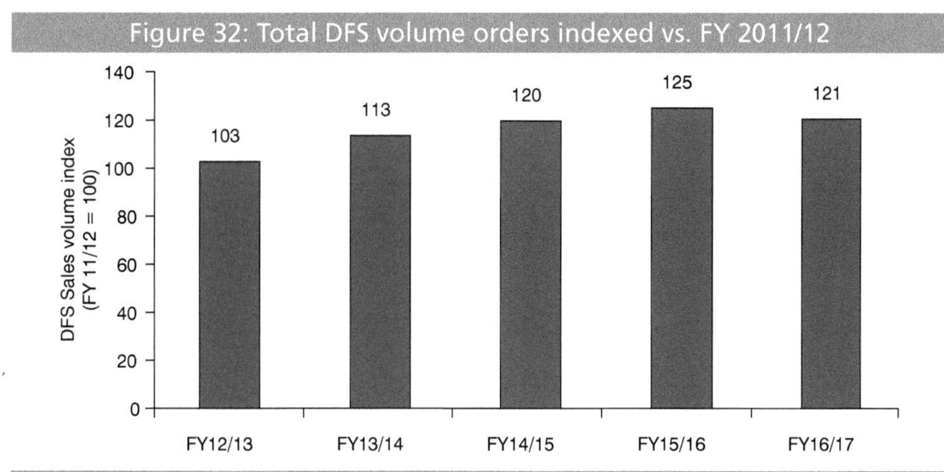

More people have visited the DFS store and website

Although DFS have only been tracking footfall since 2013, we know that since then footfall has increased 8% (Table 2).

Table 2: DFS annual footfall

	FY 2013/14	FY 2014/15	FY 2015/16	FY 2016/17
Footfall Indexed	100	103.15	107.19	108.37

Source: DFS. All stores with cameras installed since FY 2013/14

In 2017, 1 in 9 people in the market went to a DFS store; this is up 2% year on year. Web traffic has more than doubled (Figure 33). Last year 1 in 2.5 people in the market visited the DFS website.

Figure 33: DFS annual web visits

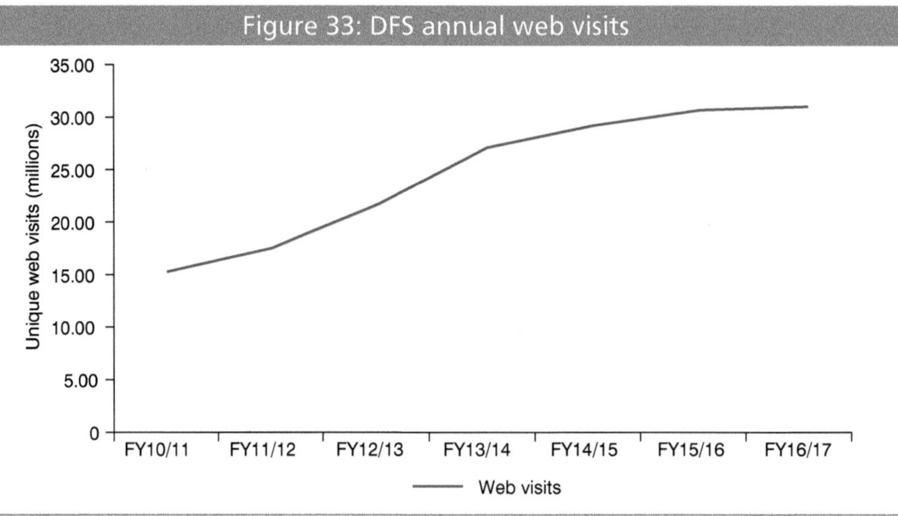

Source: DFS

Something other than category growth in digital purchasing of furniture must be responsible for this dramatic increase in DFS web visits because in 2016/17 the overall weekly average size of the digital furniture market decreased by 1%, but our web visits increased by 1%. [13]

More people considered DFS

Before we began our journey, 60% of sofa shoppers said that they would consider the brand. In the current year to date (2018), 76% of sofa shoppers now say that they would consider DFS (Figure 34).

Figure 34: 28% increase in sofa shoppers' top 3 box consideration for DFS

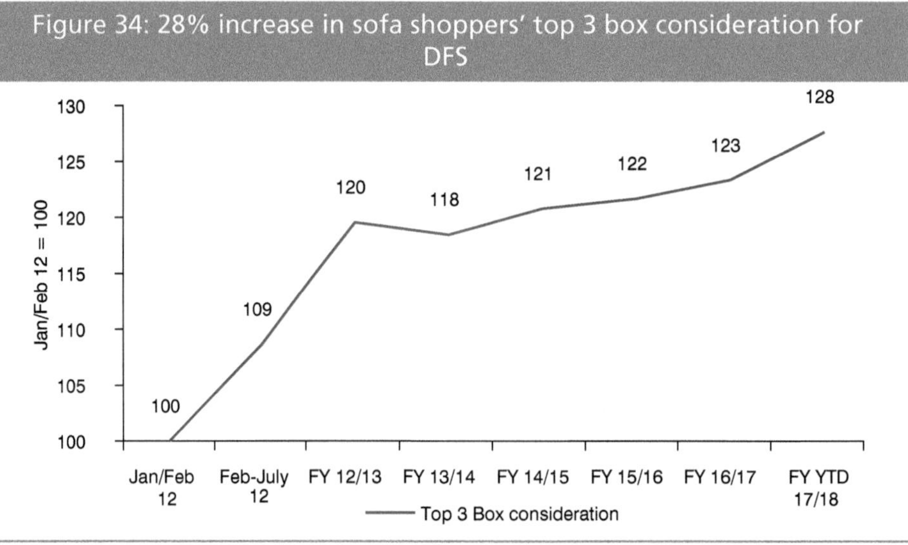

Base: Total sample of 'in-market' sofa shoppers. All YOY differences statistically significant at 95% confidence level.

More people more strongly considered DFS

Following the communication of our Team GB partnership and subsequently the 'Upholstered people' campaign with Aardman, we saw a step change not only in the number of considerers but also in the strength of that consideration, too (Figure 35).

Figure 35: DFS 45% increase in top 2 box consideration

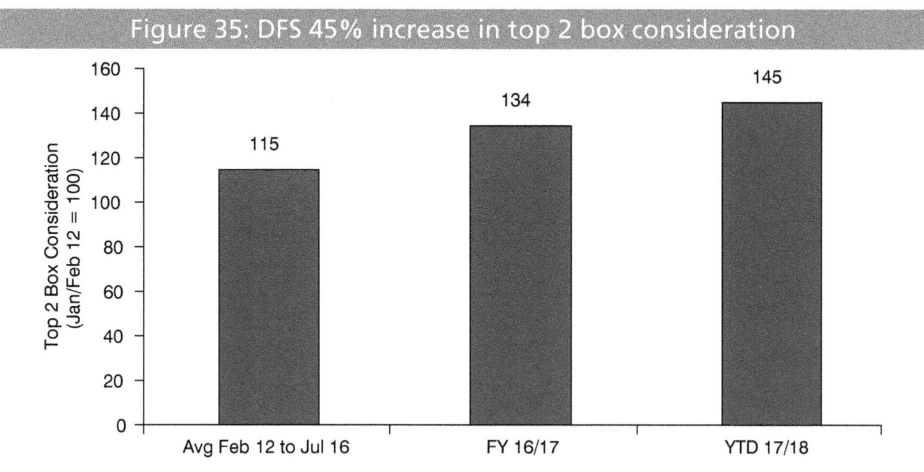

All differences statistically significant at 95% confidence level.

More 'quality seekers' considered DFS

A key marketing objective was to broaden the appeal of the DFS brand with 'quality seekers' in order to increase our penetration of this lucrative segment. Over the last six years we have not only made gains in the numbers of 'quality seekers' now more open to DFS but also to the strength of their consideration (Figure 36).

Figure 36: 'Quality seeker' DFS consideration growth

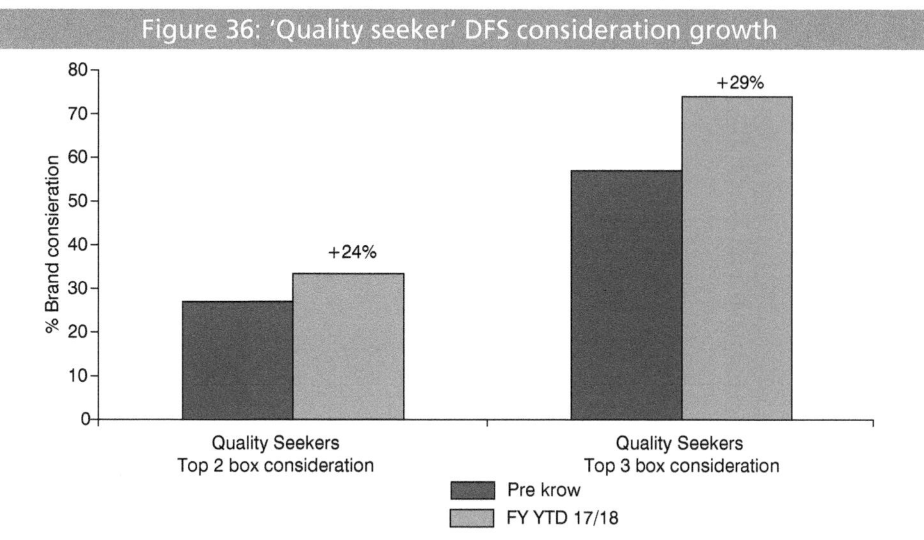

Source: Monkey See Brand and Communications Tracker, February 2012–February 2018. Base: ABC1 'in-market' sofa shoppers. All differences statistically significant at 95% confidence level.

More 'quality seekers' have now bought sofas from us

In 2016/17 we achieved our 'quality seekers' market share target a full year ahead of target. This was driven by a 32% increase in penetration (Figure 37).[14]

Figure 37: 32% increase in DFS share of 'quality seekers' spend

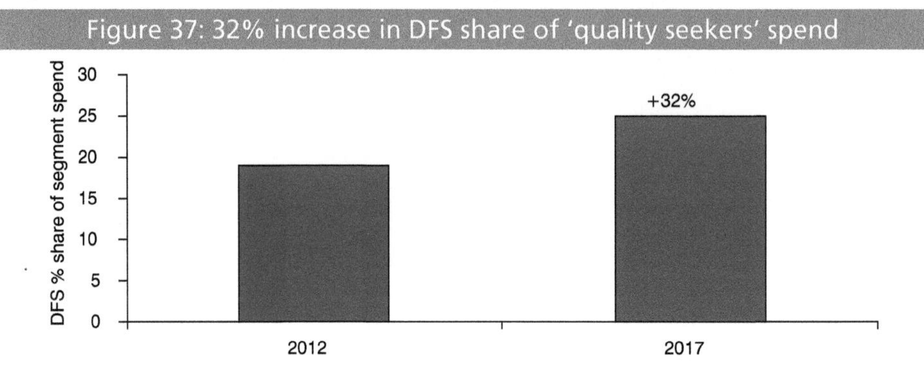

Source: DFS market tracker

More 'value seekers' more strongly considered DFS

Another key marketing objective was to strengthen our relationship with our core 'value seeker' audience. Figure 38 shows how we managed to grow the strength of their consideration for DFS by 32% over this period.

Figure 38: 'Value seekers' DFS consideration

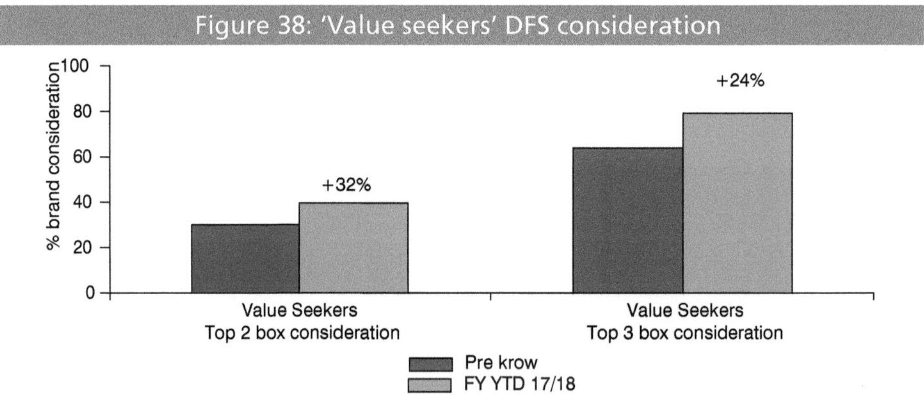

Source: Monkey See Brand and Communications Tracker, February 2012–February 2018. Base: C2DE 'in-market' sofa shoppers. All differences statistically significant at 95% confidence level.

These positive shifts protected DFS from a category-wide value decline in contribution from this segment. Between 2010 and 2017, while the sales contribution of 'value seekers' to the total upholstery category declined 38% by value, DFS experienced only a 13% decline. This would suggest that strengthening the relationship between DFS and its core 'value seeker' segment insulated DFS somewhat from otherwise challenging category dynamics (Figure 39).

Figure 39: Showing the 38% decline in the spend contribution of 'value seekers' to the category and the 13% decline to DFS sales share of segment spend

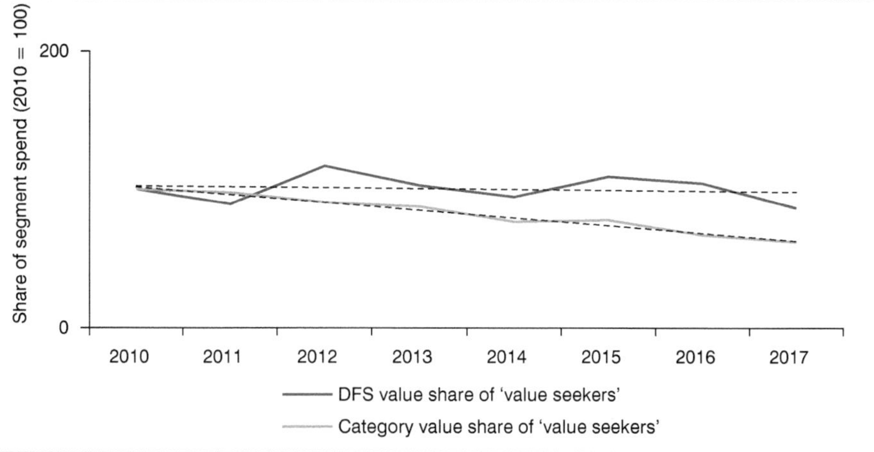

Source: DFS Market Tracker

Why improving consideration was so important to driving value for DFS

Consideration increased store footfall

Through econometric analysis we have identified that, on average, communications factors drive 30% of total footfall with consideration contributing around 9% of this (Figure 40).[15]

Figure 40: Drivers of footfall by year

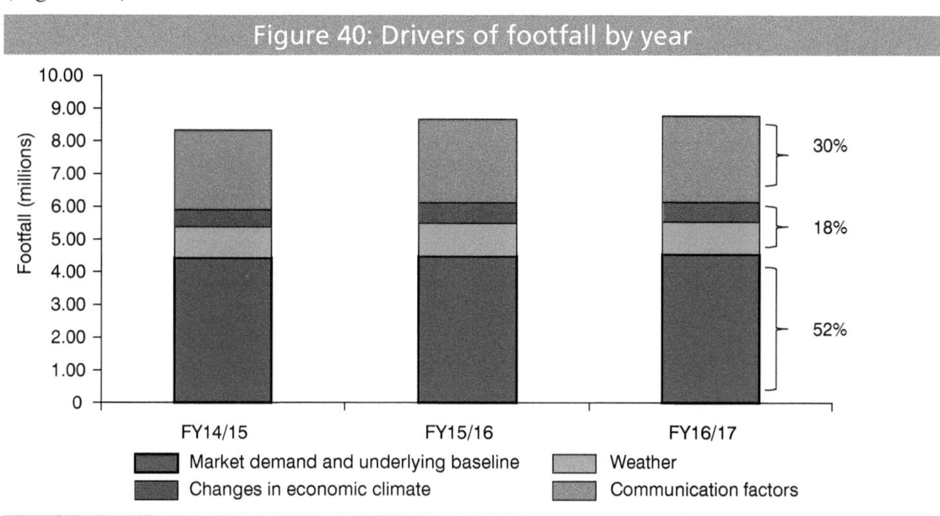

Source: MediaCom Business Science econometrics projects from FY 2011/12 to FY 2016/17

Further econometric analysis isolated that a 1% percentage point change in top 2 box consideration will cause a +0.35% change in footfall per week across all stores. On average, this accounted for 11% of footfall in any given week. Between FY 2014/15 and FY 2016/17, consideration improvements drove an additional 2.2m footfall in total (Figures 41 and 42).

Figure 41: Additional footfall driven by changes achieved in top 2 box brand consideration

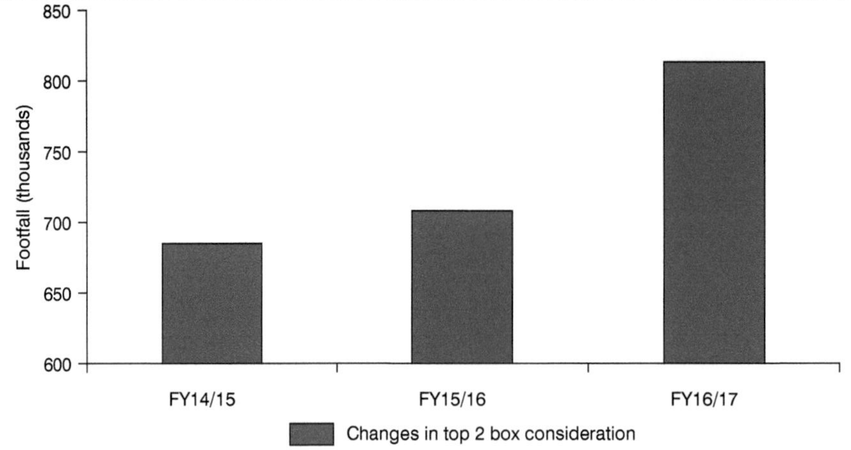

Footfall (thousands)
850
800
750
700
650
600
FY14/15
FY15/16
FY16/17
Changes in top 2 box consideration

Source: MediaCom Business Science econometrics projects from FY 2011/12 to FY 2016/17

Fig 42: Consideration-driven footfall

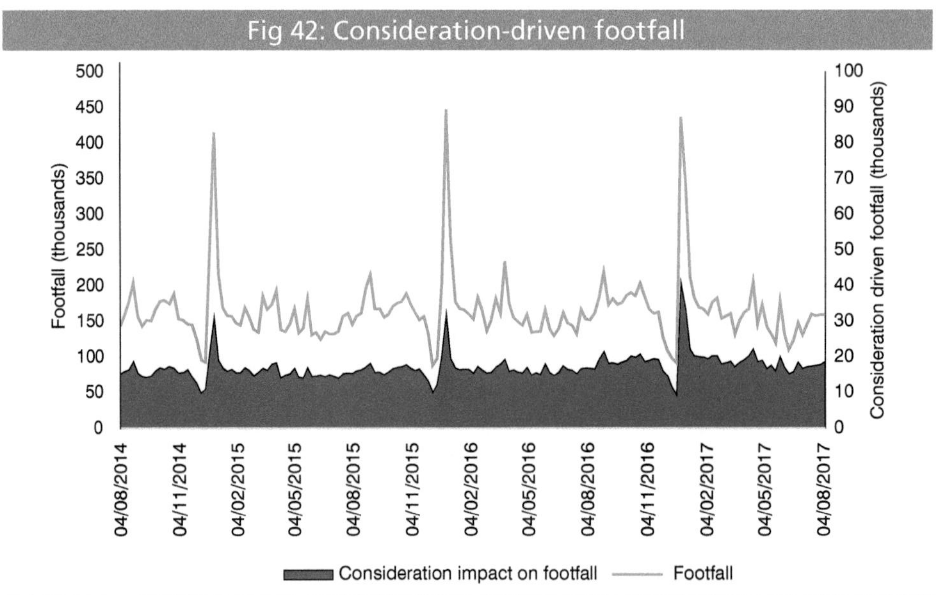

Source: MediaCom Business Science econometrics projects from FY 2011/12 to FY 2016/17

Increases in consideration improved the effectiveness of response-driving advertising

Consideration has not only had a positive longer-term effect on the brand but it has also improved the performance of the shorter-term, promotional communications by delivering more 'warmed up' consumers into the DFS stores. Our most recent econometric analysis has quantified that over the past six years, consideration improvements have driven an extra £109.2m worth of incremental sales and +£49m incremental profit (Figures 43 and 44).

Figure 43: Average consideration value vs. incremental bookings driven

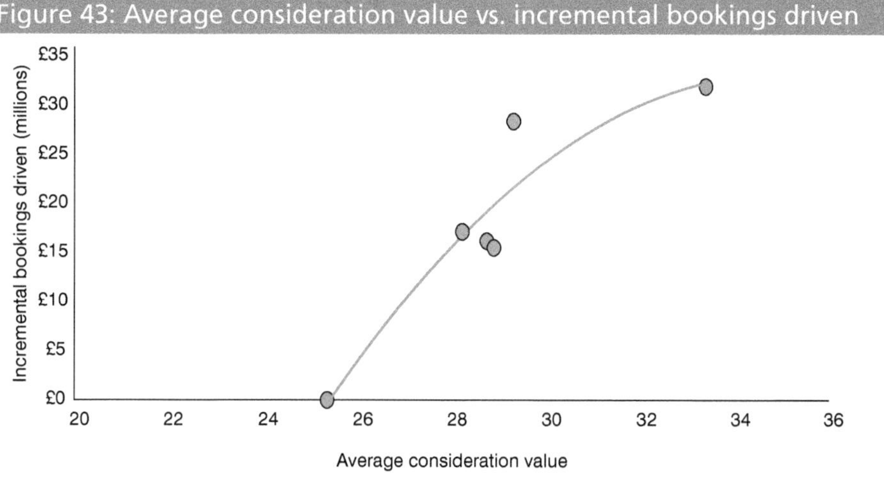

Source: MediaCom Business Science econometrics projects from FY 2011/12 to FY 2016/17

Figure 44: Average consideration value vs. incremental profit driven

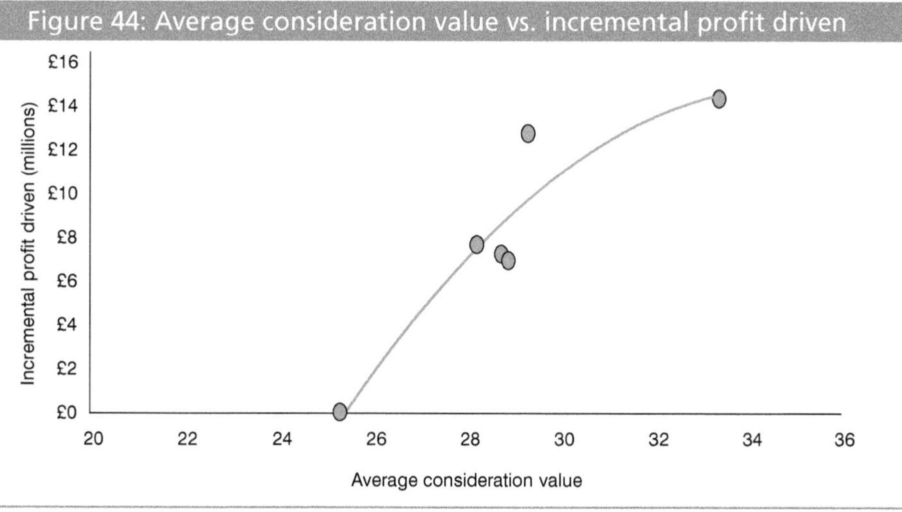

Source: MediaCom Business Science econometrics projects from FY 2011/12 to FY 2016/17

Consideration converts sales more efficiently

Econometric analysis has been used to identify that the conversion rate for a shopper saying they would consider DFS is almost double a 'non-considerer'. So increasing the number of top 2 box considerers visiting DFS has had a very valuable impact on the DFS business (Figure 45).

Figure 45: Conversion rate for consideration-driven sales vs. non-consideration-driven sales

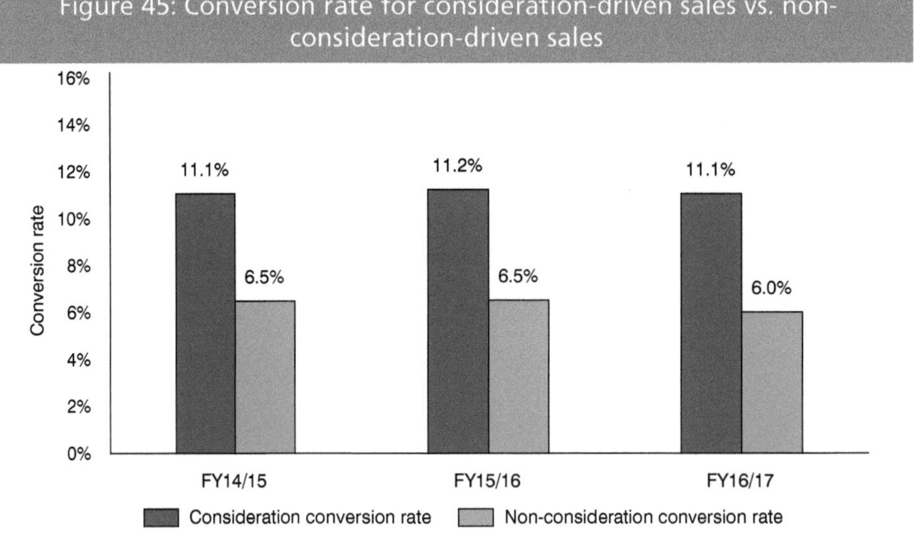

Source: MediaCom Business Science econometrics projects from FY 2011/12 to FY 2016/17

Consideration has had a very positive impact on base sales over time

When we started this journey, DFS was a value brand that relied on short-term sales activation-style advertising to fuel the business. A key communications opportunity, we believed, was to begin to emotionally prime people to be more predisposed to the brand based on valuing what it had to offer rather than just seeing discounts and price tags, and we have been proved correct. The increases we have seen in consideration have made a valuable contribution to a 23% increase in base driven sales. This equates to a 14% reduction on our reliance on short-term activation advertising to drive sales (Figure 46).

Our focus on growing brand love and consideration for DFS has not only ensured that every £1 spent worked harder and therefore enabled DFS to make media savings, but it is also stretching the longevity of our returns further than ever before for the brand.

Signs that advertising was a major driver of these business and behavioural improvements

Using advertising to build consideration was the key to achieving the commercial successes we have outlined above. This section enumerates the signs that our advertising was a driver of these significant consideration increases.

Figure 46: Base sales and profit and the positive contribution of consideration

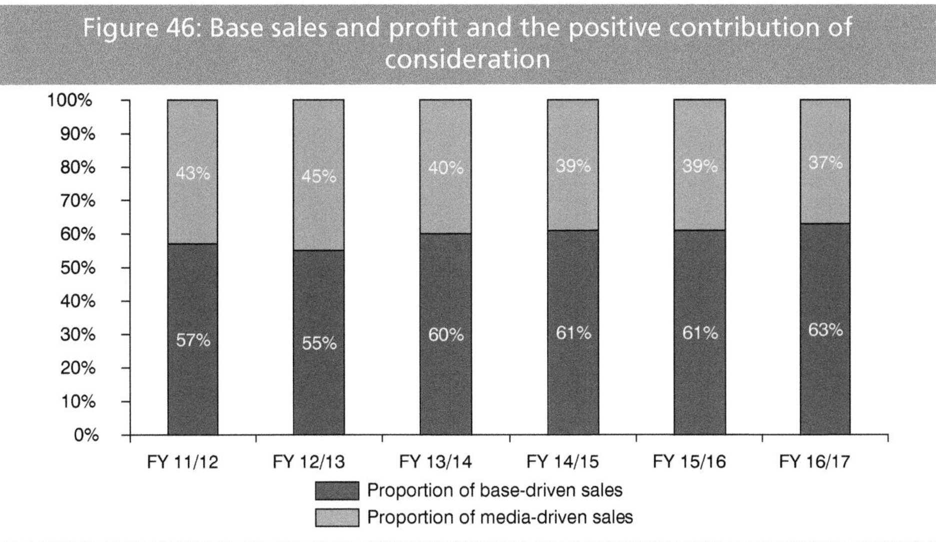

Source: MediaCom Business Science econometrics projects from FY2011/12 to FY2016/17

Fewer people claimed that advertising was a barrier to consideration

Previously, DFS advertising was seen as a barrier to conversion from awareness to consideration. According to DFS' Market Tracker research, there has been a 48% decrease in people saying that their reason for not considering DFS was because they were 'put off by our advertising'. This is more important than just being an expression of personal preference about the advertising. Improving the advertising in the subtle ways we have described has removed a 'blockage' and allowed the huge consideration gains to happen and 'flow' through to improved business performance (Figure 47).

Figure 47: 48% fewer sofa shoppers aware of DFS claimed being 'put off by their advertising' as their reason for not considering

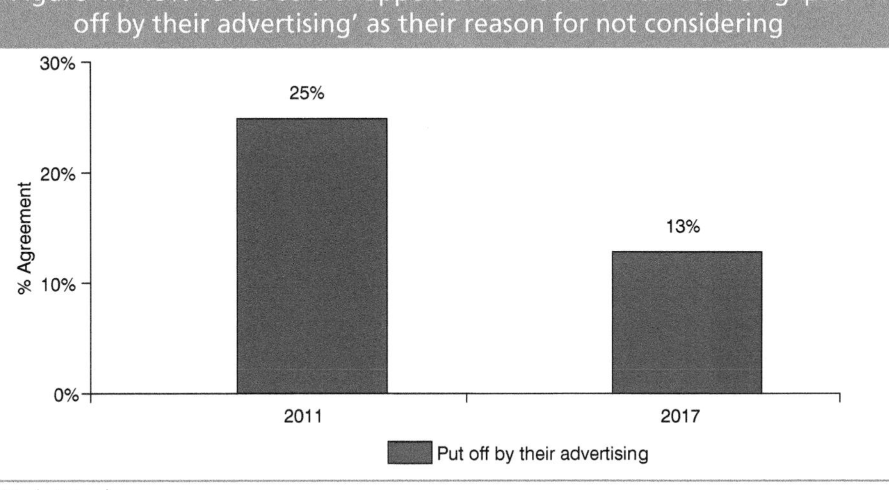

DFS Market Tracker

Advertising appeal and persuasion strongly correlate with love and consideration

Correlation analysis demonstrates the strong relationship that exists between growth in key advertising measures and DFS brand love and consideration (Figure 48).[16]

Figure 48: Annual average correlations that exist between brand and advertising tracking measures

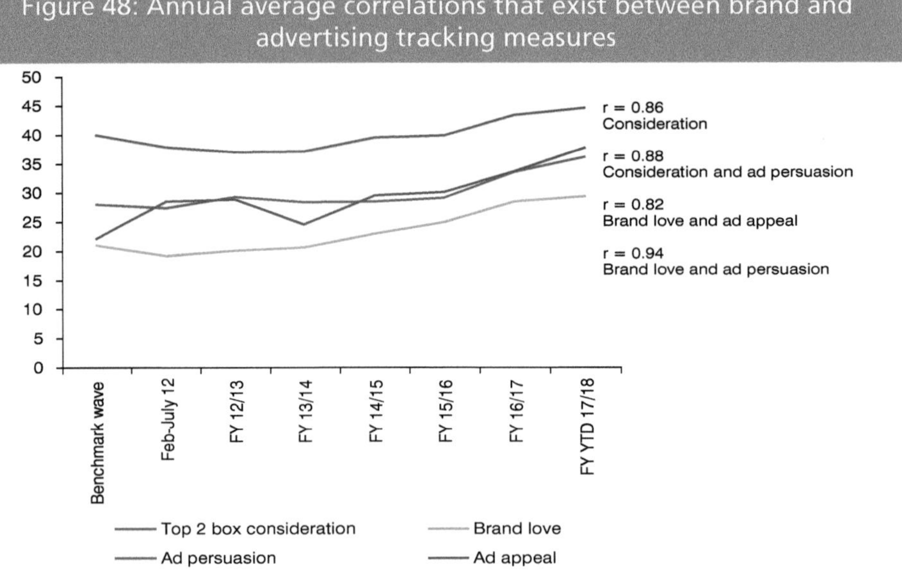

Source: Monkey See Brand and Communications Tracker, February 2012–February 2018. Base: Total sample 'in-market' sofa shoppers. All differences statistically significant at 95% confidence level.

Our advertising was designed to improve the measures we believed would drive consideration[17]

It is clear from tracking and other sources, which we report on below, that the four themes which informed our careful communications development, were recognised and 'digested' by consumers to such an extent that they appear to be drivers of the consideration improvements and the brand perception shifts we achieved. This meant that we delivered against our objectives or, in other words, that the advertising worked as intended (Figure 49).

Figure 49: A reminder of the four key themes that guided our creative decisions

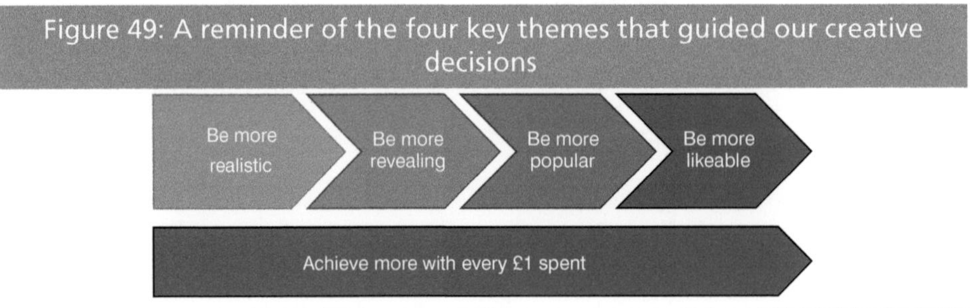

Be more realistic

More realistic presentations of family life on and around the sofas in the advertising dramatically improved consumers' identification with the DFS brand (Figure 50).

Figure 50: Sofa shoppers 89% more likely to agree that DFS is 'for someone like me'

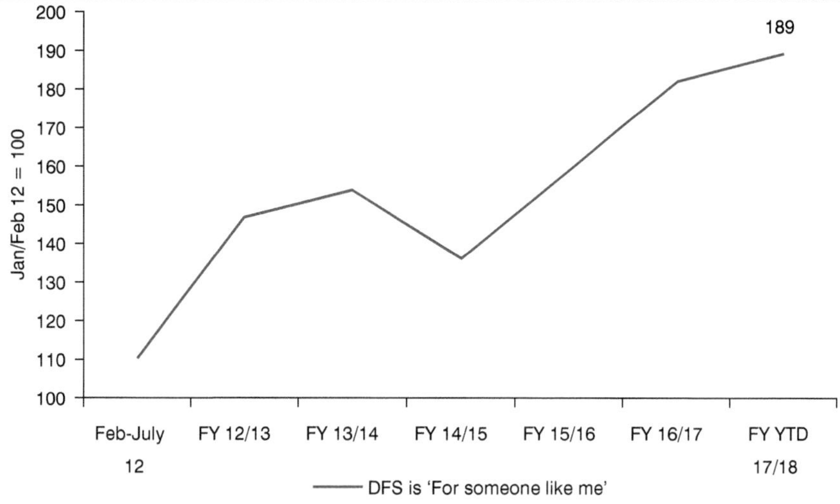

Base: Total sample 'in-market' sofa shoppers. All differences statistically significant at 95% confidence level.

Identification with the brand also had a 'rub off' positive effect on DFS range perceptions (Figure 51).[18]

Figure 51: Sofa shoppers 16% more likely to agree DFS 'somewhere I expect to find something I like' indexed vs. FY 2014/15

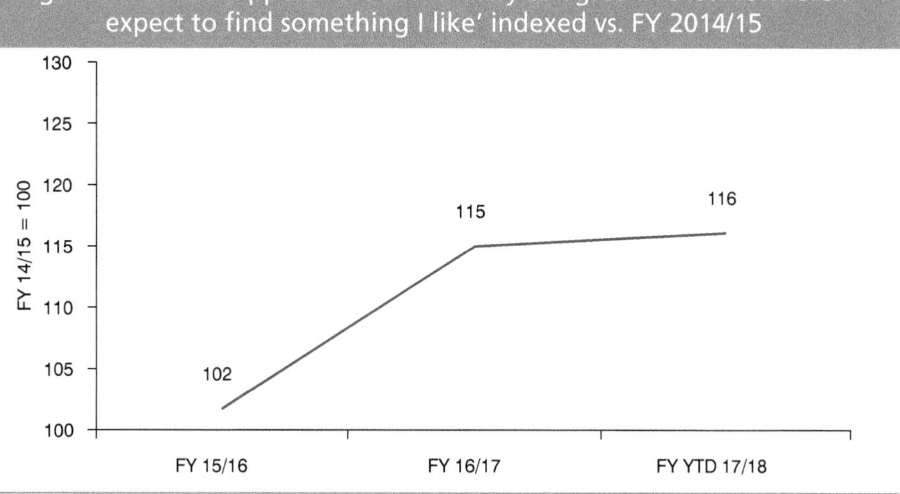

Base: Total sample 'in-market' sofa shoppers. All differences statistically significant at 95% confidence level.

Be more revealing

Weaving craftsmanship and provenance cues into promotional communications has had an impact on the equity of the brand (Figure 52), and perceptions of the quality DFS offers have also improved (Figure 53).[19]

Figure 52: Sofa shoppers growth in DFS brand association with craft and provenance stories YTD vs. FY 2013/14

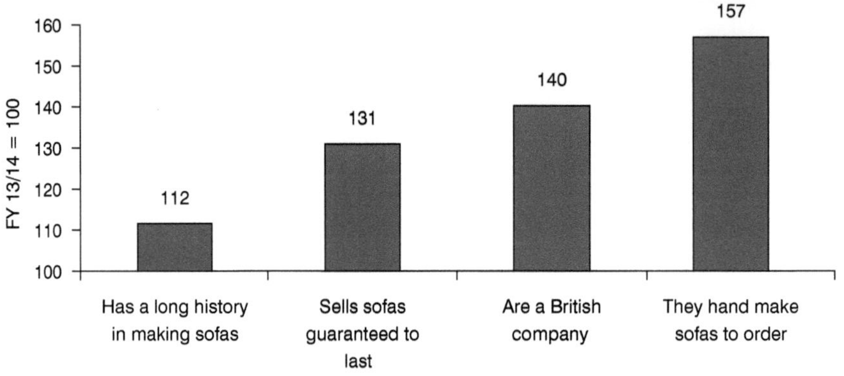

FY 13/14 = 100
160
150
140
130
120
110
100
112
131
140
157
Has a long history in making sofas
Sells sofas guaranteed to last
Are a British company
They hand make sofas to order

Source: Monkey See Brand and Communications Tracker, February 2012–February 2018. Base: Total sample 'in-market' sofa shoppers. All differences statistically significant at 95% confidence level.

Even more importantly, value for money perceptions increased at almost the same rate as the quality perceptions (Figure 53), which suggests that these two factors are linked, and that in being persuaded to adjust their perception of DFS quality, consumers also 'recalculated' the value that DFS was seen to offer. Importantly, the introduction of quality messaging not only changed 'quality seekers' perceptions of the VFM offered (+42%) but it also strengthened the relationship with the core 'value seeker' audience too (+31%).

Figure 53: Sofa shoppers' association with VFM and quality indexed vs. January/February 2012

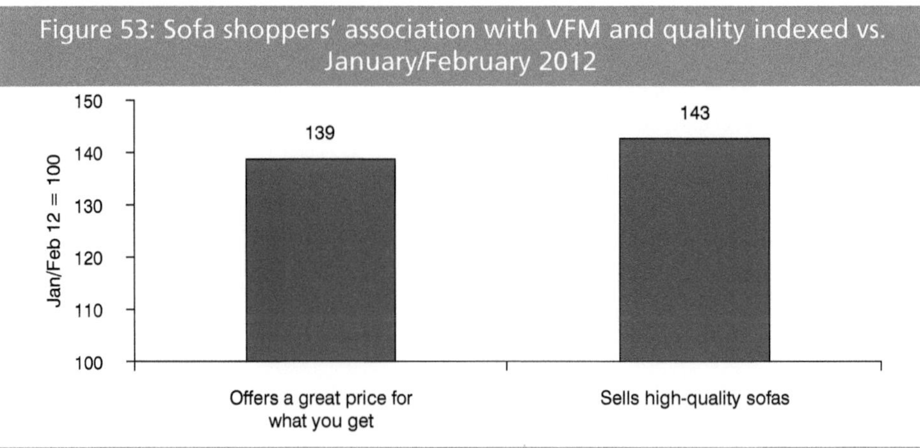

Jan/Feb 12 = 100
150
140
130
120
110
100
139
143
Offers a great price for what you get
Sells high-quality sofas

Source: Monkey See Brand and Communications Tracker, February 2012–February 2018. Base: Total sample 'in-market' sofa shoppers. All differences statistically significant at 95% confidence level.

The fact that step changes in value perception have happened in line with quality cues were being incorporated into the advertising, and then again when the Team GB sponsorship and upholstered characters were launched suggests that advertising played an important role in driving these important perceptions (Figure 54):

Figure 54: Sofa shoppers 39% more likely to agree DFS 'Offers a great price for what you get' indexed vs. pre-krow

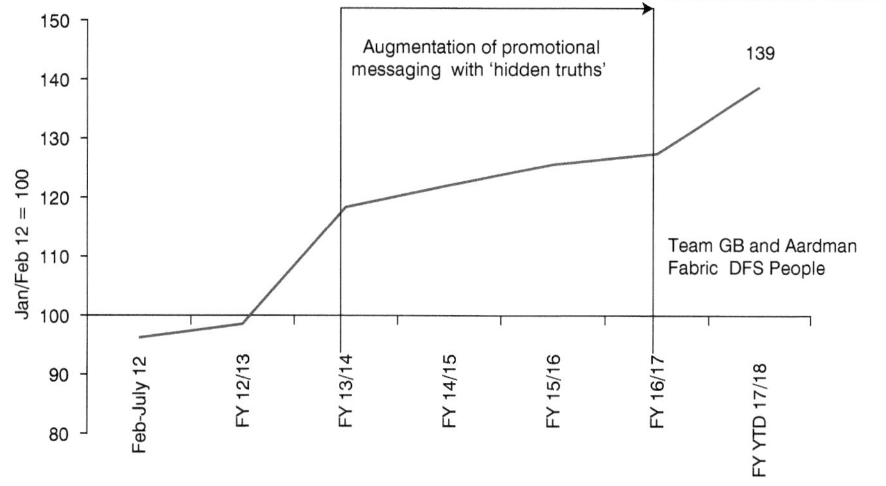

Source: Monkey See Brand and Communications Tracker, February 2012–February 2018. Base: Total sample 'in-market' sofa shoppers. All differences statistically significant at 95% confidence level.

It is also clear that these significant improvements in value were not driven by DFS lowering its prices. During this period the average price of the sofas in DFS advertising went up more times (3) than down (2) (Table 3).

Table 3: Average price of sofas advertised

	FY 2012/13	FY 2013/14	FY 2014/15	FY 2015/16	FY 2016/17	FY YTD 2017/18
Average price of sofas advertised	£825	£749	£768	£805	£717	£763

Source: DFS

Be more popular

After some early modest reputational gains associated with the new advertising, the real uplift in DFS' improved reputation occurred when the Team GB partnership was communicated in advertising (Figure 55).

Figure 55: DFS reputational gains amongst sofa shoppers % agreement indexed vs. January/February 2012

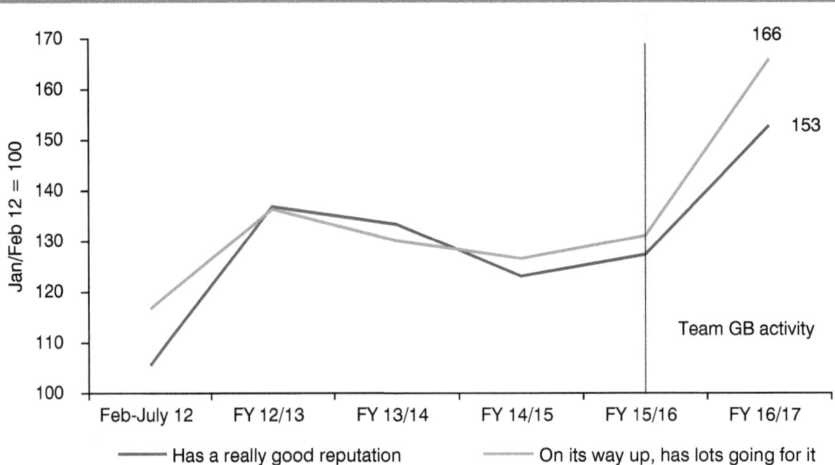

Base: Total sample 'in-market' sofa shoppers. All differences statistically significant at 95% confidence level.

Featuring the popular lifestyle 'Exclusive Brands' and their ranges in advertising has positively impacted sales. Since its launch in Dececember 2014, the Zinc Sofa from the French Connection range has featured in 28 of the 43 campaigns that we have run for DFS and has been the No. 1 best selling sofa (single product) for three years running. [20]

And partnering with BHF has gained popular attention and so far has helped to raise a very valuable, £13m (Figure 56).[21]

Figure 56: Max Whitlock and Mike Taylor of BHF celebrate the £13m fundraising milestone together in June 2017

These popular associations have contributed to an 18% improvement to DFS' acceptability ratings (Figure 57).

Figure 57: Change in percentage of sofa shoppers claiming that DFS is an acceptable choice vs. an unacceptable one

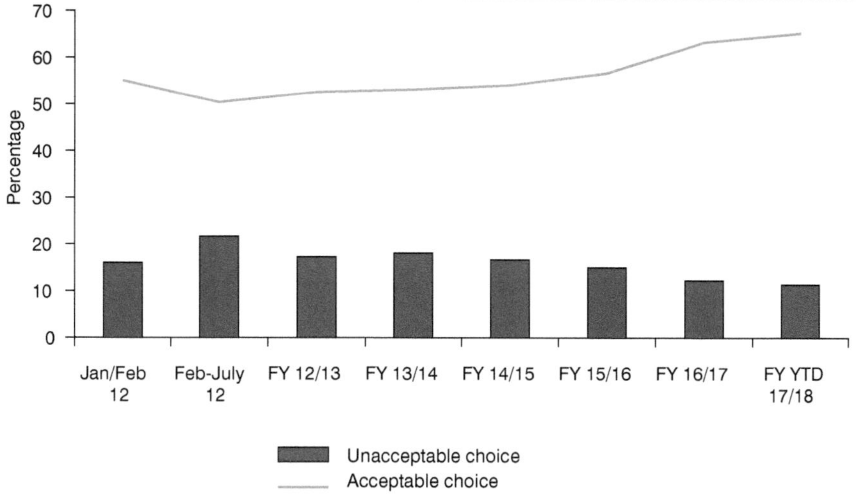

Source: Monkey See Brand and Communications Tracker, February 2012–February 2018. Base: Total sample 'in-market' sofa shoppers. YTD position significantly higher than all time periods except 16/17 at 95% confidence level.

Be more likeable

As intended, the 'new' DFS advertising has been recognised as much more appealing than the old. Both segments, 'quality seekers' and 'value seekers' agree (+75% and +60% respectively) (Figure 58).

Figure 58: Sofa shoppers claiming that they found DFS advertising to be appealling indexed vs. pre January/February 2012

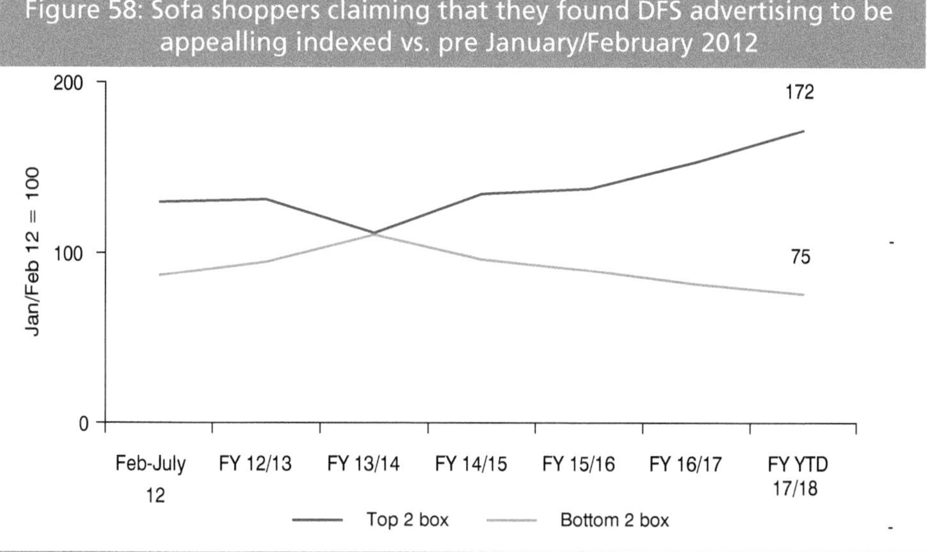

Source: Monkey See Brand and Communications Tracker, February 2012–February 2018. Base: Total sample 'in-market' sofa shoppers. All differences statistically significant at 95% confidence level.

These improvements in appeal have contributed to DFS being awarded as *Campaign* magazine's AdWatch most recognised advertiser, two years in a row (Figures 59 and 60).

Figure 59: Excerpt from *Campaign*'s AdWatch feature, December 2016

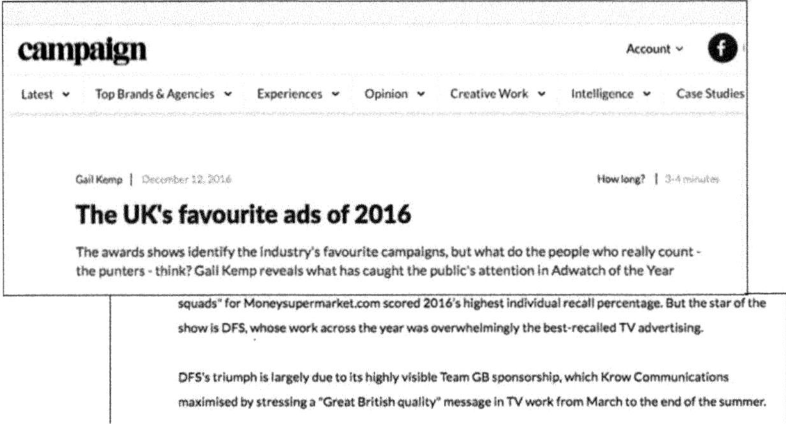

campaign

Account

Latest | Top Brands & Agencies | Experiences | Opinion | Creative Work | Intelligence | Case Studies

Gail Kemp | December 12, 2016

How long? | 3-4 minutes

The UK's favourite ads of 2016

The awards shows identify the industry's favourite campaigns, but what do the people who really count - the punters - think? Gail Kemp reveals what has caught the public's attention in Adwatch of the Year

squads" for Moneysupermarket.com scored 2016's highest individual recall percentage. But the star of the show is DFS, whose work across the year was overwhelmingly the best-recalled TV advertising.

DFS's triumph is largely due to its highly visible Team GB sponsorship, which Krow Communications maximised by stressing a "Great British quality" message in TV work from March to the end of the summer.

Figure 60: Excerpt from *Campaign*'s AdWatch feature, December 2017

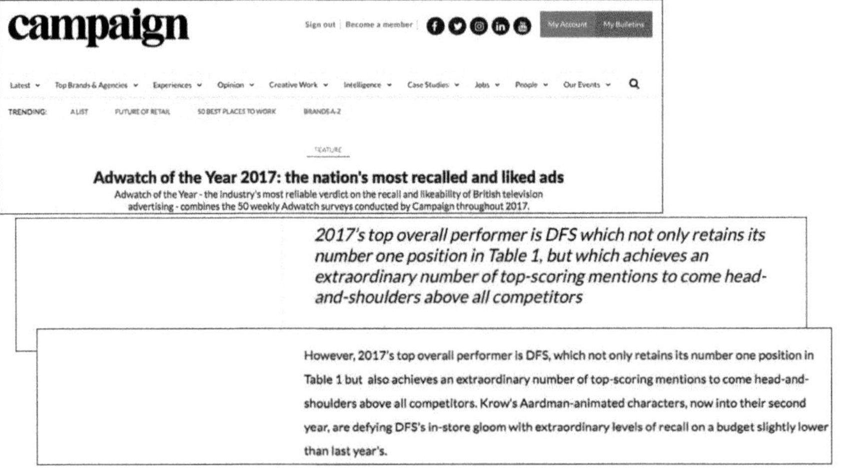

campaign

Sign out | Become a member | My Account | My Bulletins

Latest | Top Brands & Agencies | Experiences | Opinion | Creative Work | Intelligence | Case Studies | Jobs | People | Our Events

TRENDING: A LIST | FUTURE OF RETAIL | 50 BEST PLACES TO WORK | BRANDS A-Z

FEATURE

Adwatch of the Year 2017: the nation's most recalled and liked ads

Adwatch of the Year - the industry's most reliable verdict on the recall and likeability of British television advertising - combines the 50 weekly Adwatch surveys conducted by Campaign throughout 2017.

2017's top overall performer is DFS which not only retains its number one position in Table 1, but which achieves an extraordinary number of top-scoring mentions to come head-and-shoulders above all competitors

However, 2017's top overall performer is DFS, which not only retains its number one position in Table 1 but also achieves an extraordinary number of top-scoring mentions to come head-and-shoulders above all competitors. Krow's Aardman-animated characters, now into their second year, are defying DFS's in-store gloom with extraordinary levels of recall on a budget slightly lower than last year's.

This significant improvement in advertising appeal has been translated into a much deeper emotional connection with the brand, and a significant erosion of what had previously been deeply-held negative feelings toward DFS (Figure 61). Our aim to strengthen our relationship with our core 'value seeker' target has been achieved with a 61% top 2 box growth.

Figure 61: Brand love – the claimed relationship between sofa shoppers and the DFS brand

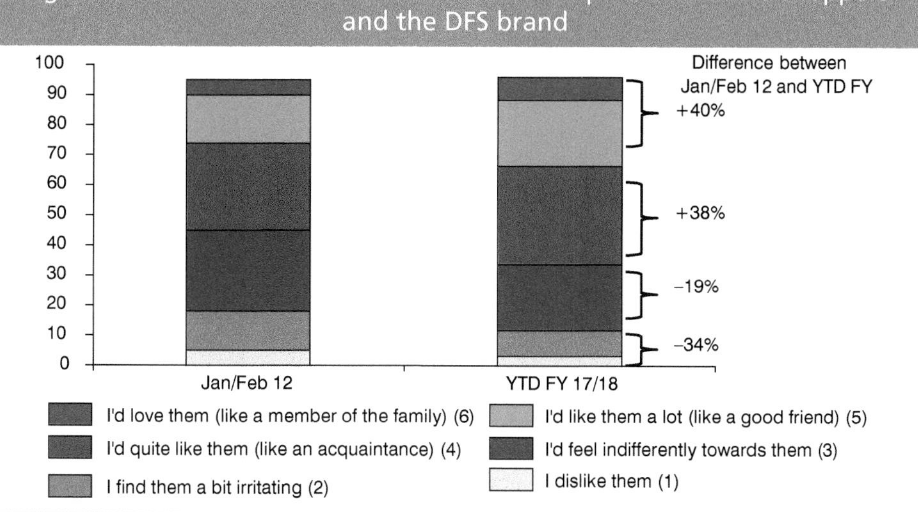

Base: Total sample 'in-market' sofa shoppers. All differences statistically significant at 95% confidence level.

An additional and impressive measure of the progress that DFS have made towards becoming well-loved is that the 'love-gap' between DFS and Britain's best-loved retailer, John Lewis, has closed year-on-year, and in total, by 52% (Figure 62).[22]

Figure 62: 52% reduction in the 'love gap' between DFS and John Lewis

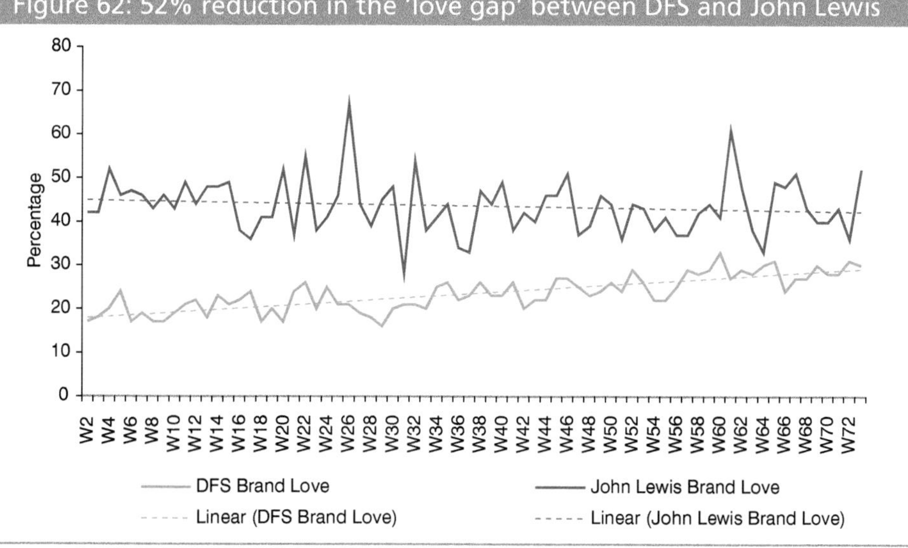

Base: Total sample 'in-market' sofa shoppers. All differences statistically significant at 95% confidence level.

And where previously, the DFS brand was negatively perceived, and even mistrusted, for its 'never-ending sale' we saw a 67% increase in people now regarding DFS as trustworthy (Figure 63).

Figure 63: Change in sofa shoppers' belief that DFS is a trustworthy brand indexed vs. January/February 2012

Jan/Feb 12 = 100
180
160
140
120
100
159
167
Team GB activity and Aardman upholstered avatars
Feb-July 12
FY 12/13
FY 13/14
FY 14/15
FY 15/16
FY 16/17
FY YTD 17/18
Trustworthiness

Base: Total sample 'in-market' sofa shoppers. All differences (except 16/17) statistically significant at 95% confidence level.

This improvement of DFS brand image did not come at the expense of a dilution of the communication of DFS' main message. On the contrary, more people believe that DFS offers great sales and promotions than before (Figure 64).

Figure 64: Sofa shoppers were 15% more likely to claim they believe that DFS 'Has great offers and sales'

Source: Monkey See Brand and Communications Tracker, February 2012–February 2018. Base: Total sample 'in-market' sofa shoppers. YTD position significantly higher than all time periods except 16/17 at 95% confidence level.

We believe that this 15% improvement is a consequence of the changes we made to emotionally prime people to value what the DFS brand offers in its sales and promotions, rather than being a coincidence.

What is also notable is that these large improvements in brand perceptions and emotional warmth have not been won at the expense of response. Today, DFS advertising encourages just as much action as it always did with 6 in 10 people saying they would do something as a result of seeing the adverts (Figure 65).

Figure 65: Ad persuasion showing 6 in 10 people said they would do something as a result of seeing a DFS advert in January/February 2012 and again, on average, YTD FY 2017/18

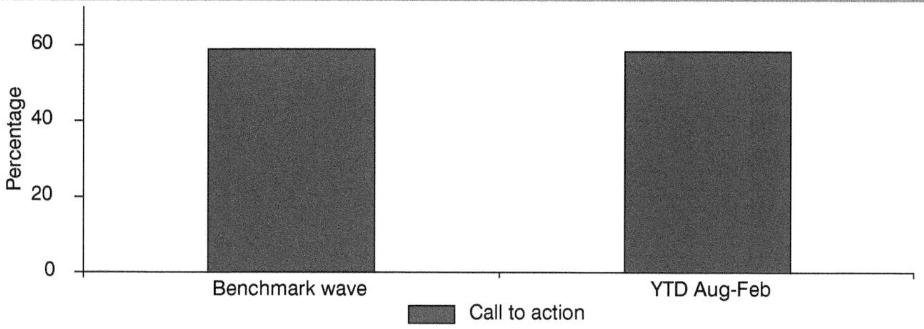

Source: Monkey See Brand and Communications Tracker, February 2012–February 2018. Base: Total sample 'in-market' sofa shoppers.

More people now recommend DFS and are likely to re-purchase in the future

Growing and strengthening a brand's emotional equity affects more than a consumer's likelihood to purchase; it can also influence their post purchase satisfaction and the potential to recommend the brand to others. Amongst those customers who are in the post-purchase honeymoon period, we have seen a 39% increase in their Net Promoter Score. More encouraging still is what happens further out from purchase: customers feel much more positively about their purchase from DFS, and this has improved by 112% (Figure 66).[23]

Figure 66: DFS Net Promoter Score over time

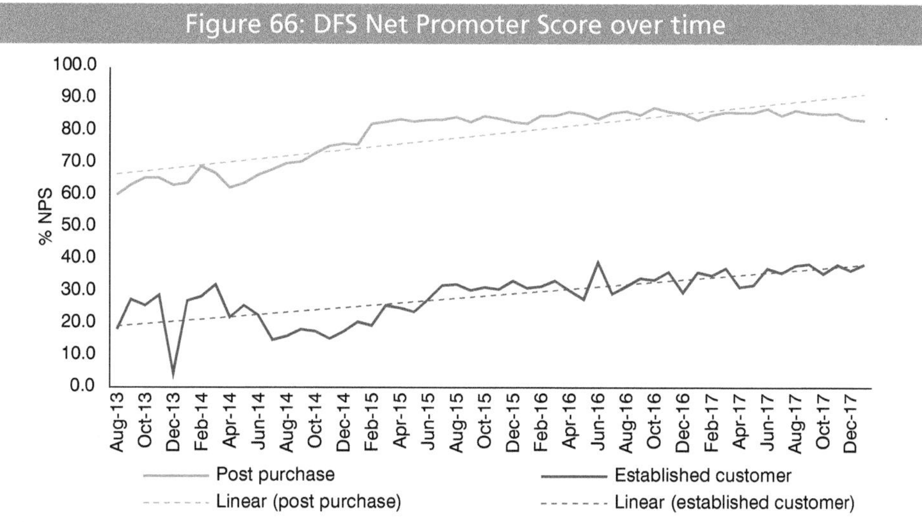

Source: NPS research conducted by research company Grassroots on behalf of DFS

With more satisfied customers, satisfied for longer and more out of market consumers with more positive associations of, and consideration for the brand then it is a viable suggestion that it shouldn't cost the business so much to bring people through the door in the first place.

A stronger brand outside of category

Our primary objective was to broaden the appeal of the brand, and grow the volume of people open to buying from DFS in order to improve the short-term effectiveness of DFS advertising. However, we also always had an eye on the bigger picture; upon the longer-term health and strength of the brand, including making a meaningful difference amongst those people (the general public) who are not yet in the market for a sofa. This is indeed what has happened. More British adults now feel much more positive about the brand (Figure 67). They also have better quality associations and would consider DFS as result (Figures 68 and 69).[24]

Figure 67: YouGov BrandIndex positive/negative brand impressions (all adults)

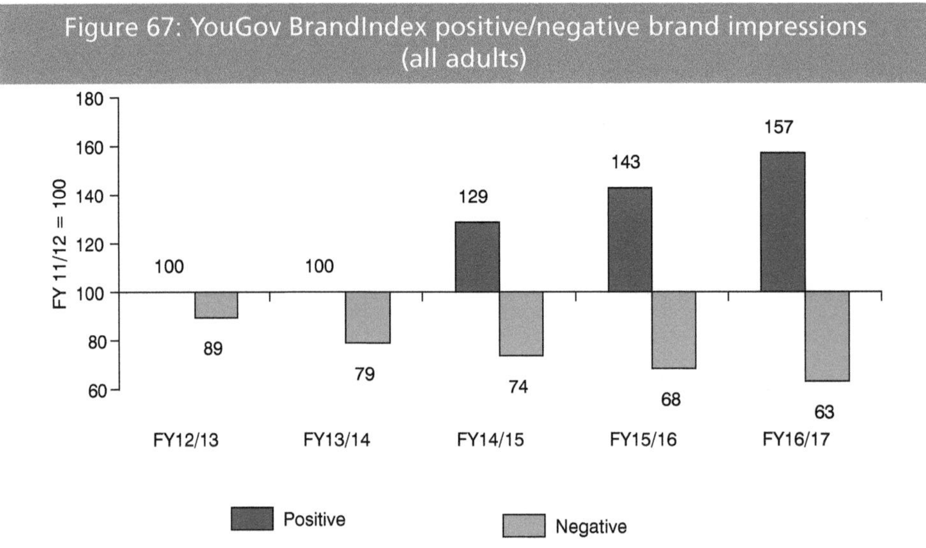

Source: YouGov BrandIndex. Base: Nationally representative adults

Figure 68: YouGov BrandIndex perception of brand quality (all adults)

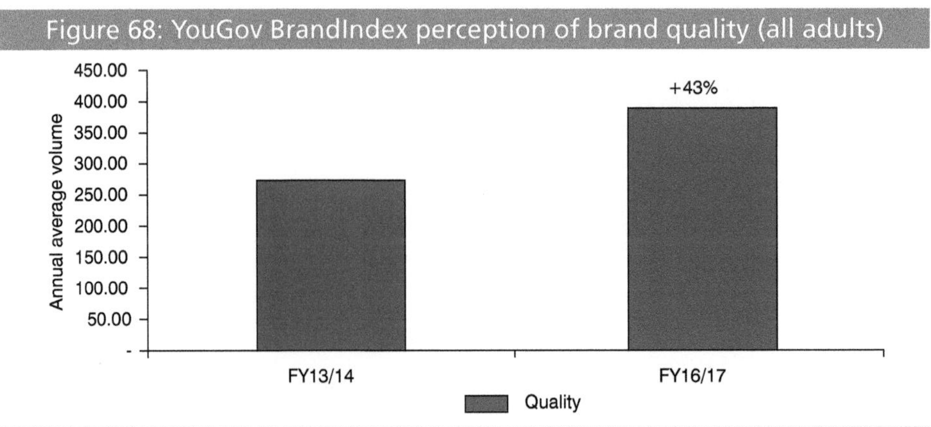

Source: YouGov BrandIndex. Base: Nationally representative adults

Figure 69: YouGov BrandIndex brand consideration (all adults)

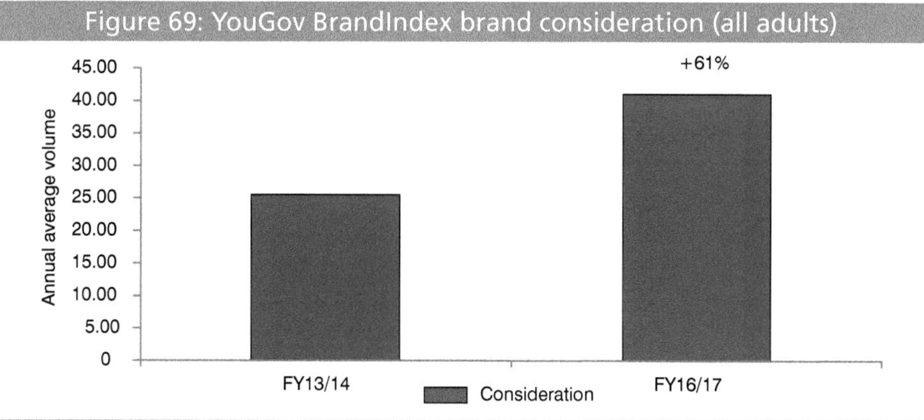

Source: YouGov BrandIndex. Base: Nationally representative adults

Discounting internal and external factors

DFS have used econometric modeling since 2011. This enables us to identify the key drivers of sales and quantify the impact that they have. The model accounts for and controls for all of the factors that could influence orders at a weekly level. For DFS, these factors are seasonality, the weather, when bank holidays, sporting events and cultural events fall, the number of new stores opened, changes to the promotional calendar, changes in the economy (which in itself is an indicator of current mortgage approval ratings), underlying market trends, movements in brand consideration, our own promotional communications and competitors activity.

The analysis allows us to determine whether each factor has a positive or negative impact on sales, and also the magnitude of that impact.

The waterfall chart below summarises the individual impact of the key drivers on sales from FY 2013/14 to FY 2016/17 (Figure 70).[25]

In the final year, due to a much tougher trading environment, which has affected many retailers we saw a decline, for the first time, in the contribution of promotional communication to total sales. However during this same period we also saw consideration uplifts that helped to offset these declines.

Crucially, the econometric modelling has allowed us to isolate and quantify the impact of our creative and strategy changes over the last six years (and separate it from other growth pillars).

The improvements made to the efficiency and effectiveness of our promotional communications and the additional contribution to both base and incremental sales as a result of consideration increases, have together, since 2011/12, helped to deliver over £530m profit for DFS, delivering a 64% improvement in profit ROI over the past six years (Figure 71).

Figure 70: Total orders waterfall from FY 2013/14 to FY 2016/17

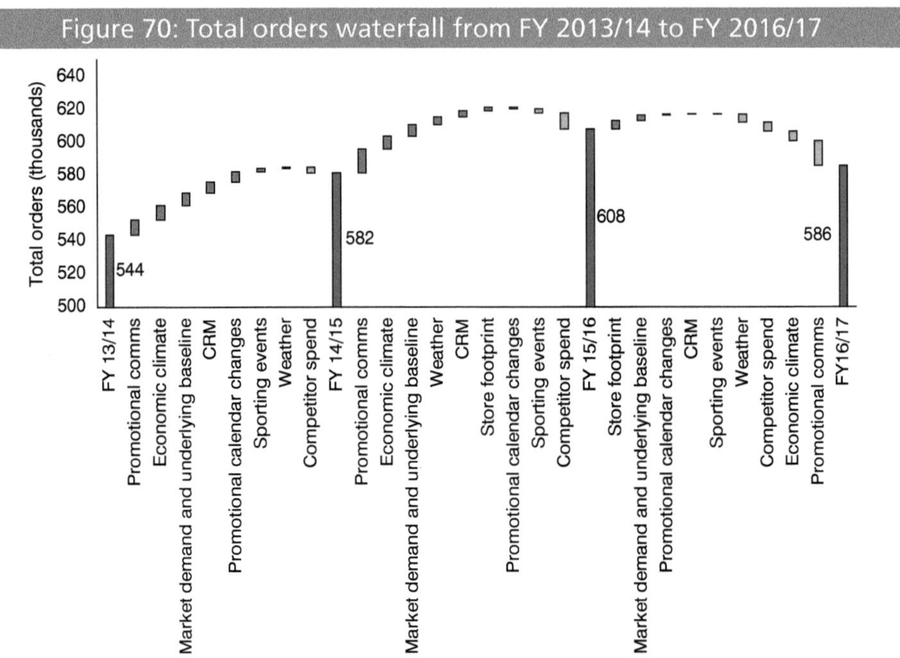

Source: MediaCom Business Science econometrics projects from FY 2011/12 to FY 2016/17

Figure 71: Profit ROI between FY 2010/11 and FY 2016/17

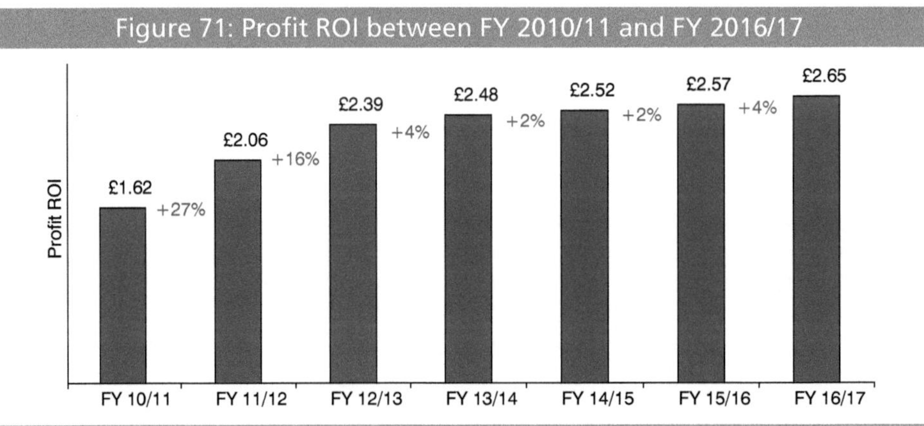

Source: MediaCom Business Science econometrics projects from FY 2011/12 to FY 2016/17

The most recent year's profit ROI of £2.65 is now exceeding the retail category average as proposed in the recently published Profit Ability study (Ebiquity and Gain Theory, 2018).

Summary

Six years ago, we set out on a journey to address the both the short- and long-term effectiveness and efficiency of DFS advertising, and to make every £1 spent on advertising more profitable.

To grow the DFS business we had to improve penetration amongst a more aspirational and affluent audience whilst strengthening our relationship with our core audience. Day-by-day, week-by-week, year-by-year, we undermined the barriers that were limiting peoples' ability to value the brand and what it had to offer.

We set out to grow love and consideration, to warm up more consumers so that when they came through the doors they would be more open to buying today but also less needing of (expensive) convincing tomorrow.

This paper has been about celebrating the enormous progress that the previously much-derided DFS has made at making significant improvements to how the brand is perceived by evolving the advertising, all the while without fundamentally changing what we said.

The net result of this careful evolution is that by turning DFS from being perceived as 'just' a value brand into a brand that people value, we have created significant value for the DFS business.

Notes

1. Latest market share data as published in DFS Annual Report 2016/17.
2. Total advertising spend (including production and all media channels including DM) FY 2005/06 through to 2009/10: £490,846,410.
3. Filby's growth pillars: Broaden appeal, UK store expansion, international roll out, full utilisation of retail space, online channel leadership.
4. 'Quality seekers' are defined as ABC1 sofa shoppers who are prepared to pay a premium for a quality product/service. Brands are important to them as signifiers of trustworthiness and quality. 'Value seekers' are C1C2DE families with young children. They are value-for-money driven and spend a lot of time shopping around for the best product at the best price.
5. The DFS Brand and Communications tracker, run by research agency Monkey See, is in field 52 weeks of the year, monitoring the health of the DFS brand and the effectiveness of its advertising. During each wave, of which there have been 73 over six years, on average 400 'in-market' respondents are interviewed ('in-market' as = either having bought a sofa in the last six months or intending to buy in the next six months). The tracker has been running since January/February 2012 when a period of benchmarking was run in order to be able to compare the performance of the DFS brand and advertising under the new creative direction introduced by krow. Where possible all tracking data included in the paper will compare brand and advertising performance of DFS to this first wave.
6. BrandIndex from YouGov is a measure of brand perception. BrandIndex continuously measures public perception of thousands of brands across dozens of sectors. Brand Impression is measured by asking sample respondents: 'Which of the following brands do you have a generally positive/negative feeling about?'
7. Source: DFS proprietary Market Tracker Lightspeed. DFS has run a quantitative study three times a year to track the health of the upholstery market since 2011. Importantly, this tracker also researches consumers' usage, attitudes and behaviours in the category. One of the questions is: 'Earlier you mentioned that you were aware of DFS but you didn't think about shopping at their store, why was that?' Respondents are given a list of multiple-choice options, one of which is 'put off by their advertising'.
8. Source: MediaCom AdvantEdge 2010.
9. On behalf of DFS, krow conducted research with YouGov's omnibus panel of nationally representative adults in August 2011. Respondents were introduced to a list of 20 'truths' about DFS and were asked the following questions: 'Which, if any, have you heard of before in relation to

DFS?'; 'Which, if any, of the following statements would make you more likely to consider DFS the next time you are shopping for furniture?'; 'Which, if any, of the following statements give you a more positive impression of DFS than you previously had?' The research findings, amongst 'quality seekers', are shown in Table 1; the truths are ranked in descending order of consideration shift.

10. DFS began its relationship with Hearst publications *Country Living* and *House Beautiful* during FY 2012/13 and then French Connection during FY 2013/14.
11. BHF offer a free removal service to any DFS customer Customers of DFS can call the BHF once they've received notification of delivery of their DFS sofa and the BHF will collect their old sofa free of charge and at a time and location convenient to the customer. Sofas are then taken to one of the BHF's 170 furniture and electrical stores across the UK and this helps to raise vital funds towards their lifesaving heart research.
12. The DFS Group announced a £1.01bn sales total in the FY2 16/17 reported results. This total includes sales from all brands within the DFS Group.
13. The size of the UK digital furniture market as calculated by HitWise.
14. In the DFS Annual Financial Report for 2016/17 (p. 14) DFS announced that the goal of achieving 25% penetration amongst 'quality seekers' had been achieved.
15. Econometric modelling of footfall has only been available since FY14/15 due to footfall camera data only being collected from all stores since FY 2013/14 'Market demand and underlying baseline' in the MediaCom econometric analysis of footfall includes: base, seasonality, sporting events and new stores.
16. A correlation coefficient of between 0.7 and +1 equates a strong positive relationship between two variables (Karl Pearson, 1896). Obviously correlation does not mean causation but rather that there exists a positive relationship between the variables in question. So, in other words, at the same time as more people were saying they liked our advertising and were persuaded by it, more people said they liked/loved the brand and would consider it more strongly.
17. Source: Bonamy Finch. In order to inform the steps in our creative journey, in 2012 (and again in 2014), Gamma analysis was carried out on our entire brand and communications tracker questionnaire to identify (and consequently creatively target) the drivers of consideration. Gamma analysis is a measure of rank correlation, i.e., the similarity of the orderings of the data when ranked by each of the quantities. It measures the strength of association of the cross-tabulated data when both variables are measured at the ordinal level. It makes no adjustment for either table size or ties. Values range from –1 (100% negative association, or perfect inversion) to +1 (100% positive association, or perfect agreement). A value of zero indicates the absence of association. In this analysis, statistical significance of changes in consideration and changes in key drivers was also used.
18. We did not start tracking 'Somewhere I expect to find something I like' until August 2014 (FY 2014/15) YTD data is significantly higher across all time periods except 16/17.
19. DFS started tracking craft and provenance associations continuously from July 2013 (FY 2013/14).
20. Source: Zinc sofa sales supplied by DFS.
21. Source: DFS & BHF.
22. Since we began tracking, we have monitored our main competitors brand health as well as our own.
23. Post-purchase NPS scores are from those customers who are contacted immediately after delivery of their sofas. Established customers NPS scores are from those customers who are contacted 3–4months later.
24. YouGov assess the quality perceptions of a brand by asking the following question on their BrandIndex survey: 'Which of the following brands do you think represent GOOD/POOR quality'. YouGov assess the likely consideration for a brand by asking the following question on their BrandIndex survey: 'When you next make a purchase, which brands would you consider?'
25. 'Market demand and underlying baseline' in the MediaCom econometric analysis of footfall includes: base, seasonality, sporting events and new stores.

GOLD AWARD
BEST NEW LEARNING

Direct Line Group

They went short. We went long

By Carl Bratton and Ann Constantine, Direct Line Group; Nic Pietersma, Ebiquity
Contributing authors: Thomas Skinner and Richard Woodward, Ebiquity; Maria-Louiza Konstantinidi, Direct Line Group
Credited companies: Direct Line Group; Ebiquity; Hall & Partners; Kantar Millward Brown

Summary

Direct Line Group (DLG) had to demonstrate the business case for marketing its multiple insurance brands: Direct Line, Churchill and Privilege. The company analysed what factors drove sales at each brand, measuring the contribution of brand and acquisition activity over the short term and the long term. It used the learnings to set investment priorities across its portfolio, including more focus on brand-building TV, improving propositions and customer service. Brand preference and consideration rose across the portfolio. Total customers increased, led by Direct Line. This case estimates DLG brands contributed £46m profit to its home and motor insurance businesses.

Editor's comment

The judges thought that this was an excellent case of an organisation adopting a systematic approach to effectiveness, using this to help manage its portfolio of brands, model brand equity and communications spend both in the short and long term. Something for everyone to learn from.

Client comment

Mark Evans, Marketing Director, Direct Line Group

This project was a huge undertaking for marketing, spearheaded by the marketing effectiveness team. It required patience and perseverance. What we built is knotty in the extreme, but has become a key platform to cement the confidence, capability and credibility of marketing within the business.

Coincidentally at the time of writing we are responding to a cost challenge. However, we are not panicking since we have the finance community saying that marketing 'is the last place we want to have to take from'. There is no greater accolade for the team than moving us from the front of the 'cuts queue' three years ago to the back of the queue today. Because we are able to articulate precisely the short- and long-term impacts of our marketing investment decisions we have changed the tone of conversation with the business. This empowers us to do the right things for our brands with a very explicit long-term perspective in mind.

This backdrop has also provided a context for genuine creativity in our communication as evidenced by bold projects such as 'Fleetlights' and 'Smart crossing' which were unimaginable a few years ago. Implicit to this we have been able to 'prove it' i.e. acceptance across the business that the art of long-term brand building is alive and well. Seemingly the more things change, the more they stay the same!

We are proud that we went long when others went short. It was painful at times given that we were moving against popular opinion. However, there is a restless ambition in the team so this journey represents how we constantly aim higher to bolster our brands and drive towards a customer-first business.

Introduction

Every marketing professional deals with them at some point in their working life. Cost challenges.

> *'The business needs £5m to pull out of 2016 ... can you get back to me by the end of the week with your suggestions.'*

Cost challenges are a fact of life, but they have been the everyday norm in the insurance sector for the last ten years. Insurance is ultra-competitive; it is as close to perfect competition as you can get. Consumers can enter their details on one price comparison website and instantly get hundreds of quotes back from across the marketplace. This is an unforgiving environment, where every pound spent on marketing needs to pay for itself.

Most direct insurers have responded to budget challenges by cutting brand advertising and shifting into short-term acquisition marketing, trying against all odds to boost short-term efficiency.

At DLG, we chose a different path. We zigged when the rest of the market zagged; we continued to invest in mass-reach above-the-line brand-building media lines when others did not. Why?

We subscribe to the philosophy that we have a duty to invest responsibly. At DLG we work with brands that have been built up through long-term investment over the last 30 years; they are assets and we see ourselves as their current guardians.

To ensure that we continue to make the right decisions for the brand, for shareholders and for our business, we set up a two-year joint marketing insight and effectiveness workstream called the Brand Equity Analysis Programme. This programme has helped us identify *c.* £46m of previously unmeasured profit contribution per year.

In this paper we present three case studies that together create a strong commercial argument for long-termism in the management of brands in the financial sector and beyond.

Case study 1: The brand glide path – Privilege Insurance

For our first study we asked the question ... what happens when we 'turn off the tap' and completely stop brand investment?

Privilege was launched in 1994 as a brand for higher-risk consumers, but soon evolved into a mass-market brand. Between 2004 and 2006 Privilege enjoyed high levels of above-the-line marketing support, featuring the slogan 'you don't have to be posh to be privileged' made famous in the UK by Joanna Lumley.

Around 2006 the insurance market was disrupted by the growth of price comparison websites, or PCWs (illustrated in Figure 1 using Google search volume[1]).

PCWs changed the existing commercial logic of insurance marketing by offering a commission-based model that was cheaper than media acquisition. Media cost per sale climbed as the size of the direct market shrank. Furthermore, on PCWs, brands that carry large marketing overheads are at a pricing disadvantage. After a portfolio review, we identified that DLG needed a 'pure PCW' brand. Privilege was given a

Figure 1: Growth of price comparison sites

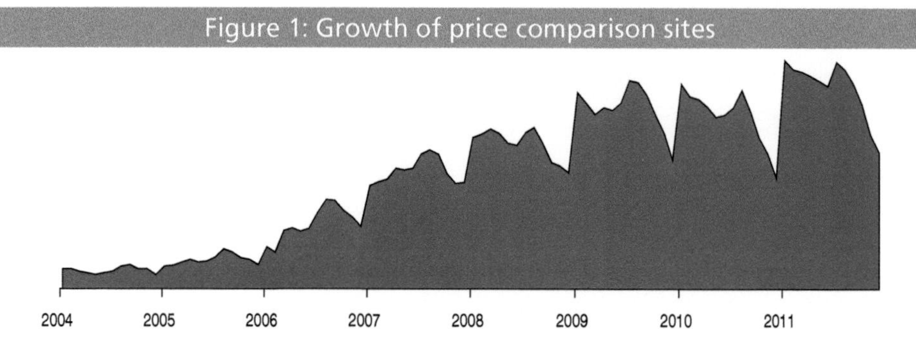

Source: Indexed Google Trends for top four brands

new strategic position – it carries no marketing overhead and is priced as keenly as possible. The brand outcome of this natural experiment is shown in Figure 2.

Figure 2: Privilege Insurance the brand glide path

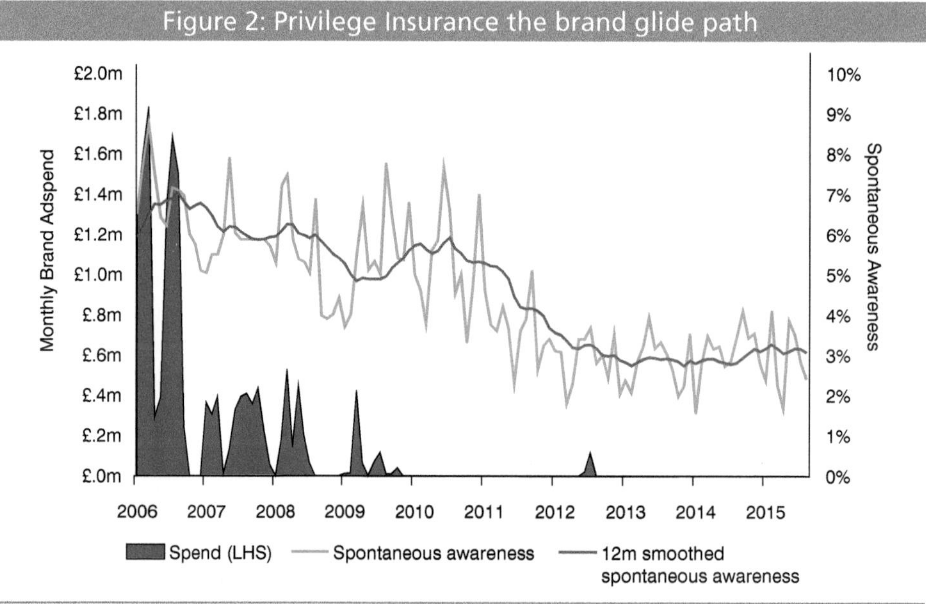

Case study 1: What did we learn?

First, when marketing investment is reduced, brand metrics such as spontaneous awareness[2] do not decline immediately. It took about three years for the brand to level off at *c.* 2–3%, where it stabilised. Second, in the period between 2007 and 2009, although the level of investment[3] was greatly reduced, even a little spend seemed to provide some 'maintenance' support.

This case study gives us a measure of what 'glide path' we should expect as a consequence of reducing marketing investment for any of our brands.

Case study 2: Brand advantage on price comparison websites – Churchill Motor

Measurement of marketing effectiveness on direct channels (like phone or web) is relatively easy, but understanding the influence of brand marketing in a PCW environment is much more difficult. Churchill's challenge is that it is both a direct brand[4] as well as a PCW brand.

Above-the-line advertising relies on a small percentage of the audience responding via website or contact centre. Measured this way, on a direct cost per sale basis,[5] Churchill brand advertising is below breakeven and looks unsustainable versus Direct Line (Figure 3).

Figure 3: Motor insurance direct cost per sale (indexed Churchill vs. Direct Line)

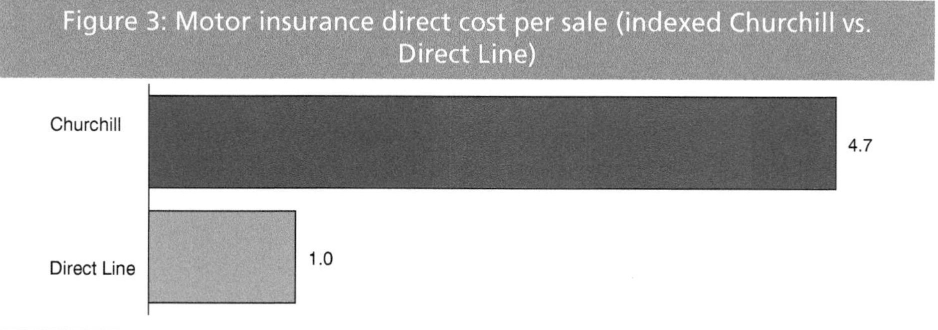

To understand the full picture though we need to know how brand equity influences consumers in the PCW environment. The consumer journey is fundamentally different on PCWs. When consumers start shopping they may not have your brand in mind at all. Once they submit their details they will be confronted with numerous options, mostly comparable in quality, and all bunched together around a similar price point.

What makes the consumer select one brand over the other? Competitiveness is tremendously important, but contrary to popular belief consumers do not always choose the cheapest brand.[6] For DLG, roughly half the sales volume on PCWs come from quotes that were not in fact the cheapest result shown to the consumer (Figure 4).

Familiarity may provide a nudge that swings consumers towards one brand rather than the rest. This dynamic is particularly apparent for insurance brands. Insurance is about trust. Consumers are anxious about poor claims handling, refusal to pay out or financial insecurity. Many will automatically exclude any unknown brand.

> *'I've never heard of these brands ... I don't want to make a mistake. I know legally an unknown brand would have to pay out, but a known brand would provide me with more reassurance.'*
>
> Andrea, Manchester

Once the consideration set is narrowed, consumers will look for a 'better brand' and are willing to pay a small price premium if necessary. Our survey data suggests

Figure 4: PCW motor insurance sales by position in results (total DLG, Churchill and Privilege)

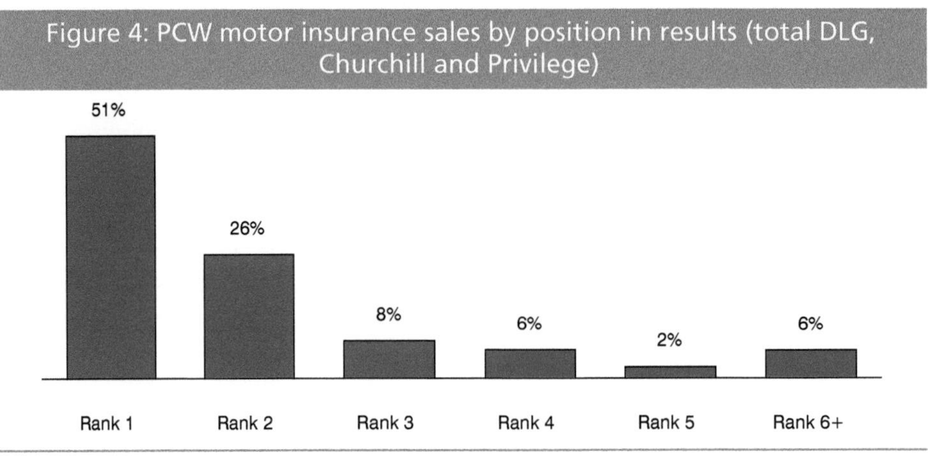

that recognisable brands are also likelier to be trusted and selected.[7] This mechanism is subtle, but as we will show it's ultimately very effective (Figure 5).

Figure 5: General insurance awareness drives trust

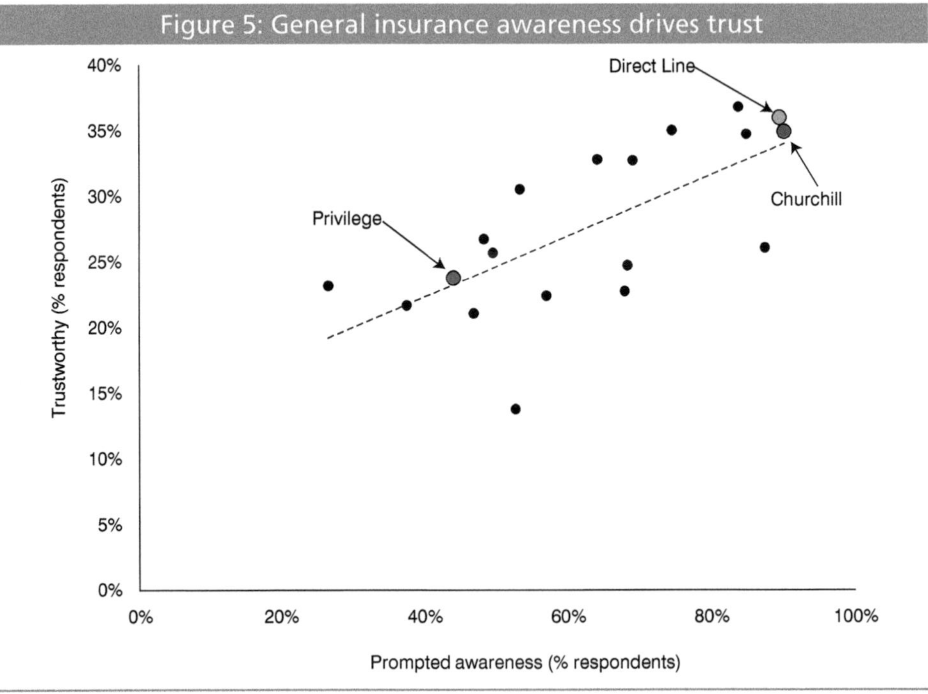

Measurement approach

We found that if a consumer is served an identical price for both brands, *c.* 83% of consumers chose Churchill. If however, Churchill has a higher price we would still see a certain proportion of consumers selecting Churchill as their preferred brand.

For example, as shown below, at a price premium in the £10–£19 range, we would still see *c.* 33% of consumers choose Churchill.

This is a well-behaved relationship that is predictable and consistent in the data – the greater the price premium, the greater the switching rate (Figure 6).

Figure 6: Motor insurance preference Churchill vs. Privilege by price comparison

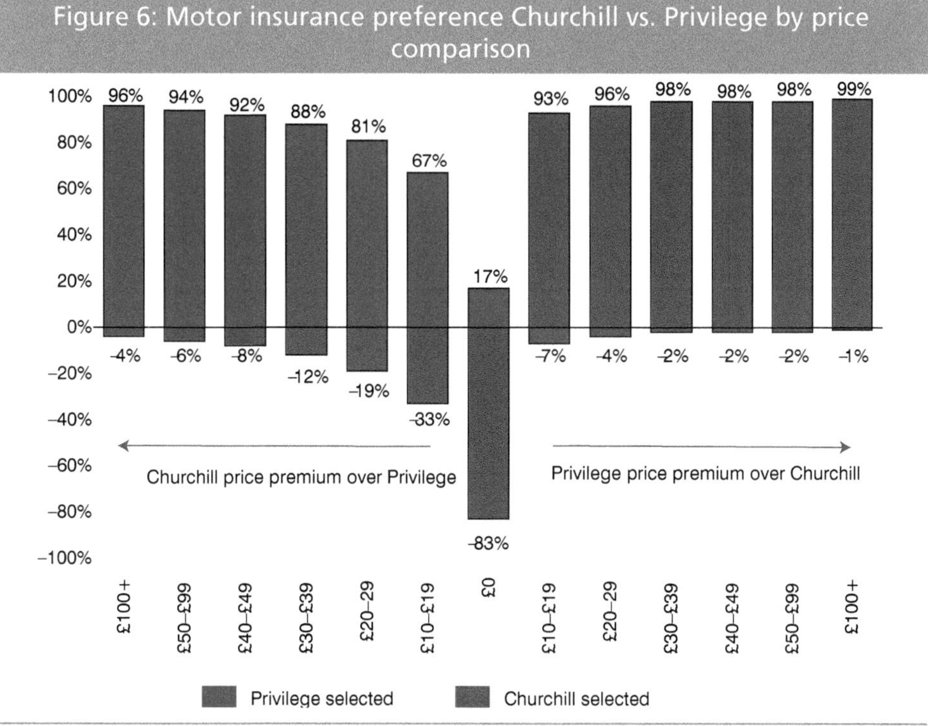

This analysis can be extended. We were able to quantify Churchill's brand advantage by matching PCW[8] data to internal data on clicks, quotes, sales and customer demographics; then we used Privilege as a 'low brand equity' reference point.

To understand the volume advantage conferred by Churchill's stronger brand equity we need to look at the click-through rate, an important metric in the PCW environment.

On a PCW, a click-through is intermediate between a quote and a sale. If a quote is more competitive it will gain a better rank position, which will improve the click-through rate.

However, because competitiveness is so important, we cannot compare click-through rate directly between Churchill and Privilege without first banding into rank. What this shows is that Churchill enjoys better click-through rates for any given rank (Figures 7 and 8).[9]

Figure 7: Click-through rate by brand and rank

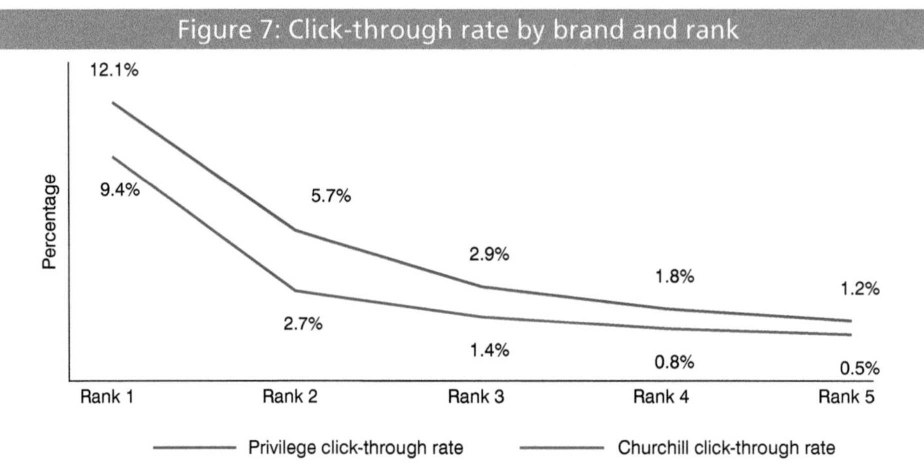

Figure 8: Click-through rate advantage Churchill vs. Privilege

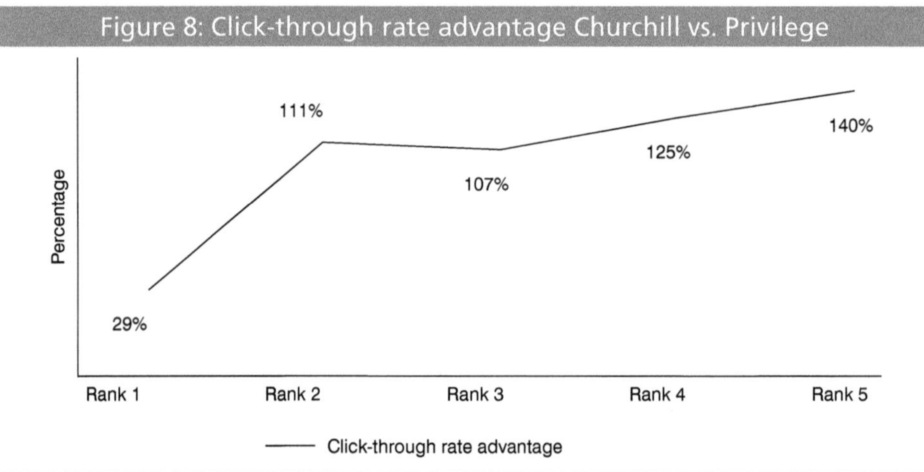

Why do consumers seem to have a preference for Churchill? More to the point, why are some consumers willing to pay a premium to be covered by Churchill? It is not service levels. Churchill and Privilege are supported by the same contact centres and claims handlers and have similar satisfaction and complaint rates.[10]

The explanation is that Churchill has enjoyed much higher brand advertising investment over the last ten years[11] which has driven its advantage. Regardless of metric, it is clear that Churchill is ahead of Privilege (Figure 9 and 10).[12]

Figure 9: Ad spend 2008–2016

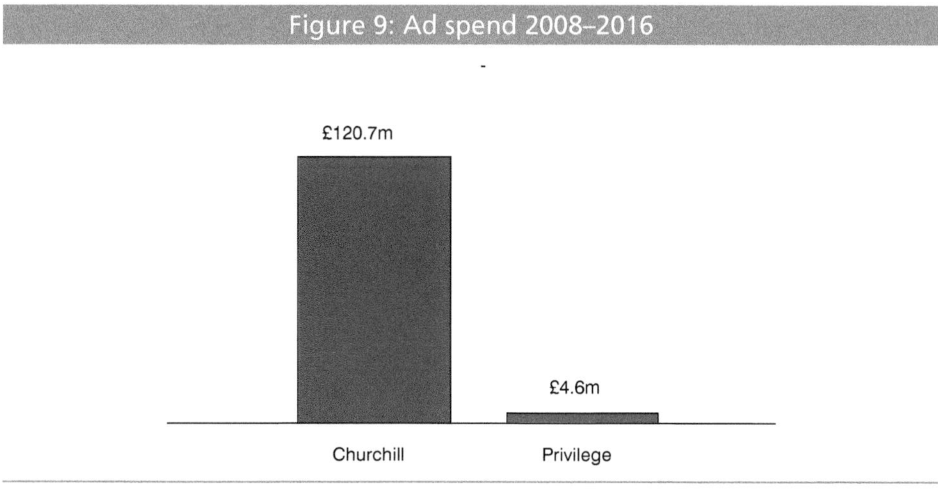

Figure 10: Brand metrics 2016

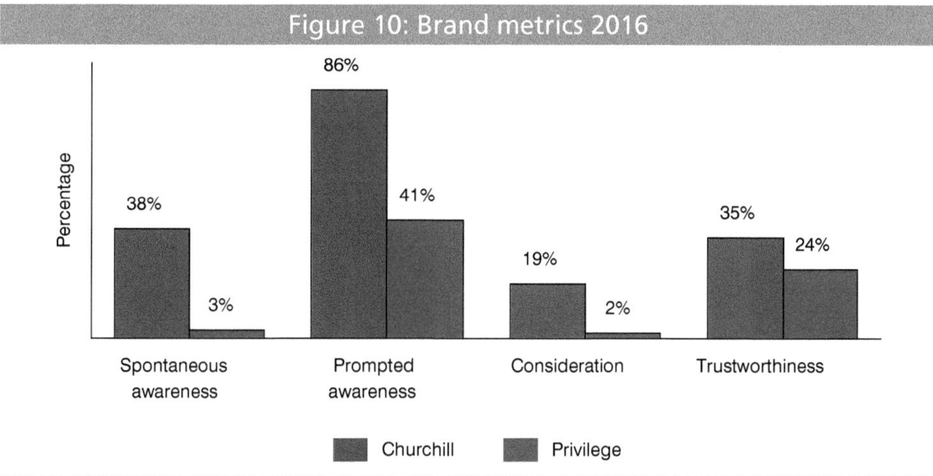

The dependent variable in our models is click-through rate for each age band and rank. Robust quantification of the size of the brand effect requires further controls which are implemented in a time-series multiple regression framework. Specifically:

- *Age banding:* splitting the data into age bands helps control for composition effects. Three groups were used: 16–34, 35–54, 55+;
- *Price point:* beyond grouping data by rank we also control for price competitiveness in both absolute and relative terms;
- *Propositions:* there were periods when either Privilege or Churchill benefitted from special offers such as free breakdown, free toys or telematics;[13]
- *Media:* time-series analysis is required to quantify the short-term benefit of marketing investment, which is a significant factor even if it is much smaller than the long-term benefits.

Our model is set up within a system[14] that includes both Churchill and Privilege data. Any difference that cannot be explained by the factors above are absorbed by differences in brand equity.[15]

This modelling approach helped us establish under what circumstances Churchill's enhanced brand equity delivers the greatest benefit. We found that brand equity gives us a bigger advantage if our price is within an acceptable range (ideally in rank 2–4) and that we are more likely to 'swing the vote' of older consumers (Figure 11).

Figure 11: Standardised impact on click-through rate Churchill brand advantage (by age and position in results)

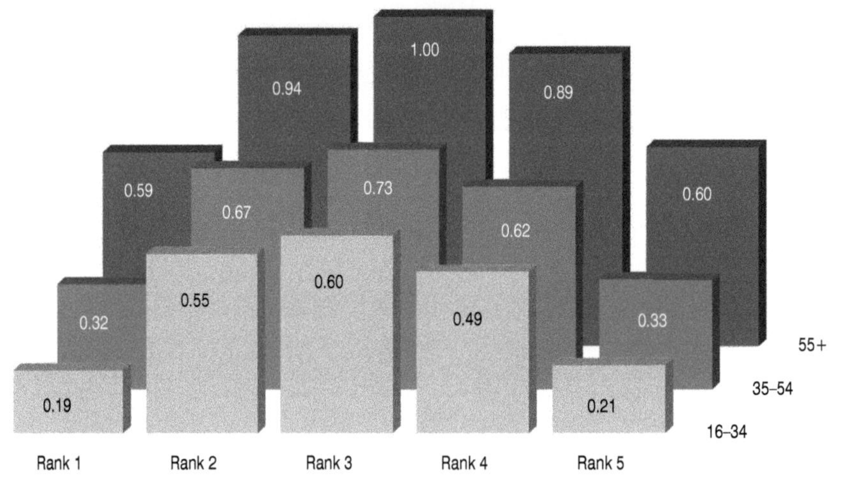

A fascinating result! But what is this worth in commercial terms?

Case study 2: What did we learn?

Of Churchill's PCW sales, 37% can be attributed to our brand advantage and a further 5% can be attributed to short-term impact of above-the-line marketing (Figure 12).

A small nudge from brand preference can have a disproportionately large effect. Our analysis suggests that if a consumer is willing to pay a premium for a brand, the most they will tolerate is typically in the £10–£20 range.[16] But even if the consumer's attachment to our brand is slight, thousands of marginal decisions go our way, ultimately delivering 37% of Churchill's sales in the PCW environment.

By isolating this impact we quantified *c.* £5.5m of previously unmeasured profit contribution (Figure 13).[17]

Figure 12: Churchill weekly sales decomposition

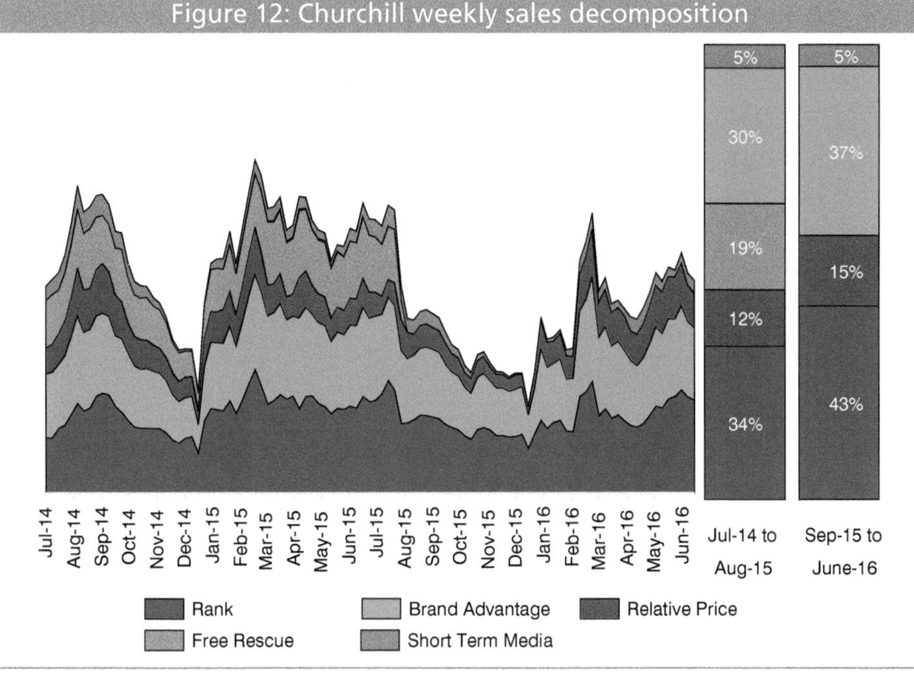

Figure 13: Churchill motor media ROI (52 weeks to March 2017)

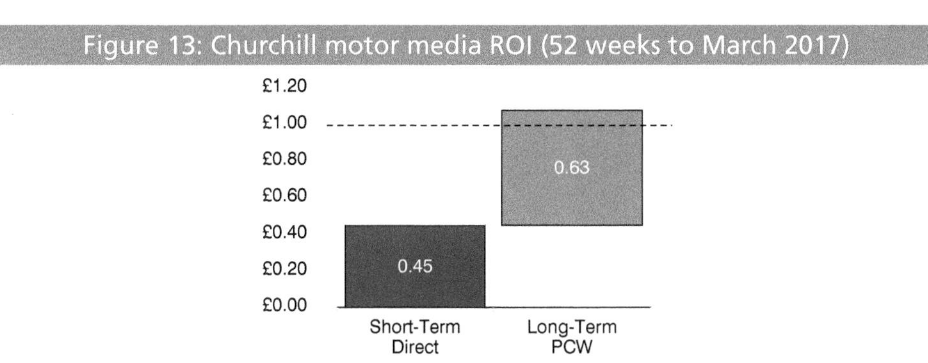

Over the same period the short-term profit contribution from brand media[18] lines was c. £2.9m at an ROI of £0.45. If we made budget decisions on a pure short-term basis we would have disinvested at this point. Having measured the long-term contribution on PCWs we get an additional ROI of £0.63.

This takes us to an ROI £1.08, which we consider commercially sustainable to continue supporting the brand.

Strategically, we could not replicate this outcome by reducing our marketing overhead and lowering our price point; our competitive set can (and do) respond to price changes almost instantly. The Churchill brand legacy is based on long-term investment and a tremendous creative asset; this builds a consumer affinity that acts as a kind of soft 'barrier to entry' that low-cost insurers cannot match.

Case study 3: Pathways to consideration – Direct Line Insurance

Our third case study is about finding the balance between brand and acquisition media lines.[19]

It is worth recapping some of Direct Line's achievements. In 2014, after four years of decline, we rebooted the brand with the 'Fixer' campaign led by Harvey Keitel. The use of a character from a Tarantino film to represent our brand was a bold choice, but we were confident that the humour and the promise of straightforward convenient insurance would resonate with our target market. Initial results were excellent. In 2016 we submitted an IPA paper that showcased early signs of success from the reboot.

The *IPA Advertising Works*[20] editor commented that '... *this case documented an extremely well-considered comeback that transformed the business from inside out'.* Since then, we have indeed gone from strength to strength.[21] We know that market trends and improved short-term media ROI is part of this success story, but we also believed that there was a brand element that we were failing to capture (Figure 14).

Figure 14: Direct Line motor and home quotes

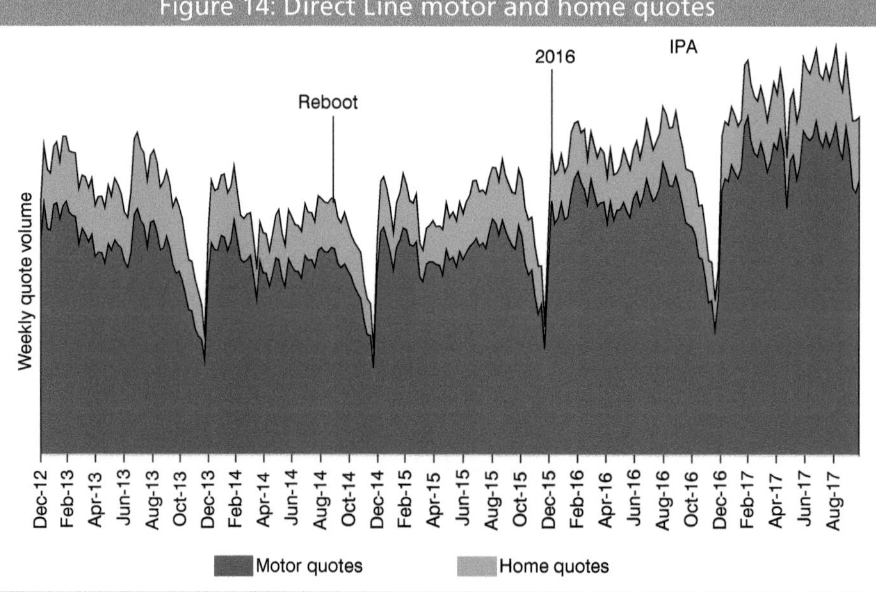

Understanding the true drivers of our growth is critical for our commercial planning. Our challenge is that, despite our growth since reboot, the short-term acquisition costs of brand media lines[22] are still much higher than we see for acquisition media lines (PPC, affiliates or DM). The cost per sale of brand media is shown indexed versus acquisition media in Figures 15 and 16.

Figure 15: Direct Line cost per sale – motor and home

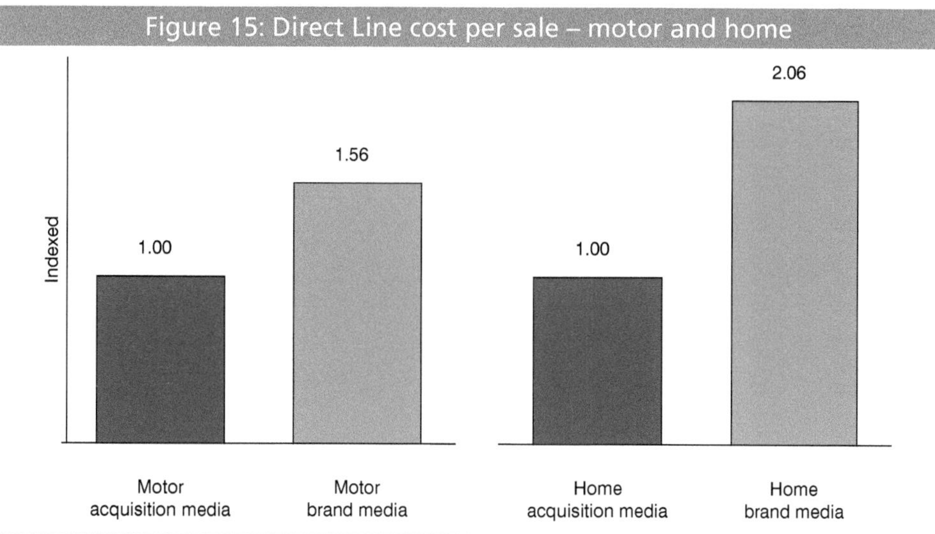

It is a fair challenge to ask whether putting c. 45–50% of our Direct Line marketing budget into what apparently looks like a less-efficient media line is the right decision for DLG. To address this we created a new measurement approach that allows us to better understand the impact of our marketing investments on long-term dynamics (Figure 16).

Figure 16: Direct Line motor spend percentage – motor and home (52 weeks to October 2017)

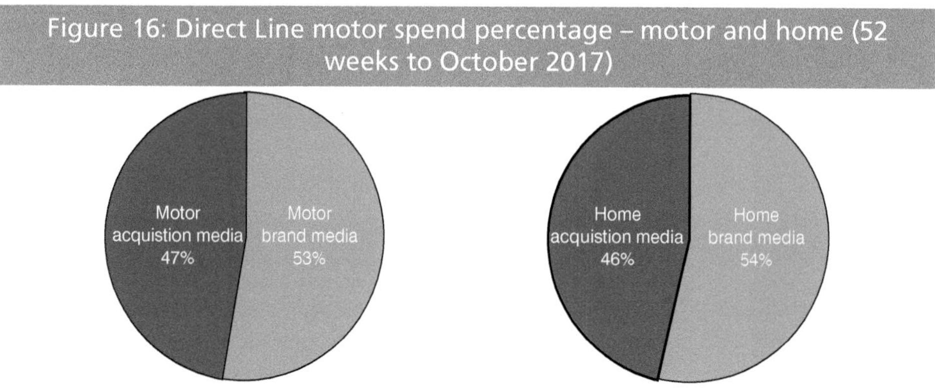

Measurement approach

The defining problem of modern commercial analysis is not that there is not enough information, but that there is too much. Brand survey data gives us an abundance of information – hundreds of metrics that can be split hundreds of ways. This creates an analytic challenge; how can we identify what element drives commercial growth?

Individually, many brand measures are statistically noisy making it hard to draw meaningful conclusions about what individual factor is driving success.

The correlation heat map shown in Figure 17 represents a subset of 72 brand metrics available for Direct Line. Red data points indicate highly correlated metrics, blue data points represent negatively correlated metrics.

Figure 17: Direct Line brand metrics correlation

This graphic illustrates two things: a) there are large red blocks of metrics that all move together and seem to be measuring some underlying factor and b) there is too much data for meaningful interpretation.

In order to make sense of the information it is necessary to reduce the number of factors we look at. This can be done using techniques such as factor analysis, principal components analysis or cluster analysis (as shown in dendrogram in Figure 18).

Reducing the dimensions of the brand dataset gives us a more natural way of thinking about human attitudes so we can identify the pathways that drive commercial growth; either directly or indirectly.

For DLG brands, the exact aggregation differs for new and existing customers, for home and motor and by period. However, the factor groupings shown in Table 1 highlight common themes that were found to be most representative across the portfolio.

The extended brand health dataset[23] could not be tested in an econometric framework.[24] The reduced factor set, however, can then be tested.

The first stage of the analysis is a 'traditional' econometric model which we use to strip out drivers like PPC, DM and the short-term impact of above-the-line media. For Direct Line motor insurance this accounts for about 41% of sales. For home insurance this accounts for 48%.

But what about the remainder? Typically this is described as 'base' sales and it would include factors such as the market, the regulatory environment and brand equity (which we believe would determine market share in the absence of price and short-term marketing).

The mechanism through which brand investment drives base evolution is not straightforward, but rather relies on both direct and indirect pathways. One fundamental finding is that consideration is directly linked to base sales, which confirms a rather classical view of how the marketing funnel works (Figures 19 and 20).

Figure 18: Dendrogram cluster analysis of brand values

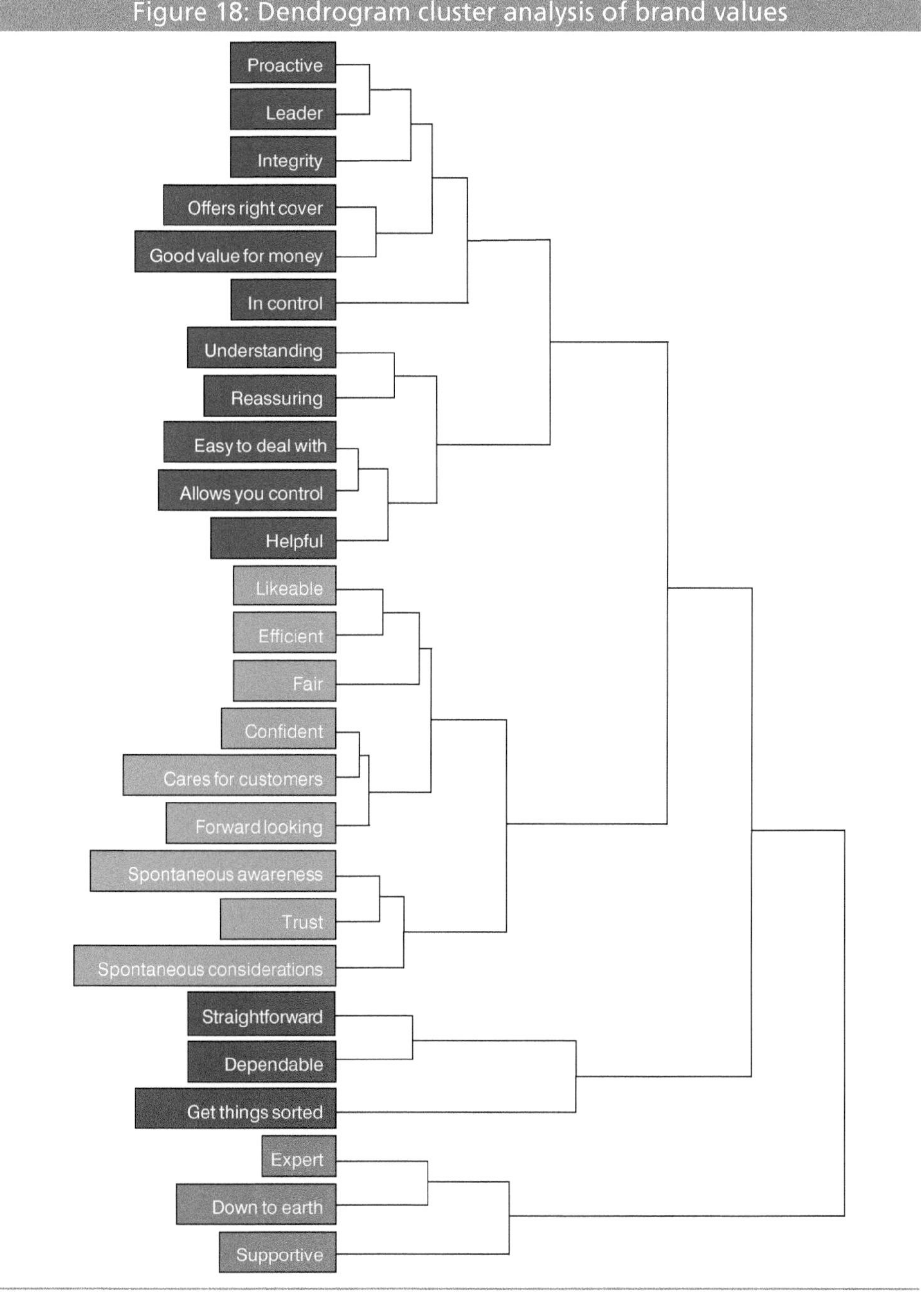

Table 1: Factor groupings		
Factor group	**Motor**	**Home**
Top of mind	Spontaneous awareness	Spontaneous awareness
	Spontaneous consideration	Spontaneous consideration
	Positive buzz	Positive buzz
Straightforward reliability	Straightforward	Straightforward
	Trustworthy	Dependable
	Dependable	Trustworthy
	Forward looking	Fair
	Proactive	
Perceptions of customer service	Easy to deal with	Easy to deal with
	Good value for money	Good value for money
	Allows you to be in control	Allows you to be in control
	Cares for customers	Cares for customers
	Integrity	Integrity
	Likeability	Likeability
	Gets things sorted	Gets things sorted
	Helpful	Helpful
	Leader	Leader
	Reassuring	Reassuring
	Understanding	Understanding
Will do the right thing		Get things sorted
		Integrity
		Good value for money
		Offers the right cover
Other factors	Customer net promotor score	Customer net promotor score
	Complaints	Complaints

Figure 19: Pathways of influence – motor

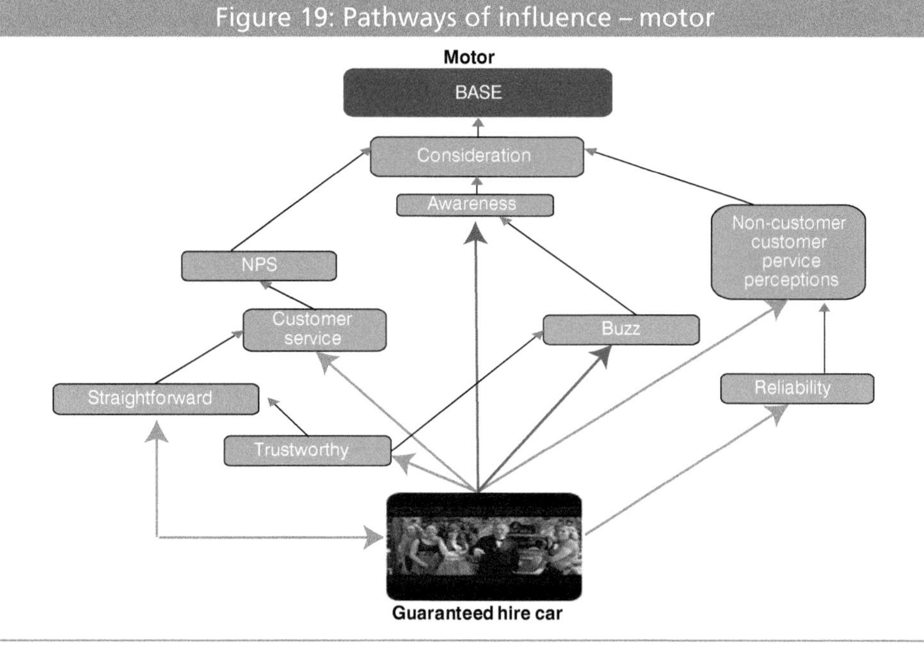

Figure 20: Pathways of influence – home

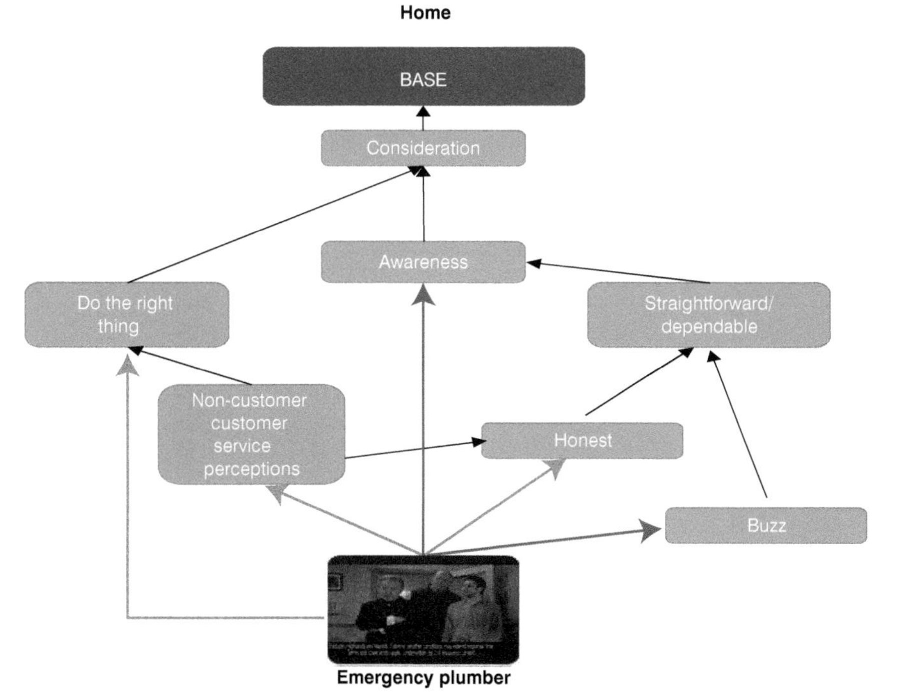

These diagrams illustrate how these pathways of direct and indirect effects drive consideration and ultimately help us explain base evolution.

Top-of-mind factors are shown with the pink arrows. For motor insurance we found that the 'Guaranteed hire car' campaign drove awareness which in turn drove consideration and base sales. Similarly we found that buzz drives awareness.

Brand-perception factors are shown in blue. The 'Guaranteed hire car' campaign directly improved perceptions of straightforwardness, trustworthiness, and customer service. These in turn helped improve the net promotor score (NPS), either directly or indirectly, which feeds into consideration. Similarly, reliability and non-customer service perceptions are positively associated with awareness.

For the 'Emergency plumber' home insurance campaign shown in Figure 22 we saw similar patterns emerge. The campaign drove positive brand perceptions on customer service, honesty and 'doing the right thing' as well as top-of-mind factors such as buzz and awareness. All of which ultimately improved base sales via consideration … the value of which is quantified in the next section.

Case study 3: What did we learn?

First, as a result of this work we now know with much greater rigour that consideration and awareness are key drivers of our base, but more importantly we have identified the levers we need to pull to move them and we know which media channels can influence our base evolution.

Second, we have identified specific long-term multipliers for Direct Line of *1.60* for motor and *1.70* for home. These are not nebulous 'industry norms' but are derived by linking our tracking data to our own commercial performance. After factoring these into our commercial planning we see that the effective cost per sale of acquisition and brand media is much more evenly balanced (Figure 21).

Figure 21: Direct Line cost per sale – motor and home (econometrics 52 weeks to October 2017)

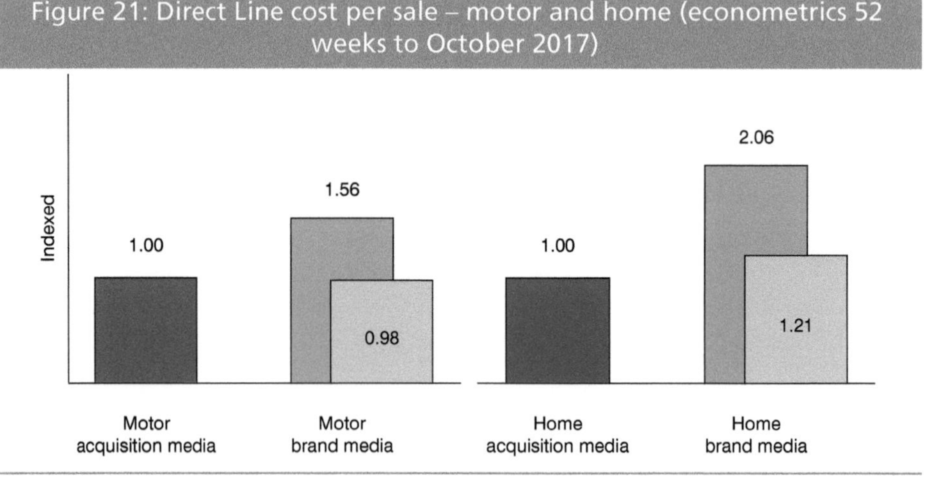

Finally, our analysis allowed us to further decompose the base and identify the contribution of brand equity. We already knew that on a short-term basis, marketing delivers around 40–50% of our sales (see below).[25] What we now know is that brand equity accounts for c. 20–25%.

Before even considering the long-term contribution, our marketing ROI[26] on Direct Line is excellent. We delivered a short-term return of £2.39 in the 52 weeks to March 2017 across home and motor (Figure 22).

Figure 22: Short-term vs. brand equity share

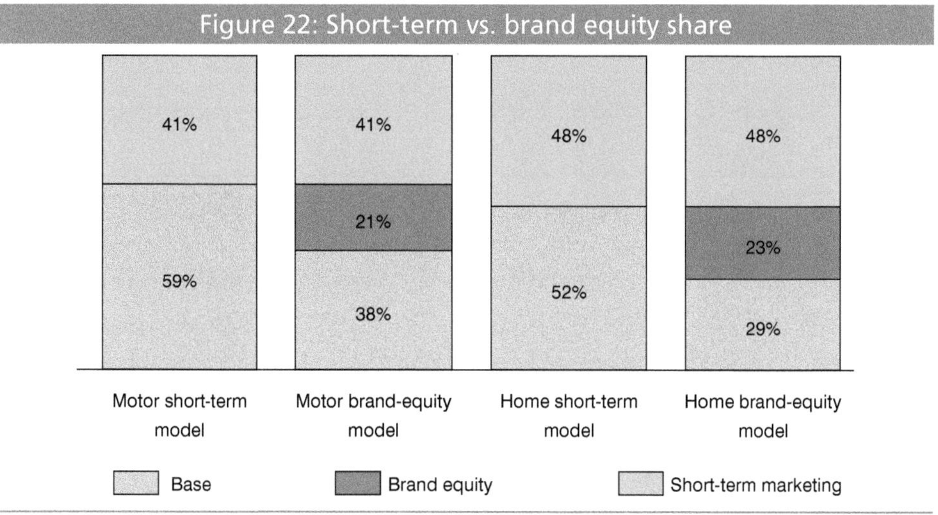

But what we found truly stunning was that the previously unmeasured profit contribution is worth c. £40.5m on a five-year NPV basis. To put this in perspective, that number alone represents about 9% of DLG's average annual profit.[27]

Implications: what we did differently

Taking the three case studies as a whole, here are four things we did differently as a result of our cumulative learnings.

We doubled down on brand-led TV marketing

As PCWs became the primary shopping channel, most insurance brands reduced investment in TV advertising. DLG didn't follow the trend. We kept TV at the heart of our media plan because we knew that it is an effective driver of brand equity in general and awareness, buzz and consideration in particular. As of 2017 our share of TV spend was twice our market share for motor, and three times for home (Figure 23).

Figure 23: TV share of voice vs. share of market – motor and home

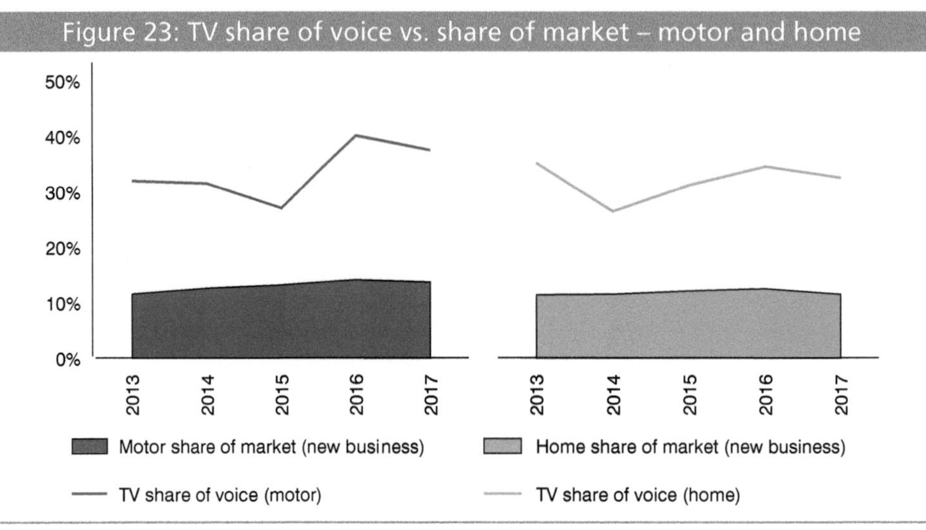

Within TV planning our strategy also changed. Historically, about half of the budget was brand (BRTV) which predominantly airs in more premium peak programming. The other half was direct response (DRTV), which is typically aired during the daytime. With a renewed focus on brand building, the balance has shifted towards BRTV. As of 2017 almost 80% of our TV budget is brand focused (Figure 24).

Figure 24: DLG TV shore by brand vs. direct response TV

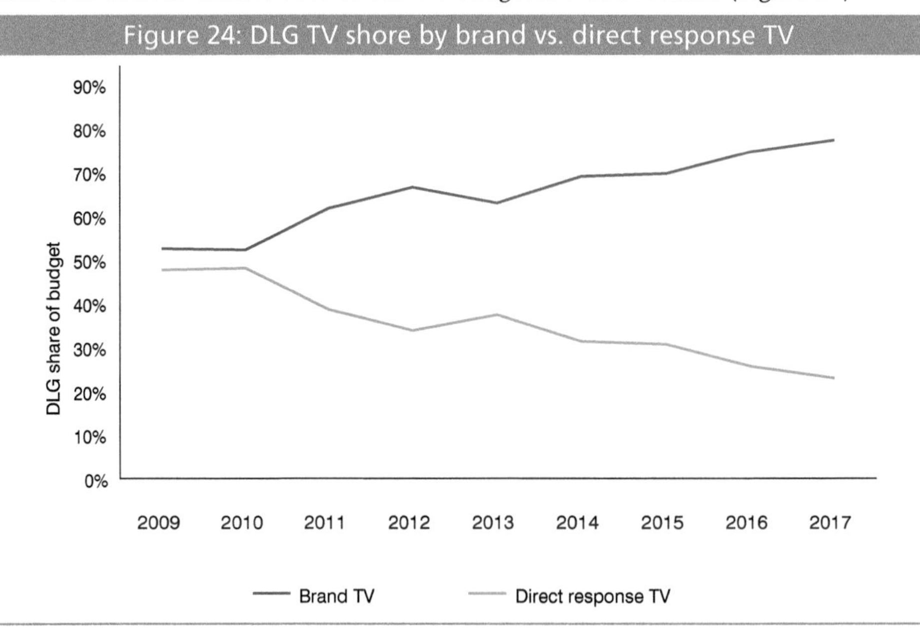

We are digital conservatives

Until very recently, the marketing orthodoxy has been that more targeting (and more digital media) is always and unambiguously a good thing, not with us! Between 2013 and 2017 we substantially reduced investment in digital display[28] and programmatic online video, both compared to previous years and compared to our competitor peer group.

What informed our divergent thinking? We devised a geotesting[29] programme to understand the incremental impact of digital. A series of tests gave us evidence of poor performance (despite excellent efficiencies being reported on a post-impression basis).

These results put us ahead of the curve. The world of marketing was shaken in 2017 when Marc Pritchard of P&G shone a light on the lack of transparency and poor efficiency of many programmatic media lines – but this was not new news at DLG.

We call ourselves digital conservatives but we are not anti-digital. We favour new, innovative and targetable media if it is cost-effective. Whatever the media line, cost-effective reach has become our imperative for all marketing investment decisions across the brand portfolio.

We could find compelling evidence for both the long-term and short-term effectiveness of media lines such as TV and radio. By contrast, our research did not support continued investment in a number of programmatic digital media lines even on a short-term basis.

The line chart in Figure 25 shows the non-response of our home and motor quote volume during an aggressive upweight of display spend across half the UK while the other half was 'dark'. Blue bars represent delivered impressions.

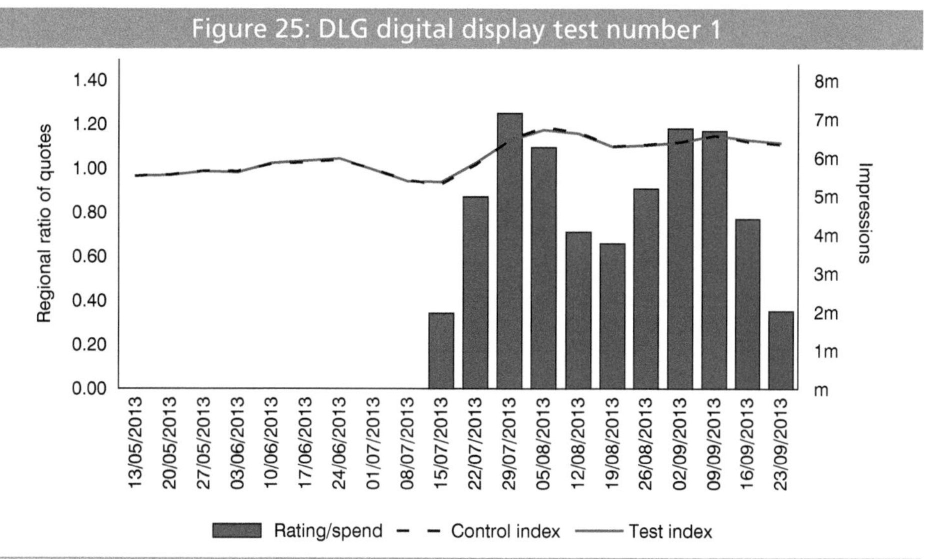

On the back of this test we reduced our display spend across the portfolio from approx. £3.5m in 2013 to no BAU[30] display spend in 2017. These savings have contributed the most to our post-IPO budget challenges and helped us defend brand budgets.

We improved our propositions and customer experience

The Brand Equity Analysis Programme demonstrated to us that our complaints, customer service perceptions and net promoter scores are all important pathways on the way to consideration.

If customers have a sub-par experience with our brands, we know that this will put our brand equity at risk, regardless of how much we invest in advertising. To protect our brand assets, we put together a programme that improved the customer experience and our propositions across the portfolio. What kind of improvements were implemented?

We reduced our reliance on discount-led advertising and strengthened our execution of the 'Fixer' positioning with a string of market-leading propositions (Figure 26).

Figure 26: Direct Line 'Fixer' campaign

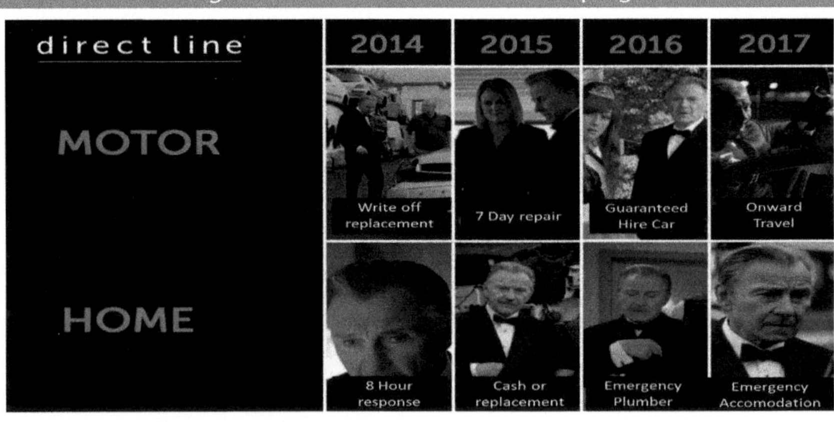

Against conventional thinking for an insurer we cancelled policy-amendment fees for Direct Line despite the commercial risks (and an annual cost of c. £7m[31]). We improved car repair turnaround time through a partnership programme with garages. The proof is in the numbers: our complaints rate fell by 48% between 2014 and 2017 (Figure 27).

We saved the dog! We continue to support a portfolio of brands

We have evidence that we should continue to support investment in the Churchill brand (Figure 28). From a short-term perspective, this investment decision would previously have been indefensible. More broadly, we understand that while there may be cost advantages to reducing the number of brands we support, we would lose out on the benefits of a 'diversified portfolio'. Our portfolio strategy is underpinned by a needs-based behavioural segmentation model.

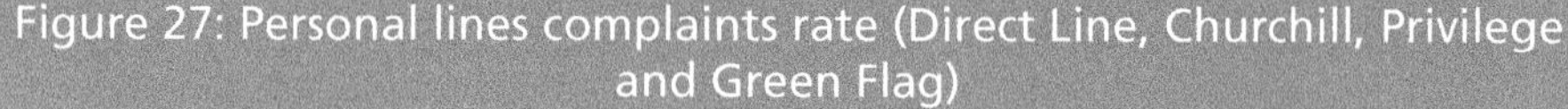

Figure 27: Personal lines complaints rate (Direct Line, Churchill, Privilege and Green Flag)

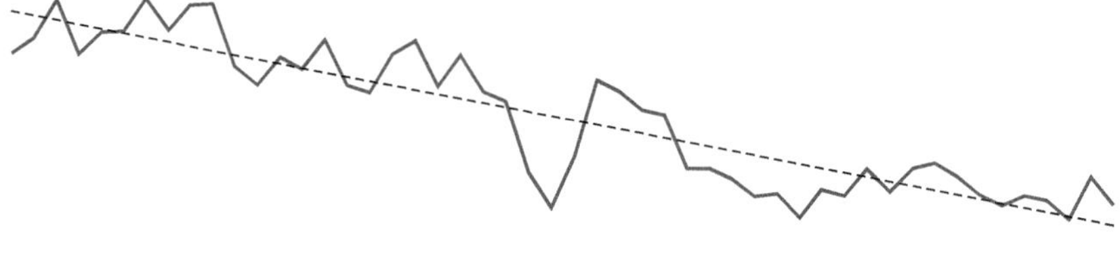

Figure 28: The Churchill bulldog

This has helped us reach consumers with different values and needs: we are able to reach customers who just want the best possible price point (Privilege); consumers who are willing to pay a premium for a brand they know and trust (Churchill); as well as consumers who simply want the best possible product and who value straightforward convenience.

Conclusion: performance of our brand portfolio (2013–2017)

Was it successful? Unequivocally yes!

Because we have played the long game and sustained brand investment over the years, Direct Line and Churchill enjoy some of the strongest spontaneous consideration scores in the marketplace.[32] We own two of the top three insurance brands in the market – an outcome that could only be achieved with a long-termist approach to brand measurement, management and investment (Figure 29).

Figure 29: Spontaneous brand consideration

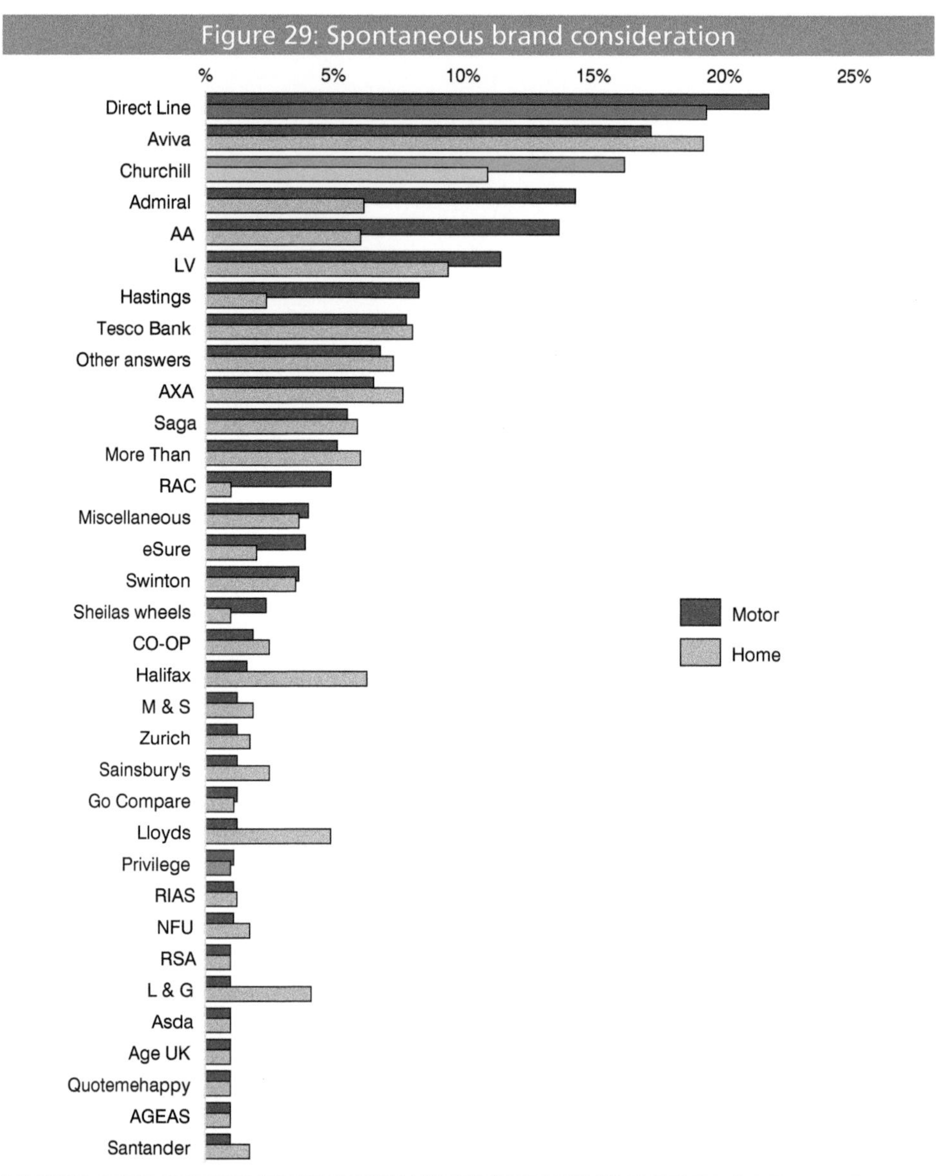

We also enjoy excellent preference[33] scores across general insurance. Again, this is the long-term payoff for ongoing brand investment and our focus on improving the customer experience (Figure 30).

Figure 30: Preference home and motor

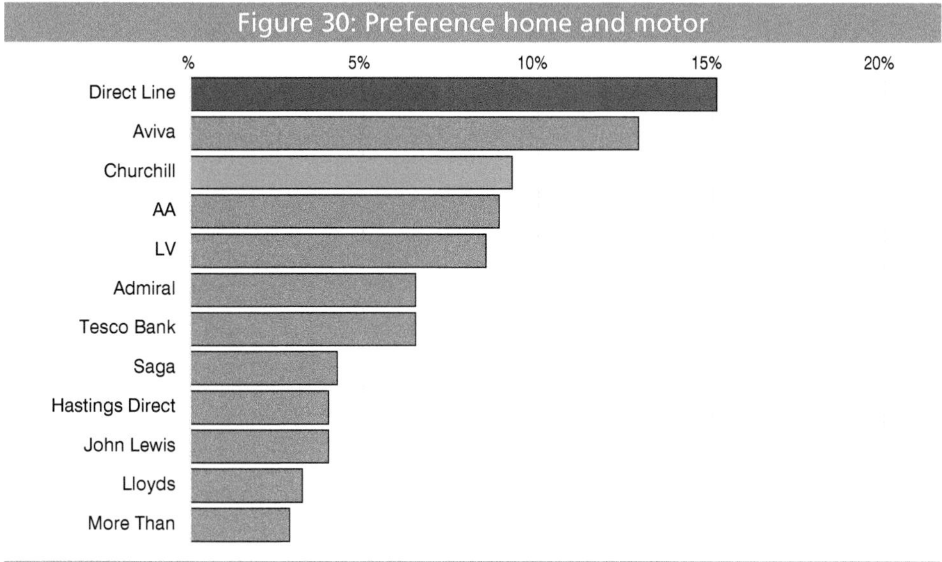

But brand equity is only a means to an end. What is the impact on our commercial performance?

As a group our book has grown and we have gained customers since 2014[34]; and we have seen particularly strong growth for Direct Line since the brand was rebooted in 2014 (Figure 31).

Figure 31: Total DLG in-force policies

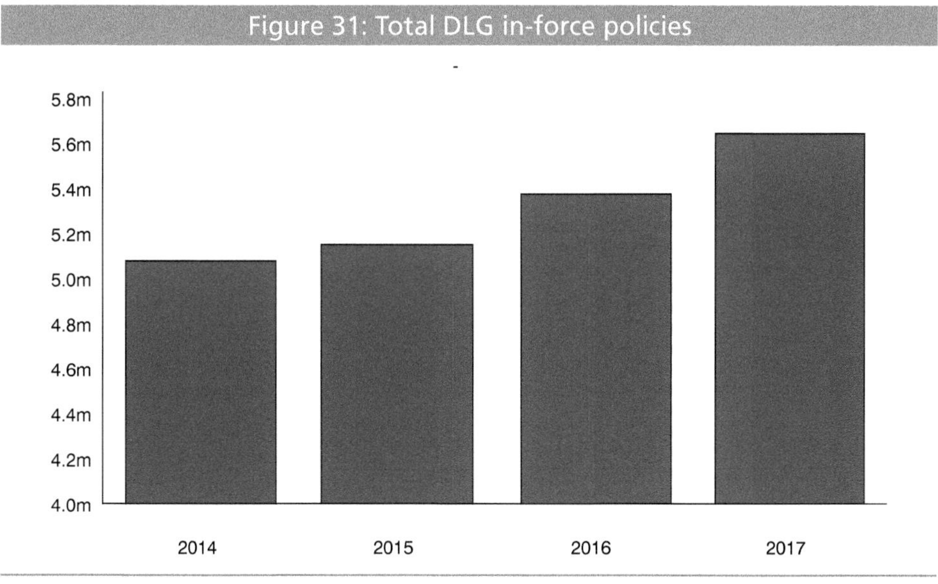

We have also seen gains in the DLG share price since our IPO – significantly ahead of the FTSE 100 (Figure 32).

Figure 32: DLG share price vs. FTSE 100 (indexed October 2012)

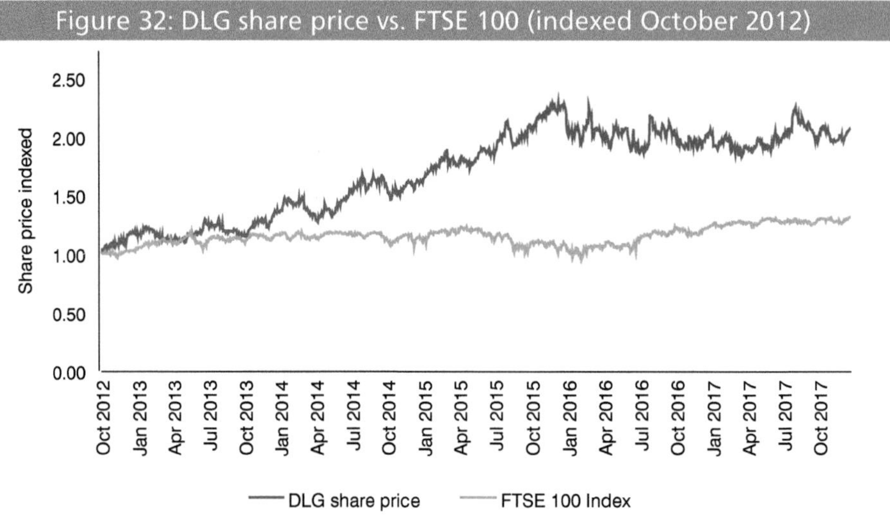

Three years ago we set out on a journey to understand whether our brand-led strategy was right for DLG when it seemed that so many of our competitors were travelling in the opposite direction.

The results are phenomenal! This paper has outlined how improved measurement has enabled us to quantify £46m previously unmeasured profit contribution on home and motor alone[35].

Proper measurement of the contribution of brand equity has fundamentally altered the strategic thinking of the business.

Through this piece of work we have been able to educate the organisation and we now have a better appreciation of the value of our brands.

When the inevitable costs challenges do come around we can explicitly quantify the long-term impact of our short-term decisions.

To put it simply, what we learned has allowed us to play the long game when others could not.

Notes

1. Source: Google Trends, 2004–2016.
2. Source: Spontaneous awareness data is based on survey based brand tracking from a number of providers. TNS 2004–2017, Nunwood 2008–2013, Hall & Partners 2013–2016.
3. Source: Spend based on internal records.
4. By 'direct' we mean that the customers gets a quote either with the contact centre over the phone, or directly on the website. Churchill's motor sales split is *c.* 40% direct to 60% PCW.
5. Source: Ebiquity short-term econometrics. Media lines include TV, radio, press, OOH, social, display and cinema. Period: 52 weeks to October 2017.
6. Source: Internal data and a leading PCW. Period March 2014 to September 2016.
7. Source: Box-Clever. Survey Date: March 2017. Sample Size: 3036.
8. The PCW data used was sourced from one of our PCW partners and has a number of limitations in place. Information was only provided on the top five positions of each query and both brand and consumer were anonymised. Exact quoted premium were provided for each position. Period: July 2014 to June 2016.

9. An implicit assumption here is that Privilege is a kind of 'non-brand' with zero equity. Clearly this is false as many of us lovingly remember the Joanna Lumley adverts that ran in the early 2000s. This is a valid criticism, but it should be noted that this will bias the results of our analysis downwards, not upwards.
10. Source: Internal data.
11. Source: Advertising spend from Ebiquity Portfolio 2008 to 2017. Media lines include estimated spend for TV, Radio, Press, Cinema and Outdoor.
12. Source: Hall & Partners. 2016.
13. Black-box devices that measure driving characteristics and feed into (hopefully) cheaper insurance premiums. Our model suggests consumers see Telematics as a 'slight negative' after adjusting for its pricing benefits.
14. Specifically we used an ordinary least squares fixed-effects panel model.
15. Technical note: the brand equity variable shares a common coefficient across Churchill and Privilege.
16. This £10–£20 figure can be derived from the hanging-bars analysis and has been corroborate by conjoint analysis conducted in 2014 by Hall & Partners.
17. Based on the last 52 weeks of the model to June 2016.
18. Including TV, radio, sponsorship and VOD.
19. You could argue that this is a false dichotomy but for the purposes of this paper we are treating brand building media lines such as TV, radio, cinema, OOH and press as 'brand' and demand-harvesting media lines such as DM, door drops, PPC and SEO as 'acquisition'.
20. *IPA Advertising Works* Volume 23, 2016.
21. Source: Internal data. Period: December 2012 to September 2017.
22. Source: Based on econometric measurement of short-term advertising effects 52 weeks to September 2017.
23. Customer Net Promotor score and complaints data sourced from DLG. Positive Buzz sourced from YouGov. All other survey data for this study was provided by Hall & Partners. Period: Jan 2013–March 2017. Sample: n=1000.
24. To do so would be committing the crime of 'over-fitting' the data.
25. Based on econometric analysis.
26. ROI calculated using a five-year net present value for each acquisition. Breakeven ROI is *c.* £1.00.
27. Source: DLG Annual Report 2017. Average declared profit before tax 2016 and 2017.
28. This includes prospecting and retargeting.
29. Implemented in partnership with Ebiquity.
30. Digital display spend is currently confined to our media testing budget (based on 2017 and 2018 plans).
31. Source: Internal data. Period: January 2014 to January 2018.
32. Our brand tracking was recently moved to a new provider and as such we cannot offer a multi-year time series view. Period: Monthly average for the period July 2017 to February 2018. Source: Kantar Millward Brown. Sample size: 1000. Question: *'Thinking about the next time you need to renew your motor/ home insurance policy, which providers would you consider?'*
33. Source: Kantar Millward Brown. Period: Monthly average for the period July 2017 to February 2018. Sample size: 1000. Question: *'If price was equal, which home and/or car insurance provider would you prefer to use?'*
34. Based on consumer panel data provided by insurance specialist Consumer Intelligence.
35. On an annual basis. This is £5.5m on Churchill motor and £40.5m on Direct Line motor and home. This is a conservative estimate as it does not include many of our other lines such as Churchill Home, Direct Line for Business, Green Flag or Privilege.

Guinness

'Made of more', 2012–2018

By Lisa Stoney, AMV BBDO
Contributing authors: Craig Mawdsley, David Edwards, Lilian Sor and Rory Gallery, AMV BBDO; Alison Falconer and Nanda Griffioen, Diageo; David Hartley, Data2Decisions
Credited companies: AMV BBDO; Carat

Summary

Guinness has a high bar for creativity and effectiveness, but by 2015 the challenge heightened: distribution was tight, the economy continued to stagnate and competition was tougher. Guinness doubled down on its 'Made of more' positioning with every iteration, creating stronger connections to culture that brought the platform to life in new and bold ways across the media mix, and genuinely resonated with its audience (from the story of Gareth Thomas to the cowboys of Compton). Ultimately, bolder work paid dividends with on-trade value share growing 8% in Great Britain and an estimated £4.13 profit returned for every £1 invested.

Editor's comment

The consistency of the commitment by Guinness to keep its brand culturally relevant and its rigorous measurement of both beautifully executed advertising and channel innovations won the admiration of the judges.

Client comment

Alison Falconer, Global Consumer Planning Director, Guinness and Beer, Diageo

This paper is a tale of iterative learning; of how magic and measurement create work that not only works, but endures. It's the story of how Guinness never settles – and the success of this strategy is indicative in this being our second 'Made of more' IPA paper. Again, we've proved iterative creative development helped us build market share and claim the highest profit ROI ever reported in the IPA beer category.

As we stated: it is a bold claim to be 'Made of more' – you have to live up to it, to be prepared to never settle for ordinary, to push from good to great to best ever. This doesn't mean repeating a formula. It's about consistency of spirit and meaning, but never being afraid to question whether we could have done better. If we could have reached more people. If we hit all the right notes.

But with the right tools in place, the right people and the right learnings we will continue to adapt 'Made of more', making it more effective every time. Creativity has more power with the wisdom of measurement: by using data and cultural/audience learnings to get to the nub of what has worked in the past in order to optimise for the future. For us, measurement isn't about right and wrong, it's about finding opportunities to help all of our teams make future decisions. This is why our work gets bolder, and why we've sought to embed our brand in culture.

This is evidenced across our IPA papers, starting with 'Clock' and 'Cloud', and through to planning our next campaign after 'Compton cowboys'.

In 2016, Guinness won a Gold IPA Effectiveness Award for 'Made of more' and the effect it had in market between 2012 and 2015.

It was the story of iterative executional development to build market share and the highest profit ROI ever reported in any IPA paper in the beer category.

But Guinness is a brand that never settles.

Brands grow through consistency. Sticking to ideas and building over time. But this shouldn't mean repeating a formula. Success can be a trap.

This paper is about absolute consistency of spirit and meaning. Committing to an idea over time. But it's also a paper about avoiding the traps of success. Of never standing still.

We have reaped further rewards from consistency, taking success and beating it. Taking the best beer category profit ROI ever reported in an IPA paper and beating it.

As a result, Guinness has regained its place as the third favourite draft beer in Britain.

The origins of 'Made of more'

Guinness is the most distinctive beer in the world: which is both a blessing and a curse.

It originated in 1759 in the brewery of Arthur Guinness at St. James' Gate, Dublin (Figure 1). It's now brewed in 60 countries and available in over 150.

Figure 1: St James' Gate Brewery in Dublin

As a dark stout, its distinctive black liquid is set in contrast to the creamy white head (Figure 2).

Figure 2: A glass of Guinness

Guinness isn't served in the same way as a regular beer: you get the perfect pint when poured in two parts over 119.5 seconds.

Because of this, Guinness had traditionally focused on dramatising product truths (Figure 3).

Figure 3: Past Guinness advertising

(Left) Guinness' first-ever ad which focused on perceived medicinal benefits; (centre) Guinness' famous Gilroy work claiming 'goodness' in the drink; and (right) our 'Good things come to those who wait' campaign which celebrated the 119.5 seconds it takes to pour the perfect pint.

Our communications often differed by market as Guinness has different products and formats across the world. In Europe and America it is mainly Guinness Draught (the famous pint with the creamy head), in Africa and Southeast Asia, Guinness is bottles of Foreign Extra Stout – stronger-tasting stout, originally created to survive long shipping (Figure 4).

Figure 4: Guiness formats across the world

By 2011 we were supporting five different positioning statements globally: an approach that was no longer viable. Our core markets of Great Britain and Ireland would now be treated as one, with shared communications working to one idea.

The move to one global brand positioning

We needed to increase effectiveness and efficiency of communications. One global platform would allow us to create communication of greater quality.

Our new approach would move away from the drink and instead focus on the shared attitude between brand, product and drinker.

We built on three truths (Figure 5).

Figure 5: Guinness is a beer made of more, for people made of more, and we tell stories of how unexpected character in people and beer enrich the world around us

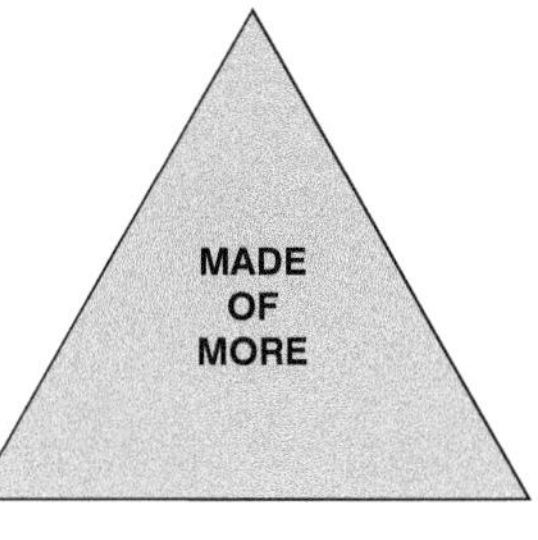

Purpose pays

'Made of more' is a platform with purpose that triggers competitive advantage. In our 2016 IPA Effectiveness Awards paper, we showed how Guinness built on the success of our early iterations of 'Made of more' in GB and Ireland to develop campaigns which more effectively communicated the brand's distinctiveness and salience.

The progression of 'Made of more' (see appendix for video links) (Figure 6).

Figure 6: 'Made of more' progression

Through continual dedication to this strategy we delivered improving returns, with an overall profit ROI of £3.88 for every £1 invested: almost twice the category norm (Figure 7).[1]

Figure 7: Pre vs. post 'Made of more' profit ROI

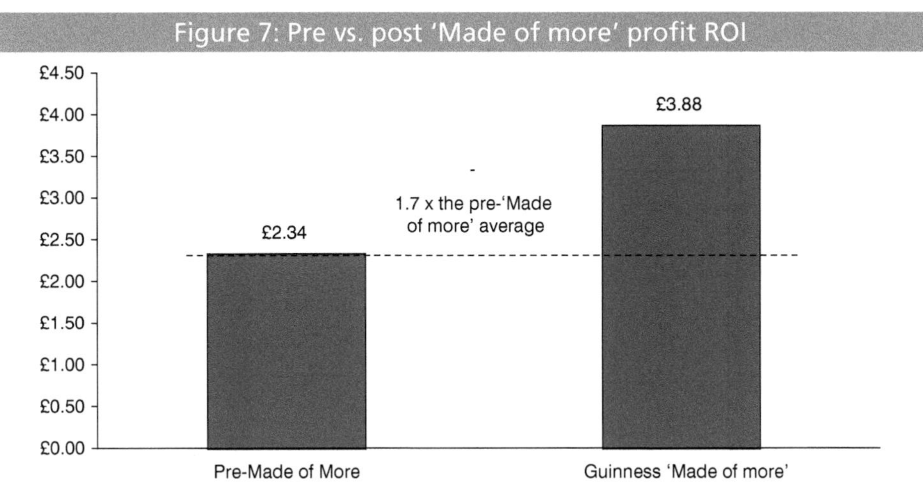

Source: Data2Decisions econometric modelling

'Made of more' enabled us to achieve great success, because we committed to constant improvement, never settling for average.

Settling wasn't an option as the landscape (culturally, economically and politically) became even more challenging after 2015.

Challenge 1: The beer market was declining in GB and Ireland

In the run up to 2015, the beer market had been continuing downwards (Figure 8).

Figure 8: Beer sales GB and Ireland 2012–2014

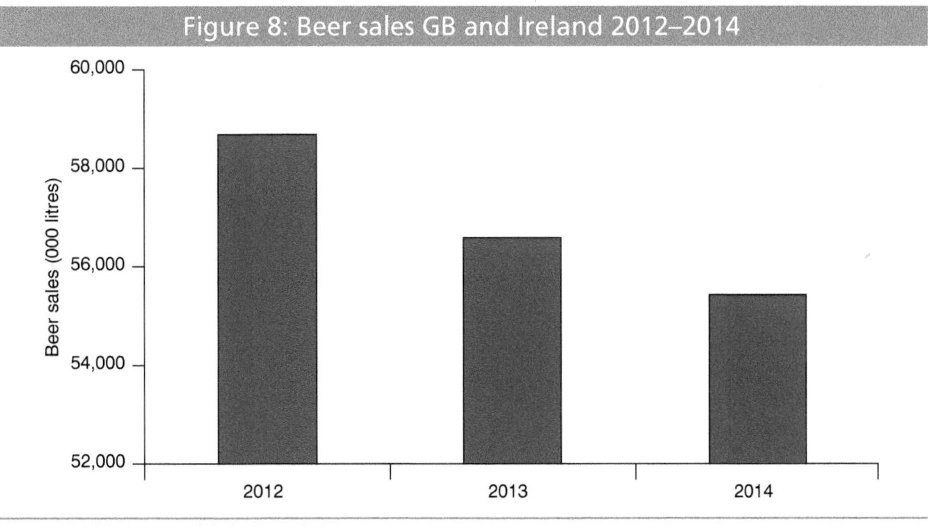

Source: British Beer and Pub Association

This was keenly felt by Guinness, as stout sales were declining ahead of the rest of the beer market (Figure 9).

Figure 9: Beer vs. stout sales decline

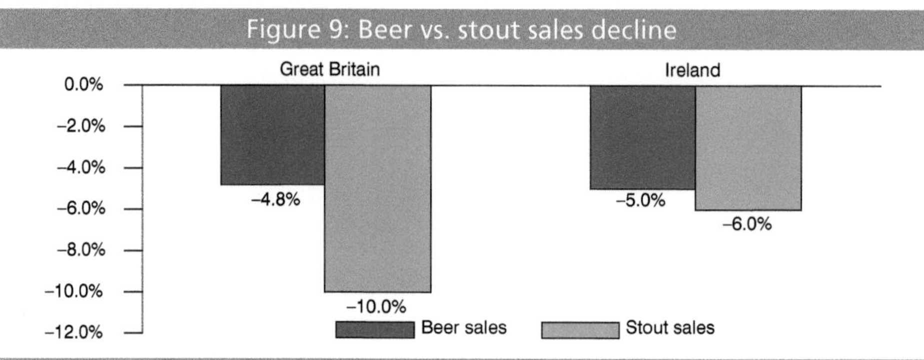

Source: USA Today and Daily Telegraph

Challenge 2: The market was shifting to off-trade.

The recession and the collapse of the 'Celtic Tiger'[2] changed drinking habits. People were going out less, so more inclined to drink at home. This contributed to significant pub closures across GB and Ireland (Figures 10 and 11).

Figure 10: Numbers of pubs in GB 2008–2017

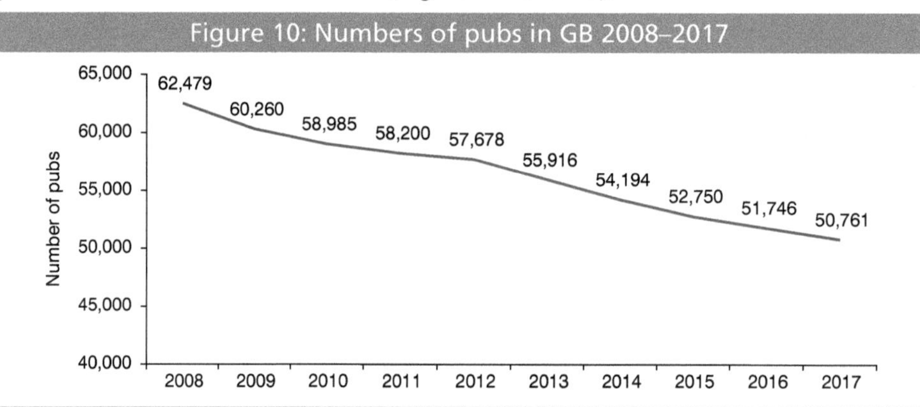

Source: Camra[3]

Figure 11: Numbers of pubs in Ireland 2007–2017

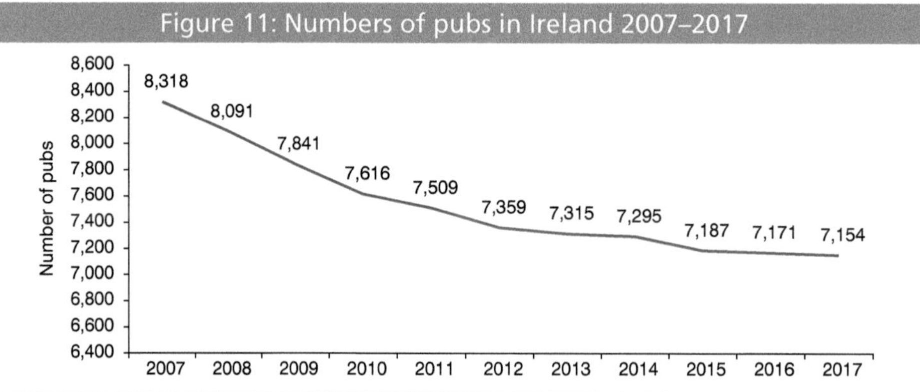

Source: Irish Revenue Commission[4]

This was a significant problem given Guinness sales are skewed to on-trade, with our signature draft considered best enjoyed in the pub (Figure 12).

Figure 12: Guinness pub/in-home (on-trade vs. off-trade) split

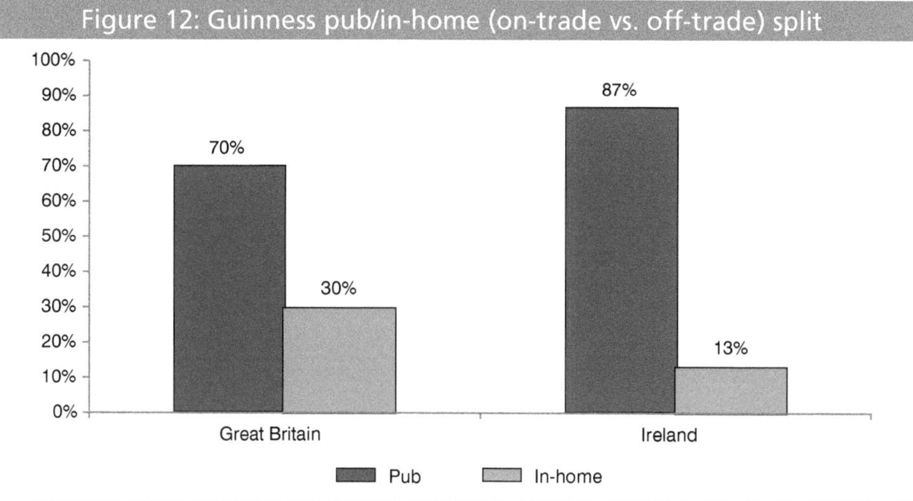

Source: Nielsen & Data2Decisions Econometric Modelling

Challenge 3: The market was increasingly competitive

A typical pub now has 36 brands to choose from (though it can be as high as 50–60[5]) (Figure 13).

Figure 13: Range of brands in a typical pub

Source: JD Wetherspoon

This is partially due to the rise of premium lagers (Figure 14).

Figure 14: Beer market: actual volume change (hectolitres)

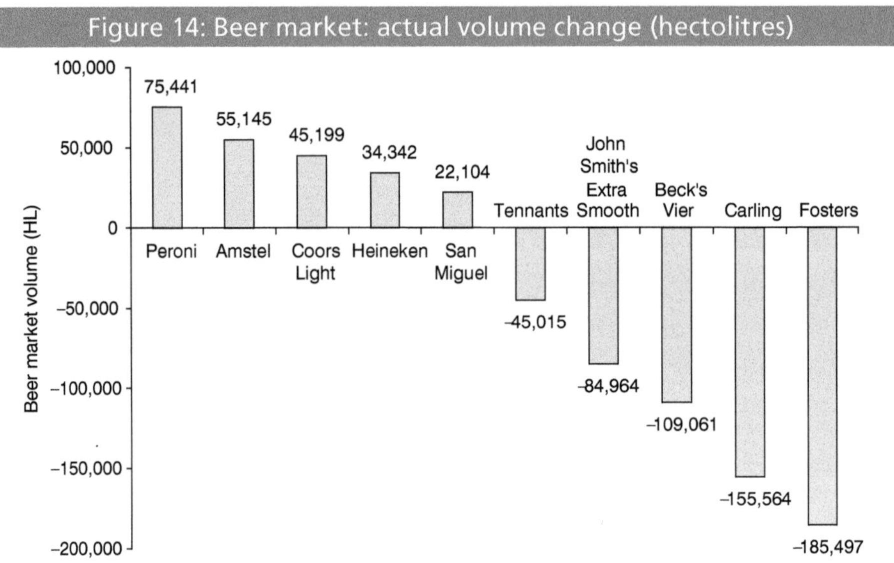

Source: CGA BrandIndex MAT data to P06 (13 June 2015)

But also craft: mainstream drinkers experimenting with more interesting, better tasting beer. By 2016 craft beer penetration would be higher than stout[6] and by 2017 worth almost £1bn (Figure 15).[7]

Figure 15: Craft beer growth 2015–2017

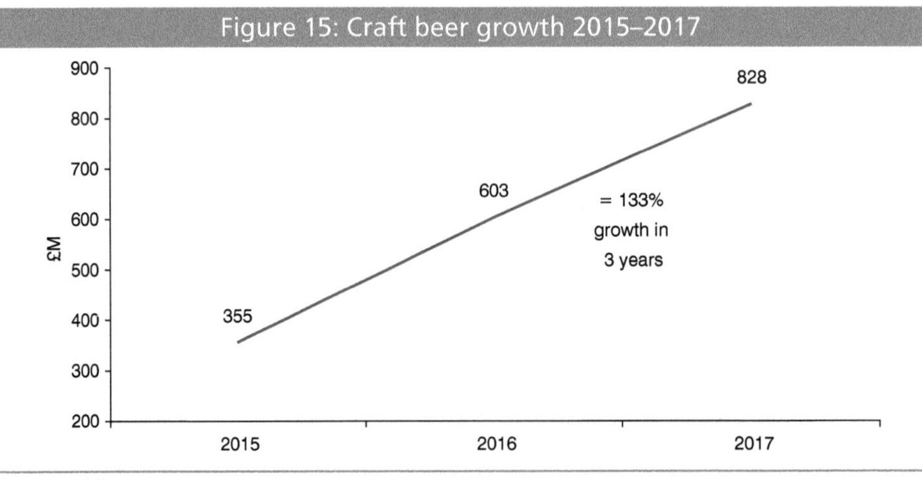

Source: Nielsen

As a more robust-tasting beer, this was a threat to Guinness.

We needed to keep 'Made of more' fresh and relevant, evolving to suit the new context.

Our objectives

Guinness couldn't rely on category growth to reach targets.

We had bucked the trend through commercially successfully communications in the few years prior to 2015, but things were getting tougher.

Communication objective

Drive brand fame through highly creative, more culturally relevant communications.

Marketing objective

Use brand affinity to remain competitive and resonant: see improved saliency and ensure our key affinity statements.

Commercial objective

Increase the efficiency of our ROI (vs. pre-'Made of more' and vs. competitors), and maintain revenue growth and value share in the face of rising costs.

Finding our edge

In true Guinness tradition, we sought to isolate what had worked to make the next better. By 2015, we were four years into 'Made of more' and 'Sapeurs'[8] had been our best yet (Figure 16).

Figure 16: The Sapeurs celebrating in our 2014 Guinness advert

Post-testing revealed our life lesson, encapsulated in the Invictus quote, 'I am the Master of my fate, I am the Captain of my soul', is what resonated most. A relevant cultural tension: in tough economic times we reminded people they control their own destiny.

We needed to liberate 'Made of more' to play a role in culture

'Made of more' has never been about jumping on a cultural bandwagon: but it could be a tool to remind people that you can always carve your own path in life. For our next iteration, we identified the connection between 'Made of more', audience, and culture (Figure 17).

Figure 17

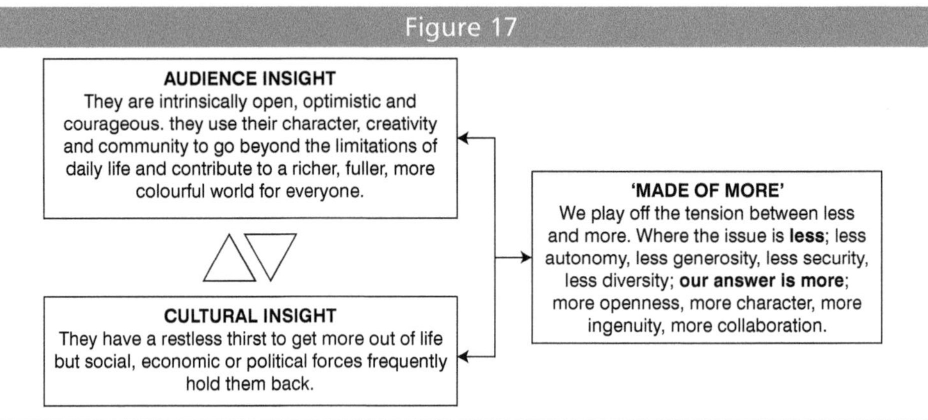

Coupled with our Sapeurs learnings this formed the basis of the next 'Made of more'.

The next chapter – 'Made of more' 2015–2018

'Made of more' 2015

The Rugby World Cup

In the Autumn of 2015, Guinness faced a direct challenge to brand and business in GB and Ireland. Heineken had sponsorship of the Rugby World Cup, banning any sight of Guinness from the stadiums (Figure 18).

Figure 18: Heineken advertising their sponsorship of the 2015 Rugby World Cup

The connection between Guinness and rugby runs deep, built on shared values: it is always a big sales moment.

But we had something Heineken didn't: 'Made of more'

Most rugby marketing focuses on shallow truths of rugby: physicality and masculinity. We decided to be bold, to go against the grain and uncover rugby stories that went beyond mere rugby physicality; stories that would be culturally resonant and timely.

We challenged conventional views of men and masculinity, in two 'Made of more' stories.

'Never alone', featuring Gareth Thomas

In addition to the Rugby World Cup, 2015 was the year Ireland chose to legalise gay marriage. Despite this, homosexuality is still far from an easy topic for many in the world of sport.

In the teeth of our biggest competitive showdown yet, we told the story of rugby's first openly gay player who kept his sexuality secret for years. He found the courage to confront his demons and 'come out', with the encouragement of his team mates (Figure 19).

Figure 19: 'Never alone'

Never Alone (Gareth Thomas)
60"
This advertisement is about the courage, and strength of character Gareth Thomas exhibited on the road to greatness.

We see Gareth Thomas from behind, alone in the stadium, reflecting on his personal hardships.

GT: Everything that I went through out there was nothing compared to the demons inside. In my darkest hour I turned to my teammates.

Gareth Thomas emerges from the tunnel with the hand of a team mate on his shoulder. The camera turns to his face, determined as he leads Wales out on the pitch.

Telling them that I was gay, that was the toughest thing I've ever done. But when I needed them the most, they were there for me.

The frame cuts to TV footage of an elated Thomas scoring a try with the Welsh team around him

AV: https://youtu.be/xFTUTfiUMeM

'The right path', featuring Ashwin Willemse

Research had revealed our target audience felt powerless against the forces that conspired to hold them back: lack of employment opportunities caused by the economic downturn.[9] It was (and is) a crisis that has marked an entire generation.

We found common ground between this and the little known story of Springbok Ashwin Willemse who had to choose between two paths: a notorious Cape Town gang, and rugby. Our story celebrates his choice to defy his circumstances (Figure 20).

Figure 20: 'The right path'

The Right Path (Ashwin Willemse)
60"
This advertisement is about overcoming your circumstances and the bold choices made to achieve something greater.

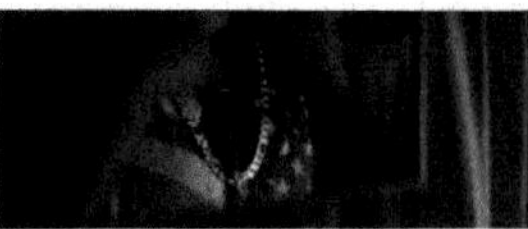

Ashwin Willemse. comes home and changes out of his rugby kit, into a chain and white sneakers.

AW: In my life I had to choose between two teams.

He walks through the township, picking up a package from a gang, but is ambushed whilst delivering it.

One had all the power.

They told me what to do. They told me who to be. But in my time of need they were gone.

After the attack his rugby team is around him, helping him back to his feet as runs back out to play rugby in the township.

The other was always there for me. They gave me strength. They carried me forward. Together we showed the world who I could be.

As he receives a pass, the image transforms to TV footage of Ashwin scoring a try in Springbok colours.

AV: https://youtu.be/534aGB00VC4

This activity was accompanied by out-of-home (Figure 21).

Figure 21: Guinness OOH ads 'Socks' and 'Mouth guard'

To be relevant in culture, it had to be timely

Heineken may have been closer to the pitch, we were closer to the game with reactive social content that solidified the link between rugby and Guinness, examples of great character 'Made of more' (Figure 22).

Figure 22: Guinness social posts

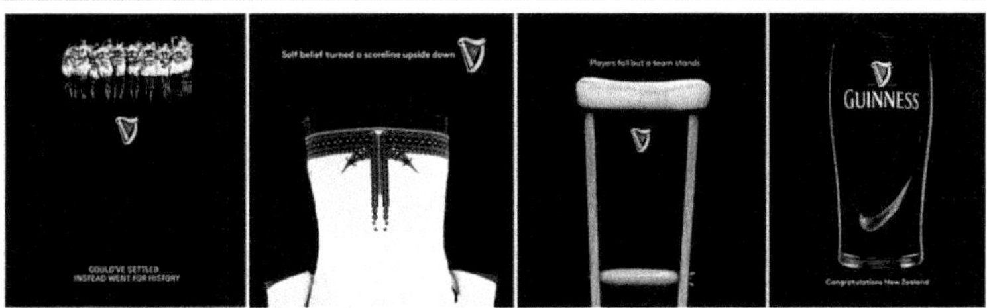

(L-R) The Japanese team celebrating after their shock defeat of South Africa in the last minute; Romania's biggest comeback in World Cup history defeating Canada; Ireland's defeat of France was slightly marred by four major injuries; and NZ snagged the Cup.

Our final battleground was the physical world

If we couldn't win on the pitch, we would win in the pub. The first drink set the tone for match day so we launched The Guinness Lineout: a shared sampling mechanic for groups of four friends watching the match together in 10,000 sport-watching pubs (Figure 23).

Figure 23: The Guinness Lineout

Our resolve to tell stories that elevated and played a role in culture paid off with revenue and profit ROI increasing (Figures 24 and 25).

Figure 24: GB 'Made of more' ROI

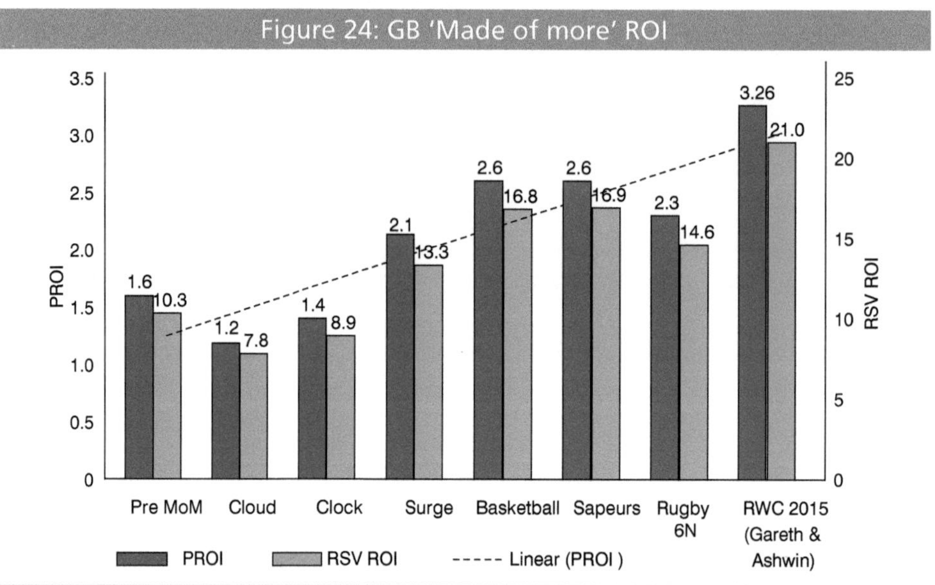

Source: Data2Decisions Econometric Modelling

Figure 25: Ireland 'Made of more' ROI

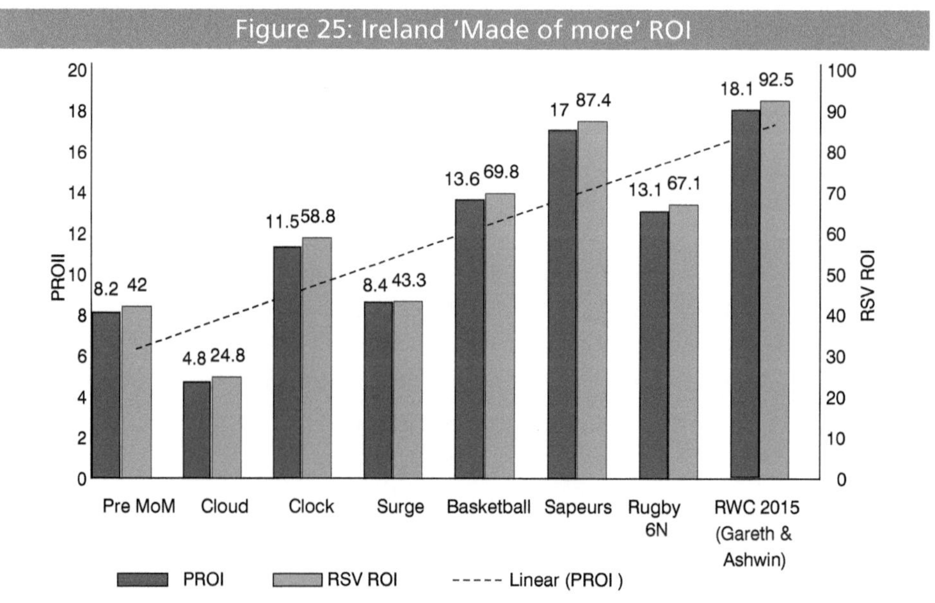

Source: Data2Decisions Econometric Modelling

The continuity of 'Made of more' enabled us to refresh the rich brand associations established in the previous few years and enhance ROI as a result. We had learned the value of continuing to be bold, using the stories of individuals who had the courage to challenge accepted norms, and linking those to debates in culture.

The value lay in a story with a bigger, broader, more powerful truth that applied to any one of our drinkers. Now we needed to go further.

'Made of more' 2016

It was time to beat 'Sapeurs' as our most successful brand film (Figure 26).

Figure 26

AUDIENCE INSIGHT

They are intrinsically open, optimistic and courageous. they use their character, creativity and community to go beyond the limitations of daily life and contribute to a richer, fuller, more colourful world for everyone.

After scouring the globe, one story beat the rest.

'Intolerant champion', featuring John Hammond

Tapping into the spirit of 'Made of more' and celebrating those who decide to carve their own path, we found a story to inspire people with the sentiment that:

It's what you do in life that truly defines who you are (Figure 27).

Figure 27: John Hammond surrounded by musicians

This spirit was encapsulated by John Hammond: one man with passion for music of black origin so he toured the bars and clubs of Harlem, seeking undiscovered talent for his radio show.[10] He stood up to prejudice in the 1930s, championing the potential of black and white artists working together: he opened ears to jazz and eyes to prejudice (Figure 28).

Figure 28: 'John Hammond'

John Hammond
60"

In this advertisement we learn about the pursuit of passion in spite of what society tells you to do.

Black New Yorkers dance to a frenetic Jazz track, as headlines report a ban on black musicians on radio.

VO: When Jazz first hit New York, New York hit back.

John Hammond walks into a radio station, recording live on air a band made up of black and white musicians.

VO: One man heard no colour in music. All John Hammond wanted was great Jazz.

As the band plays, listeners revel in the music, as one reads about Hammond defying the ban on black musician on radio. The dancing stars again as Hammond laughs on at the music.

AV: https://www.youtube.com/watch?v=S4y6kBYF084

Our story of Hammond (told through TV and an online documentary) launched against racial turmoil in the US: 2016 was the year of the Oscar's Whitewash. For the second year in a row, every actor nominated was white (Figure 29).[11]

Figure 29: When nominees for the 88th Academy Awards met for a luncheon in early February, the Oscars' diversity issue was in full view

This backdrop demonstrated Guinness' belief in character, integrity and communion: a reminder that a single person can contribute to a more colourful world (Figure 30).

Figure 30

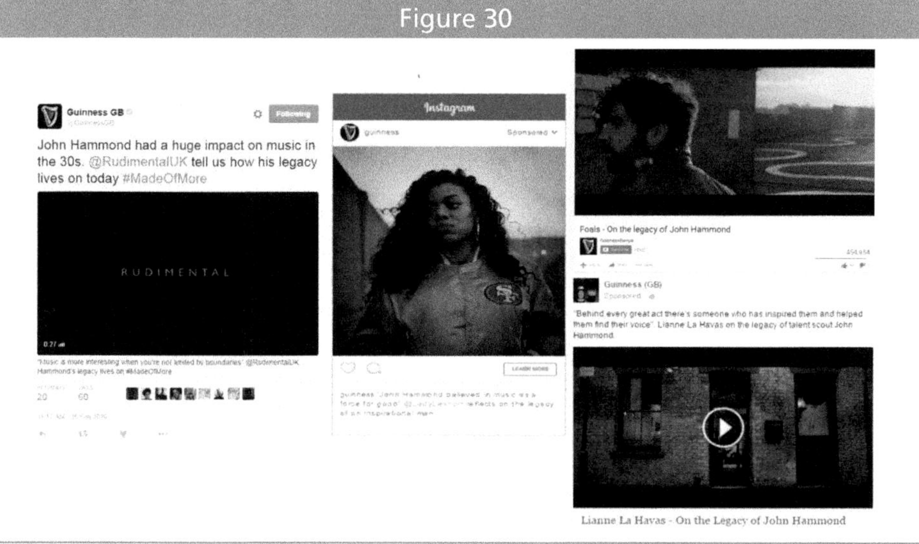

To bring our message directly to our audience, we live streamed two 'Creative Bravery' Summits[12] via Periscope, sharing perspectives of the creatively brave in music, art, dance and, of course, brewing (Figure 31).

Figure 31: Creative Bravery Summit

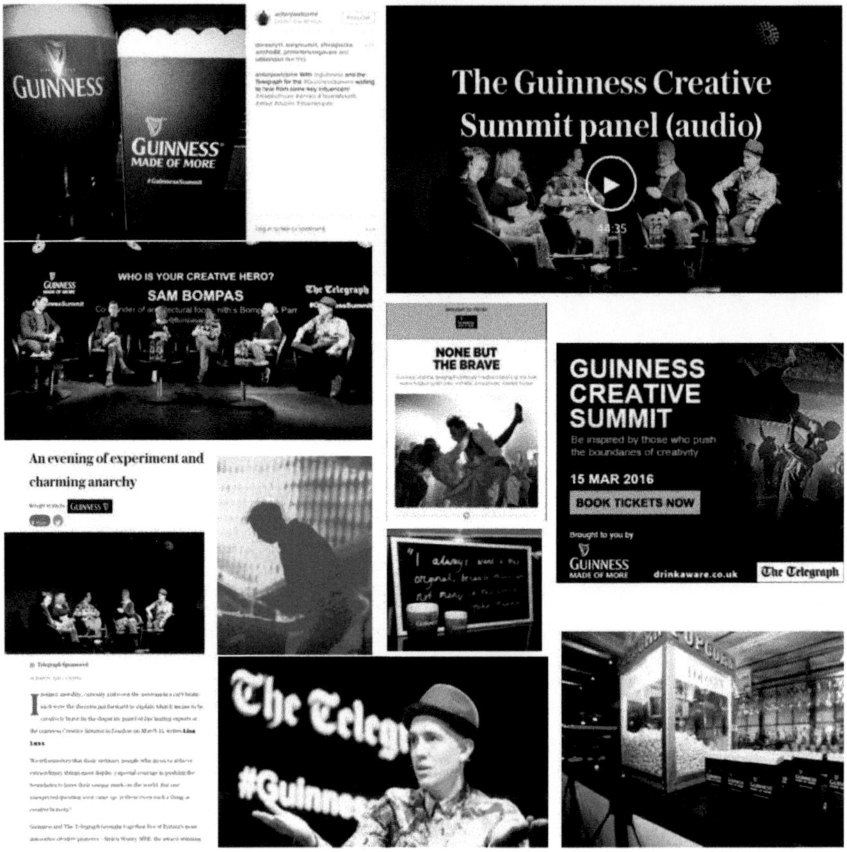

We continued to innovate, being the first to launch a 60-second film exclusively on Instagram in GB and Ireland (Figure 32).

Figure 32: Guinness first to launch 60-second film on Instagram

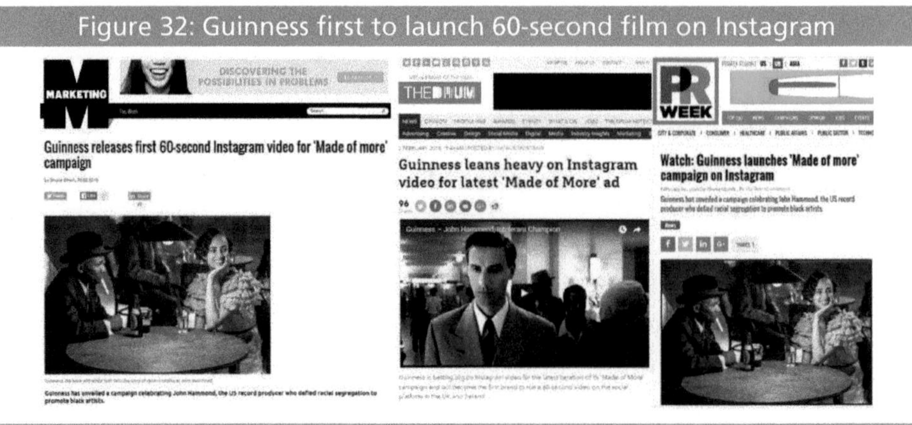

It worked. ROI continued to grow across both markets (Figures 33 and 34).

Figure 33: GB 'Made of more' ROI

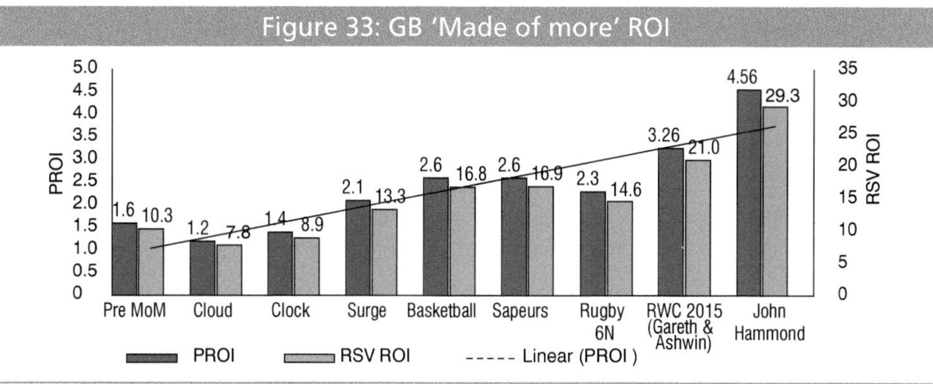

Source: Data2Decisions Econometric Modelling

Figure 34: Ireland 'Made of more' ROI

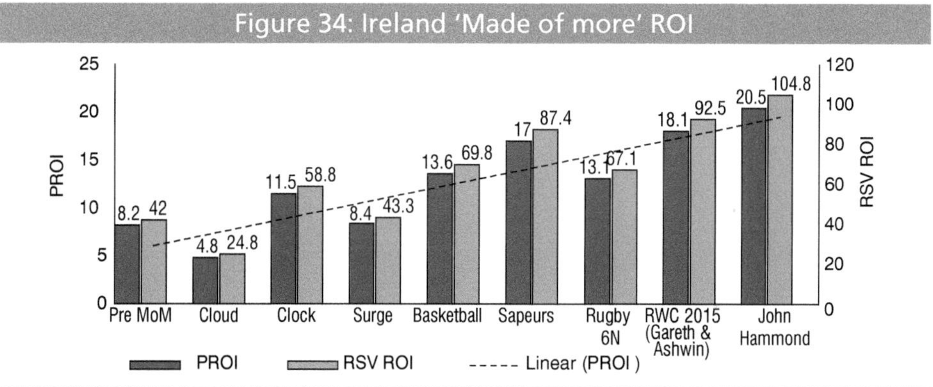

Source: Data2Decisions Econometric Modelling

The 'John Hammond' campaign unlocked the power of engaging our audience in deeper stories, and finding lateral connections to culture. It was a story that resonated with our audience because it reminded them we can all play our part in creating a more vibrant world, regardless of how much society pushes back.

We would take this depth of storytelling even further in our next idea.

'Made of more' 2017

We wanted to bring the story closer and make it more relevant to our audience, invigorating 'Made of more' through a real-time story that could directly inspire drinkers.

Compton cowboys

Refreshing our audience insight confirmed that, more than ever, we're feeling as though our future is out of our hands, and out of our control.[13]

Enter 'The Compton cowboys': young men whose passion is to ride horses in South Central LA, a region better known for its tales of crime and violence. These Compton natives carved out their own path – instead of joining a gang, they chose to ride horses and inspire those around them (Figure 35).

Figure 35: 'Compton cowboys'

Compton Cowboys
60"

This advert is about a group of urban cowboys who have found their own path in life.

A cowboy rides a trotting horse through a Compton street in Los Angeles, USA, catching glances from windows and cars.

VO: In Compton, you join a gang, or you find another way to survive. You gotta make your own path.

Our rider is joined by his fellow cowboys, riding through the local community.

A lotta horses round here are throwaway horses. My horse was headed to the slaughter house.

The horses in stables are being groomed and cared for. The riders gallop down an urban river bank.

I've seen horses bone dry, skinny, haven't eaten in weeks. And we bring them back to life.

They joke after a hard day's riding and Guinness is handed around. The cowboy finally gallops off.

I think maybe, did I save the horse or did the horse save me?

AV: https://youtu.be/9HWnO5XZf2M

Making difficult choices in challenging circumstances, supporting one another and providing hope to a community are universal themes. 'Made of more' in every way: the cowboys' sense of positivity, spirit of fun and camaraderie make for uplifting characters (Figure 36).

Figure 36: Two of the Compton cowboys laughing over a pint of Guinness

Bringing the cowboys to our audience

We wanted our audience to feel this was their story and so it was the most integrated communications plan we had launched. We applied two principles:

1. *Deep and wide:* Mobile and social allowed us to reach a large number of people; content and stories enabled people to dig deeper into these stories
2. *Multiplatform = Multiformat:* Use a range of formats in interesting and engagng ways to surprise and cut through the online noise

Everyone could experience the story behind Compton through mini-documentaries (Figure 37).

Figure 37: Compton mini-documentaries

The Two Sides of Compton
Contrasts the image of Comption as a scene of crime and violence with the brotherhood and peace of the cowboys.

The Horses of Compton
Tells the story of the unique relationship between the cowboys and their horses.

The People of Compton
Delves into the hope and sense of community that the Compton cowboys offer and share with those around them.

The Cowboys of Compton
Brings key themes from the story together: positive choices, brotherhood and caring for horses.

Our four in-depth stories behind the Compton cowboys were housed on YouTube. And bespoke social content. This content lived across Facebook, Instagram and Snapchat (Figure 38).

Figure 38: Bespoke social content

It has become a best-practice case study used by both Google and Facebook (Figure 39).

Figure 39: The 'Compton cowboys' campaign ecosystem

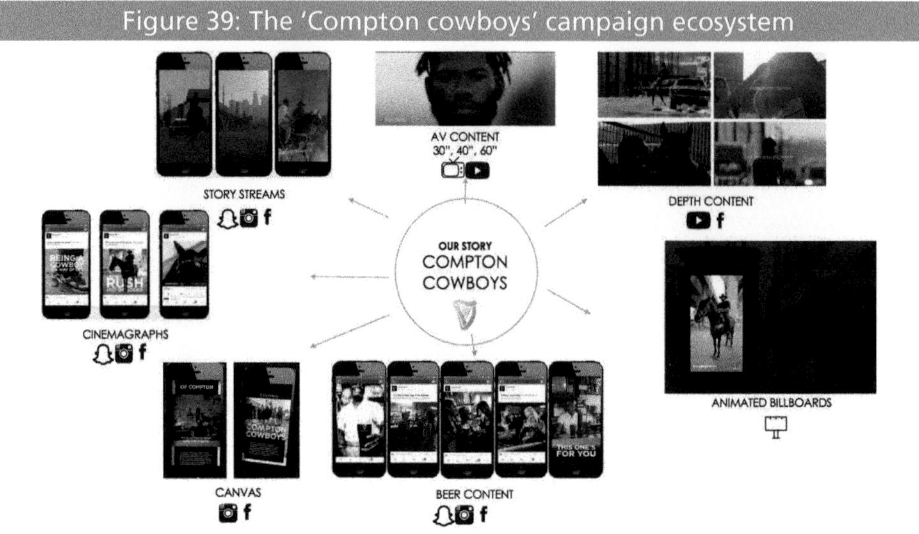

All signs indicate our upward ROI trajectory will continue

The 'Compton cowboys' campaign is too recent for us to have full econometric analysis and ROI.[14]

But we believe it will *at least* be in line with the enhanced ROI performance reported elsewhere in the paper, because:[15]

- media share of voice for Guinness remained the same for 'Cowboys' as it had been for previous campaigns;
- our Kantar Millward Brown post-testing showed that the campaign was highly regarded by drinkers;
- our equity scores have remained strong.

And perhaps most significantly, in GB, Guinness has now regained third position in draft beer for the first time in ten years.[16]

A return on investment 'Made of more'

The econometrics show that commitment to long-term strategy and creative bravery has paid off over time. We see a steady build in ROIs, now our work is up to *1.9 times* as effective in GB and *1.7 times* as effective in Ireland as pre-'Made of more' campaigns.

Revisiting our objectives

Our communications objective

Did we drive brand fame through highly creative, culturally relevant communications that would resonate with drinkers?

People loved the work

Qualitative research demonstrated the popularity of our work (Figure 40).

Figure 40: Kantar Millward Brown post-test evaluation

'Never alone'	'The right path'	'Intolerant champion'	'Compton cowboys'
'It made me appreciate Guinness more for being forward-thinking and inclusive'	'Guinness is a brand with character'	'Stands out from the crowd, innovative and you have to be a certain kind of person to appreciate it'	'an interesting and different ad that intrigues in the very best traditions of Guinness adverts'
'The brand represents strength of character and inclusiveness'	'The story of triumph against the odds'	'It reminds me how different Guinness is to other drinks'	'Stand out, so distinctive … like Guinness really'
'Best ad I have ever seen, I remember how Gareth Thomas felt pride'	'Was enthralling from start to finish'	'It is inspiring and highly creative and energetic'	'It's just so cool'
'It pushes real boundaries (gay sports stars)'	'I liked the ad, and I like the idea that Guinness might be involved in helping underdogs'	'Moral strength to defy odds … feels like Guinness'	'Amazing … the story and characters are so surprising '
'it is for people who are not scared to be brave and have some bottle'	'You will always be part of a team with Guinness' 'Inspiring'	'I would immediately remember it next time I see it'	'So completely different to any ad and conveys a really worthwhile message'

'Made of more' made (more) waves in culture

'Gareth' and 'Ashwin' clocked over 38 million video views across GB and Ireland.[17] The 'bravery' of the campaigns drove coverage across the world (Figure 41).[18]

Figure 41

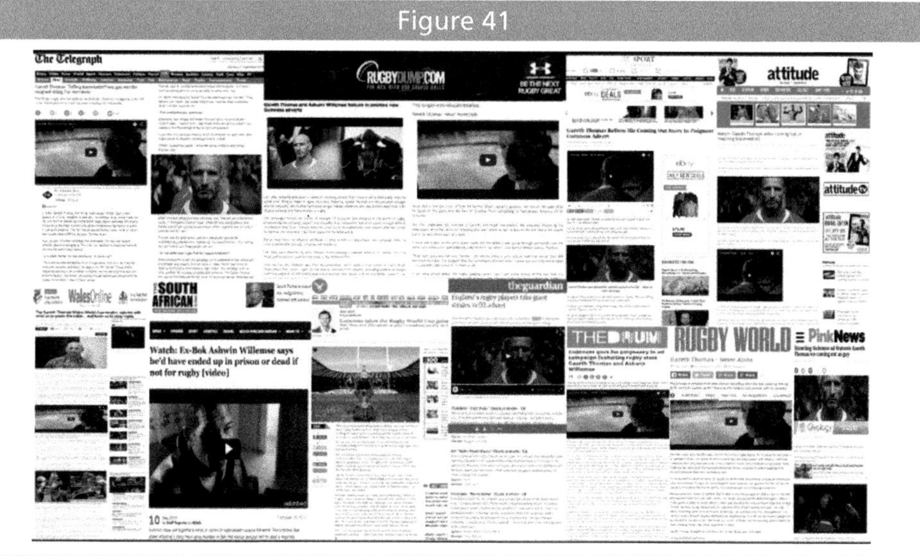

In a moment backing the Irish gay marriage vote, Gareth Thomas was a guest on Ireland's iconic The Late Late Show reaching 650,000 viewers in a single night. Host Ryan Tubridy: 'The ad has completely struck a chord with the nation' (Figure 42).

Figure 42: Gareth Thomes on The Late Late Show

We defeated the official sponsor, Heineken, in winning the Rugby World Cup.[19] A YouGov study showed we were the brand most associated with the event (Figure 43).[20]

Figure 43: No 1 brand associated with Rugby World Cup

24 September

1	Guinness	17.0%
2	Heineken	16.7%
3	O2	15.1%
4	Land Rover	12.8%
5	Royal Bank of Scotland	12.2%
6	Emirates	8.9%
7	Mastercard	8.8%
8	Canterbury of New Zealand	8.6%
9	Coca-Cola	7.6%
10	SSE	7.3%
11	Lucozade	5.7%
12	DHL	4.9%
13	Adidas	4.1%
14	Samsung	4.0%
15	BMW	1.2%
16	Fuller's	1.1%
17	Beats by Dre	0.5%

4 November

John Hammond's story was picked up by contemporary artists, told and retold across scores of media sources, most notably through Lianne La Havas (our LoveLive partner) (Figure 44).

Figure 44

Events from the Brit Awards to the Manchester Film Festival used it as part of their own communications (Figure 45).

Figure 45

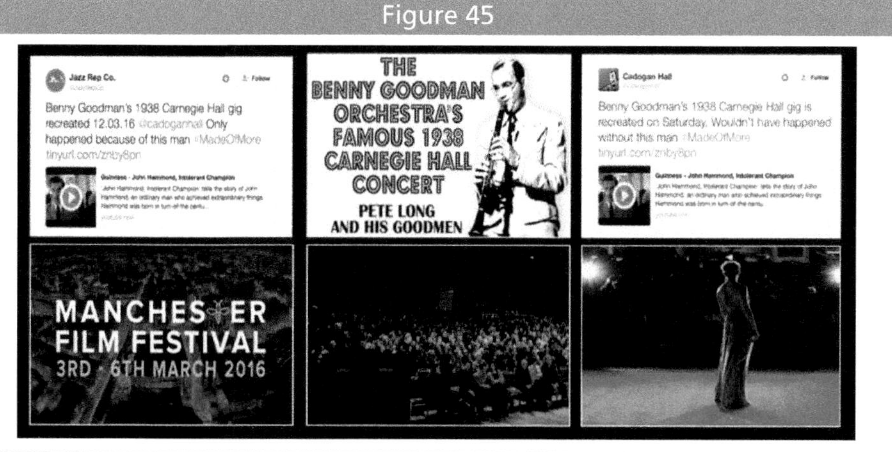

The 'Cowboys' triggered an outpouring of positivity from the public, the news and industry, all sharing our ad (Figure 46).

Figure 46

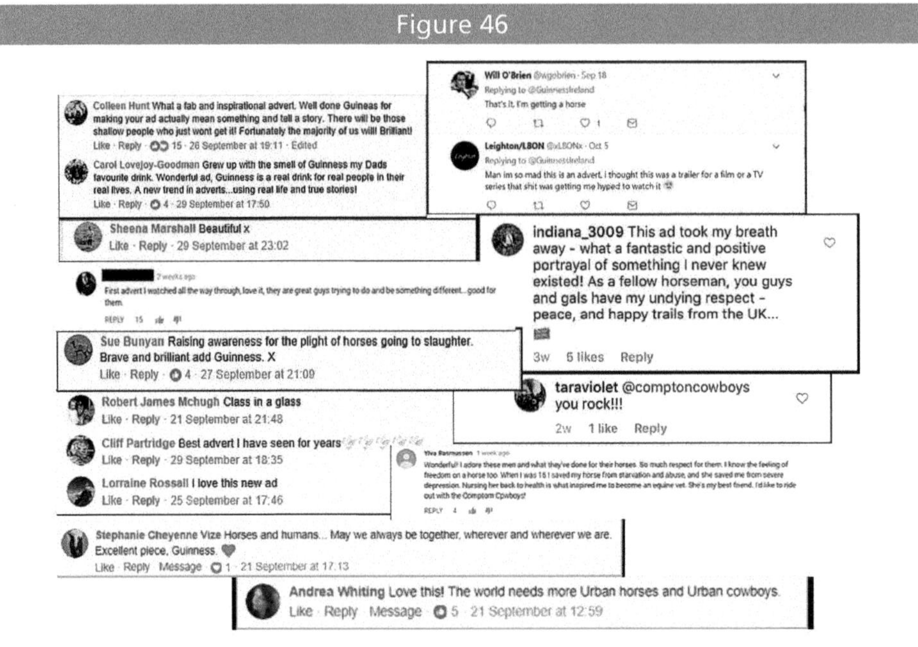

The public was so interested in their story and characters that they sought the 'Cowboys' out on social media (Figure 47).

Figure 47

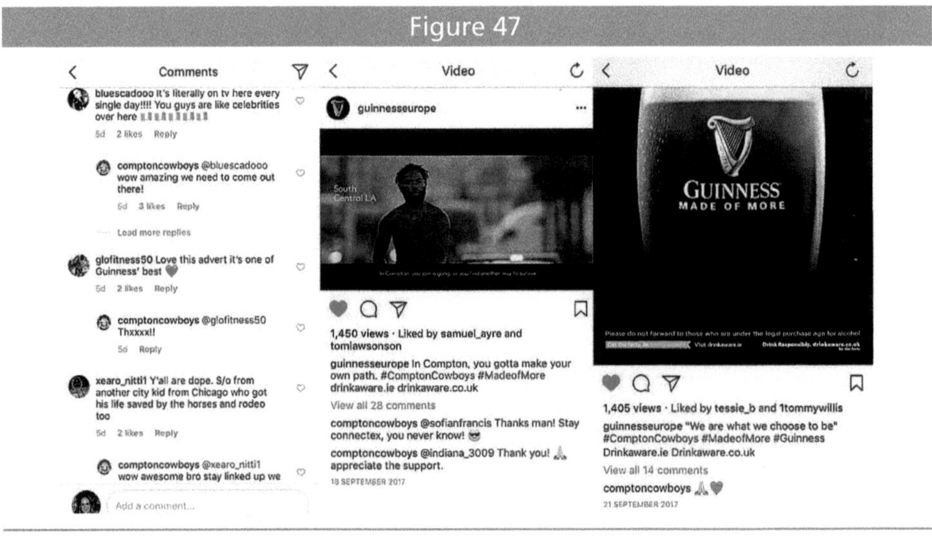

It wasn't just another ad, it was a 'Made of more' story (Figure 48).

Figure 48

CREATIVE

Guinness' 'Compton Cowboys' Campaign Challenges Stereotypes to Enrich All of Our Lives

AMV BBDO, 5 months ago

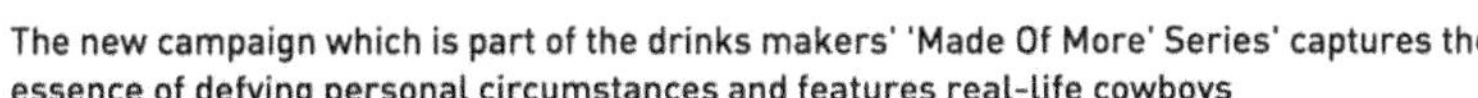

The new campaign which is part of the drinks makers' 'Made Of More' Series' captures the essence of defying personal circumstances and features real-life cowboys

The release of a new Guinness advert, portraying the story of 'The Compton Cowboys', which will air for the first time in the UK today. The new release is the next chapter of the iconic 'Made of More' series, which champions real people who have shown unexpected character to enrich the world around them.

Source: LBB Online[21]

'Made of more' had brought unique, culturally relevant stories to the fore, and they were picked up, retold and elevated in culture

Gareth went on to create a BBC show. In 2017, 'Gareth vs. Homophobia: Hate in the Beautiful Game' discussed the lack of openly gay professional sportsmen (Figure 49).

Figure 49

John Hammond's story has become more relevant every year, as the 'Whitewash' debate spread from the Oscars to the Grammys (Figure 50).[22]

Figure 50

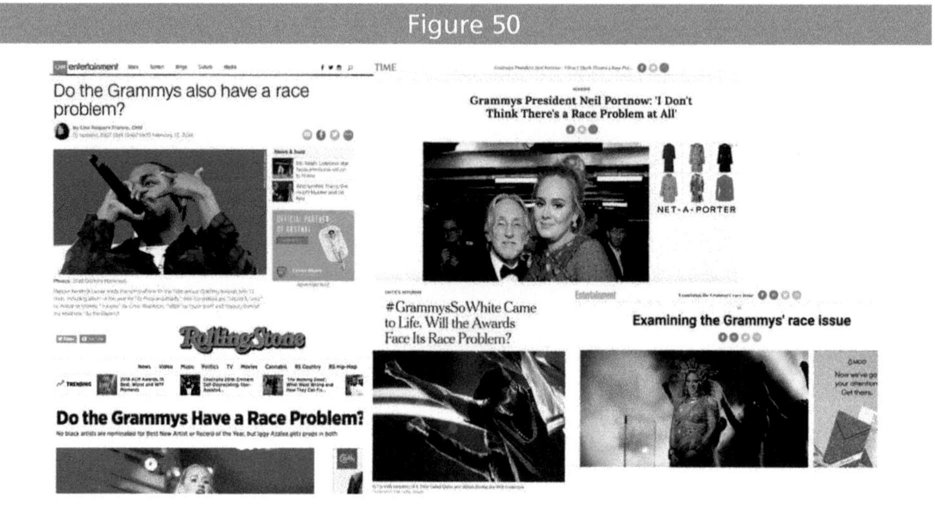

In April 2017 (seven months after our campaign launched) 'The Compton cowboys' featured in *The New York Times* in an article shining a light on African-Americans battling racial stereotypes (Figure 51).[23]

Figure 51

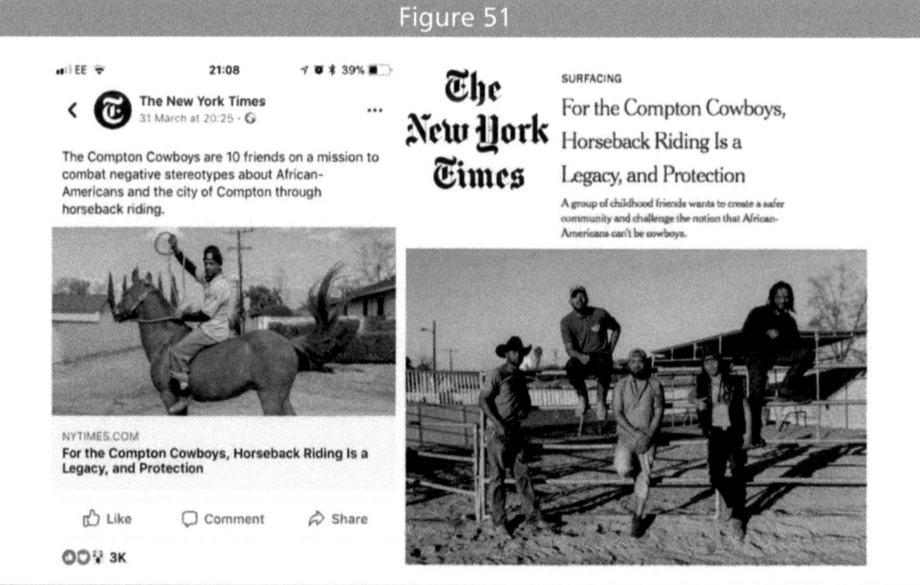

People were genuinely interested in the backstory behind 'Made of more'.

Gareth and Ashwin's self-narrated five-minute online documentaries generated over 3.1 million unique views, with 400,000 organic views of Gareth's story (Figure 52).[24]

Figure 52

Our Hammond ad brought viewers into a wider ecosystem, where more than 80% of visitors went on to explore our documentary and LoveLive content (Figure 53).[25]

Figure 53

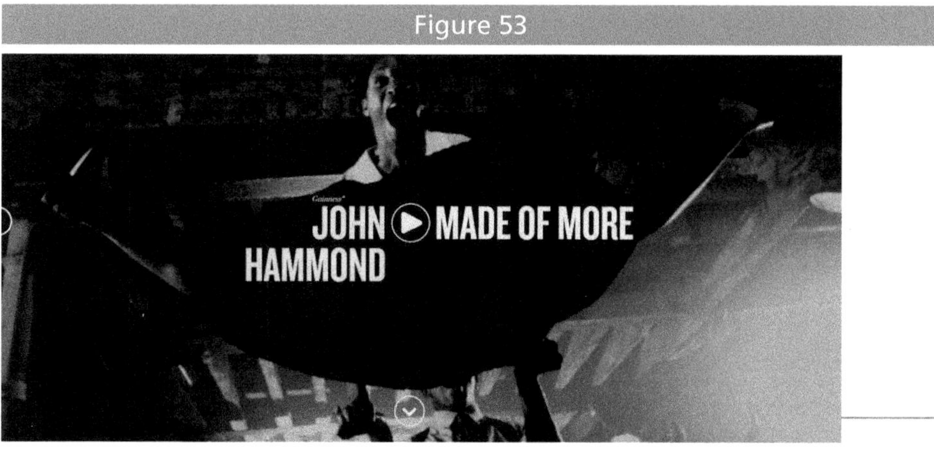

In-depth stories behind the Compton cowboys held viewers' attention for up to 2.07 mins,[26] and our highest performing content, 'Cowboys of Compton' had no paid support (Figure 54).

Figure 54: Average YouTube view time (in-depth content)

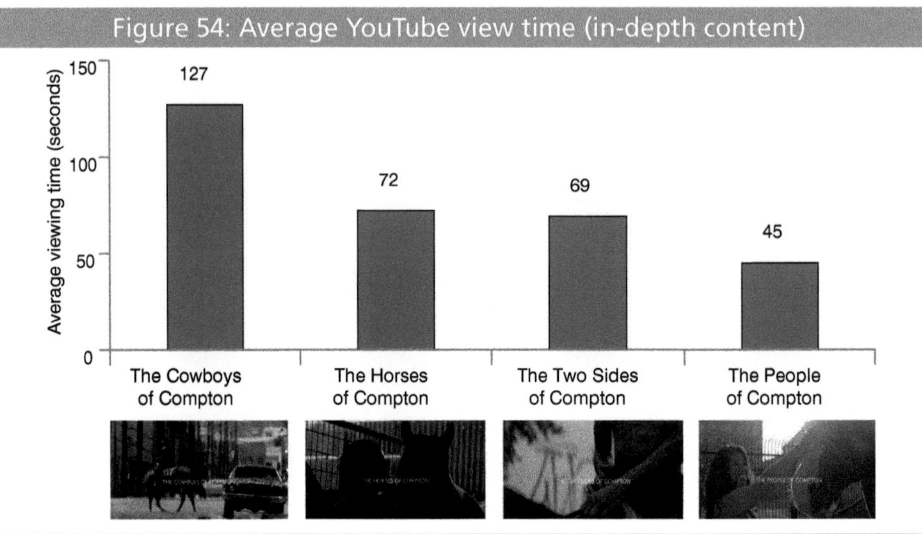

Source: YouTube, Carat

'Made of more' gives Guinness permission to entertain

'Compton cowboys' revealed that our branded videos significantly outperformed non-branded versions. This proved the strength of the Guinness brand as a content creator (Figure 55).

Figure 55

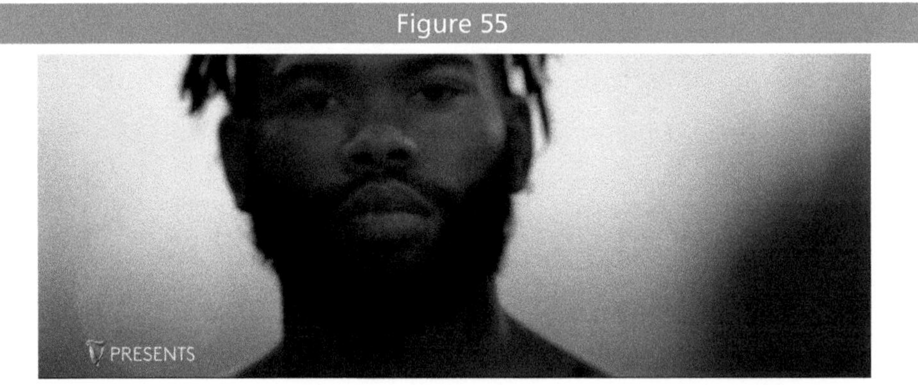

Award juries loved our work

The 'Made of more' work detailed in this paper received 148 creative awards including wins at all major international award festivals. It has won 13 Cannes Lions, including Gold in the illustrious Glass Lions for Gareth's 'Never alone'.

Our marketing objective

Did we see an increase in brand fame and affinity to the Guinness brand?

We did.

It's worth noting we have not shown pre-'Made of more' metrics, unlike in our 2016 paper, as Kantar Millward Brown slightly tweaked the metrics, meaning comparing 2017 to 2012 is not like-for-like. As with our 2015 metrics, our 2017 metrics will undoubtedly have surpassed this, hence we have used 2015 as our benchmark to ensure the veracity of this paper and our data.

In order to stave off the threat posed by competitors, it was important to be seen as more distinctive than the rest of the category. Both markets saw an uplift (Figure 56).

Figure 56: Guinness is a distinctive brand

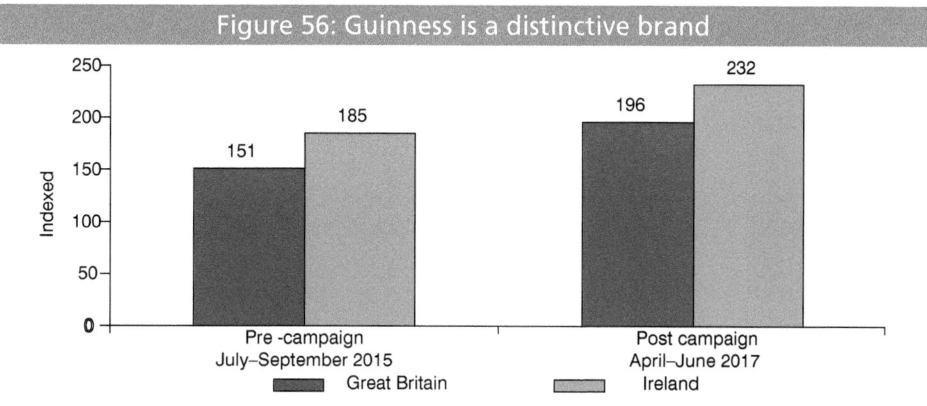

Source: Kantar Millward Brown. Note these figures are measured as indices rather than percentages and are benchmarked against the category average.

Our cultural traction and creative success enabled us to achieve this objective. In a more competitive environment, saliency was key. Brand fame can be evidenced in improvements between pre and post campaign dips (Figure 57).

Figure 57: Salience

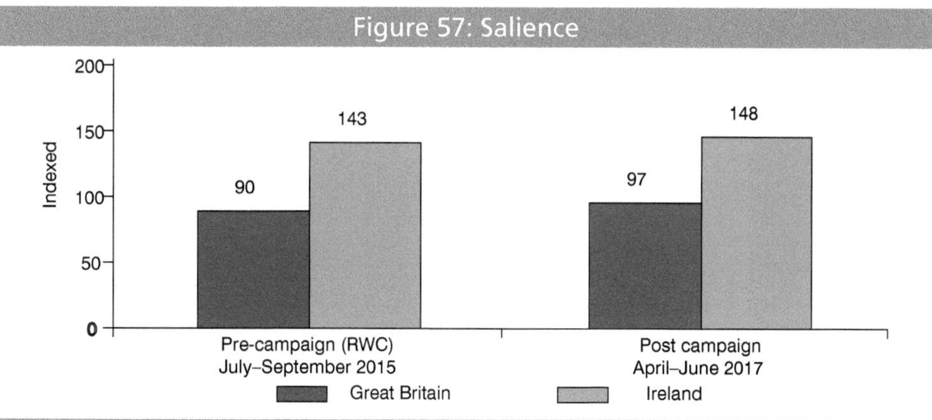

Source: Kantar Millward Brown. Note these figures are measured as Indices rather than percentages and are benchmarked against the category average.

A significant increase in pre and post dips in both markets across the metric 'Guinness is a brand that is leading the way' (Figure 58).

Figure 58: Guinness is a brand that is leading the way

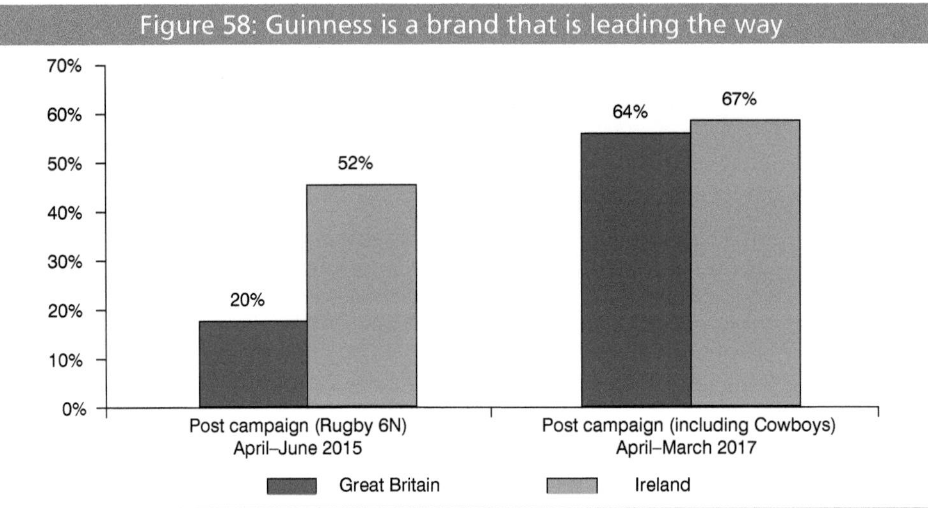

Source: Kantar Millward Brown. Note these figures are measured as percentages.

Our commercial objective

Did we see an improved ROI in addition to maintaining revenue growth and value share in the face of rising costs?

Data2Decisions has conducted econometric modelling on the effect of the campaign.

Revenue ROI

Our *revenue ROI is £22.06 per £1 spent*. Much higher than pre-'Made of more' campaign average revenue ROI (£12.01).

We increased our return on investment versus pre-'Made of more' work with a more profitable return than our competitors, growing sales and share (Figure 59).

Figure 59: Pre vs. post 'Made of more' revenue ROI

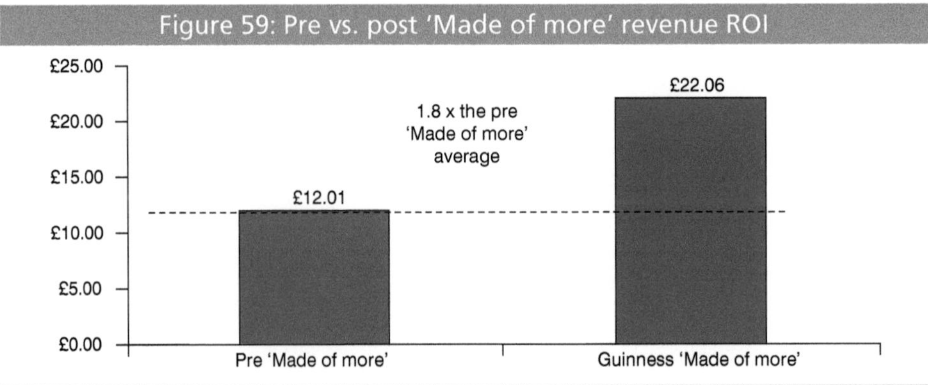

Source: Data2Decisions econometric modelling

This is now the second-highest recorded revenue ROI for a beer brand in the IPA awards – behind only Foster's 2014 Grand-Prix-winning campaign (Table 1).

Table 1: Beer category IPA Awards by revenue ROI

Brand	Year	Revenue ROI
Fosters	2014	£32
Guinness	2018	£22.06
Guinness	2016	£19.90
Coors Light	2016	£17
Stella Artois	2000	£12
Budweiser	2002	£6
Bud Ice	1998	£5
Stella Artois	1996	£5
Marston's Pedigree	1994	£4
Stella Artois	1992	£2

Source: WARC/IPA

Profit ROI

The total profit ROI is £4.30 per £1 spent

Overall, 'Made of more' has now delivered a profit ROI 85% higher than campaigns prior to its introduction (Figure 60).

Figure 60: Pre vs. post 'Made of more' profit ROI

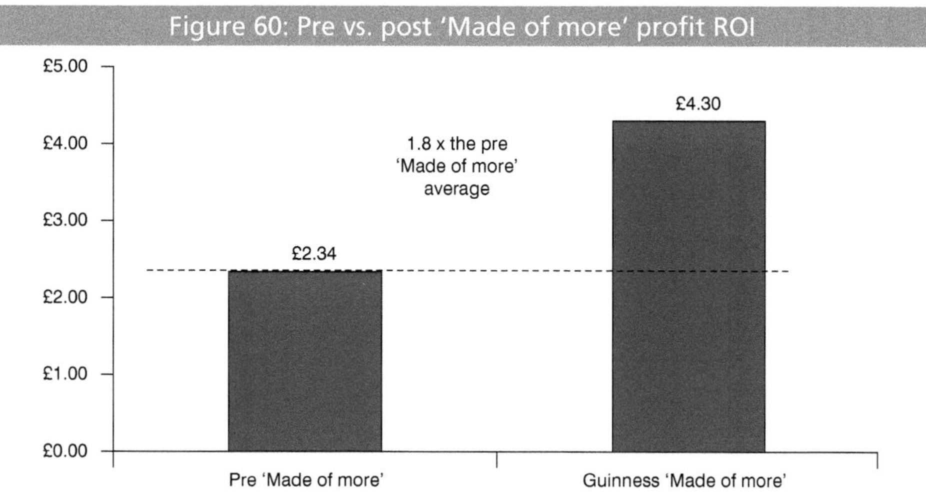

Source: Data2Decisions econometric modelling

This is also higher than the £3.88 profit ROI reported in the 2016 IPA paper (Figure 61).

Figure 61: Percentage growth in ROI 2015–2018

10%
5%
0%
9
ROI growth

Source: Data2Decisions econometric modelling

This campaign outperforms profit ROIs from other beer brands in the Data2Decisions database, with a profit ROI 1.8 times the category norm (Figure 62).[27]

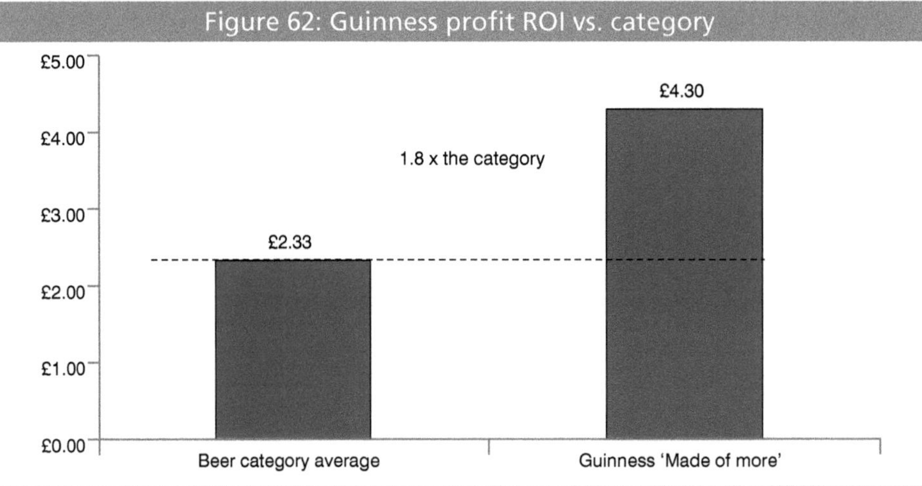

Figure 62: Guinness profit ROI vs. category

Source: Data2Decisions econometric modelling

This remains the most profitable beer campaign in the history of the IPA awards. In another illustration of the tougher competitive context since 2015, VCCP's excellent Coors Light work had shown a profit ROI of £4.13 in the 2016 IPA Effectiveness Awards, but our latest work for 'Made of more' has edged ahead of that (Table 2).

Table 2: Beer category IPA Awards by profit ROI

Brand	Year	Profit ROI
Guinness	2018	£4.33
Coors Light	2016	£4.13
Guinness	2016	£3.88
Carling	1996	£2.08
Stella Artois	1992	£1.92
Marston's Pedigree	1994	£1.64

Compared to work before 'Made of more', ROI has now almost doubled.

Market share

Our on-trade value share in Ireland has remained steady at 32% (it's tough to grow from such a high share), but has grown by 8% in GB (Figure 63).

Figure 63: Guinness value share (%) GB

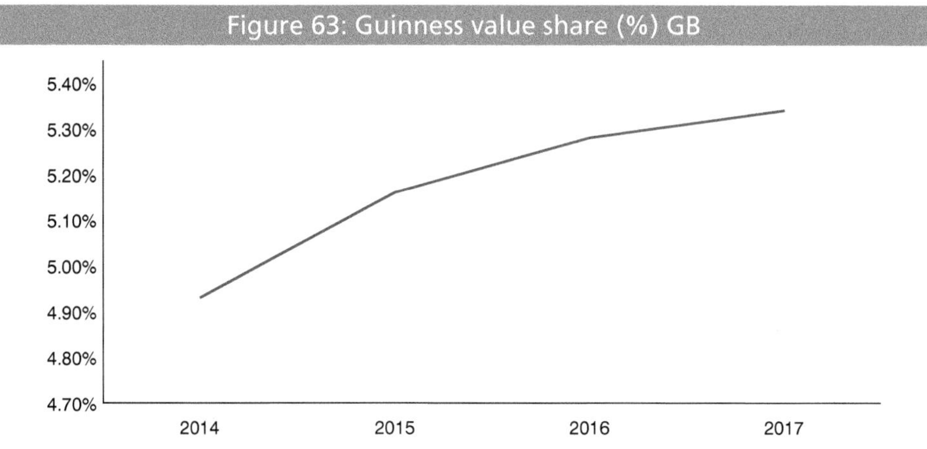

Source: Nielsen

Also in GB at this period, we saw a marked decrease in price elasticity (Figure 64).

Figure 64: GB Guinness Draught price elasticity

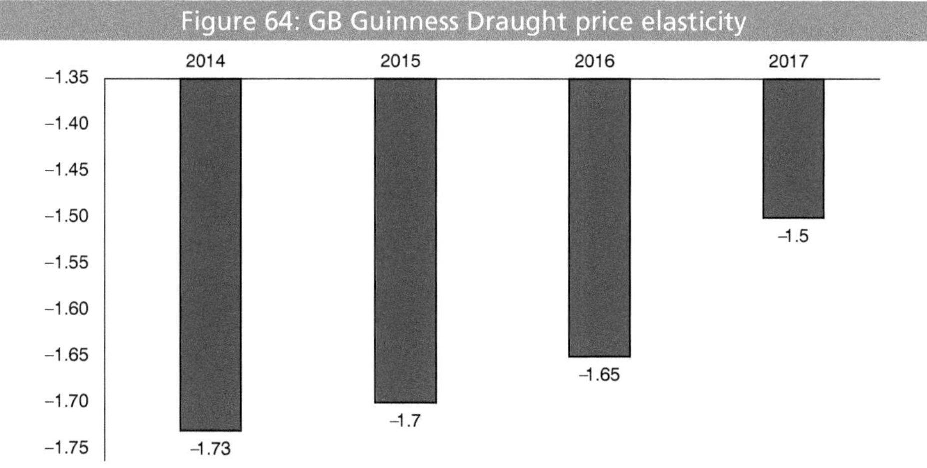

Source: Data2Decisions

Discounting other factors

Econometric modelling conducted by Data2Decisions has isolated the effect of the communications when calculating the ROI. This section demonstrates how none of the other key sale drivers could have been responsible for the continued success in commercial results for Guinness.

Price

There has been little change in the price index of Guinness versus the rest of the market since the start of 'Made of more' in both markets. The average price of a pint of Guinness has increased slightly vs. the market average putting downward pressure on sales (Figure 65).

Figure 65: Guinness Draught price index vs. market average

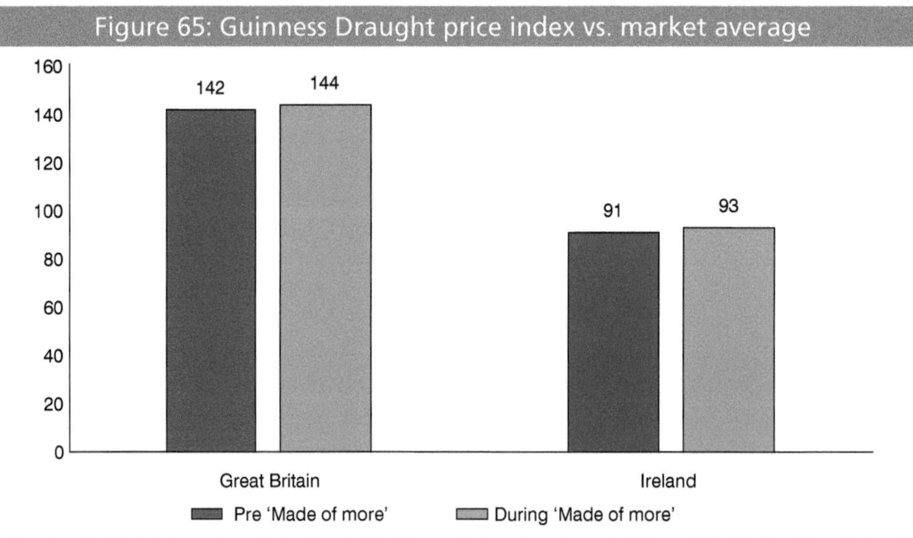

Source: Nielsen/CGA

Price promotions

In this paper we have focused on the impact of our campaign on draught Guinness sold in pubs and bars (the on-trade) as this channel accounts for at least 80% of Guinness sales. We have excluded a detailed examination of the off-trade in this paper in part due to the complexity of the range of products and pack sizes sold though this channel and the vast array of price promotions that inevitably increases the complexity. Due to alcohol restrictions, price promotion in the on-trade in alcohol is minimal.

In-outlet activations

Guinness has invested in a number of in-outlet activations in the on-trade (pubs and bars) over the analysed period with marketing materials distributed to pubs around key events including major rugby tournaments and matches. The impact of these activations on sales has been captured in the econometric models.

Product

Guinness launched a range of new products over the period including a range of new porters, a golden ale and a new lager. We have not included sales from these products as part of our volume sales, value share or ROI calculations, even though 'Made of more' campaign will have driven additional sales for these products.

Distribution

Distribution in Ireland has remained steady at a very high level, but declined in GB (Figure 66).

Figure 66: Guinness Draught on-trade WTD distribution

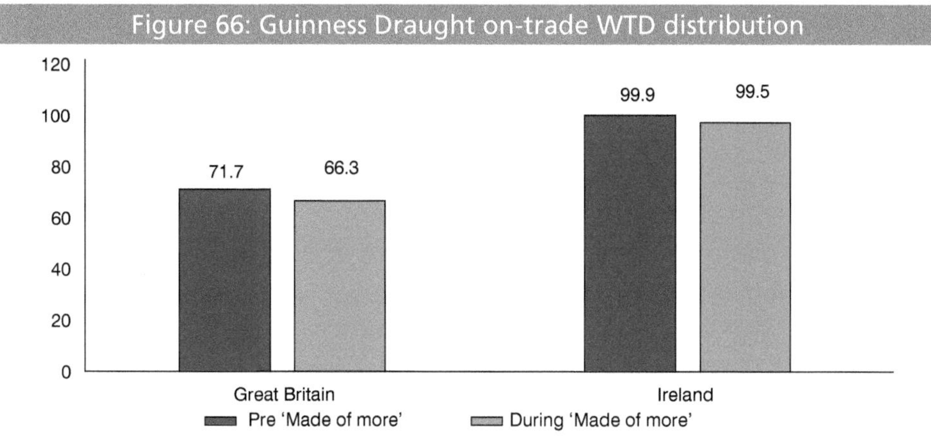

Source: Nielsen /CGA

Number of pubs

Success cannot be attributed to a growth in the number of pubs. As mentioned earlier in this paper, pub numbers continued to decline in both markets.

Economy

The effect of economic growth has been captured in the econometric models. We have also shown that market share has turned around for Guinness in both markets since the start of 'Made of more', which accounts for any change in overall beer consumption driven by macroeconomic factors.

Spend level/SOV

Media-spend levels for Guinness have remained consistent across 'Made of more' with no sustained share of voice advantage for Guinness during the campaign (Figure 67).

Figure 67: Guinness share of voice

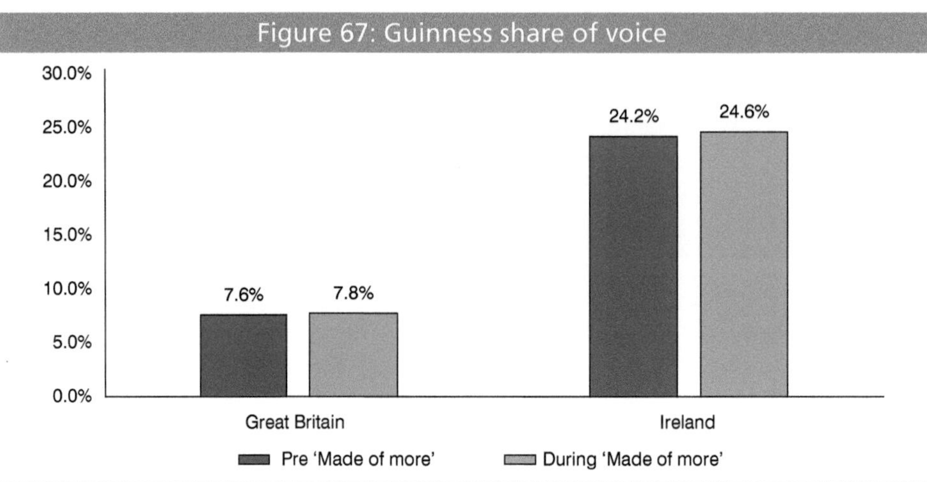

Source: Carat/Nielsen Addynamix

Weather

Weather does influence Guinness sales over time. The effect of this is measured in the econometric models. Colder weather increases Guinness sales, warmer weather dampens them. Average temperatures were slightly higher in GB and flat in Ireland (Figure 68).

Figure 68: Average temperatures

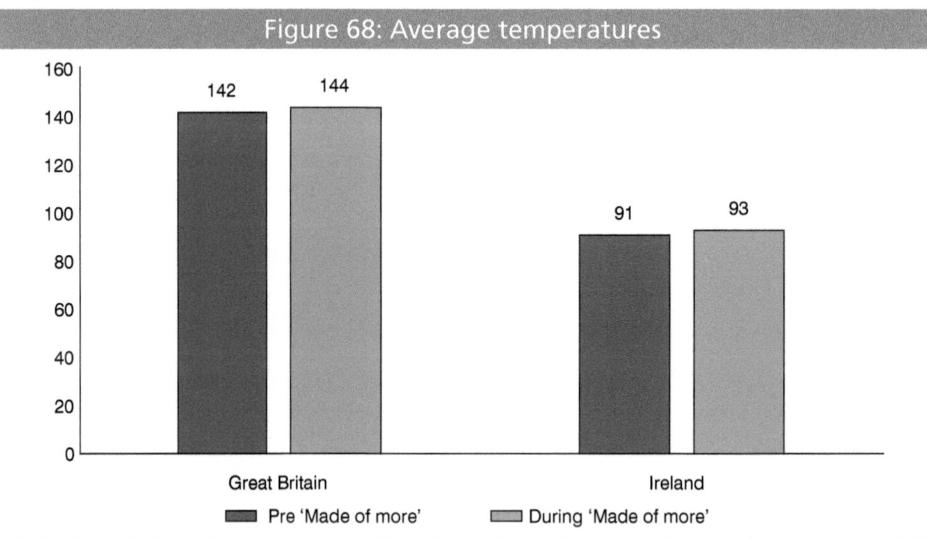

Conclusions

It's a bold claim to be 'Made of more'.

A claim you can only make if you're willing to live up to it. To never settle for ordinary, to push from good to great and from great to best ever.

Guinness is not the only brand that can do this. The lessons are there for all to see in the IPA Effectiveness Awards over the years. Invest in emotion. Invest in consistency. Keep it fresh. One of Byron Sharp's rules in *How Brands Grow* is *'be consistent whilst keeping the brand fresh and interesting'*.

Knowing it is one thing. Doing it is quite another.

'Made of more' is an example of the business benefits that come from creativity, from daring to be bold – because boldness is what sits at the heart of this: our bravery and willingness to share our point of view on subjects from sexuality to gang violence and disability.

All because we believe in celebrating that which makes the world more characterful and more vibrant.

Here's to the next five years.

Appendix: 'Made of more' work to date

Basketball: https://www.youtube.com/watch?v=iiB3YNTcsAA
Sapeurs: https://www.youtube.com/watch?v=66HuFrMZWMo
Jonny Wilkinson: https://www.youtube.com/watch?v=lJhw0FeKaU0
David & Goliath: https://www.youtube.com/watch?v=JyE56rF6mU8
Mind over Matter: https://www.youtube.com/watch?v=wHu6ZM7gDbs
Irrepressible Spirit: https://www.youtube.com/watch?v=oK9ioFs1i20
Never Alone: https://www.youtube.com/watch?v=xFTUTfiUMeM
The Right Path: https://youtu.be/534aGB00VC4
Intolerant Champion: https://www.youtube.com/watch?v=S4y6kBYF084
Compton Cowboys: https://youtu.be/9HWnO5XZf2M

Notes

1. Source: Data2Decisions econometrics, cited in IPA 2016, 'An Effectiveness Story Made of More'.
2. The Celtic Tiger was a period of unprecedented economic growth in Ireland. It began around 1995, and ensured Ireland at one point became one of the wealthiest countries in Europe. This came to a dramatic end in 2008 and the effects are still being felt today.
3. Data comes from: 'Euro Crisis Even Staggers Irish Pubs'. http://www.usatoday.com/story/news/world/2012/09/25/ireland-economy-pubs/1588187/ and 'British Beer Sales Plummet'. http://www.telegraph.co.uk/finance/newsbysector/retailandconsumer/9626126/British-beer-sales-plummet.html
4. Source: http://www.drinksindustry.ie/assets/Documents/The%20Economic%20Contribution%20of%20the%20Drinks%20Industry%202013x.pdf
5. Source: Diageo.
6. Source: Kantar Millward Brown; Nielsen, 2016.
7. Source: Nielsen, 2016.
8. The Sapeurs, 'The Society of the Elegant Persons of the Congo', are a real group of men who are ordinary people by day, but by night dress to the nines in flamboyant suits, coming together to bring joy to their community.
9. Source: http://www.thejournal.ie/esri-report-great-recession-1919516-Feb2015/
10. John Hammond stood alone in New York against the practice of segregating black and white musicians and audiences. He discovered and brought the likes of Billie Holiday, Count Basie and

Benny Goodman to world attention – names that went on to help write the history of twentieth century music.

11. That's 20 best actor, actress, supporting actor and supporting actress candidates in Sunday's telecast, with zero people of colour.
12. The Creative Summits provided an interactive platform to tell the Hammond story and drive depth and relevancy, with authentic representations of creative bravery in popular culture.
13. This has been magnified by social, political and continued economic unrest in western countries, and particularly GB and Ireland.
14. Our econometric analysis is completed by Data2Decisions at the end of our financial year, every year, which runs from June to July. We will receive the next wave of data in August 2018.
15. All of these statements are backed by Nielsen data, Kantar Millward Brown data and Data2Decisions.
16. Source: Diageo.
17. Of the 9 million on YouTube, 700,000 were purely organic. Source: Carat Media Agency.
18. Source: Freuds PR & WH PR.
19. http://www.thedrum.com/news/2015/10/30/heineken-rubbishes-report-which-shows-guinness-outgunned-it-rugby-world-cup
20. The second independent research source is Millward Brown who reported that 77% of people felt that the campaign demonstrated that 'Guinness really understand rugby'.
21. Source: https://lbbonline.com/news/guinness-compton-cowboys-campaign-challenges-stereotypes-to-enrich-all-of-our-lives/
22. https://edition.cnn.com/2016/02/12/entertainment/grammys-race-feat/index.html
    https://www.nytimes.com/2017/02/13/arts/music/grammys-adele-beyonce-black-artists-race.html
    http://time.com/4671779/grammys-president-no-race-problem/
    http://ew.com/music/2017/02/16/grammys-race-issue/
23. https://www.nytimes.com/2018/03/31/us/compton-cowboys-horseback-riding-african-americans.html
24. Source: Carat Media Agency.
25. Source: Carat Media Agency.
26. Carat Media Agency.
27. Our pre-'Made of more' ROI was only £0.01 higher than the category average.

Lidl

How Lidl grew a lot

By Justin Clouder, TBWA\London
Contributing authors: Elliott Millard, Starcom; Ian Sippitt, Lidl UK; Stephen Gausden, Ebiquity
Credited companies: TWBA\London; Starcom; Lidl UK; The Effectiveness Partnership

Summary

Shoppers were sceptical about Lidl's value model, assuming that cheaper meant worse. To address this perception and increase household penetration, Lidl adopted a more mass-reach strategy. Between 2014 and 2017, campaigns focused on revealing truths about the brand and its products, backed with increased media spend. Following the activity, Lidl's market share peaked at 5.3%. This case estimates that £2.7bn of direct and long-term sales were generated, with a £398m net profit delivered over four years.

Editor's comment

The judges liked how rigorously this paper applied the 'laws of growth' across communications over time, moving from short-term activation to a blend of brand and response, combating misperceptions about the brand, migrating the media mix into national investment and achieving sustained long-term growth.

Client comment

Claire Farrant, Marketing & Advertising Director, Lidl

The case history shows the potential rewards that can be achieved when you commit to consistent and heavyweight advertising investment. We had the confidence in Lidl's ability to challenge the conventions of the grocery market and by investing in broad-reach media, at levels ahead of our market share, we have driven mass penetration over the long term. We continue to derive the benefits of us taking the 'long view'. In an increasingly competitive market, we have held our nerve about the importance of long-term advertising communication and its ability to deliver a tangible return on investment.

Introduction

Lidl took 20 years from the opening of its first UK store in 1994 to reach a market share of 3.1%[1] at the start of 2014.

But in just four years since then Lidl has added a further two points of market share to hit a peak of 5.3% in September 2017, larger than Waitrose.[2] That's an additional £2.5 billion of sales, a dramatically increased rate of growth (Figure 1).

Figure 1: Lidl market share growth from 1994 to the end of 2017

Source: Kantar Worldpanel, Grocers' share of total till roll.

Following a successful regional test in 2013,[3] from 2014 Lidl made a big investment in advertising. Unpicking the contribution of this advertising investment to Lidl's astonishing growth requires the isolation of advertising from various other effects. We will do that.

We will show that Lidl's big investment in advertising delivered big results – £2.7 billion of direct and long-term sales and £398m of profit over four years, at a profit ROMI of £1.38. We will show that advertising is responsible for a quarter of Lidl's sales growth.

While these numbers are extraordinary, the Lidl advertising story is surprisingly simple, with success informed by the well-established rules of growth described by Byron Sharp[4] and the Ehrenberg-Bass Institute, and by Les Binet and Peter Field[5] for the IPA:

- penetration rules – brands grow by attracting more customers, loyalty follows;
- new customers are drawn from the whole market, especially the largest competitors;
- emphasise broad reach media and invest in 'excess share of voice' (ESOV);
- a combination of messaging addressing brand perceptions and messaging driving direct effects, helps deliver both strong short-term sales and long-term brand strength.

Our case in a nutshell

This is a 'before and after' story.

Before 2014, Lidl focused on short-term deal and offer marketing – 100% activation.

After, there was a big investment in high-reach advertising media, especially TV, with messaging tackling brand perception (and misperception) alongside price and promotions, designed to work over all timeframes.

In the post-crash years from 2008 to 2013 Lidl's growth picked up, but was mainly dependent on shoppers who had discovered Lidl for themselves. Despite a favourable climate for discounters, misperception roadblocks (explained below) prevented the wider shopping public from trying Lidl.

The 2014 move to national advertising,[6] and a shift to high-reach media broke through those roadblocks and unleashed massive growth in penetration, contributing to average annual sales growth from 2014–2017 of 15.5% (versus 9.5% in the preceding five years) (Figure 2).

Figure 2: Lidl sales growth, penetration, basket size and frequency indexed vs. 2008

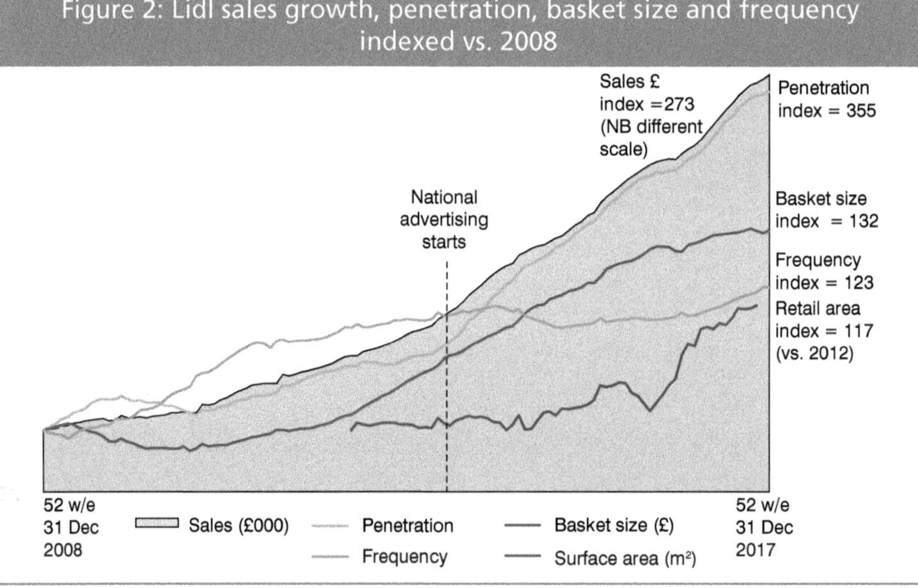

Source: Kantar Worldpanel; Lidl (total retail floor space indexed vs. 2012)

A sharp uptick in penetration and sales can be seen from the moment national advertising started. Retail space barely grew until a surge in 2017 (and we will isolate its effect later).

Penetration drives growth. Advertising drives penetration. This is a study in how advertising helps brands grow.

Part 1: Setting the scene

A Lidl bit of history

Lidl's roots go back to a wholesale business in 1930s Germany, but it was not until 1973 that the first store named Lidl was opened.

Lidl was a discount retailer from the start and has stayed true to this philosophy ever since. Everything is optimised to make the experience as efficient as possible, meaning a ruthless focus on keeping costs and prices down.

A typical Lidl store is approx. 1,100m^2 and sells approximately 2,300 products. A typical Tesco supermarket (not an Extra, which is even larger) is approximately 2,700m^2 and sells approx. 40,000 products. Two completely different models, but – as we will see – competing for the same customers.

Lidl came to the UK in 1994, and grew slowly until the economic shock of the 2008 recession, when sustained pressures on living standards combined with changes in consumer shopping habits led more shoppers to try the discounters.

While there was then solid growth (averaging 9.5% a year from 2009–2013), negative perceptions amongst the uninitiated held Lidl back.

The misperception problem

Everyone likes the idea of getting great-quality food for less. Who wouldn't? But shoppers were sceptical. The belief that 'you get what you pay for' is deeply engrained. The discounter model was not understood, so assumptions were made: cheaper = worse.

Brand tracking did not start until November 2014, but as this was only shortly after national advertising started the relevant measures from that month still reflect the problem: Lidl was bottom of the pile (Figure 3).

Figure 3: Key perception measures for grocery retailers, November 2014

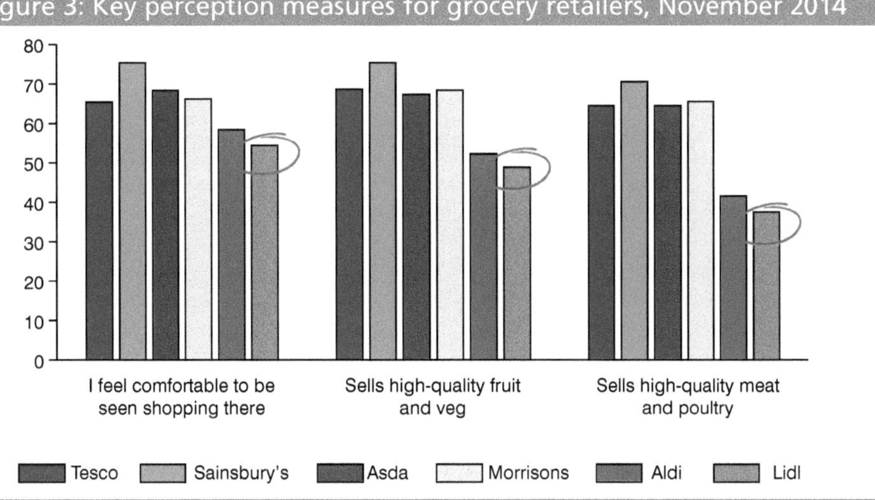

Source: Hall & Partners Tracking November 2014. Base: all current grocery shoppers (all/partly responsible for decision making), nationally representative demographic quotas. Top 2 box agreement percentage

A cruel video spoofing Lidl shoppers brutally summarised the problem (Figure 4).

Figure 4: Screenshot from "I love shopping at Lidl" spoof video mocking Lidl and Lidl shoppers

And Lidl's marketing at the time frankly wasn't helping (Figure 5).

Figure 5: Example of Lidl print advertising from c. 2012

Advertising's challenge was to change this misperception. And to do that, the advertising strategy needed to change.

A roadblock to growth

The grocery retail market is a classic example of Ehrenberg's 'double jeopardy' rule – bigger brands have more customers and those customers are slightly more loyal, with high correlation between penetration and share, as illustrated in Figure 6, which plots household penetration against market share for 2013, the year before Lidl started national advertising.[7]

Lidl was not competing in a discounter niche, it was just small – with fewer, less loyal shoppers (spending less and visiting less often).

Figure 6: Grocery market share (annual grocers share of total till roll) vs. annual household penetration, 2013

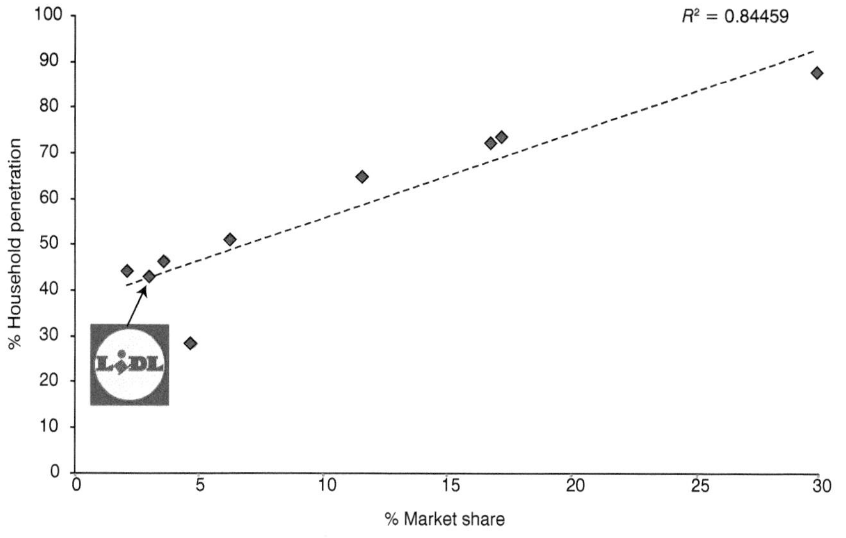

Source: Kantar

Lidl aspired to sit in the mainstream, alongside the Big 4, and that depended on increasing household penetration. But the perception that Lidl was not a suitable destination for the typical family to buy its groceries was a significant barrier to growth.

Removing this roadblock of misperception was the No.1 role for communications.

More customers needed...but who?

This is not a market that can be expanded: everyone buys food. New customers had to come from other retailers.

Customers didn't need to stop shopping at their existing grocery retailer, they could instead add Lidl to their repertoire, either expanding their number of trips or moving some trips to Lidl. But one way or another, if Lidl was to grow it had to attract new customers to take business from the rest of the market.

The natural assumption might be that the target should be cost-conscious or less well-off shoppers. After all, Waitrose shoppers wouldn't come to Lidl, would they?

Actually, they would. And in numbers proportionate to the relative market shares of Waitrose and Lidl: this is another example of the grocery retail market following Ehrenberg rules of growth, in this case 'duplication of purchase'.

Figure 7 shows that customer duplication between grocery retailers increases with market share and is overall very high – for instance, Tesco has around 28% market share yet 75% of everyone's customers also shop there in the course of a year (for shorter periods the level of duplication is lower but the pattern is the same).

Figure 7: Duplication of shoppers between grocery retailers in 2017

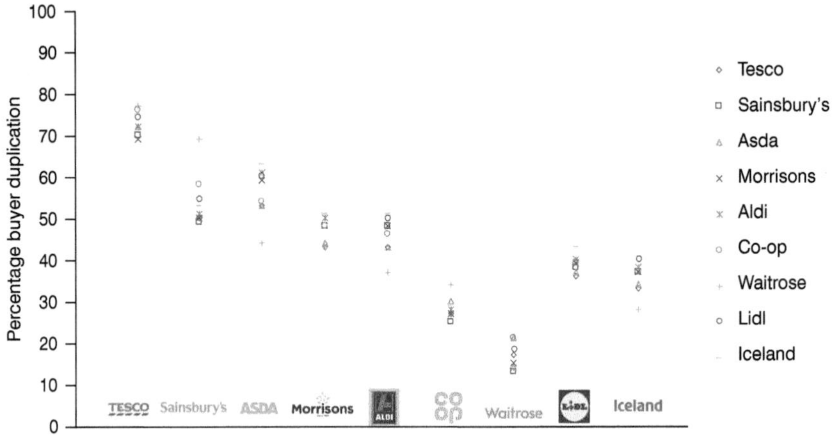

Source: Kantar Worldpanel

This market dynamic meant that Lidl needed to increase its duplication with all competitors to maximise growth, and most notably from the Big 4 in volume terms.[8]

This high duplication was an opportunity. Polygamy, not monogamy, is the norm for grocery shoppers. Lidl was not asking people to forego the Big 4 entirely (this would be unrealistic), merely to move some trips and some spend.

It might still be expected that some retailers would disproportionately appeal to certain demographics and attitudinal groups. But again, the answer is contrary to received wisdom, with the actual picture reflecting another Ehrenberg law: customer profiles in a market seldom vary much. Figure 8 illustrates this point.

Each data point on the top chart is a retailer's performance in a demographic segment, indexed against the market.

Each data point on the bottom chart is a retailer's performance on a 2017 TGI attitude statement, indexed against the market.

There are small differences to be found if you hunt for them, with minor targeting efficiencies on offer. But similarities are far greater than the differences: the vast majority of data points bunch closely either side of an index of 100:

Beyond media stereotypes there is no such thing as a Lidl shopper, or a Waitrose shopper, or a Tesco shopper, in the sense that the shoppers of one retailer differ greatly from those of another.

So there was no mileage in targeting specific demographic or attitudinal segments. The whole market was open to Lidl: everyone's shoppers were available to us. But of course our shoppers are also available to everyone else. We are all fishing in the same big pond.

This could not be a surgical strike: growth depends on reach and scale.

Lidl needed to wage war on the whole market.

Figure 8: Retailer demographic and attitudinal profiles vs. market average

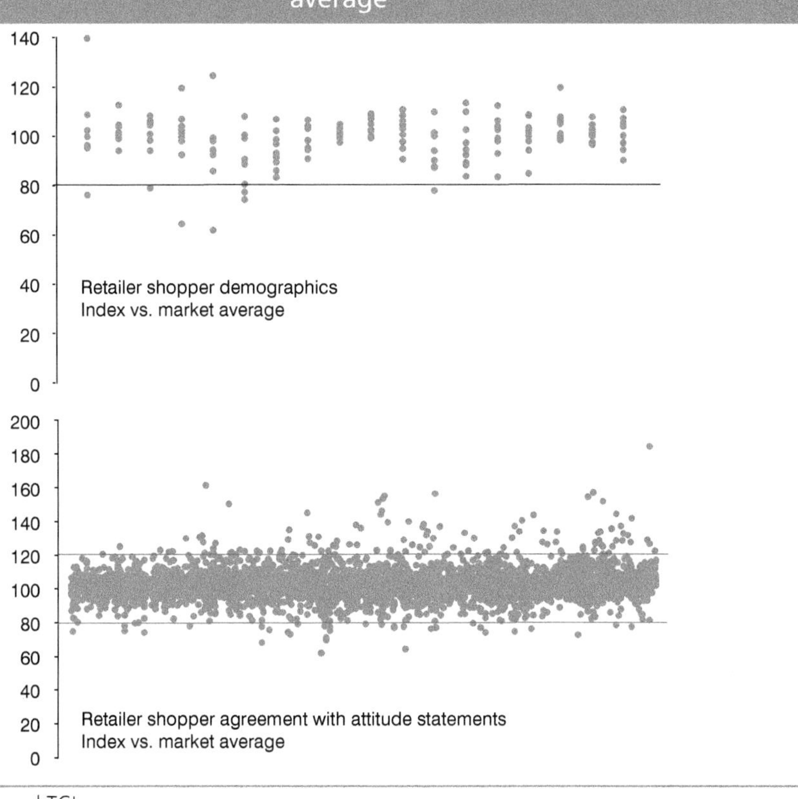

Source: Kantar and TGI

Part 2: Realising the mainstream opportunity

Lidl's war: terms of engagement

Growth depended on increasing penetration, which required attracting shoppers from all rival grocery retailers.

There was no specific demographic or attitudinal segment to target.

There was no retailer from whom Lidl could steal disproportionate share.

We needed to address the misperception roadblocks – low prices means poor quality – preventing people from coming to Lidl, even when they were aware of us.

And we needed to do so on a mass scale, waging war on a £100bn market which touches every household in the country multiple times a week.

Translating these to campaign objectives, informing all activity 2014–2017:

- *Business objective*: accelerate growth in sales and market share.
- *Marketing objective:* grow mass household penetration – attract customers from everywhere.

- *Communications objective:* dispel the myth that Lidl's low prices come at the expense of quality.

A new approach to media

These objectives demanded a complete change in media approach:

- mass penetration growth requires mass reach;
- mass reach requires mass investment.

A major investment in 'excess share of voice' (ESOV) – over-investment in share of voice versus share of market – was a necessary part of the new approach (as demonstrated by Binet and Field for the IPA). It is a harsh truth that raw spend matters.

Lidl embraced this requirement, at times matching the spend of much larger competitors, an extraordinary commitment for a relatively small brand in a market of behemoths, let alone one without a history of national advertising (Figure 9).

Figure 9: Lidl ESOV 2011–2017

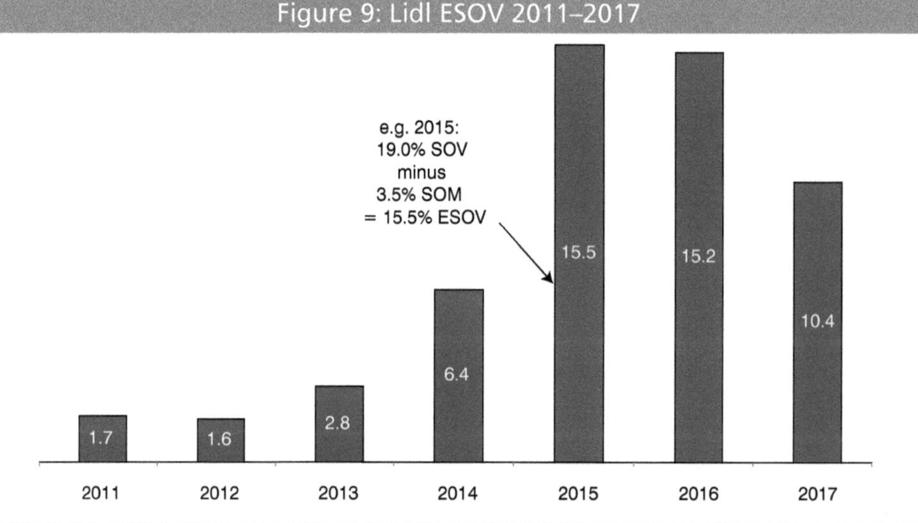

Sources: Kantar and Nielsen. Figures shown are the amount by which Lidl's share of voice during the year exceeded its market share at the start of the year.

The increased budget driving ESOV was primarily invested in TV and was incremental, with press spend maintained (while reducing as a proportion of a rising total). Radio and other media (notably outdoor and digital) have also played a larger role over time (Figure 10).

For twenty years Lidl spent all its budget on short-term, sales-driving activation advertising. Spending the majority of a greatly increased budget on national mass-reach media, using creative intended to address long-term perception challenges, represents a significant shift.

A key effect of this change in media strategy was a huge increase in the number of people exposed to Lidl advertising. As an illustration of this, Figure 11 shows the average weekly 1+ reach of Lidl's TV advertising among the housewives with children buying audience.

Figure 10: Lidl media spend and split by media, 2011–2017

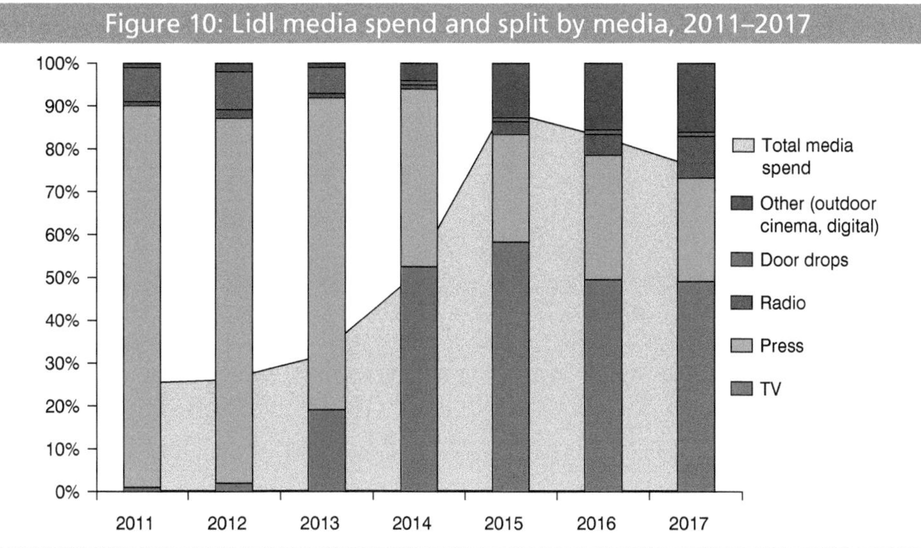

Source: Nielsen

Figure 11: Lidl TV advertising average weekly 1+ reach among housewives with children buying audience

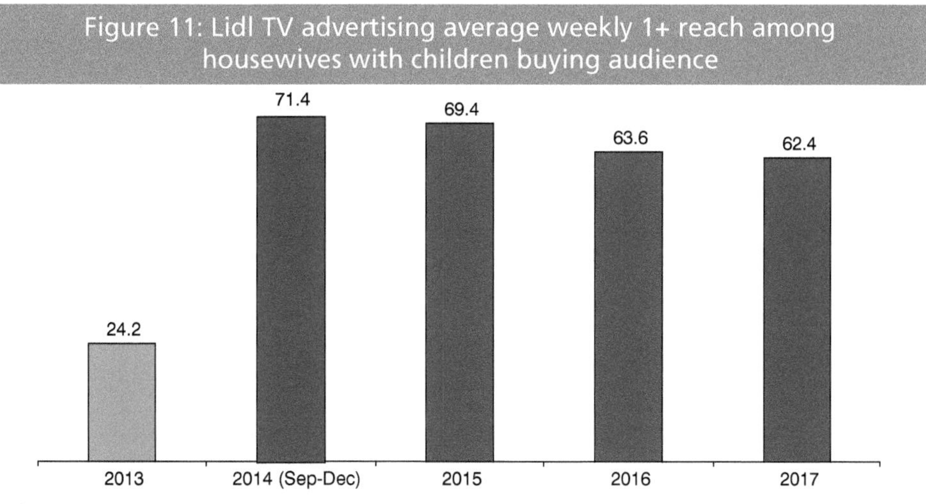

Source: BARB

The very high 2014 figure is a result of a very large campaign launch spend. The slight reduction from 2015 to 2017 is a result of a slightly reduced spend, optimisation and small declines in average levels of TV viewing.

A new creative strategy

With TV at the heart of the media plan, the creative had to deliver a powerful and compelling truth, and we had one: the perception that 'low prices mean poor quality' was simply not true.

We took this head-on in our creative brief: *'Tell people the truth about Lidl'*.

But that truth could not simply be asserted. A truth is most powerful if discovered for yourself, or if you see people like you discovering it, particularly if that truth is surprising.

It took great confidence for a brand new to national advertising to show customers being surprised at the quality of the produce. But that simply reflects the rock-solid truth underpinning the campaign: the products are good quality ... as well as being low priced.

It also reflects the determination to defy convention which sits at the heart of Lidl's disruptive business model and would be carried into its communications.

The first national campaign (in September 2014) featured a *farmers' market*, complete with stalls all selling (unbeknown to the people exploring them) Lidl produce. Only when the delicious food had been sampled, delighted in and bought was its source revealed, much to the surprise and delight of the shoppers.

The genuine surprise of the participants powerfully demonstrated the *#LidlSurprises* endline.

This was the first of a series of executions, including a *country house* where invited locals were served a sumptuous Christmas lunch, and a *pub* where customers were invited to pay what they thought their Easter food was worth, only to be given plenty of change when it was revealed (to much surprise) that all the food had been Lidl produce (Figures 12–14).

Figure 12: Sample screenshots from 'Market' (September 2014)

Figure 13: Sample screenshots from 'Country House' (Christmas 2014)

Figure 14: Sample screenshots from 'Pub' (Easter 2015)

In the next #LidlSurprises iteration (from mid-2016) doubts about quality were confronted by inviting sceptical shoppers who had expressed some concern or cynicism about a Lidl product to feature in an ad bringing them face-to-face with a Lidl supplier, or (in shorter executions) inviting a supplier to address the concern directly to camera.

When experiencing the truth of Lidl's sourcing and quality, our sceptics became advocates, just as had those attending the farmer's market in 2014 or the Easter pub in 2015.

This campaign continues to run, with 10 executions to date covering steak, turkey, mussels, broccoli, kale, strawberries, wine and more, each starting with a sceptical comment and ending with a persuasive and engaging TV ad ... and a new advocate (Figures 15–17).

Figure 15: Sample screenshots from 'Mussels' (July 2016)

Figure 16: Sample screenshots from 'Turkey' (November 2016)

Figure 17: Sample screenshots 'Jersey Royals' (May 2017)

Alongside this, building on strengthened quality perceptions, the TV brand narrative has emphasised how much more (in terms of equivalent quality products) your money buys you at Lidl versus other retailers: 'Big on quality, Lidl on price' (BOQLOP).

Each BOQLOP execution (over 40 to date) calls out a product and price from a rival grocery retailer, demonstrates how buying the equivalent[9] from Lidl leaves enough left over to buy an entire meal. It's a message rooted in low price, demonstrating range and delivered in an engaging way, all while being uncompromising in its competitive punch.

BOQLOP comparisons cover meals (e.g. fish and chips), occasions (e.g. movie night) and topical themes (e.g. healthy breakfast in January) (Figures 18–20).

Figure 18: Sample screenshots from 'Tesco Sunday Roast' (January 2017)

Figure 19: Sample screenshots from 'Sainsbury's Healthy Breakfast' (January 2018)

Figure 20: Sample screenshots from 'Morrison's Movie Night' (February 2018)

Price-promotional and category-specific activations run alongside this brand narrative throughout the year in print and TV, taking the fight to Lidl's rivals on a daily basis (Figures 21 and 22).

Figure 21: Sample screenshots from 'Nappies' (June 2017)

Figure 22: Sample screenshots from 'Valentine's Day' (February 2017)

Since 2014 Lidl has continued to surprise. And sales have continued to rise.

Part 3: The results

We greatly accelerated sales growth, driven by growth in consumer penetration

As we stated at the outset, this paper is a study in how advertising helps brands grow.

Penetration drives growth. Advertising drives penetration.

Figure 23 shows a clear sharp uptick in both penetration and sales from the start of investment in national advertising. Lidl was growing before then but at an annualised rate of 9.5% from 2009–2013; between 2014 and 2017 growth was running at 15.5% pa.

Figure 23: Lidl sales growth, penetration, basket size and frequency indexed vs. 2008

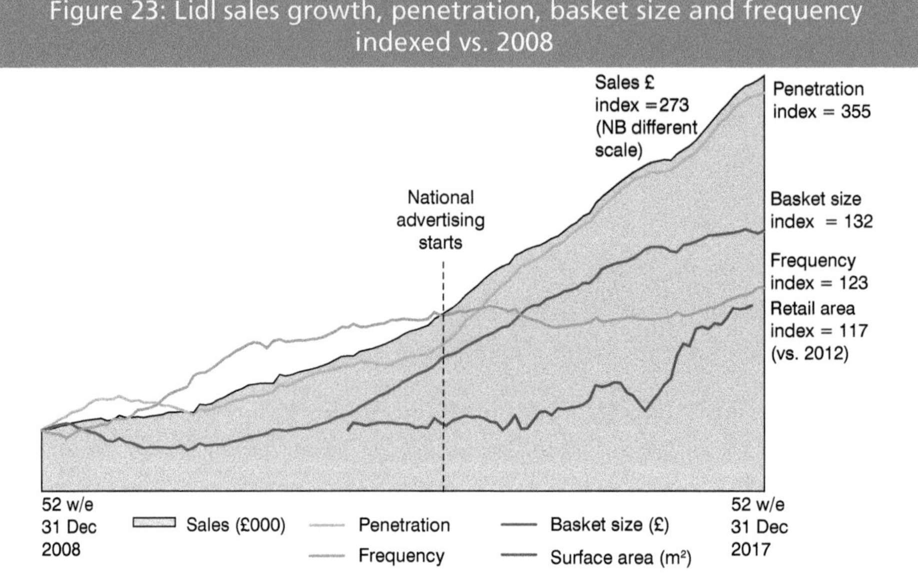

Sources: Kantar Worldpanel; Lidl (total retail floor space indexed vs. 2012

Relatively little of this growth was driven by frequency of visit (largely flat since 2010), or by store growth (which did not grow significantly until 2017). Basket spend has grown, but at a much slower rate than penetration.

Lidl brand share grew sharply in line with penetration

Annual market share and household penetration figures for 2008–2017 (Figure 24) show a marked jump from 2014 onwards.

Lidl was growing before 2014, but at a slower rate. National advertising investment from 2014 onwards turbo-charged this growth, primarily by sharply accelerating penetration growth (a 4.3 percentage point jump in 2014 and more than 10 percentage points in four years 2014–2017).

We steadily grew customers per square metre

Shopper numbers grew significantly from the start of national advertising. This was not matched by growth in total retail space, hence growth in shoppers per square metre (Figure 25).

Since late 2016 Lidl has been opening new stores at a ferocious rate. New stores tend to be slightly larger, explaining the small drop in shoppers per square metre during 2017. But shopper growth is still strong – and still being driven by advertising.

Lidl now has more customers per square metre than key rivals

Despite the sharp increase in Lidl floor space during 2017, Lidl has now more customers per square metre than market leader Tesco and fellow discounter Aldi (Figure 26).

Figure 24: Lidl market share and household penetration, 2011–2017. 52-week grocers' share of total till roll

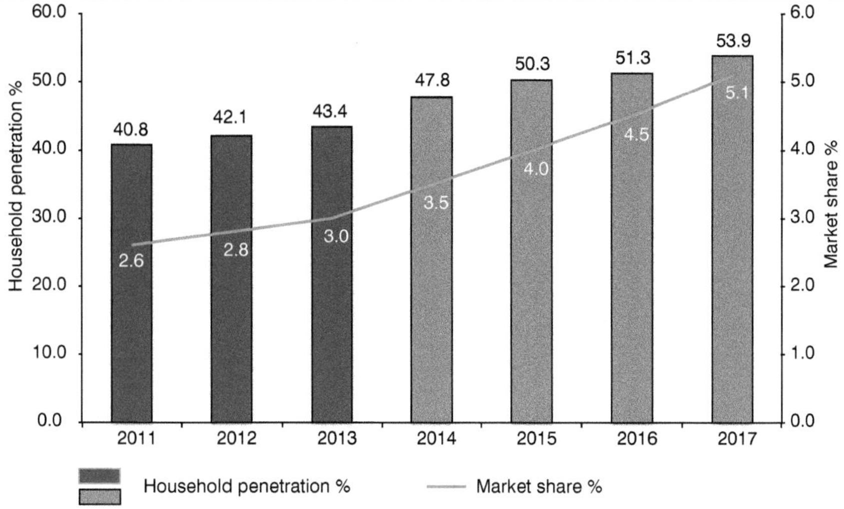

	2011	2012	2013	2014	2015	2016	2017
Household penetration %	40.8	42.1	43.4	47.8	50.3	51.3	53.9
Market share %	2.6	2.8	3.0	3.5	4.0	4.5	5.1

Source: Kantar Worldpanel

Figure 25: Lidl shopper numbers, shoppers per square metre and total retail area, indexed vs. 2012

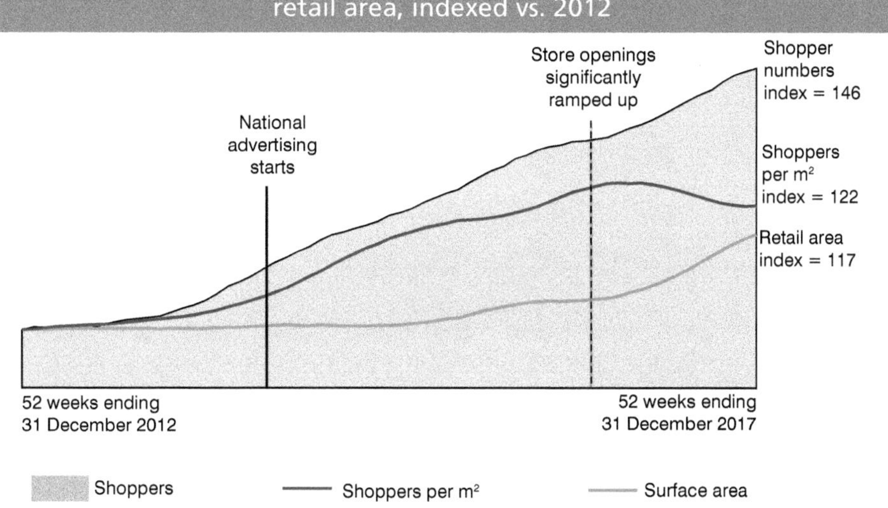

Source: Kantar Worldpanel; Lidl

Figure 26: Lidl shopper numbers, shoppers per square metre and total retail area, 2017 indexed vs. 2012

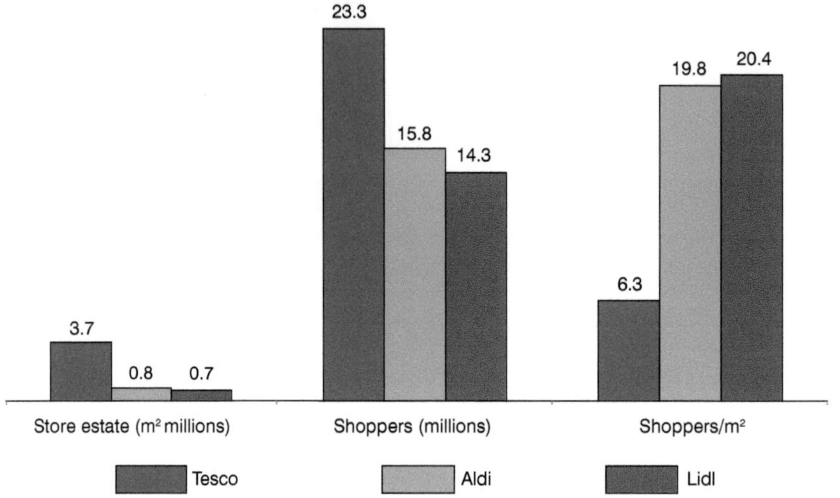

	Tesco	Aldi	Lidl
Store estate (m^2 millions)	3.7	0.8	0.7
Shoppers (millions)	23.3	15.8	14.3
Shoppers/m^2	6.3	19.8	20.4

Source: Kantar Worldpanel; Lidl

We took business from every retailer – especially the Big 4

A snapshot of Lidl's sales in early 2018 compared to the same 12-week period in 2014 shows Lidl taking business from every single grocery retailer (Figure 27).

Figure 27: Lidl net spend switching (£m) 12 weeks ending 28 February 2018 vs. 12 weeks ending 4 March 2014

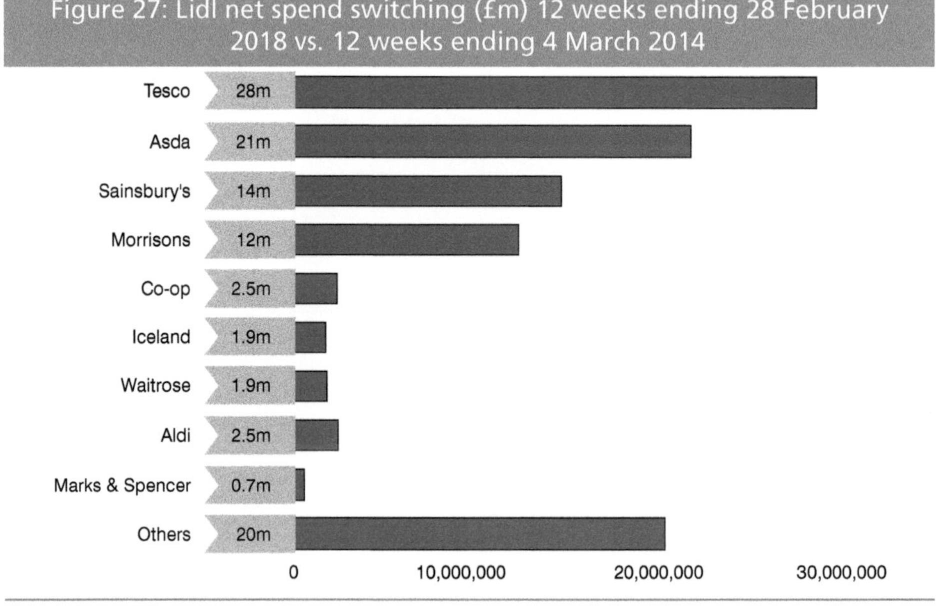

Source: Kantar Worldpanel

This is net switching of grocery spend – Lidl has net revenue inflows from all, £28m per quarter from Tesco and £21m from Asda (reflecting their market share), but also from fellow discounter Aldi.

We changed consumer perceptions, becoming salient to more and more shoppers

For a discounter, shopper confidence (measured by willingness to recommend) and quality perceptions (particularly for fresh produce) are challenges which never go away, but represented the roadblock to growth that we had to remove.

Since mid-2016 our tracking has shown a majority willing to recommend Lidl to friends and family and, from early-2017, a majority agreeing that Lidl's fresh produce is of high quality.

This battle is never won. But for over 50% of grocery shoppers quality perceptions are no longer a block to coming through Lidl's doors (Figure 28).

In line with this, the YouGov BrandIndex showed immediate jumps in both key value and quality ratings, which have been sustained at the new level by continued investment (Figure 29).

Isolating advertising's contribution

Lidl use econometrics to measure all factors contributing to sales and growth. The model isolates the contribution of: sales directly driven by advertising, store estate growth, brand momentum (longer-term effects) and other factors including competitor activity, price effects and range changes (these are listed together as 'other' for simplicity and confidentiality) (Figure 30).

There is an immediate increase in the contribution to sales from advertising with the start of national support.

'Brand momentum' is a measure of long-term brand strength. The two key drivers of this are store estate growth and advertising. Additional modelling attributes 28% of brand momentum to TV advertising, which gives us a measure of the long-term effects of sustained advertising support in addition to the direct sales driven (Figure 31).

From this modelling we can thus isolate both short-term direct sales effects of advertising and the longer-term brand effects.

Figure 28: Lidl brand tracking

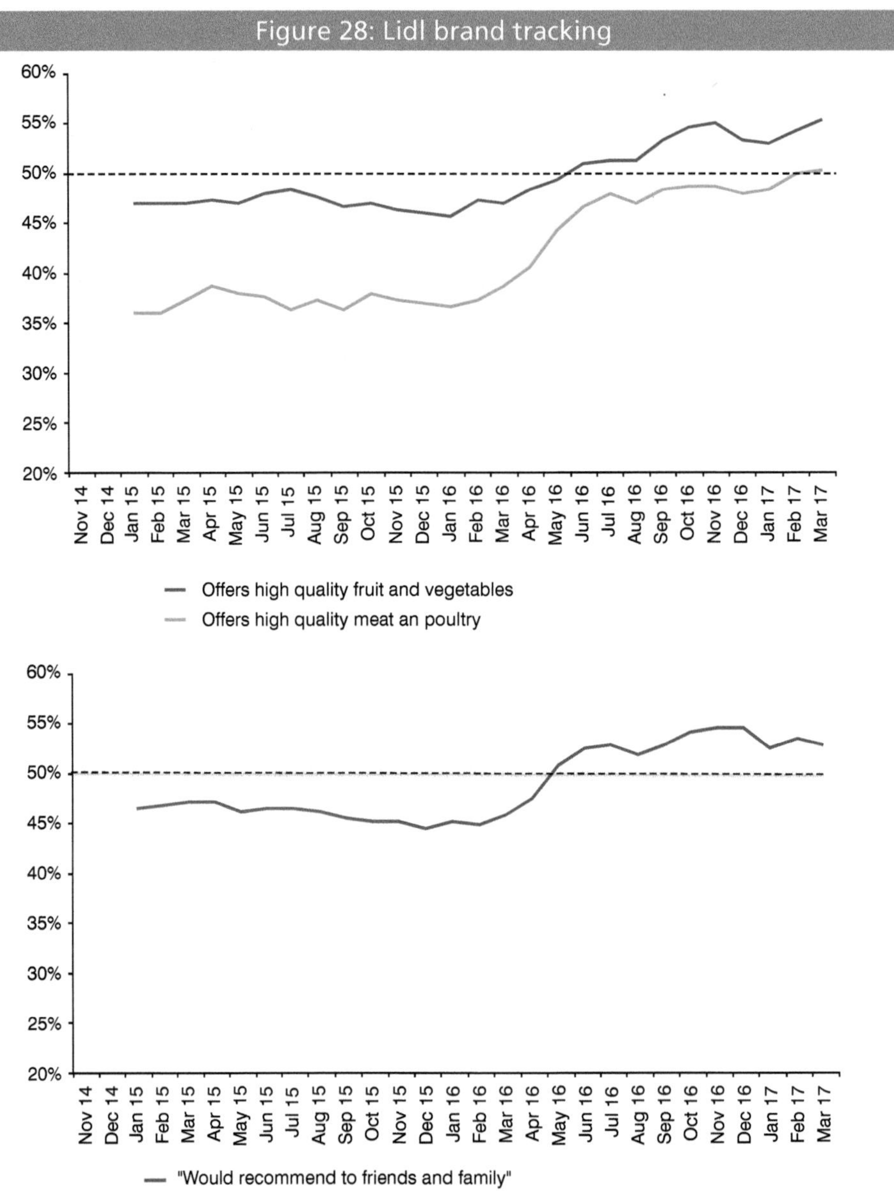

Source: Hall & Partners. November 2014– March 2017, rolling 3-month averages. Top 2 box (of 5) agreement with statement. Base: all grocery shoppers. NB Tracking methodology changed from April 2017 and the new measures are not directly comparable.

Figure 29: Lidl value for money and quality perceptions 2009–2017

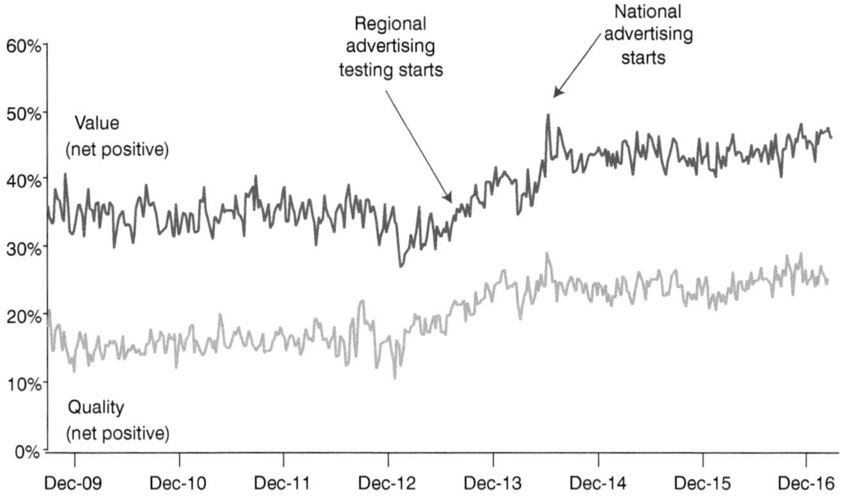

Regional advertising testing starts

National advertising starts

60%
50%
40%
30%
20%
10%
0%

Value (net positive)

Quality (net positive)

Dec-09 Dec-10 Dec-11 Dec-12 Dec-13 Dec-14 Dec-15 Dec-16

Q: *"Which of the following brands do you think represents GOOD/POOR quality"*
Overall % score is "good quality" mentions minus "poor quality" mentions divided by total number answering.

Q: *"Which of the following brands do you think represents GOOD/POOR value for money. By that we don't mean cheap or expensive, but the brand that offers a lot for the price paid."*

Overall % score 'good value' mentions minus 'poor value' mentions divided by total number answering.

Source: Ebiquity/YouGov BrandIndex. Base: all adults (no shopper filter). Rolling 4-week sample. Percentage score is 'good' minus 'poor' divided by number answering.

Figure 30: Lidl econometric model showing contribution to revenue of various factors, January 2013 to October 2017

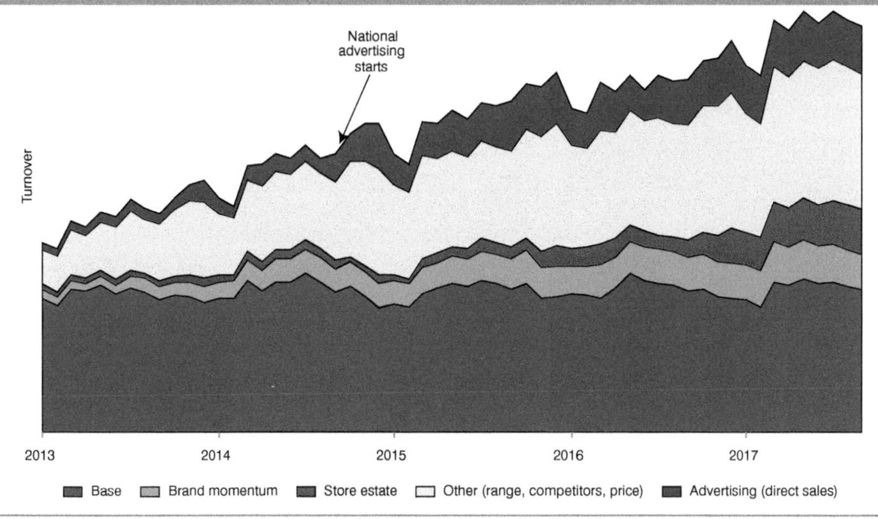

Source: Ebiquity.

Figure 31: Illustration of further modelling of brand momentum, isolating the contribution of TV advertising

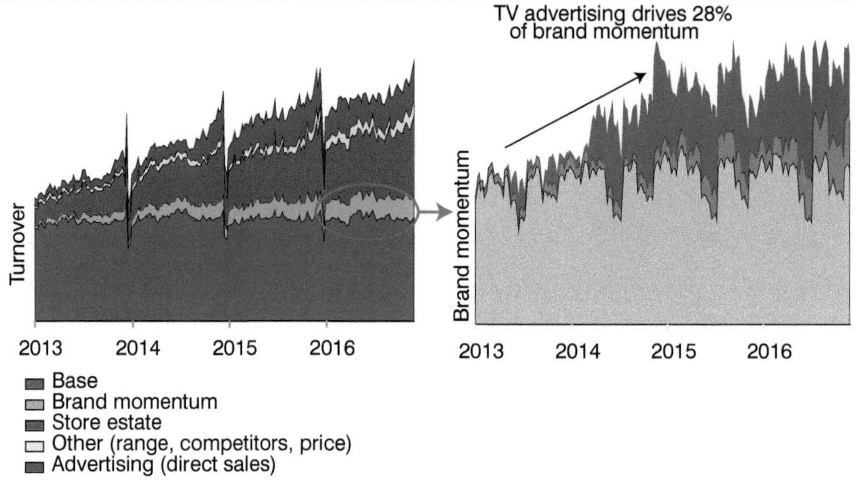

TV advertising drives 28% of brand momentum

Turnover

Brand momentum

2013 2014 2015 2016

2013 2014 2015 2016

Base
Brand momentum
Store estate
Other (range, competitors, price)
Advertising (direct sales)

Source: Ebiquity

Advertising's total contribution to Lidl's growth

Lidl's annual sales grew by £2.56 billion between 2013 and 2017 (Figure 32).

Figure 32: Lidl total sales calendar year 2013 and calendar year 2017

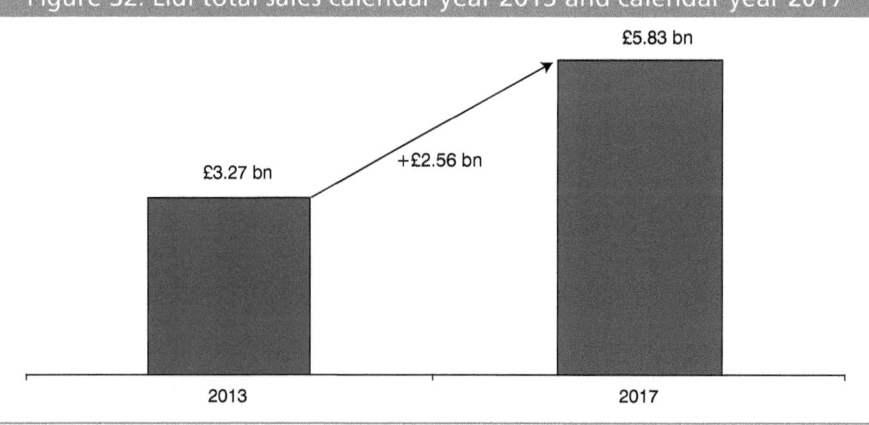

Source: Kantar Worldpanel

Econometrics can isolate the contribution of advertising to this growth by breaking out the various contributing factors over time.

The econometrics waterfall chart in Figure 33 breaks down Lidl's £2.56bn turnover growth since 2013. The figure for each factor is the amount of incremental turnover contributed by that factor.

For the sake of confidentiality and simplicity only advertising, estate size and brand momentum are broken out, with other factors combined.

Figure 33: Contributing factors to Lidl growth 2013 to 2017

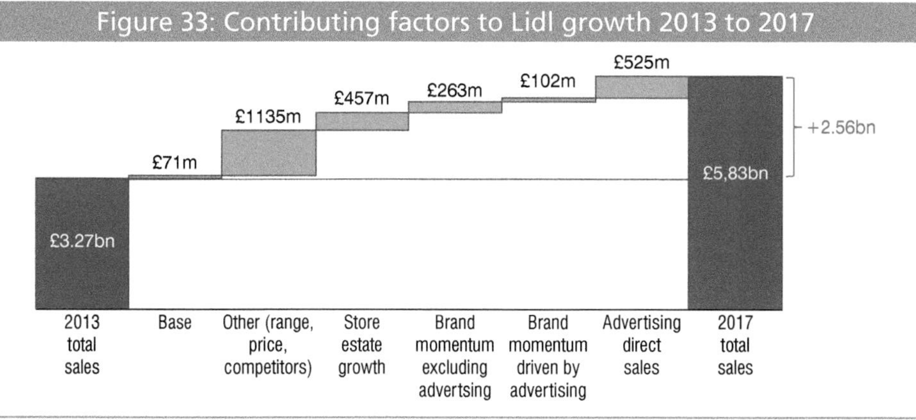

Source: Ebiquity

Between 2013 and 2017 Lidl grew from a £3.27 billion business to a £5.83 billion business. Econometrics attributes 20.5% of that growth (£525m) to sales directly driven by advertising.

The long-term impact of advertising on brand momentum contributes a further 4% of the total growth (£102m).

Advertising thus delivered *24.5%* of Lidl's annual revenue growth between 2014 and 2017, an incremental contribution of *£627m.*

Advertising investment has generated strong payback in both short and longer-term

The section above isolates the contribution of advertising to the difference in turnover in 2017 compared to 2013 – advertising's contribution to growth.

We can also quantify the total contribution of advertising investment to Lidl sales revenue in *each individual year* from 2014–2017 – advertising's contribution to sales.

This is shown in Figure 34.

Figure 34: Direct and long-term sales driven by advertising each year 2013 to 2017

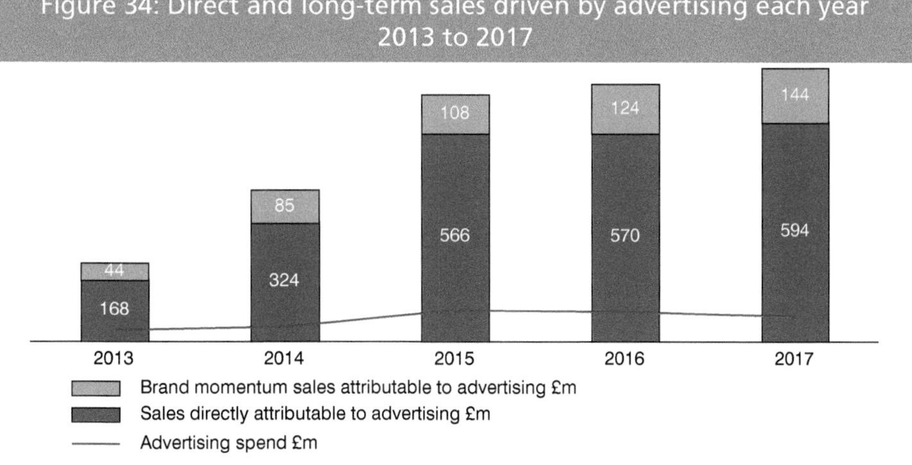

Source: Ebiquity/Kantar/Nielsen.

Both direct sales and long-term sales from brand momentum sharply increased with the move to national advertising in 2014. Note that both types of sales effect increased each year, despite the media budget falling slightly in 2016 and 2017:

We promised at the start of this paper that all the numbers herein would be extraordinary.

Over the four years 2014–2017 combined, advertising delivered:

£2,238 million in direct sales
£503 million in sales from brand momentum
=
£2,741 million total sales revenue

Marketing investment at scale – ESOV delivering strong ROMI as well as growth

Lidl do not reveal their margins, even to their agencies, so to calculate a profit ROMI we have taken an industry-standard gross margin figure of 25% as a benchmark.

We have not applied a contributory margin figure since Lidl's largest fixed costs (estate and staff) do not vary with incremental or decremental sales.

The resulting profit ROMI figures are shown in Figure 35. The calculation is as follows:

Total sales revenue driven × 25% (gross margin) = gross profit contribution.
Gross profit contribution less advertising spend = profit net of advertising spend.
Net profit divided by advertising spend = profit ROMI.

Figure 35: Profit ROMI for Lidl advertising 2013–2017

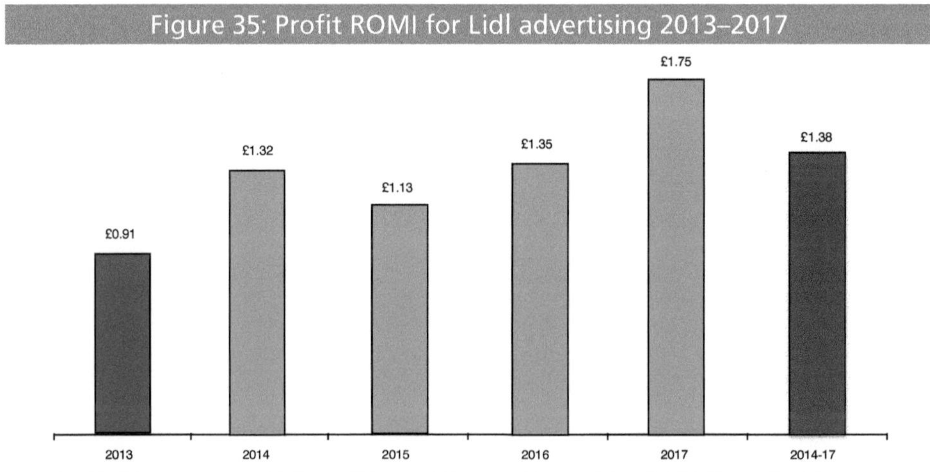

Source: Ebiquity/Nielsen

ROMI does not fall despite big increases in budget

As we have seen, a key part of Lidl's growth strategy was investing in ESOV, with an average annual media budget in 2014–2017 – 2.5 times higher than in 2013.

ROMI is an efficiency measure not an effectiveness measure and can be maximised simply by spending less, making a campaign seem more efficient yet delivering less in absolute sales terms. Conversely an increase in budget can deliver greater absolute sales contribution while appearing less efficient as ROMI falls.

In this case both absolute sales contribution (effectiveness) and ROMI (efficiency) have increased despite big incremental media spend.

Lidl's change in approach delivered an *average* profit ROMI *51.6%* higher in 2014–2017 than in 2013, while delivering *3.5* times as many sales, from *2.5* times the media spend.

Lidl's advertising investment has found the marketing effectiveness sweet spot, becoming both *more effective* (absolute customer, sales and profit growth) and *more efficient* (ROMI).

The bottom line

Lidl's big investment in advertising delivered big results.

In four years 2014–2017, advertising delivered:

£560 million in gross profit from direct sales
£126 million in gross profit from sales from brand momentum
=
£686 million gross profit contribution
=
£398 million profit (net of advertising spend)

How Lidl grew a lot bigger: learnings

Every market sector has its own particular dynamics and challenges, but this is a textbook example of the applicability of the common rules and paths to growth identified by Ehrenberg-Bass, and by Binet and Field.

To grow, you need more customers.

Those customers are currently using your competitors in predictable market-share-driven proportions.

You need to reach as many of those potential customers as possible, with strong investment in broad reach media and messaging which combines long-term brand effects with short-term sales impacts.

You will grow faster by investing in share of voice well in excess of your market share – spending big to win big.

You need a compelling creative narrative rooted in the truth of the brand, which you must not be afraid to let speak for itself.

All this is as true of a small German discount grocery retailer taking on market-leading behemoth such as Tesco as it is of a small challenger brand in any other sector.

Except Lidl isn't so small any more.

Notes

1. All sales, market share, penetration, basket size and frequency data in this paper is from Kantar Worldpanel. Data used is share of grocers within total till roll. Till roll includes everything sold in the store (including non-food items).
2. Waitrose went ahead again over Christmas. The two brands are neck-and-neck at the time of writing in March 2018.
3. Regional upweight test, including TV, documented in Lidl's 2014 IPA Effectiveness Awards entry.
4. Byron Sharp, *How Brands Grow*, 2010.
5. *Media in Focus: Marketing Effectiveness in the Digital Era*, with a focus on evidence from 2012–2016 (published by the IPA, June 2017).
6. This followed a regional test of TV advertising in 2013, as already noted.
7. The outlier (bottom left) is Waitrose, who have higher market share than their low household penetration would suggest, because they are notably more expensive. The pattern shown here is the same over time and for different periods (4-week, 12-week).
8. It might be expected that, with a similar retail proposition, there would be high duplication between Lidl and Aldi – this is not the case, in part due to store numbers and locations, which overlap significantly less than either does with the Big 4 from which both draw the majority of their sales growth.
9. That is, equivalent in terms of quality, which has to be substantiated to the satisfaction of Clearcast each time.

L'Oréal Paris True Match

How L'Oréal Paris UK True Match climbed to No.1 by making everyone feel 'Worth it'

By Emily Ellis and David Frymann, McCann London; Vasileios Kourakis, L'Oréal
Credited company: McCann London

Summary

The UK market for foundation make-up was growing, but the True Match brand had been stuck in fifth place for three years. It aimed to attract 256,000 new customers and become market leader within a year. Conventional wisdom dictates that mass marketing should focus on the majority for the biggest returns. Unfortunately, this leaves minorities feeling ignored, especially in mass cosmetics. True Match saw an opportunity to recruit consumers who felt excluded from the category because of their skin tone, or the industry's ideas of beauty and functional messaging. Partnering with 23 diverse influencers – each with a True Match shade and personal story to share – the brand communicated it was suitable for every kind of face, for every shade. Mass media followed – all under a new L'Oréal end line: 'Because we're all worth it'. The brand's value share leapt into first place, further increasing its lead in Year 2. Estimated short-term revenue ROI was £2.90 for every £1 invested, and the strategy was rolled out to 15 countries.

Editor's comment

The judges appreciated the huge changes L'Oréal needed to embrace in this campaign to move from fifth to first place in the UK. True Match's strategy was a brave move which addressed those who felt excluded from the make-up category, by creating communications which embraced both mass and personalised approaches to help everyone feel celebrated, beautiful and 'worth it' with a foundation for every kind of face, every shade, age, and gender.

Client comment

Adrien Koskas, Managing Director, L'Oréal CPD UKI

As the biggest beauty brand in the world, it is our responsibility to drive attitude changes in the industry. Through this campaign, we are changing what the beauty industry is about: the inclusivity of beauty, the connection of beauty, as well as the way we portray women – and men.

Introduction

This case shows how L'Oréal Paris UK addressed the pain experienced by those who felt excluded from the make-up category. Conventional wisdom dictates that mass marketing should focus on the majority for the biggest returns. Unfortunately, this leaves anyone who doesn't fit the beauty industry's conventional slim/white/flawless model feeling ignored. The problem was particularly acute in the make-up category. With the widest foundation range, but not the biggest share, L'Oréal Paris True Match saw an opportunity to help everyone feel celebrated, beautiful and 'worth it' with a foundation for every kind of face, every shade, every age, and every gender.

Taking an inclusive leadership stance by placing great value on those who felt marginalised had a powerful and genuinely resonant impact in four ways:

1. *for the business*, which saw True Match leap from fifth to first in terms of market share, with a short-term campaign ROI of £2.90 and a long-term ROI of £5.20;
2. *for consumers*, who now all felt 'worth it';
3. *for L'Oréal Paris UK,* which committed to being even more inclusive;
4. *and the make-up category*, which changed its approach to communications forever.

Business context: True Match flagging in fifth

With 50 products sold every second, L'Oréal Paris is the world's leading beauty brand. The brand is famous for an enviable list of celebrity endorsers and its legendary signature: 'Because you're worth it'.

With superior science at the heart of everything it creates, L'Oréal Paris Research Laboratories develop beauty products to cater to every need: from make-up to skincare, haircare, styling, hair colour and male grooming. Critical to its success is the mass make-up category which consists of four distinct segments: eye,[1] lip,[2] nail varnish, and face.[3]

Across all L'Oréal Paris categories, communications have followed a successful formula: celebrity endorsement coupled with superior science messaging, aka 'the science bit'.

In 2016, the UK make-up category was worth more than £2 billion (luxury and mass market) and was experiencing strong growth of over +8%.[4] This was largely due to the emergence of new, exciting brands such as NYX Professional Make-up and Make-up Revolution and exciting new sub-categories and trend products such as contouring (*c.* 200% growth), highlighting (*c.* +200%), brow (*c.* +50%) and setting spray (*c.* +600%).[5]

Within mass make-up, foundation is a key segment. In 2016, it was worth £147 million and was growing at a rate of 2.8%.[6] The market is very fragmented, with the leading brand having only 6.8% market share and the top five accounting for 31.7%[7] of the market.

L'Oréal UK's flagship foundation brand is called True Match and can be found in Boots and Superdrug, along with fierce competition for attention and shelf space from brands such as Rimmel and Maybelline. From 2013–2015 True Match sales were increasing, but so was the category. In fact, from a value market share point of view, whilst its share was rising slightly, True Match was persistently flagging in fifth position for three years in a row (Figures 1–3).

Figure 1: Mass foundation market value

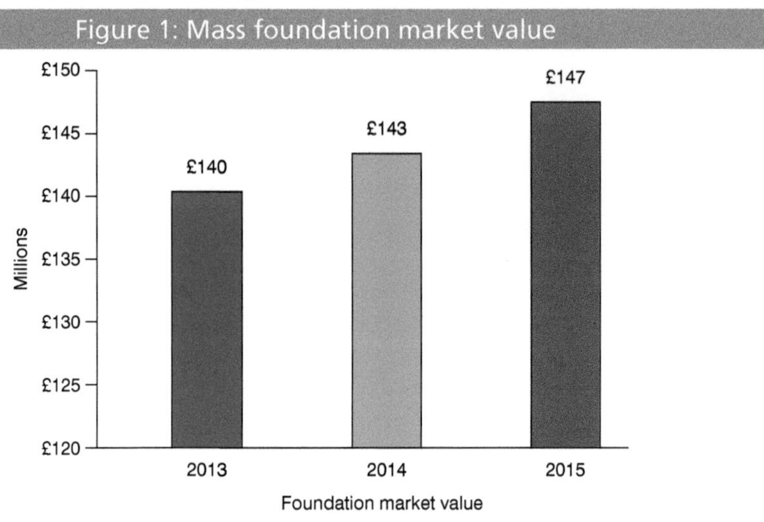

Source: Nielsen 2016

Figure 2: True Match value sales

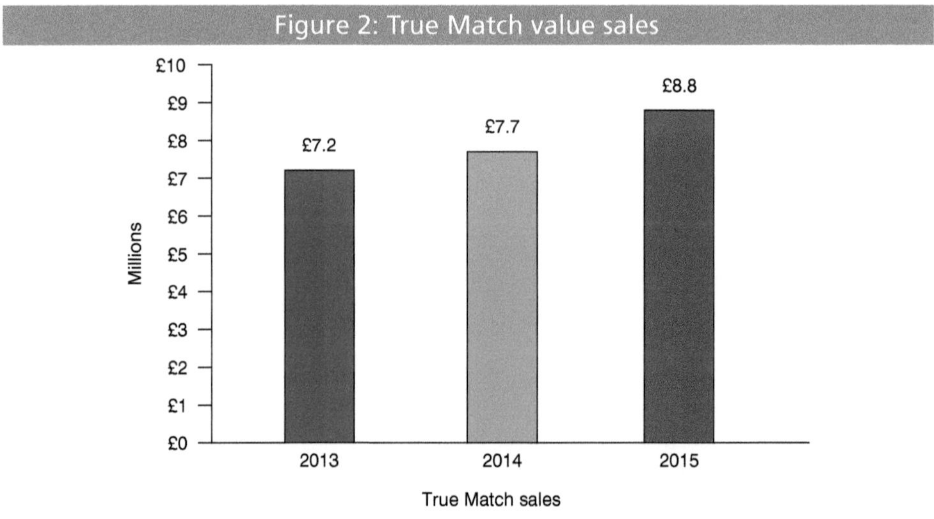

Source: Nielsen 2016

So, why were we persistently fifth?

The two main factors influencing purchasing decision for the foundation category are price and having the right shade (Figure 4).

Figure 3: True Match and competitor market share 2013/2014/2015

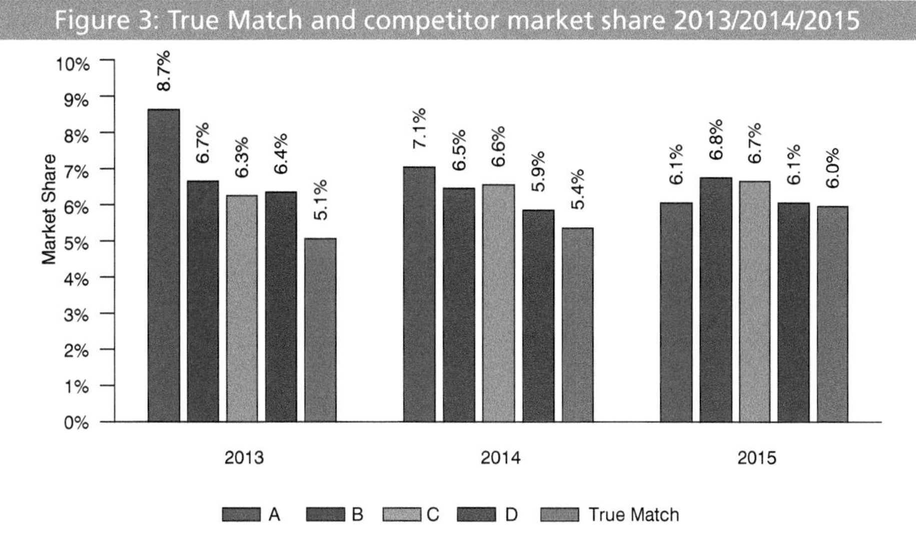

Due to confidentiality, brand names have been disguised due to Nielsen restrictions

Figure 4: Factors influencing foundation purchasing

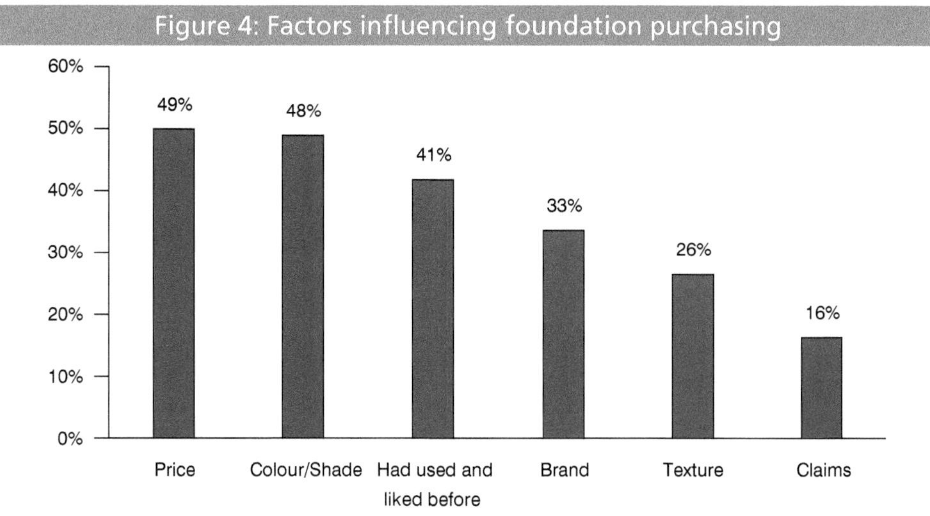

Source: Mintel (2016) Colour Cosmetics UK report: 645 female internet users aged 16+ who have bought base make-up (foundation) for themselves in the last 12 months

We were confident that True Match had great product quality (Boots reviews are persistently high at 4.3*/5*)[8] and that we had the largest shade range in the mass market, so it seemed that True Match should have been performing better than it was.

However, as the premium offering of the mass market, True Match had a premium price tag to overcome. Furthermore, a bit more digging showed that our average distribution was falling well below our main competitors (Table 1).

Table 1: True Match: the most shades, but the lowest share, lowest distribution and highest price

Product name[9]	Average unit price	Number of shades	Market share (2016)[10]	Average weighted selling distribution (2016)[11]
B	£6.40	7	6.8%	51
C	£6.10	12	6.7%	50
D	£6.54	11	6.1%	47
A	£6.40	16	6.1%	44
True Match	£9.09	21	6.0%	25

True Match's lacklustre performance was either down to its price, distribution, or its communications model – or all three. As we couldn't easily change the price or distribution, we focused on the communications model.

L'Oréal Paris' traditional model of celebrity endorsement and superior science wasn't enough to overcome its higher price point and lower distribution, even with celebrities such as Blake Lively and Eva Longoria.

However, considering the market leaders had less than 7% market share each, it appeared that no brand was truly connecting with its audience in a meaningful way.

Why was no brand connecting with everyone?

In 2018, diversity is expected in businesses, products and communications. However, prior to 2015, it was distinctly lacking in the UK mass beauty market. The sense of frustration in social media was palpable and newspapers were fuelling the fire with attention-grabbing headlines (Figure 5).

Whilst there was a clear consumer need, why was no business jumping on this opportunity?

No brand was addressing the issue because it didn't appear to be financially viable to target a relatively small percentage of the population. This left minority audiences having to track down niche specialist players, or being forced to pay up to 80%[12] more for luxury foundations.

Mass market brands tend to follow the principles of *How Brands Grow* by Byron Sharp, focusing on an average representation of the many, because the biggest returns tend to be generated by focusing on majority audiences. Unfortunately, even though the ethnic population in the UK runs into millions, in percentage terms it's only 13%[13] making it appear financially unviable for mass market foundation brands to target them (Figure 6).

Figure 5: Negative PR around lack of diversity

Figure 6: The UK is 87% white

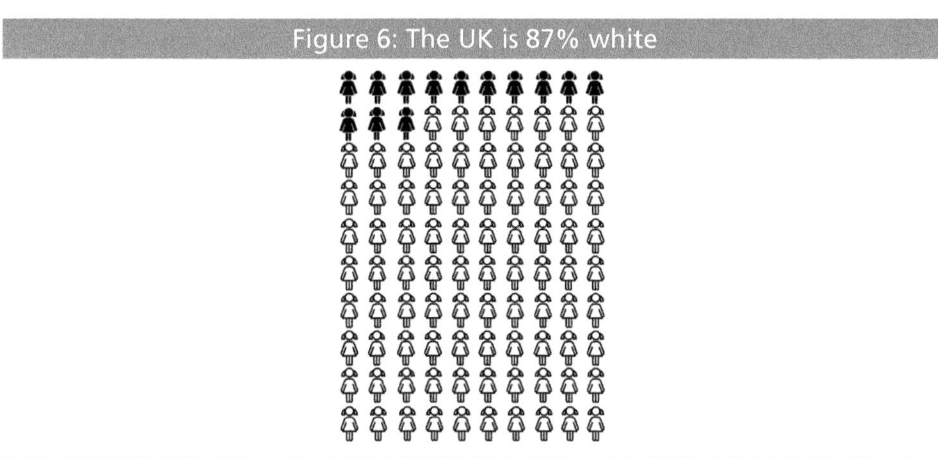

Challenge

Could True Match find a way to turn a niche issue for only 13% of the population into a mass opportunity to leapfrog the competition?

To make the challenge even more difficult, could the brand climb out of fifth place with the highest price point and the lowest distribution in the market?

Objectives

Business objective

Reach No. 1 (from fifth) market share position in mass-market foundation with 7% value share, requiring a 17% sales increase. 2015–2016.

Marketing objective

Increase penetration by recruiting 165,000 incremental consumers, requiring a sales uplift of 17%, 2015–2016.[14]

Communications objective UK

Establish True Match as 'the brand for me (whatever my skin tone)', specifically shifting the three key drivers of brand equity: emotional proximity, differentiation and relevance.[15]

For each of these we had a corresponding metric to shift:

- '*Brand I feel close to*' pre-campaign just 7% agreed (emotional proximity)
- '*Brand that caters to all women*' pre-campaign just 33% agreed (differentiation)
- '*Makes products that meet consumers' needs perfectly*' pre-campaign just 18% agreed (relevance)

Strategy: From niche issue to mass opportunity

Why does foundation matter so much?

Functionally, foundation as the name suggests, is the bedrock of any make-up routine. A good foundation should be invisible: covering, blending and smoothing out any imperfections to give your face a flawless base. It makes sense then that shade is a key driver in choosing your foundation, but we didn't realise quite how important it was until we got under the skin of the issue.

Qualitative[16] research showed us that foundation is a product laden with emotion, it is literally the foundation of the face you present to the world, and yet it's the one piece of make-up you don't want anyone to notice. In fact, it's hard to overestimate the importance of finding the shade that feels wholly a part of you. The wrong shade, even if slightly out, can leave you feeling flawed and self-conscious, rather than flawless and self-confident.

It's easy to understand why ethnic minorities were upset about the lack of darker shades in the mass market. That's why L'Oréal Paris was proud to create two new darker shades, increasing its range from 21 to 23 to ensure the widest number of people in the UK could find their perfect shade.

However, there was a tricky tension: having darker shades would appeal to the relatively small number of people with those shades, but simply having darker shades for a minority audience wouldn't guarantee mass-market leadership.

More dark shades ≠ Mass market leadership

So how could we reinvigorate the story of our entire range?

The answer wasn't as black as white as we originally thought.

When we reviewed foundation advertising prior to 2015, we were surprised to see a sea of single, white female faces and product ranges focused only on lighter skin tones. It was obvious that people with darker skin tones were absent from the category (Figures 7 and 8).

Figure 7: L'Oréal Paris True Match 2015

Figure 8: Competitor advertising 2015

Bloggers and journalists with darker skin tones captured this frustration:

'The immediate psychological response to the deficiency is a desire to seek solace in minority-owned brands that cater to us, and to cast away those that neglect us.'[17]

'I vividly recall being overlooked at the counter,' she says. 'That is an experience where, no matter how tall you are, you end up feeling a little bit smaller.'[18]

What we were hearing was a deep-rooted, industry-wide problem of people feeling excluded from the category. This led to our first thought on the insight:

'Being ignored is the worst feeling ever.'

However, with 'exclusion' in mind we realised that this problem was bigger than skin colour.

It wasn't a niche issue at all, but an issue that would resonate with anyone who felt overlooked by the perfect, slim, white version of beauty portrayed by the category. In fact, if you didn't fit this conventional model (as the majority of the UK doesn't) it was obvious you would feel forgotten or unimportant.

'We are on the verge of a very, very serious problem. The world of vloggers and YouTubers has created a perverse, homogenised sense of distorted "beauty" with no diversity or reality. The girls have neon-white eyes and crazily flawless skin. Brands will promote those images and re-gram them, but it's a long, long way from the norm. Society is losing all perspective on the diversity of beauty and it's contributing to an alarming growth in dysmorphia.'[19]

This journalist highlighted the problem perfectly, whilst questioning the world that the beauty category had helped to create. Our *powerful, uncomfortable insight* was broader than we originally thought:

'Being ignored is the worst feeling ever, no matter who you are, where you're from or whatever your skin colour.'

It would take a bold client to face this, but what did this mean for True Match? We saw a big opportunity because the category was ignoring people in three ways:

1. *Skin colour:* The first was obvious – we needed a campaign to show we had a shade for each and every skin tone across the spectrum.
2. *Beauty model:* Industry communications were leaving many feeling marginalised.
3. *How they felt:* There was a huge disconnect between how emotional people felt about foundation and the category's reliance on mostly functional messaging.

In short, True Match wanted all those who felt excluded by mass market foundation to feel included, to create a story as powerful as our range that would truly resonate with our audience and help grow our market share.

As the brand that believes 'you're worth it', we needed to ensure that meant every one, not just the chosen few.

Strategic big idea

True Match helps everyone feel worth it with a foundation for every kind of face, for every shade, every age and every gender in the UK.

Bringing the big idea to life: 23 shades, 23 stories

To create the most inclusive and talked about campaign the foundation category had ever seen, we partnered with 23 influencers to represent not just every shade, but all those who felt excluded by this category, whatever their ethnicity, gender, ability or social status.

In 2018 where 'diversity' and 'inclusivity' are the most zeitgeisty buzzwords in the industry, this pioneering and inclusive campaign might seem old hat; but in early 2016, in a whitewashed foundation category, this was revolutionary.

Our campaign line was: 23 shades, 23 stories.

With our diverse cast of influencers, we captured 23 powerful stories of frustration and joy: from TV presenter AJ Odudu, who expressed her frustration that growing up there was no make-up for her, to male beauty blogger Gary who felt he would never be accepted for his love of make-up, as well as quadriplegic blogger Jordan who, like everyone else, needs a perfect base for her entire look (Figure 9).

Figure 9: 23 Shades

The idea of putting diverse influencers and their 23 stories at the heart of our campaign was a break-through not just for L'Oréal Paris but for the beauty category, which usually relied on a small number of flawless white models and celebrities such as Eva Longoria and Blake Lively, to represent the majority.

It was not only the right thing to do, but the smart thing to do for a number of reasons.

Embracing 23 influencers was a winning tactic

1. *A breakthrough way to achieve mass reach:* With 23 influencers, we were using what is normally only seen an engagement channel as an effective way to reach a combined following of 19 million.
2. *Driving 'Brand I feel close to':* Unlike distant models, influencers are seen as human and approachable. This was essential to achieve our 'brand for me' communications objective, along with:

3. *Driving 'Brand that caters to all women':* We partnered with 23 influencers, one to represent each shade and all those who felt excluded, something the competition couldn't do because no brand has as big a range as True Match
4. *Driving 'Products that suit consumers' need perfectly':* our spectrum of influencers, each trusted by their loyal followers could show that whoever you are and whatever your skin tone, True Match can match it perfectly.

Over 18 hours of open, honest and poignant interviews we captured 23 stories. We heard heartfelt accounts of the pain of feeling marginalised, the importance of foundation and its intrinsic link to identity, no matter what the ethnicity, ability, gender, or status. A far cry from the cold, functional, celebrity endorsed communications the category was used to.

Bringing the campaign to life and real life to the campaign

Example 1: AJ Odudu, shade 10C

She is a TV presenter, DJ and blogger. Growing up she didn't actually wear any make-up because the two stores near her that sold make-up never sold it in her shade (Figure 10).

> *'It's really frustrating when you really want to buy make up and play with it, the same as my friends at school, but you just can't.'*

Figure 10: AJ Odudu

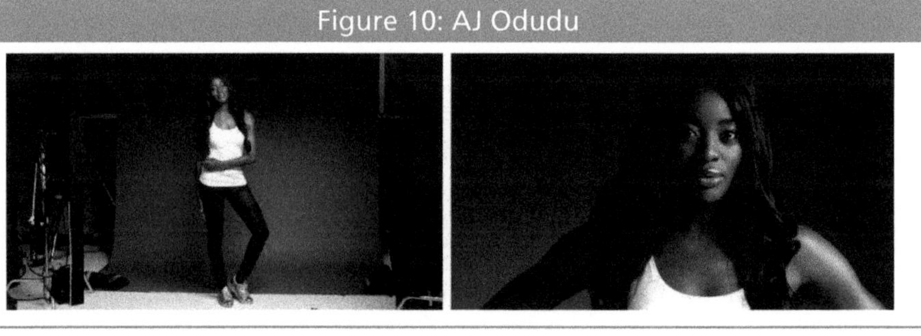

Example 2: Jane, shade 4N: owner of BritishBeautyBlogger.com

She thinks we've spent a long time accepting one vision of beauty and yet beauty is not one thing, it has many faces (Figure 11).

> *'Our country is hugely culturally diverse and of course we need to have foundations in every single skin tone that we possibly can.'*

Figure 11: Jane

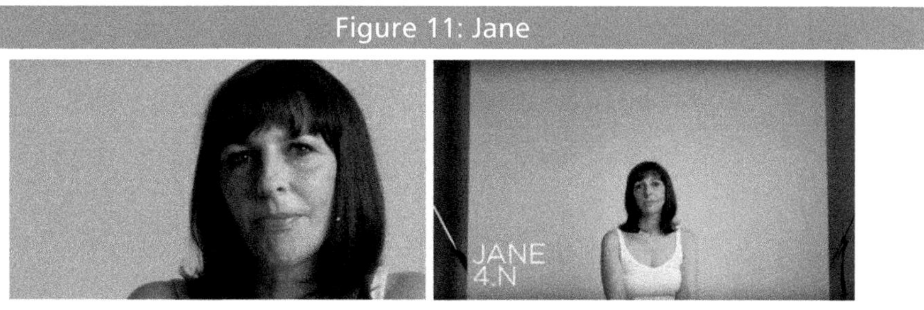

Example 3: Gary, shade 9C: beauty blogger and make-up artist

Gary's story is about feeling different and excluded for wearing make-up. He used to carry make-up wipes around with him [to remove it at any time] because he was scared of people judging him (Figure 12).

'When you have the right base it's just like a whole puzzle coming together.'

Figure 12: Gary

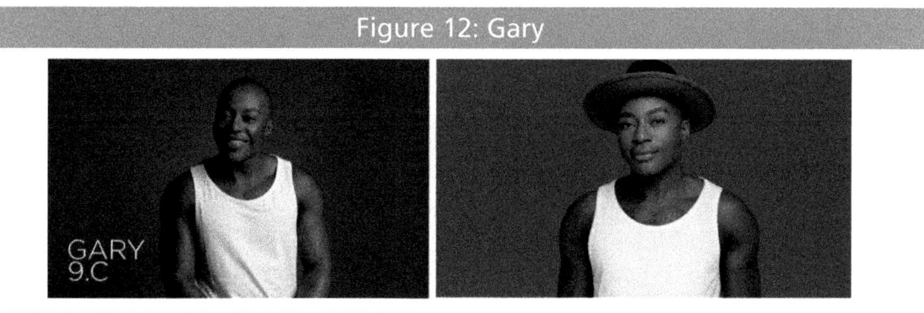

Now we had the content, next we needed the campaign.

Communications strategy: Taking the beauty world by storm

Figure 13: Communications roll out

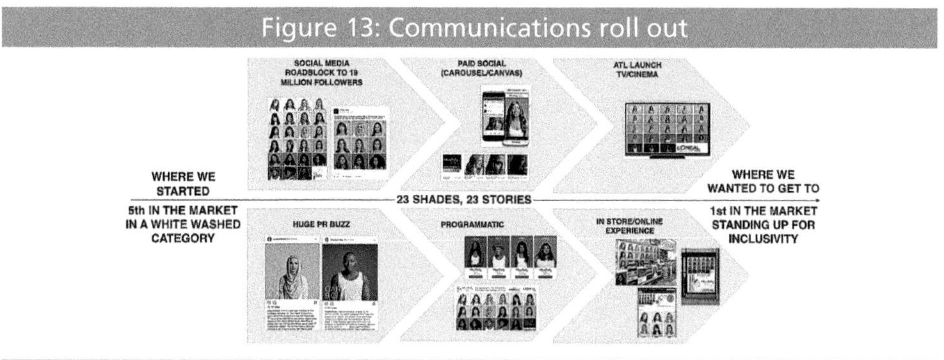

The campaign roll-out took the beauty world by storm (Figure 13), whilst we delivered against two key tasks:

1. Ensure everyone feels included

To show that we had a shade for every face, we wanted the campaign to be seen by as many people as possible.

We launched with a *social media roadblock* with each of our influencers posting their story simultaneously to all their *19 million followers*, across all their social platforms. A clever way to use what is normally only seen an engagement channel as an effective way to reach millions of consumers around the UK (Figure 14).

Figure 14: Influencer social post examples

We then released edits of the most emotive stories across all key channels to ensure mass reach: TV, cinema, YouTube, Instagram and Facebook with dynamic digital display, carousel and canvas formats.

Figure 15 shows an example carousel format and Figure 16 an immersive canvas format.

Figure 15: Carousel format example

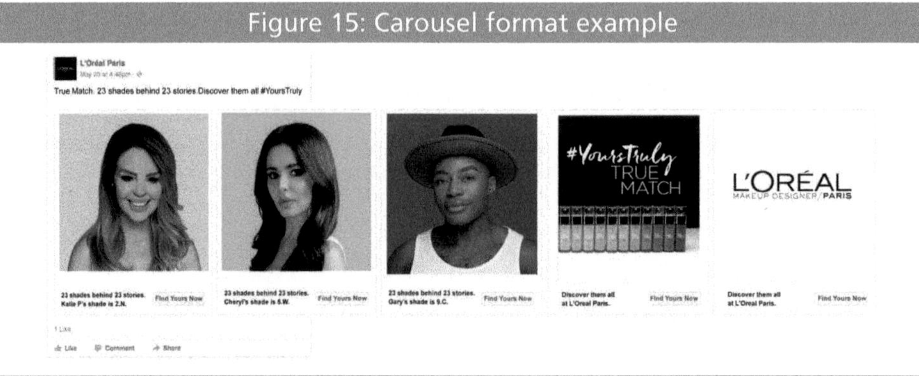

To ensure even greater coverage, we included the first man to star in a UK make-up campaign. A PR first that ensured the press took notice of True Match (Figure 17).

Figure 16: Canvas example – explore all the shades and click through to each of the individual influencer stories or click to purchase

Figure 17: PR around Gary's story

2. Recruit specific skin tones through precision targeting

As well as mass recruitment, our programmatic plan included targeting four segments (Fair Skin Tones, Switchers, Dark Skin Tones and True Match Fans). Dynamic, shade-appropriate creative drove consumers direct to store locations to find their True Match or to online e-commerce (Figures 18 and 19).

Figure 18: Dynamic, shade appropriate creative examples

Figure 19: In-store activation

To bring everything together, the True Match campaign marked a historic brand shift to a more inclusive statement

To highlight the brand's commitment to the beauty of all, not just the few, we updated the iconic L'Oréal Paris end line: from 'Because you're worth it' to 'Because we are all worth it.' A move which has since been rolled out across all UK categories (Figure 20).

Figure 20: L'Oréal Paris end line progression

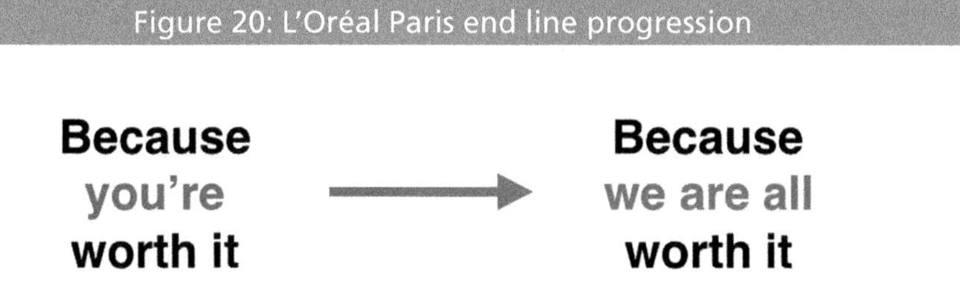

Results: From fifth to first in market share

In summary

Table 2: In summary

	Objective:	Result:	
Business:	Fifth to first with 7.0% value market share for 2016 17% sales increase (2016 v 15)	✓	2016: Not only 1st place but with a phenomenal 7.7% value market share 29% sales increase (2016 v 15) 2017: the success continued taking us to 9.7% value market share 26% sales increase (2017 v 16)
Marketing:	Recruit 165,000 new users	✓	2016 FY: Recruited 286,000 new users 2017 FY: Recruited 332,000 new users
Communication:	Shift KPI metrics for: • "Brand I feel close to" • "Brand that caters to all women" • "Makes products that meet consumers' needs perfectly"	✓	Shifted KPI metrics for: • "Brand I feel close to" from 7%-13% • "Brand that caters to all women" from 21%-42% • "Makes products that meet consumers' needs perfectly" from 18%-25%

In detail

Business: We surpassed all expectations. Our objective was to become the No.1 with 7.0% market share but we achieved 7.6% value market share, taking us from fifth to first place in 2016.[20] In 2017, our success continued with True Match achieving a 9.7% market share – pulling us even further away from the competition (Figure 21).

Figure 21: True Match and competitor market share

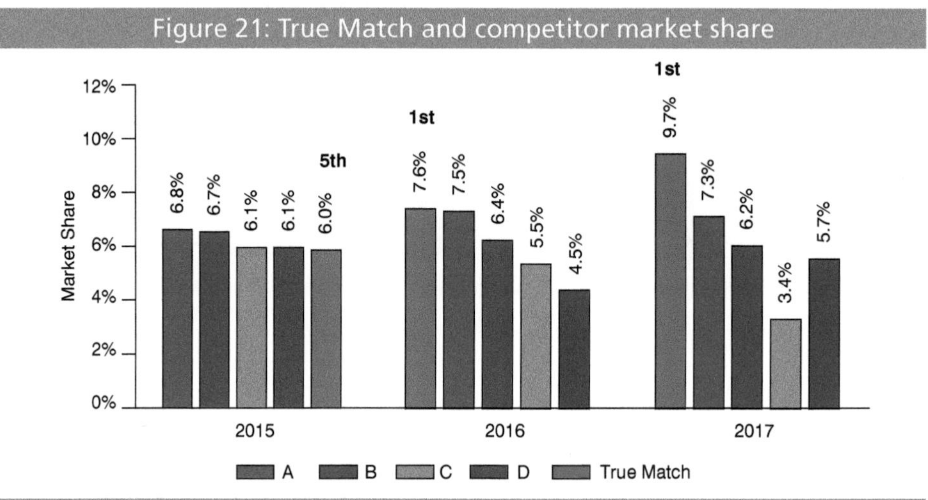

Source: Nielsen 2016

We set out to achieve a 17% value sales increase from 2015 to 2016, but actually achieved an incredible 29% increase, in a market that only increased 6%.[21]

True Match value sales grew over five times faster than the market in 2016

Figure 22: Foundation market value

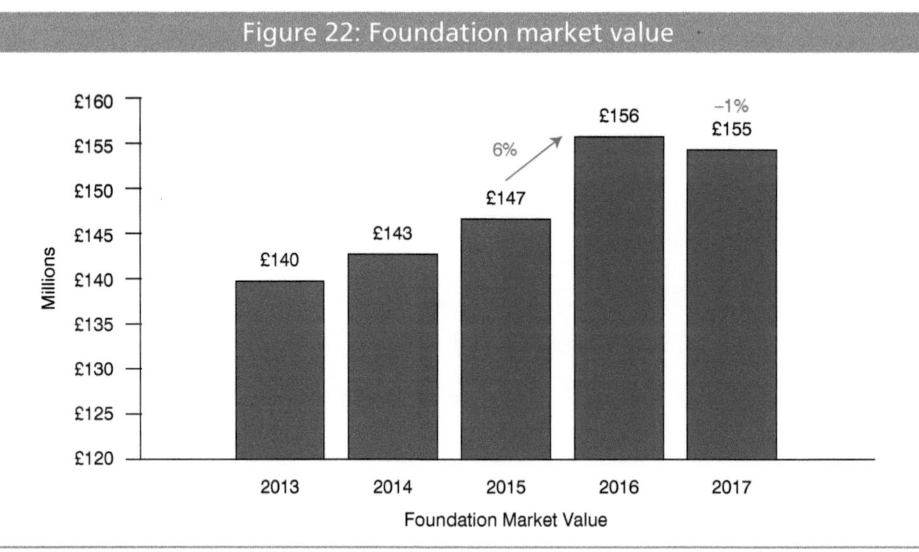

Source: Nielsen 2018

Figure 23: True Match value sales

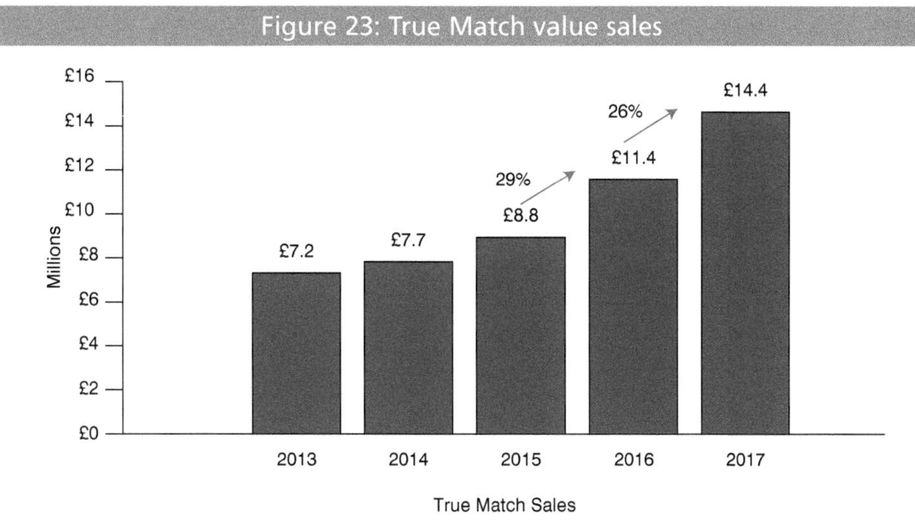

Source: Nielsen 2018

Marketing objective

For a 17% sales-uplift we needed to recruit approximately 165,000 incremental consumers. We smashed the objective, attracting 286,000 new users in 2016. Furthermore, in 2017 we recruited an additional 332,000 incremental consumers (Figure 24).

Figure 24: True Match users

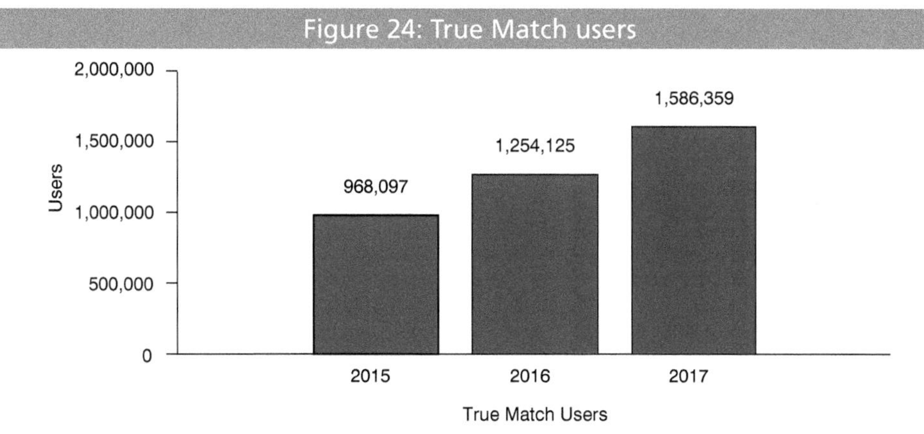

Source: Nielsen 2018

Communications objective

Establish True Match as the 'brand for me (whatever my skin tone)', specifically shifting three key drivers of brand equity: emotional proximity, differentiation and relevance.[22]

We shifted all brand metrics, doubling the score for 'brand I feel close to' and 'brand that caters to all women' and achieving 1.5 times growth on 'brand that meets consumers needs perfectly' (Figures 25–27).

Figure 25: Shift in 'brand I feel close to'

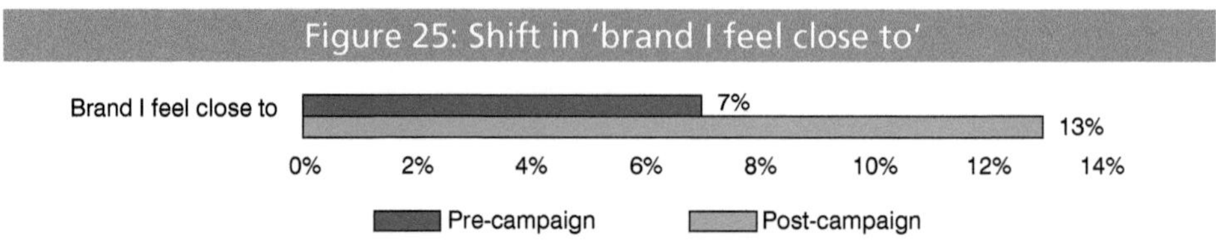

Source: IPSOS Brand Image Study post-campaign evaluation October 2016 (pre-campaign = L'Oréal Paris Masterbrand/ post-campaign = aware of True Match campaign)

Figure 26: Shift in 'brand that caters to all women'

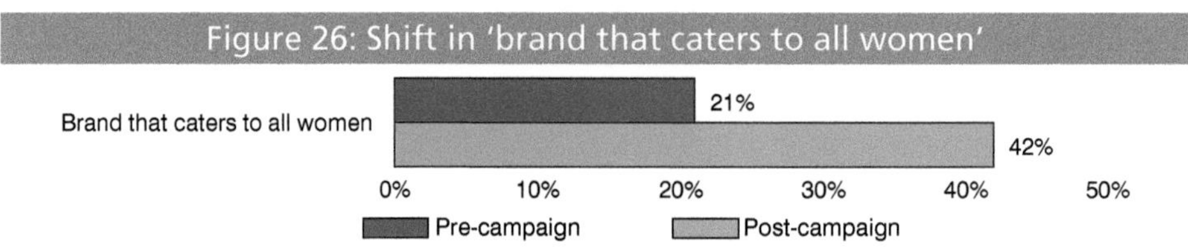

Source: IPSOS Brand Image Study post-campaign evaluation October 2016 (pre-campaign = L'Oréal Paris Masterbrand/ post-campaign = aware of True Match campaign)

Figure 27: Shift in 'brand that meets consumers needs perfectly'

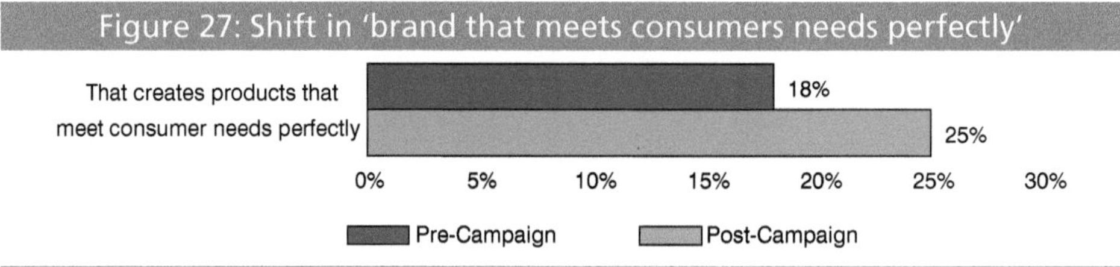

Source: IPSOS Brand Image Study post-campaign evaluation October 2016 (pre-campaign = L'Oréal Paris Masterbrand/ post-campaign = aware of True Match campaign)

Econometric results

In order to isolate the true impact of the campaign, L'Oréal commissioned an econometrics study with Nielsen in 2017, covering marketing activity from April 2014 until end of April 2017 for key retailers, Boots and Superdrug.[23]

At campaign launch as well as for subsequent bursts, True Match was on promotion at all key retailers with significant in store support.[24] In Boots and Superdrug, which account for 85% of tracked sales, there was a '3 for 2' promotion across all make-up products as well as an additional promotion for True Match. L'Oréal conducted store-level modelling at retailer level to disentangle the impact of this activity, as well as any changes in distribution, competitor media, promotional activity and seasonality.[25]

The econometric results demonstrated the power of the idea, with a short-term revenue ROI of £2.90 for every £1 spent and a longer-term ROI of £5.20.[26] This is the one of the highest ROIs for the beauty industry, comparing very favourably with previous IPA beauty winners (Figure 28).

Figure 28: Short-term ROI vs. previous IPA winners since 2010

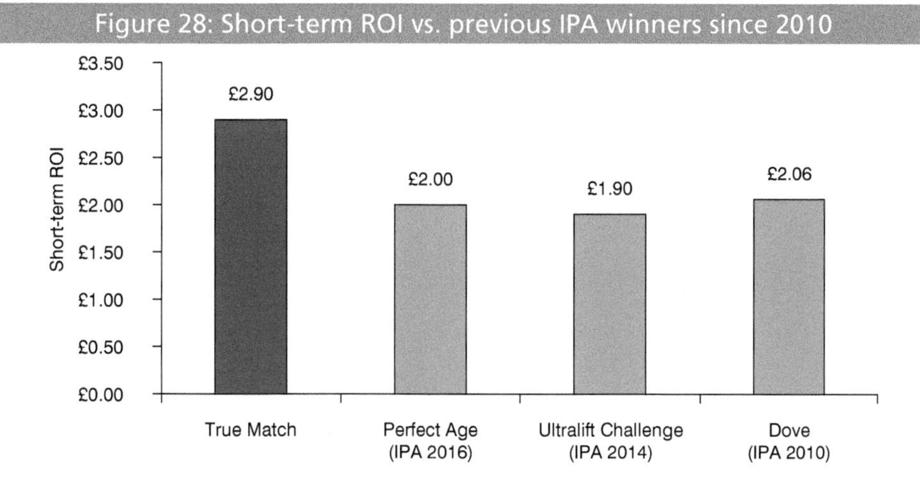

Source: IPA database

Short-term campaign effect on sales

The advertising made a significant contribution to sales, driving 19% of sales in 2016 which is phenomenal for the beauty industry (norm for FMCG is around 5%.)[27] During the campaign the contribution to sales was 22%, while for the January burst the contribution was 16% (still three times higher than the norm).

Long-term campaign effect on sales

The long-term multiplier was derived using data from the ad card switching info gathered from March 2017 to March 2018. The long-term multiplier methodology estimates the number of purchases each new user is expected to make in the three years after initial purchase, in this case it was calculated as 1.80.

With a short-term ROI of £2.90, the long-term ROI is expected to be £5.20.

PR and influencers coverage

During the campaign and for the following six months, the PR media equivalent was *c.* £120,000 vs. £56,000 for the previous six-month period. With twice the usual PR coverage, econometrics showed this had a significant impact on sales. During the campaign, the influencer engagement numbers[28] were four times higher than normal for 36 weeks during and after the campaign with 1,600,000 vs. 400,000 in the previous 36 weeks.

Google Brand Lift testing highlighted the strength of the campaign

L'Oréal conducted a Google Brand Lift/Copy Quality test during the first and the second bursts with very promising results. During the first burst we scored a 19% uplift in brand favourability[29] and 13.5% lift in purchase intent[30] – both of which

Figure 29: True Match foundation sales volume (modelled universe)

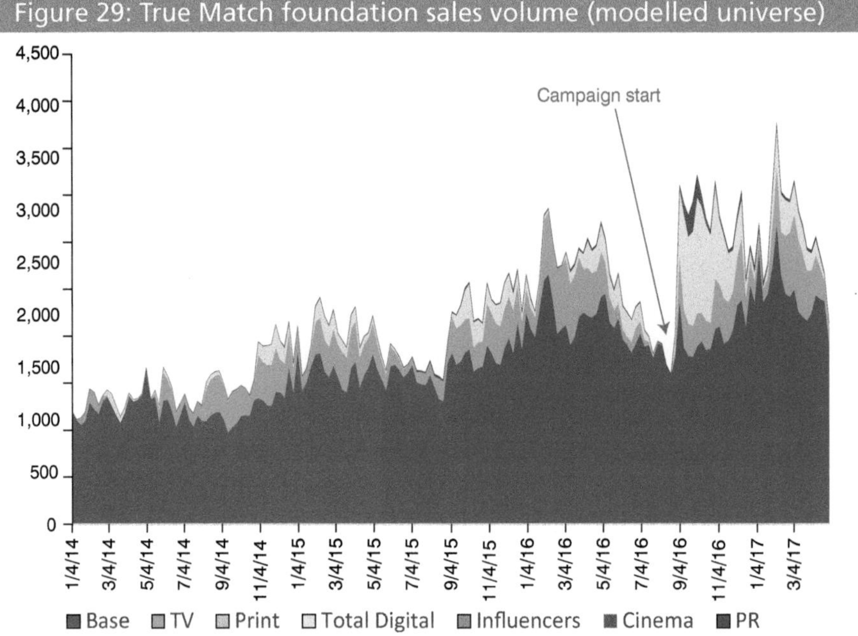

Source: Nielsen Marketing Analytics

are best in class according to Google benchmarks. The brand awareness test in the second burst delivered a phenomenal uplift of 34% which is also best in class.

Dispelling doubts

Didn't L'Oréal just buy their success with a big media spend?

No. From 2015 to 2016 the media spend increased slightly, but the amount was not significant enough to merit the level of growth accomplished. Due to the success of the campaign, L'Oréal Paris increased the spend in 2017 but the incremental budget was less than £300,000. Whilst we can't show media figures due to confidentiality, we can show the ROI which showed amazing returns across 2016 and 2017.

Wasn't the growth all down to the two new shades?

No, in fact the two new shades 10W and 10C only contributed to 3.6% of the increase[31] seen across the entire portfolio. This demonstrated that it was the campaign, not NPD, behind the growth. (Table 3)

Didn't L'Oréal just put it on constant promotion?

Promotional and in store activity during the campaign was aligned with previous years and was accounted for in the econometric modelling.[32]

Table 3: True Match volume sales per shade			
Shade	**Pre-campaign**	**During campaign**	**Difference**
Warm Beige 1.C	24,907	41,240	16,333
Rose Vanilla 2C	24,027	37,557	13,530
Nude Beige N4	19,082	25,003	5,921
Warm Ivory 3W	18,826	24,354	5,528
Nude Ivory 1N	15,726	20,881	5,155
Cappuccino 8N	5,537	8,460	2,923
Sand 5N	9,668	12,542	2,874
Deep Cool 9.C	1,456	4,121	2,665
Vanilla 2N	10,789	12,981	2,192
Honey 6N	4,147	5,791	1,644
Espresso 10.C *NEW*	759	2,297	1,538
Caramel 6.5N	6,080	7,491	1,411
Golden Amber 7W	3,769	5,129	1,360
Golden Ivory 1W	9,917	11,228	1,311
Deep Gold 10W *NEW*	1,206	1,991	785
Warm Sand 5.W	2,309	2,948	639
Rose Beige 3C	13,541	14,134	593
Toffee 8.W	4,159	4,543	384
Linen 1.5N	2,427	2,758	331
Rose Sand 5C	1,755	1,866	111
Rose Amber 7C	1,564	1,177	–387
Cream Beige 3N	12,507	12,005	–502
Linen Nat Gold 4W	7,723	6,153	–1,570

Didn't L'Oréal increase its distribution?

Distribution changes are accounted for in the econometric modelling (Table 4).

Table 4: L'Oréal True Match distribution changes			
	2015	**2016**	**2017**
L'Oréal True Match	21	25	28

Wasn't True Match's UK share increasing anyway?

Whilst True Match gained value share from 2013–2015, it was still stuck in fifth place. In 2016, True Match leapt to number 1 and its rate of increase in market share accelerated three times in 2017.

Figure 30: True Match value share increase

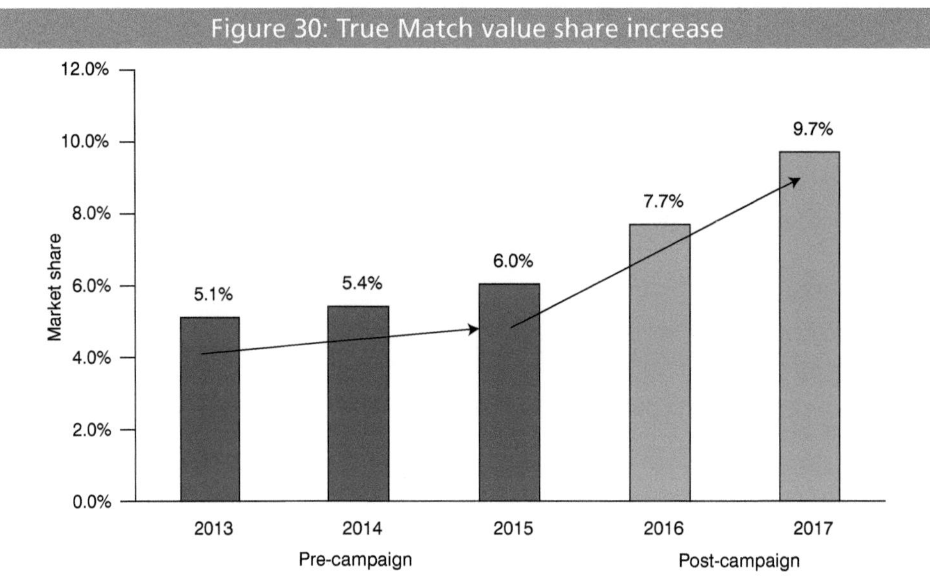

Seasonality?[33] *Competitors? Trends?*

All accounted for within econometric modelling.

Campaign halo

Across the portfolio

Econometric modelling showed the campaign not only delivered the highest ROI for True Match and had a significant impact on sales, but it also drove sales in other segments of the cosmetics category. In particular it had a significant impact on other L'Oréal Paris foundation franchises and face products as well as mascaras and other eye products.

Global rollout

After the success of True Match in the UK, the campaign was rolled across 15 other countries (Figures 31–33), with similarly impressive results. Sales in Ireland rose 16% and France rose 12%, whilst Australia achieved its highest share.

Figure 31: DPS Australia

Figure 32: DPS France

Figure 33: DPS USA

Competitors followed suit

The True Match campaign sparked a number of copycat campaigns, further highlighting that the old model of exclusivity was outdated (Figures 34–36).

Figure 34: Lancôme celebrated 40 shades of foundation, with 40 influencers (one for each shade), February 2017

Figure 35: Clinique Even Better Glow foundation, February 2017

Figure 36: Bare Minerals Bare Pro foundation, September 2017

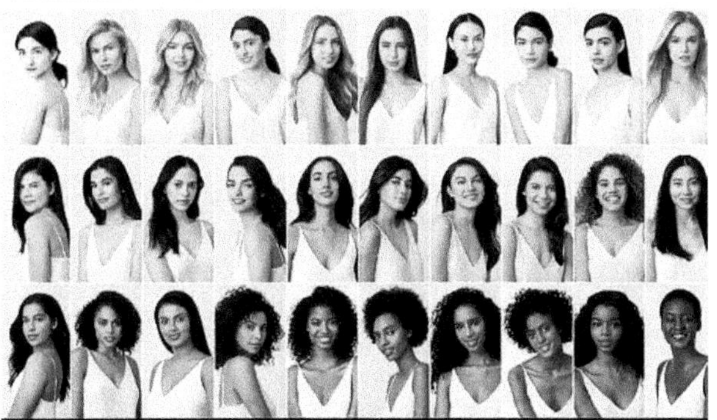

A new communications model for L'Oréal UK

After the success of True Match, L'Oréal Paris UK adopted an ongoing commitment to an inclusive influencer-led approach to communications in other categories, including flagship haircare brand Elvive, which saw double digit growth in 2018 (Figure 37).

Figure 37: L'Oréal Paris Elvive campaign

A new era for L'Oréal UK

L'Oréal Paris has always believed in the power of self-worth, but this hasn't always been delivered in a visible and meaningful way. However, the shift to 'All worth it' created the perfect opportunity for L'Oréal Paris to show that these were more than just words with its first CSR campaign with The Prince's Trust in 2017 (Figure 38).

Figure 38: L'Oréal Paris Prince's Trust campaign

PR to make us proud

As well as achieving our brand KPIs, we were particularly proud of all the positive PR, which also helped drive brand reappraisal.

Figure 39: L'Oréal Paris PR

Conclusion

L'Oréal Paris True Match was languishing in fifth place for the three years prior to our game-changing campaign, which saw the brand surpass all expectations when it reached first place in 2016 and then widened its lead in 2017. The brand recognized the pain of feeling excluded from the foundation category and was inspired to make everyone feel worth it, not just the chosen few. It was powerful in four ways:

1. *for the business,* which saw True Match climb from fifth to first in market share, with a short-term campaign ROI of £2.90 and a long-term ROI of £5.20;
2. *for consumers,* who now all felt 'worth it';
3. *for L'Oréal Paris UK,* who committed to being even more inclusive;
4. *and the make-up category,* which changed its communications forever.

Notes

1. Including mascaras and eye shadows.
2. Including lipsticks and liners.
3. Including foundation, powders and concealers.

4. These figures are approximate as they are from proprietary sensitive data.
5. These figures are approximate as they are from proprietary sensitive data.
6. Nielsen 2016.
7. Nielsen 2016.
8. In 2018 – but there has been no product renovation.
9. Due to confidentiality, brand names have been disguised (letters in line with Figure 3).
10. Mintel 2016.
11. L'Oréal CMI.
12. Independent Superdrug study found that the average price of foundation in the luxury market is £25 (compared to below £10 for mass).
13. Latest census https://www.ons.gov.uk/census/
14. Kantar panel data.
15. Three key drivers identified by L'Oréal's Consumer Product Division.
16. L'Oréal CMI.
17. https://jezebel.com/the-makeup-industrys-frustrating-cycle-of-struggle-and-1782880385
18. https://www.racked.com/2015/3/10/8176275/beauty-industry-women-of-color-makeup-Make-up
19. https://www.theguardian.com/lifeandstyle/2015/dec/06/body-image-healthy-fashion-models-young-people-rosie-nelson
20. Nielsen 2016.
21. Nielsen 2016.
22. Three key drivers identified by L'Oréal's Consumer Product Division.
23. Results became available October 2017.
24. Heavy promotions and off shelf investment, hotspots, and in store gondola ends.
25. This activity is all included within the 'base' of Figure 29.
26. Due to strict client confidentiality in a highly competitive market, and the use of named sales data, we are not permitted to reveal comprehensive profit figures.
27. Nielsen Norm 2015.
28. Tracker (Engagement is measured by views/shares/likes/comments).
29. Favourability is a measure of respondent overall opinion of the brand.
30. The plan in which a person intends to buy a particular good or service sometime in the near future.
31. L'Oréal CMI.
32. Promo mechanic and in store accounted for in econometric modelling.
33. Econometrics factored in seasonality by week and by month.

Suzuki

Suzuki Saturdays

By Rachel Courtney, Chris Herbert and Simon Harwood, the7stars
Credited companies: the7stars; ITV

Summary

Suzuki's share of the UK market languished at 1.3% at the end of 2015. Consumer insight, motor reviews and dealer feedback indicated there was an opportunity to emphasise the fun in driving Suzuki cars. To highlight enjoyment and grow consideration, Suzuki formed a content partnership with ITV's 'Saturday Night Takeaway', spanning talent, licensing, broadcast sponsorship, and content creation. Following the launch of #SuzukiSaturdays, brand consideration reached a record 44%, while increased share of market made Suzuki the fastest-growing UK car brand for two years running. This case estimates the approach paid back £207m in incremental revenue.

Editor's comment

The judges especially admired the way the solution took on the tough commercial context of residing in fourteenth place in a declining market. This challenge was met through an innovative modern approach to channel planning of sponsorship, which made it closer to a TV show, using intelligent analysis to understand when audience momentum and buzz meant content would have most impact.

Client comment

Tammy Charnley, General Manager, Marketing, Suzuki

Advertising in the automotive category had become stale. Moving away from the category conventions was a brave move for us, especially as a challenger. We recognised the need to build our brand and we took a long-term approach to this from the outset. It meant holding our nerve at times and not reacting to short-term conditions.

'Suzuki Saturdays' took an entirely new approach to content creation and distribution. We worked directly with the producers of 'Saturday Night Takeaway', using their transferable skills in production and talent management to create standout assets. From this, we've learnt to be more agile in the way we develop ideas and let them grow over time. The sense of fun we've worked hard to build isn't just a tone of voice, it has evolved over the years and is now ingrained in all that we do as a brand. It's reflected not only in our brand assets, but it has also changed the way we engage our dealer network and, in turn, the dialogue they have with customers on the shop floor.

Throughout the course of the campaign, we learnt a lot about what our audience liked and were responding well to. We used this to inform and adapt our media and creative approach, avoiding wear out. We also learnt a lot about ITV's creative and production process, and in turn, ITV were invited into our world. 'Suzuki Saturdays' was a direct output of shared appreciation and understanding of each other's craft.

We've learnt to take calculated risks and push boundaries, stretching ourselves and our agency partners. This resulted in award-winning communications that really helped Suzuki stand out in the category. Our communications punched well above their weight, made significant shifts in brand metrics but also sold record numbers of cars in the process.

Introduction

Suzuki operates in an extremely competitive UK market. At the end of 2015, their share of market lagged behind at 1.3%.[1] Suzuki were only going to get noticed if we did something which truly stood out. Stood out against the endless car ads featuring cars driving through hills, through cities. Stood out from the miles per gallon, safety and financing messages.

In early 2016 Suzuki needed to deliver sales of its new family SUV, the Vitara.

Years of consumer insight, motor reviews and dealer feedback led us to one singular insight – Suzuki cars are fun to drive. Being fun to drive pays off commercially with an incredible 70% test drive to conversion rate.

But truly being fun is difficult. You can't just sponsor fun, you have to make people laugh!

We partnered with the UK's leading commercial broadcaster, ITV, which gave us unprecedented access to the 'Saturday Night Takeaway' IP as well as Ant & Dec, forming a partnership that spanned talent, licensing, broadcast, and content creation.

This was the start of #SuzukiSaturdays. A car campaign which took a completely different approach to creative, content and media and sold out of cars in the process. It was entertaining, culturally relevant and spread like a TV show.

The campaign was responsible for delivering Suzuki record car sales for the past two years, making Suzuki the fastest growing car brand in the industry. The activity delivered an incremental £207m sales revenue and delivering a payback of £17.88 for every pound spent.

> *'Moving away from the automotive conventions was a brave move for us a brand, especially as a challenger. This sense of fun isn't just a tone of voice, its evolved over the years and is now ingrained in all that we do as a brand.'*
>
> Tammy Charnley, UK General Manager, Marketing

Lost among the pack

Suzuki Cars UK operates in an industry with 30+ other major brands each vying for attention. Of the top 30 brands, 23 have a market share of no more than 5%. It's a market with a lot of extremely closely matched brands.[2] To say it is a market which has become very competitive would be an understatement! At the end of 2015 Suzuki had a market share of 1.3%, putting the brand firmly among the also-rans.

Suzuki's spend was slightly below its share of market, at fourteenth position[3] versus competitor brands (Figure 1). Even if Suzuki did have more marketing budget available, experience showed that simply increasing media budget to shout louder or more often hasn't converted to a growth in market share which can offset increased spend.

Figure 1: Media spend for the automotive market full year 2015, showing Suzuki in 14th position

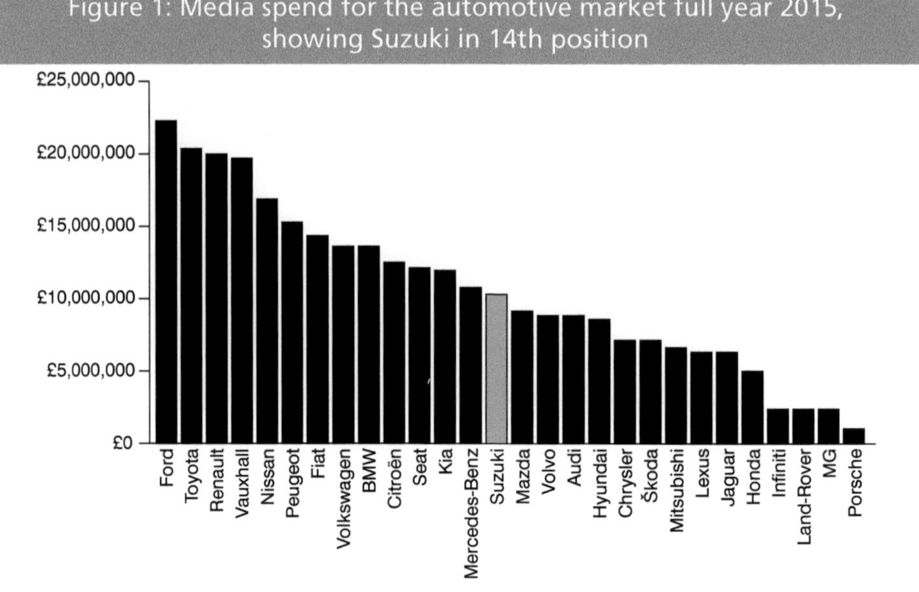

Brands which had been successful within the industry clearly stood out as being different.

Suzuki had long suffered the 'middle market' problem. Trusted European premium brands dominated at one end, and at the other, the traditional Japanese 'high-tech, low-cost' position, had been claimed by the Korean brands Hyundai and Kia.

Consecutive periods of declining growth had all but eroded Suzuki's marketing budgets and share of voice.

We had to do more with less, bring fame to the brand's car range and make the case for more investment.

Three objectives, one BHAG

As we headed into 2016, we had a clear overall business objective – sell more cars.

The 'big hairy audacious goal' was set at selling *37,000 cars* over the year. To reach it would have represented an all-time high for Suzuki car sales in the UK.

We were also set a specific goal of selling *9,500 Suzuki Vitaras*, an old classic 4×4 which had reinvented as a family SUV and relaunched in late 2015.

In addition to sales, our 2016 approach had to drive greater *awareness, consideration and positive opinion* of Suzuki as a brand. The focus being on setting Suzuki up for continued growth rather than trying to hit a record level of sales one year, only to see them slump the next. All brand metrics were to be measured in Suzuki's ongoing brand tracker carried out by The Nursery.

The Suzuki Vitara had been warmly received by motor journalists but again we faced the problem of an extraordinarily competitive market.

So we began by accepting the hard truth behind the brand.

Suzuki resonated with quirky people who didn't take themselves or their cars too seriously.

Owners are more likely to be 'the fun one in the group' who want something different to the status quo to be found in their neighbours' driveways (Figure 2).

Figure 2: Social media monitoring of Suzuki owners reveals their fun side

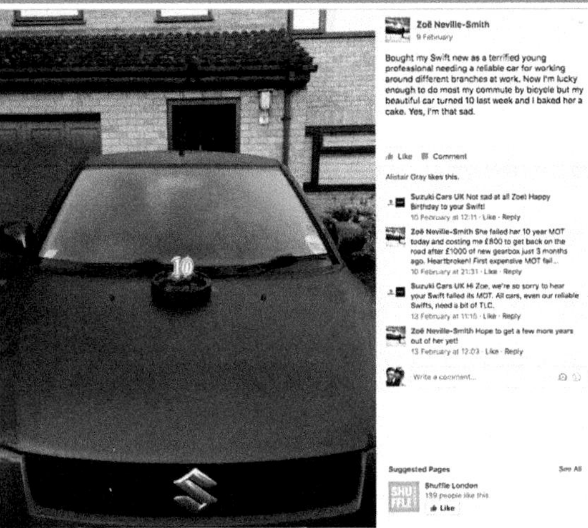

For them, 'why' they travelled, was even more important than 'how' they travelled. The purpose trumped the pleasure. This attitude to driving was most prevalent in the surprisingly neglected family car buyer segment of the market (Figure 3).[4]

So we committed everything to them.

Figure 3: Brand personality analysis by The Nursery with 'friendly', 'lively', 'reliable' and 'sociable' top-performing scores for Suzuki

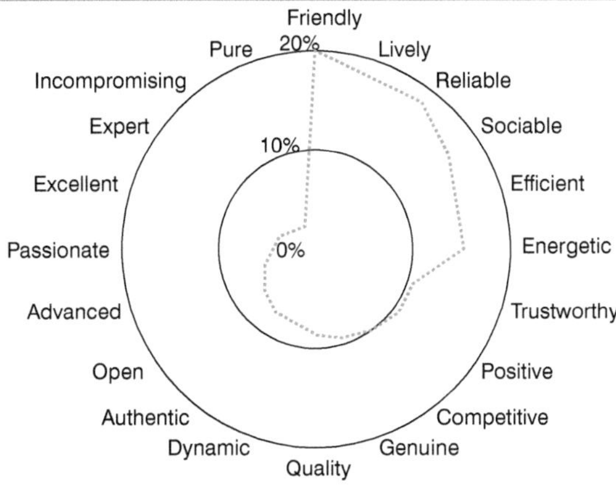

Source: The Nursery

Ironically, with less driving tech at the wheel, what also stood out to them was just how fun Suzuki's were to drive.

And being fun to drive translated to sales – the sale rate after a test drive was second to none at 70%.[5] Our communications had to show just how fun Suzukis were both as a brand, and as a car to drive.

While people are inundated with messages of efficiency, safety and technology; fun is rarely used when marketing affordable cars. We realised that we could distinguish Suzuki by giving it a fun tone of voice which is right for our cars, our audience and taps into British culture.

But truly being fun is difficult in real life.

You can't tell people you're fun, you have to make them laugh, and humour is a very subjective thing, it doesn't always travel well.

We had to be humorous, in touch with British culture and aimed squarely at families.

The solution

We knew that we had to do something radically different. We needed to create something that didn't look like any other car advertising.

So we created a campaign which didn't look like other media campaigns. It wasn't confined to the same formats, didn't rely on the same messages. It was entertaining, culturally relevant, and spread like a TV show.

Our strategy was to create fame and show the brands 'fun' personality by connecting with popular family entertainment that was truly our own and not a badging exercise of someone else's content.

ITV's iconic Saturday night entertainment programming was tonally perfect at this – delivering a style of humour which appealed to our family target. Yet we didn't want any entertainment sponsorship that could easily be misattributed to any other family-fitting car brand.

We wanted to find a way to engage with the crown jewels of ITV, which wasn't the shows but their talent – more specifically, Ant & Dec (Figure 4).

Figure 4: Ant & Dec

We wanted to use Suzuki as a vehicle to tell their jokes and deliver their famous pranks.

To give Suzuki a platform proven to get the country giggling, the7stars would strike a deal with ITV AdVentures to use IP from Ant & Dec's 'Saturday Night Takeaway' ('SNT'). This would give unprecedented access to Ant & Dec and allow the use of pranks and challenges seen in the show to be adapted and used as part of our campaign – a UK TV first.

Not only would this allow us to sponsor the duo in their biggest ITV show, it also allowed us to use their own production teams and writers to produce content for Suzuki featuring Ant and Dec being themselves, that could run across Suzuki's paid, owned and earned channels. By securing unparalleled access to ITV's leading talent we were able to produce regular features using IP taken from the show itself.

Capturing the fun

We captured hours of footage featuring Ant, Dec and two Suzuki Vitaras in a series of skits, challenges and pranks.

1. *Ant vs. Dec:* where they joined 'Little Ant & Dec' to take on head-to-head challenges, such as popping balloons in Vitaras (Figure 5).
2. *Chat Nav:* Ant & Dec secretly voiced a spoof live Sat Nav that talked with drivers about their clothing, driving skills and pedestrians (Figure 6).
3. *I'm A Celebrity, Get Out of my Ear:* where the boys hid in a backroom, voicing silly commands into earpieces of Suzuki sales people, getting them to sniff tyres, jump through driver windows and lie on bonnets (Figure 7).

Figure 5: Ant vs. Dec

Figure 6: Chat Nav

Figure 7: I'm a Celebrity, Get Out of my Ear

It was content which ticked all the boxes: genuinely entertaining to watch, laugh-out-loud funny and featuring our product in a way which added to the story rather than shoe-horned in. But none of that would matter if we stuck it all in traditional advertising formats, people could still ignore it.

So rather than plan a traditional media campaign, we took guidance from content producers, looking at how TV series are distributed.

#SuzukiSaturdays was born

We produced 10 short films for TV, each to be aired only once. These spots focused on Ant & Dec's pranks and worked as short sketches where the Vitara was always part of the fun (Figure 8).

Figure 8: Suzuki Saturdays film

Figure 9: Sponsorship bumpers for Suzuki Saturdays

Two of these spots were teased each week on Suzuki's Twitter and Facebook channels, before being aired in full on ITV each Saturday. Sitting as mini episodes of a show within key primetime family programming. Once aired each short film was placed on Suzuki's YouTube channel for the catch-up viewers. A paid for YouTube strategy made the content easy to find.

On 20 February 2016, series 13 of 'Saturday Night Takeaway' launched, featuring Suzuki sponsorship bumpers which extended the fun of the show into the ad break (Figure 9).

To take advantage of the social chatter in the afternoon prior to each episode of the 'Saturday Night Takeaway', we released a longer film from our own seven-part exclusive online series – 'Suzuki's Saturday Afternoon Takeaway' – through Suzuki's YouTube and Facebook channels (Figures 10 and 11).

Figure 10: Use of 'SNT' IP in Suzuki's website

Figure 11: Use of 'SNT' IP in Suzuki's social channels – Twitter

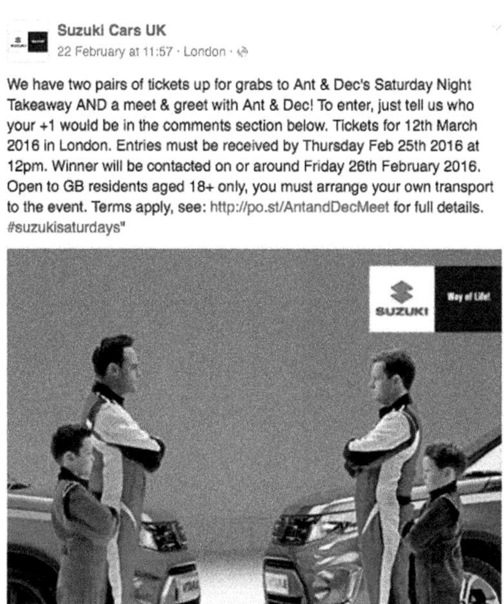

This extensive sponsorship and licensing deal also meant that the fun could live off screen too, so #SuzukiSaturdays was taken around the country in a nationwide roadshow. Dealers jumped at the opportunity to embrace the Ant & Dec antics on the shop floor with many making localised #SuzukiSaturdays events (Figure 12).

Figure 12: Use of 'SNT' IP in Suzuki's roadshow events

We knew that this partnership had to build Suzuki's credibility as a fun brand over time, so the partnership was brokered over two years. This demonstrated real commitment from both the brand and the talent, maximising the authenticity of the endorsement.

The plan 2016

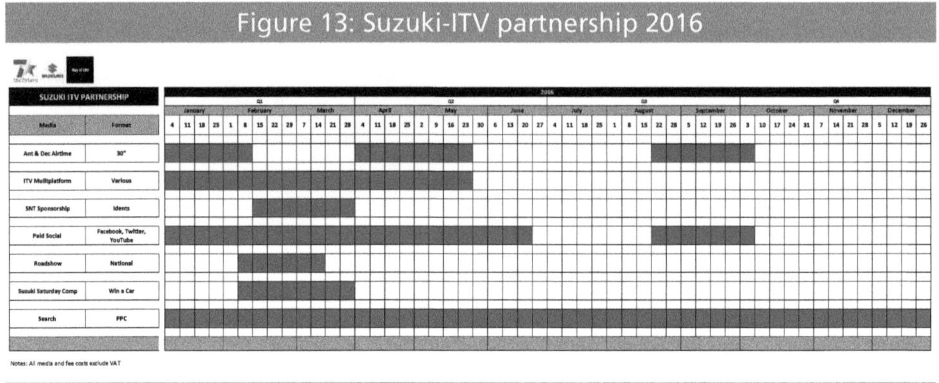

Figure 13: Suzuki-ITV partnership 2016

Building on the fun

In 2017 we continued to deliver hilarious content broadcast live as an integral part of ITV's Saturday night entertainment and distributed across social channels (Figure 14).

We further developed our approach by bringing in many shorter pieces of content which had performed particularly well at launch.

These meme-style pieces of social content were used on Saturdays during the build-up to and throughout the show being on air.

We involved the Suzuki dealer network too, inviting them to audition and take roles in the latest series of ad spots.

We kept the campaign close to the show by constructing these features around a series of initiation tests for the newest 'Saturday Night Takeaway' presenter – Scarlett Moffatt (Figure 15).

We knew from social listening that excitement for 'Saturday Night Takeaway' started to build from 2:00 pm each Saturday afternoon so we started to seed our content out from this point.

With access to pre-production meetings, bespoke creative was planned in advance and promoted online each Saturday evening at relevant moments of that week's show.

Figure 14

Figure 15: Scarlett Moffat

The plan 2017

Figure 16: Suzuki–ITV partnership 2017

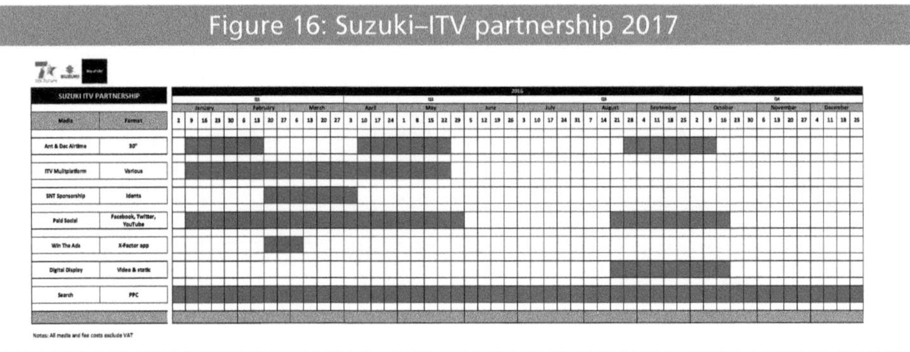

Results

Our results prove that when done right, content can drive conversion, even for high-ticket items such as a new car.

Beyond the BHAG

Remember, we were set three objectives for 2016.

The 'big hairy audacious goal' was set at *selling 37,000 cars* over the year – an all-time high for Suzuki car sales in the UK.

Suzuki posted *record UK car sales* for the year 2016, selling *38,190 units.*[6] That is 3,700 more than in 2015 and 1,890 ahead of the 'wildest dreams' target set for 2016. In fact, car sales exceeded forecasts to the extent that Suzuki literally ran out of cars. There was a three-month waiting list for a Vitara by the end of Q1 2016.

Suzuki car sales overall were up 14% versus total automotive market growth of 4% for the same period.

But it was in 2017, the second year of the partnership, that the long-term commitment really started to reap rewards.

While the rest of the market slumped in 2017, hit by poor consumer confidence and flagging new car sales, the brand has continued to post record sales numbers.

Suzuki sales grew by a further 6% whilst the car market overall was down a further 5.7% in 2017 (Figure 17).

Figure 17: Rolling 12 months registration volume showing Suzuki outperforming the car market

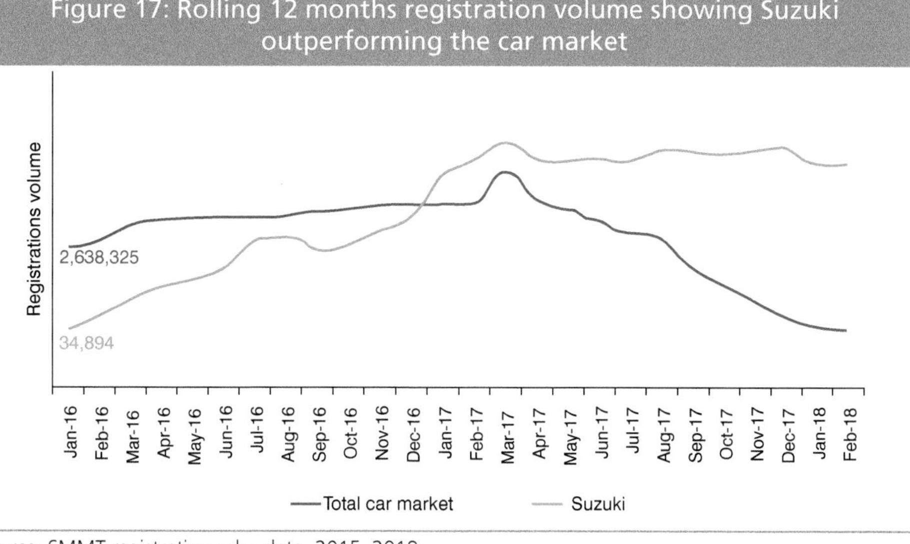

Source: SMMT registration sales data, 2015–2018

The increase in sales volume drove value for the Suzuki brand. Total Suzuki market share increased consistently from January 2016 when the campaign started, rising from 1.3% to 1.6% over the campaign period (Figure 18).[7]

Figure 18: Rolling 12 months Suzuki market share by month

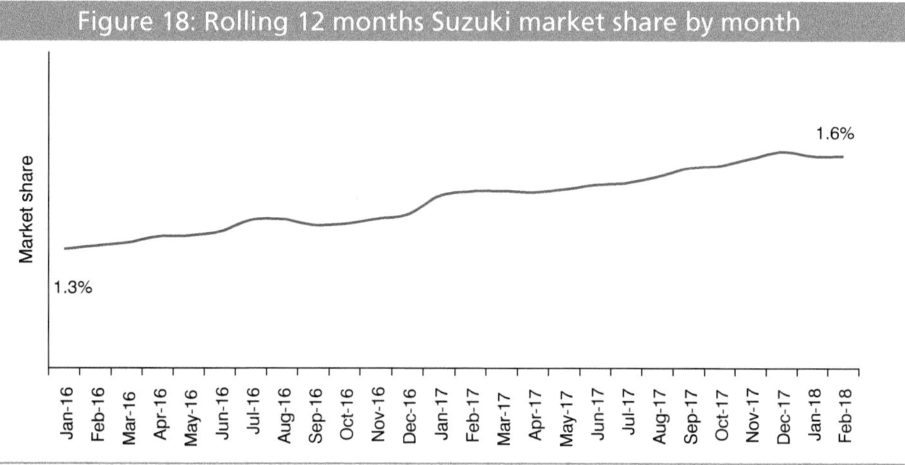

Source: SMMT registration sales data, 2015–2018

V for Vitara

We were also set a specific goal of selling *9,500 Suzuki Vitaras.*

Across 2016, the Suzuki Vitara sold *11,500 units.* That's more than 20% ahead of the annual volume target for this model (2016 sales results).

The sales rate for the Vitara (the model featured in the campaign) rose 38% between Q4 2015 and Q1 2016, selling just shy of 3,500 units in Q1.

The rolling sales data demonstrates that since 2016 when the campaign launched, sales of the Vitara outperformed the total crossover market and like-for-like crossover models.

Vitara's share of the SUV and Crossover segment rose by 26% over the campaign period (Figure 19).

Figure 19: Rolling 12 months registration volume showing Vitara outperforming the crossover segment and like-for-like models

Registrations volume
373,190
6,600
Jan-16 Feb-16 Mar-16 Apr-16 May-16 Jun-16 Jul-16 Aug-16 Sep-16 Oct-16 Nov-16 Dec-16 Jan-17 Feb-17 Mar-17 Apr-17 May-17 Jun-17 Jul-17 Aug-17 Sep-17 Oct-17 Nov-17 Dec-17 Jan-18 Feb-18
Total crossover market
Crossover market value like for like
Vitara

Source: SMMT registration sales data, 2015–2018

Sales revenue of the Vitara increased over the same period, despite like-for-like models within the crossover segment seeing a *decline*. This demonstrates that the uplift was not driven by Vitara taking its 'fair share' of an overall increase in segment revenue.

In a shrinking market, the Vitara stood out as the star performer (Figure 20).

Figure 20: Rolling 12 months retail sales volume showing Vitara value outperforming the crossover segment and like-for-like models

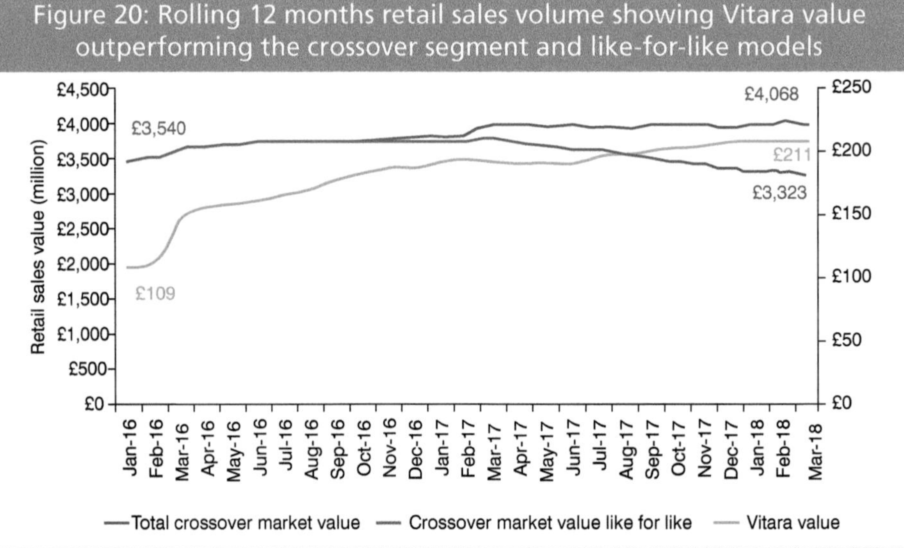

Softer metrics rising in line with sales

The third objective was to increase *awareness, consideration and positive opinion* of Suzuki as a brand.

Brand consideration reached 44% during the campaign,[8] the highest it's ever been. Positive opinion of Suzuki rose from 9% to 14% in only three months (Figure 21).

Figure 21: Overall opinion of Suzuki

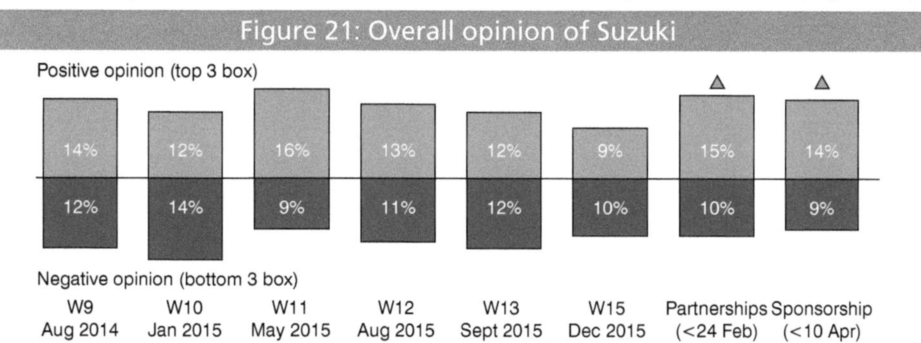

Source: The Nursery 'What is your overall opinion of the brands below?'. Base: all market aware and shown brand, Suzuki ratings (815, 398, 405, 797, 397, 1193, 1413). ▲ = significant differnce at 95% CI vs. December 2015.

YouTube were quick to spot how well the content was performing on their platform and quickly implemented a brand uplift study to track the effectiveness of the Ant & Dec creative on their channel.

Across multiple metrics, Suzuki have achieved best in class results – summarised below (Figure 22).

- *Week 1 Brand Lift Survey*: Best in class results for ad recall (31.7%) and consideration (16.4%).[9]
- *Week 2 Brand Lift Survey*: Best in class results in brand favourability for viewers of the ad (29%).
- *Week 3 Brand Lift Survey*: Best in class results in purchase intent for viewers of the ad (45.2%).

Figure 22: Brand ad recall and consideration lift measured by YouTube Brand Lift Survey

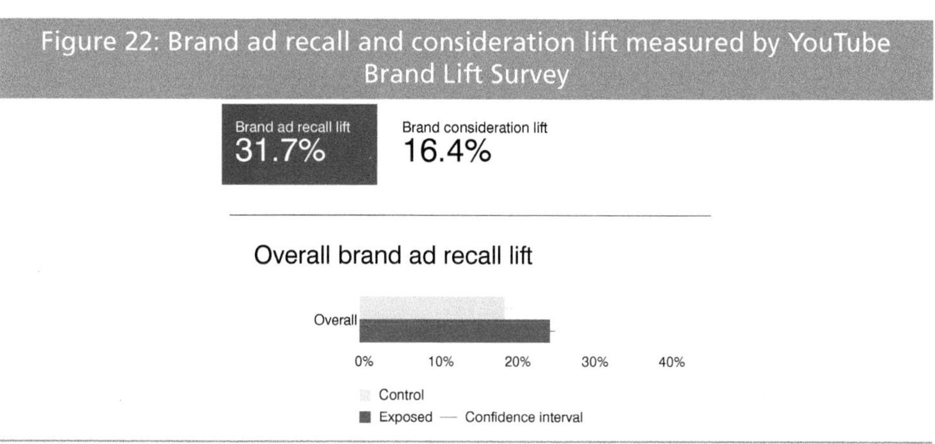

We exceeded our three objectives but what would have happened to sales without the partnership activity?

We need to be able to rule out other factors such as seasonality, market share effects, improvements to website, dealership experience and shifts in total market demand.

We did this by modelling the relationship between the year-on-year difference in media spend verses the year-on-year difference in registrations, ruling out market fluctuations.

Comparing the pre-partnership period and extrapolating this relationship we were able to estimate the total registrations by month during the partnership period. Figure 23 demonstrates the expected new registrations in absence of the partnership activity.

The partnership drove an incremental 13,795 registrations with a value of £206,905,471. This equates to an ROI figure of £17.88.[10]

Figure 23: Modelling the incremental new registrations for Suzuki verses expected

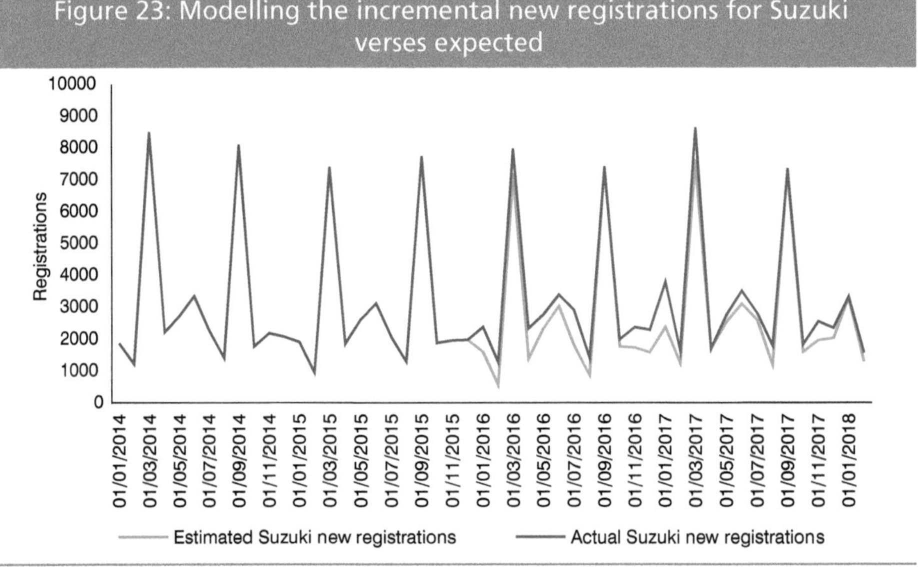

We were also able to model the effect on brochure requests and test drive requests. The activity drove an additional 7,951 brochure requests, an uplift of 21.95% (Figure 24).[11]

Figure 24: Modelling incremental brochure requests for Suzuki verses expected

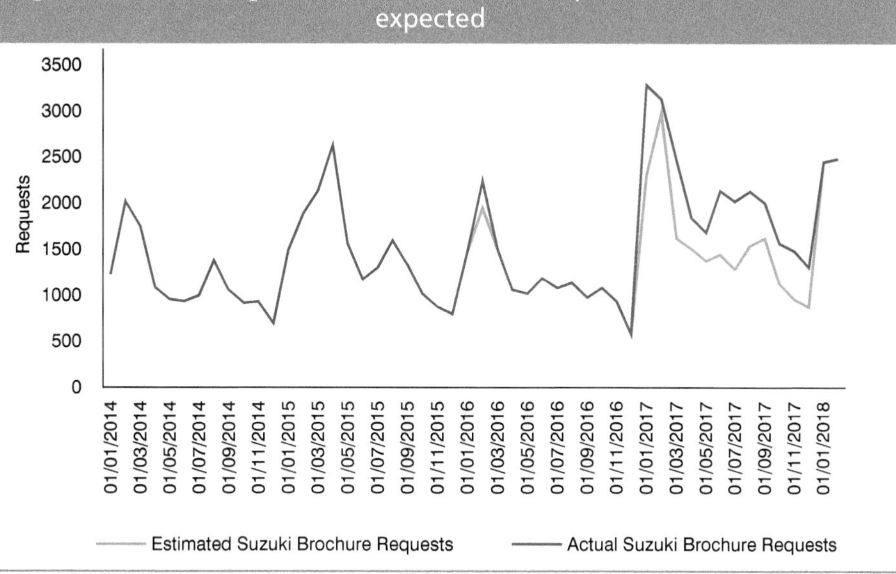

Sources: SMMT new registration data, Suzuki actual sales data, Google Analytics

Likewise, for online test drive requests, the activity drove an additional 497 requests which is an uplift of 12.25%. Note that most test drive requests are booked by phone or in-dealerships so the majority of test drives are offline requests (Figure 25).

Figure 25: Modelling incremental test drive requests for Suzuki verses expected

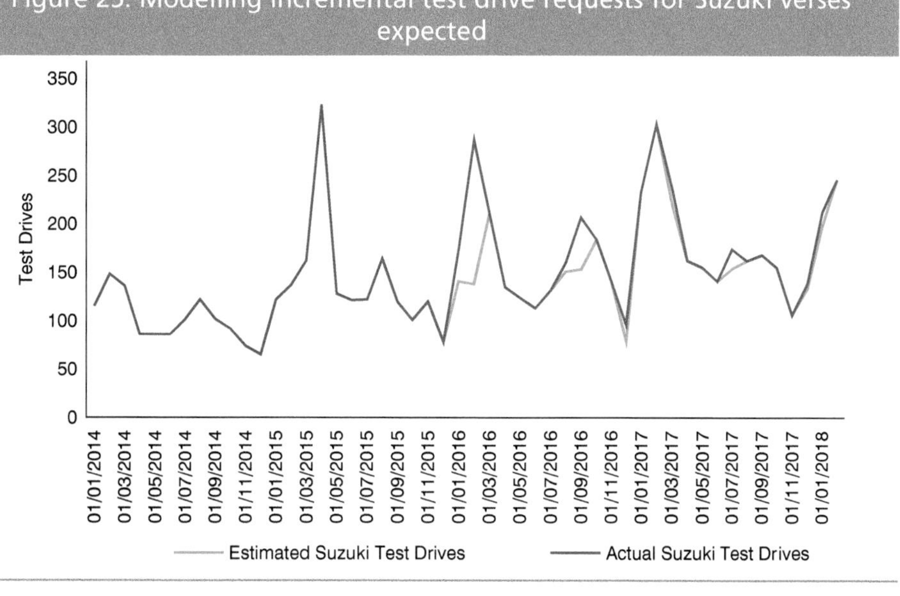

Additional manifold effects

The visibility of the campaign also drove some manifold effects beyond the three key objectives set at the start of 2016.

Over the first three weeks – user searches for 'Suzuki Vitara' increased by up to 7,656% for viewers exposed to the ad.[12]

We also saw user searches for 'Ant & Dec Suzuki' increase by 3,248% during the same period.

The partnership activity helped to drive increased morale and motivation amongst the dealer network. Giving the Suzuki commercial team new incentives to encourage support from the dealers. It also gave the marketing team the opportunity to engage the dealer network by giving them the opportunity to star in the creative.

In taking the partnership into dealerships we had re-energised a key consumer touchpoint, critical to converting test drives into sales. Suzuki were voted joint second by National Franchised Dealer Association (NFDA), keeping company with Mercedes and Lexus – the number one non-premium brand in the survey.

Conclusion and learnings

#SuzukiSaturdays is a campaign that took an entirely new approach to sponsorship. We delivered fun, fame and fortune for the brand by moving beyond bumpers and idents. The inclusion of licensing and content creation as well as an exclusive talent deal with Ant & Dec helped bring this car brand new fame and sell out of cars in the process.

We learned that it is possible to use a partnership to not only lead effective change in brand metrics but to directly sell high volumes of an incredibly considered purchase.

Suzuki is now the fastest-growing automotive brand in a context of a declining market.

Entertainer, not advertiser

This partnership enabled us to take a series of pranks and challenges adapted from regular features and IP from 'SNT' and inject it into branded content. Suzuki gained unprecedented access to behind-the-scenes production, rehearsals and filming of live 'Saturday Night Takeaway' episodes. Suzuki's content is produced with this insider view to ensure its relevant and reactive to the live show format, becoming a natural extension of the show itself.

Tailor content to the format

Our content and distribution strategy meant that the assets were carefully shot and tailored to different placements, playing to the strengths of each channel. Short-form versions were teased out on Twitter in advance and extended edits were released on Suzuki's Facebook and YouTube channel post transmission.

Long-term commitment pays off

With so many moving parts, this significant partnership was brokered over a minimum of two years. It was important to allow real commitment from both the brand and the talent, maximising the authenticity of the endorsement.

In that time, we learnt a lot about what our audience liked and were responding well to. We also learnt a lot about ITV's creative and production process, and in turn, ITV were invited into Suzuki's world. Suzuki Saturdays was a direct output of shared appreciation and understanding of each other's craft.

> *'This campaign was very different to our usual, and it was a huge decision to go with it but I'm very glad we did. The return we've had is more than we would ever have hoped for. The partnership has been a great example of how a national advertising campaign can drive through the line engagement. What's great to see is that we've made engaging and entertaining content that our audience have really engaged with, and we're thrilled this is connecting customers with the brand in a fun and memorable way.'*
>
> Dale Wyatt, Director, Suzuki Automotive Division

Notes

1. SMMT registration sales data 2015.
2. SMMT registration sales data 2015.
3. Addynamix media spend January–December 2015.
4. The Nursery, attitudinal research – Suzuki vs. the market, 2015.
5. Suzuki sales/test drives average conversion rate 2014–2015.
6. SMMT registration sales data 2016.
7. SMMT registration sales data 2015–2018.
8. The Nursery, brand tracking, 2016.
9. YouTube, Brand Lift Survey: ad recall consideration, brand favourability, purchase intent.
10. Sources: SMMT new registration data, Suzuki actual sales data.
11. Sources: SMMT new registration data, Suzuki actual sales data, Google Analytics.
12. Google Analytics, 2016.

GOLD AWARD

The AA

From spark-plugs to singalongs

By Tom Sussman, adam&eveDDB
Contributing authors: Nick Hirst and Les Binet, adam&eveDDB; Sara Donoghugh, Pearl Metrics; Simon Bielby, Carat
Credited companies: adam&eveDDB; Carat; Agenda21; Data2Decisions; Old Street Data Science; Oliver; Splendid; The Automotive Association; YouGov

Summary

Like many brands, the AA had been focusing on efficient delivery of short-term results via direct, targeted comms. This seemed to be working – profit was growing. But a new team looked beyond short-term results and discovered a worrying picture of market share and membership decline, driven by increased price sensitivity and falling salience. So the AA overhauled its marketing and reinvested in brand communications. The resulting campaigns rebuilt salience and image, increasing both acquisition and retention. The strengthened brand enabled the group to raise prices – driving stable revenue growth and delivering a profit ROMI of £2.23 for every £1 invested.

Editor's comment

The judges especially appreciated the shift from a declining business focusing on short-term metrics, response activities and buying new sales, moving into a mass emotional approach to rebuild brand equity and sales. This paper acts as a great proof of the value of brand building in a membership business.

Client comment

Cheryl Calverley, Marketing Director, The AA

The transformation journey for the AA has been tackled on many fronts, but by far the most commercially significant has been the transformation in brand and communications strategy. There were three big learnings from this journey I'd call out.

1. Attitudes, values, needs and desires drive people's relationships with brands, and thus their propensity to buy. Talking to their sense of self and identity is highly commercially effective, even in incredibly rational 'nuts and bolts' categories such as breakdown cover.
2. Emotional advertising is highly data-driven. It's only with deep and robust, rational data and analytics that a business can have the confidence to leap into an emotional communications strategy.
3. Media mix is your body language. Delivering an emotional campaign effectively relies on big, emotive channels, on a one-to-many basis. Rational message matrices are seductive in their complexity – we all like to think we're the cleverest marketer in the room, but the clever marketer says one thing, beautifully, to as many people as possible.

The campaign has given us, as a business, the confidence to believe in the effectiveness of our brand, and more importantly our new strategy, with a focus on our new target audience of 'freedom seekers'.

Introduction

In recent years, most of us have been convinced of the effectiveness of mass-reach, emotional brand-building communications (Figure 1).

Figure 1: The growing literature on the power of emotion, scale and long-term thinking in brand building

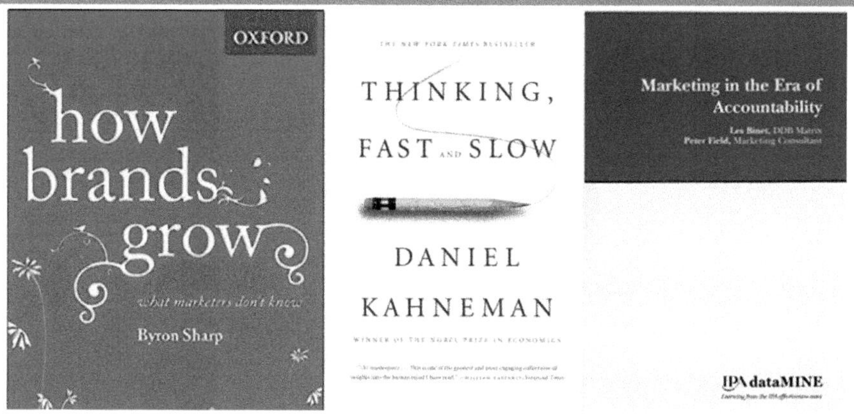

Many of us, however, may have concluded that, whilst this all sounds great in theory, it just isn't right for us in practice.

Because, away from the theory, we face real-world pressures: from our competition, from our KPIs, from our bosses, and from our bosses' bosses, the shareholders.

And one pressure dominates above all others: the imperative to deliver short-term results.

Faced with this pressure, 'brand building' can start to feel like an indulgence.

By 2014, the AA had adopted this attitude for over a decade.

In this paper, we show how this apparently sensible short-term approach allowed the AA to slip unwittingly into a decade-long commercial decline.

We also show how these underlying problems were masked by the brand's impressive short-term successes, and how it was only after looking beyond these short-term metrics that the truth began to emerge.

Finally, we'll show how a complete marketing overhaul, and in particular a return to emotional brand-building communications, reversed these fortunes and delivered the AA back into growth.

Background

When the AA and adam&eveDDB first got together in 2014, life looked great

The AA had just been crowned the most trusted brand in the UK, cementing its place as a genuine national treasure (Figure 2).

Figure 2: The AA named one of Britain's most trusted brands

UNITED KINGDOM

Loulla-Mae Eleftheriou-Smith | April 10, 2014 How long? | 1 minute

AA, Post Office and Boots named UK's most trusted brands

The AA, the Post Office and Boots have been named the top three most trusted brands in the UK, according to BrandAsset Valuator (BAV).

It was also a clear category leader with 3.8 million personal members and 2,700 patrol vans on the road.[2]

The AA also seemed to be delivering some impressive commercial results, with profit going through the roof (Figure 3).

Figure 3: AA EBITDA, financial year (FY) 2009–15

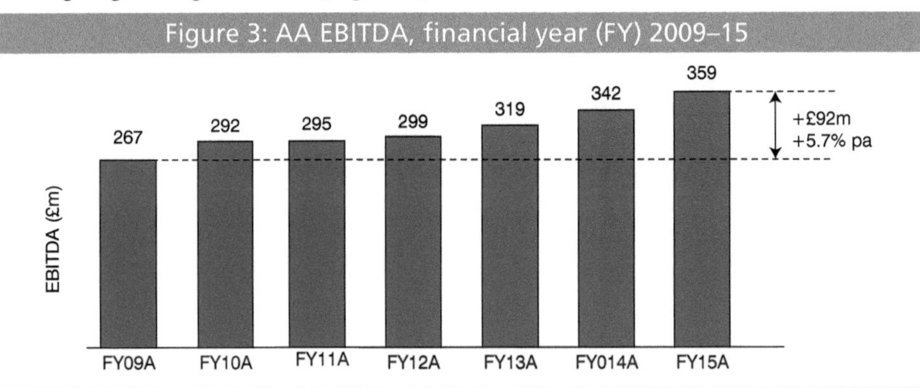

Source: AA

This growth was helped along by a membership base that seemed happy to pay more when renewing every year. In fact, in the previous six years, the average renewal price had increased a whopping 40% (Figure 4).

Figure 4: 'Roadside' average transaction value, FY 2009–15

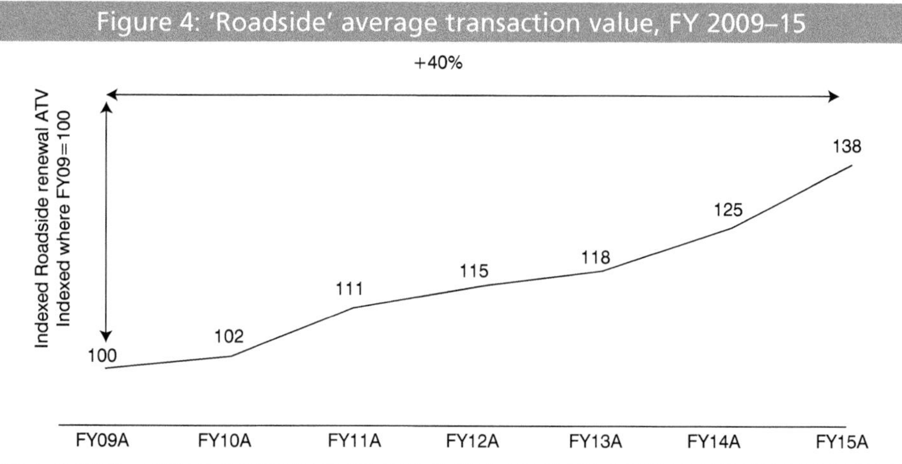

Source: AA

Furthermore, this growth had been delivered with apparently greater and greater efficiency in communications.

This meant there was another factor contributing to the impressive EBITDA growth: the slashing of marketing expenditure over the previous decade (Figure 5).

Figure 5: AA marketing expenditure ('Roadside'), 2004–2014

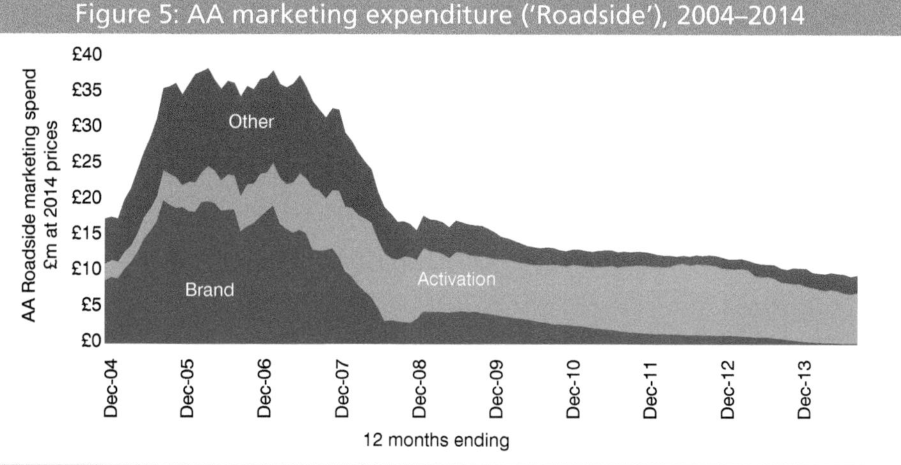

Source: Addynamix and ONS

This decreasing budget was also being spent with an increasingly narrow focus.

Acquisition-driving communications had been progressively cut falling by 34% since 2011 alone to accommodate a new emphasis on more immediately efficient retention campaigns (Figure 6).

Figure 6: Marketing spend split by retention/acquisition objective, 2011–2015

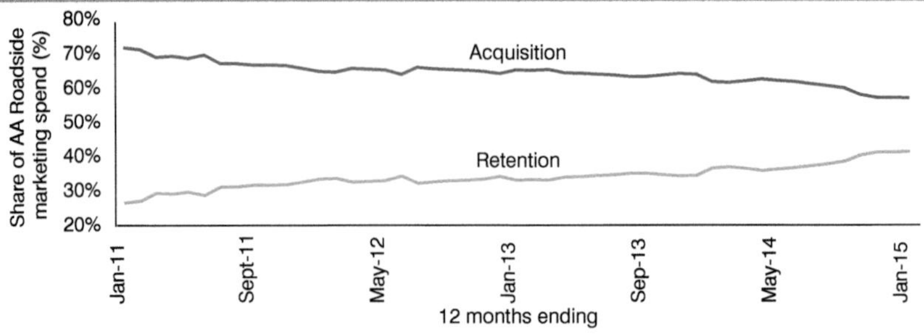

Source: AA

Moreover, investment in brand building had been entirely withdrawn.

By 2014, the AA's media plan had become completely dependent on direct-response media, with an overriding bias towards direct mail (Figures 7 and 8).

Figure 7: Marketing spend split by brand/activation, 2004–2014

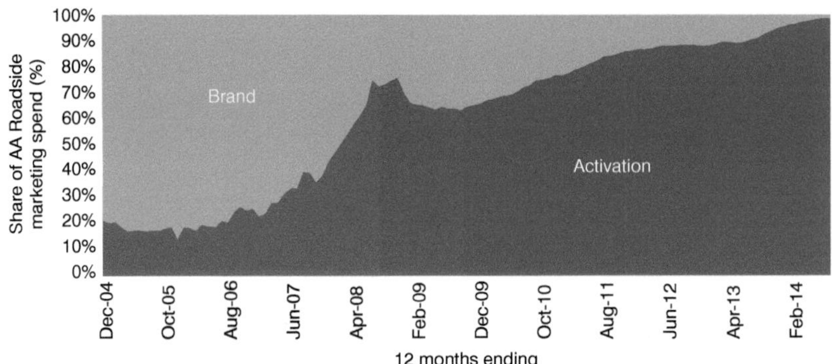

Source: Addynamix

Figure 8: Marketing spend split by channel, 2010–2014

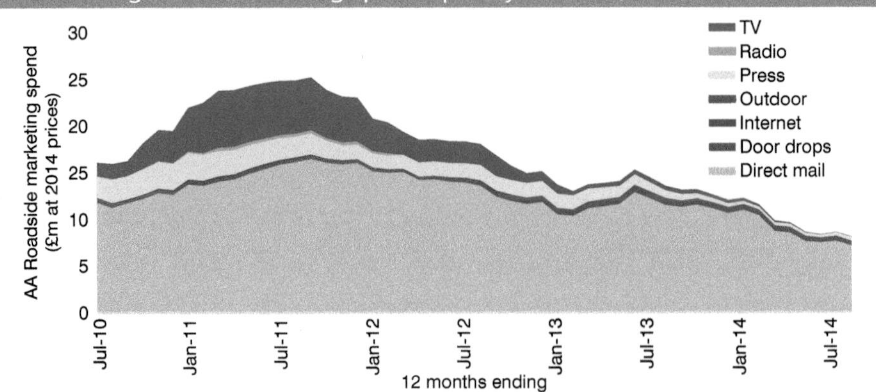

Source: Addynamix and ONS

As with every other brand in the breakdown category, short-term marketing efficiencies were being valued above all else.

In some ways this approach was hard to argue with. The AA had eschewed the expensive and imprecise world of brand communications, focusing instead on cross-selling to its huge member base. It was an enormously efficient approach and the profits that followed were impressive.

But this short-termist, tunnel-visioned approach worried us.

So we dug deeper into the AA's long-term brand and commercial data.

It was then that things started to look less rosy...

The problem

The AA's impressive short-term profit figures hid a completely different story.

Historic data revealed that the current marketing approach had not just abstained from building the AA's brand it had neglected it to the point of crisis.

Over the previous 10 years, as brand-building campaigns had been cut and membership communications prioritised, salience had dwindled dramatically (Figure 9).

Figure 9: Spontaneous brand and advertising awareness, 2005–2014

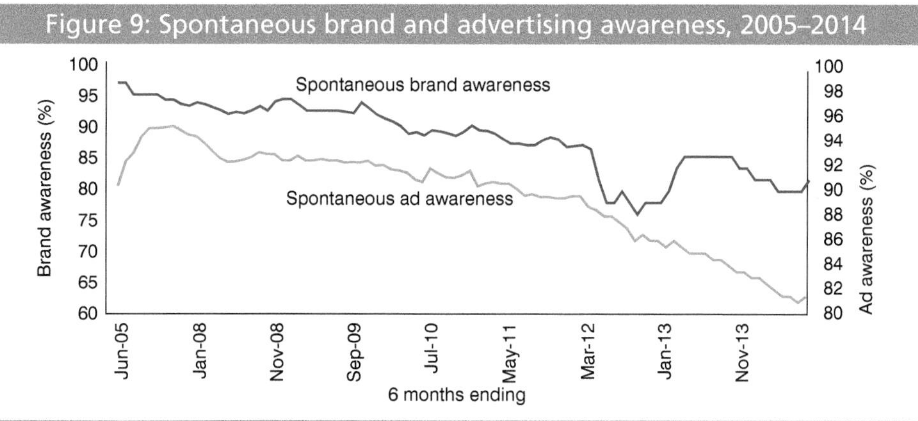

Source: AA

In fact, 8% of people now claimed they'd never heard of the AA at all.[3]

This marketing approach had also resulted in a long-term decline in brand perceptions.

Since 2008, the AA had become weaker across every single tracking metric (Figure 10), and 60% of people no longer agreed that the AA was the nation's best breakdown provider.

As a result, interest in the brand weakened and there were signs of commoditisation.

Searches for the AA had fallen dramatically over time and were now below generic category searches (Figure 11).

Figure 10: Changes in AA tracking metrics, 2008–2014

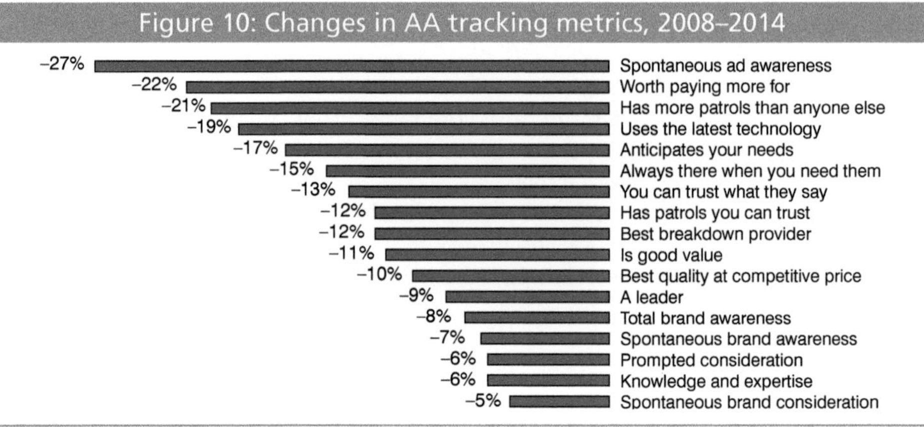

Source: AA brand tracking

Figure 11: Searches for 'AA' and 'breakdown', 2005–2014

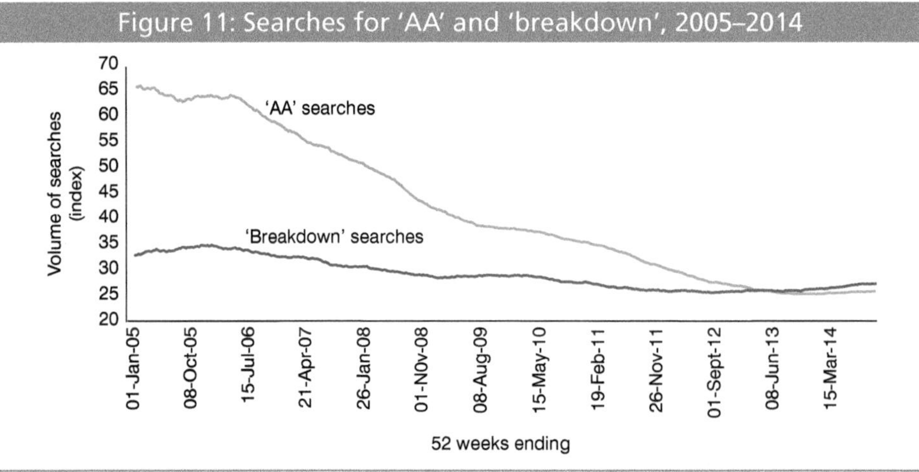

Source: Google Trends

These deteriorating brand measures were worrying in themselves, but their effect on the AA's membership acquisitions and retention was even more concerning.

Despite EBITDA growth, acquisitions of new members had been falling since 2012 and, by 2014, sales of core products were down 29% on their peak (Figure 12).

This meant that, although it was still a clear market leader, the AA's share of new business had now plummeted below the RAC's (Figure 13).

Additionally, a weaker brand meant decreased pricing power.

The AA had been forced to lower prices and increasingly resort to giving away membership for free. The average new business price was now down by 19%, since its peak five years earlier (Figures 14 and 15).

Figure 12: New business sales by product area

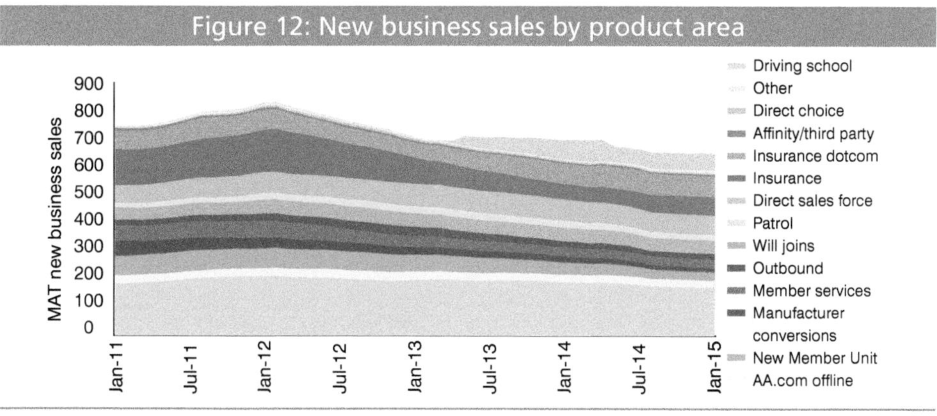

Source: AA

Figure 13: Share of new business ('voluntary'– or paid – breakdown cover), 2010–2014

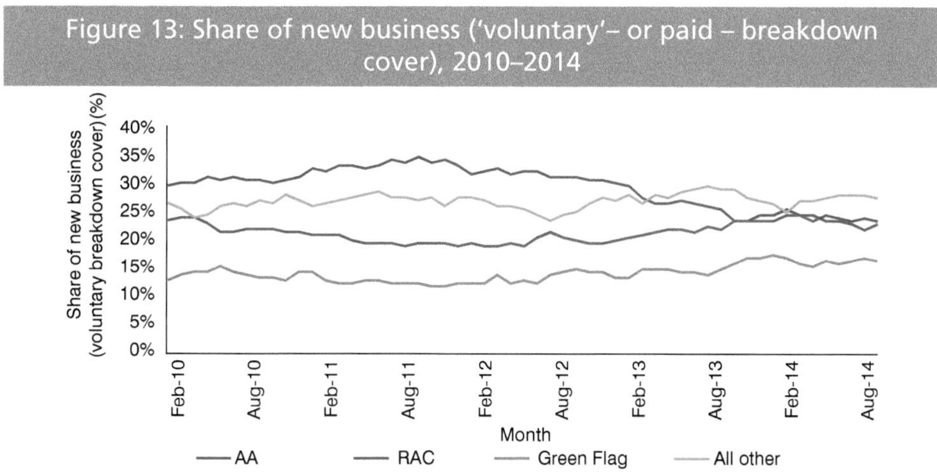

Source: AA

Figure 14: New business price index, 2007–2013

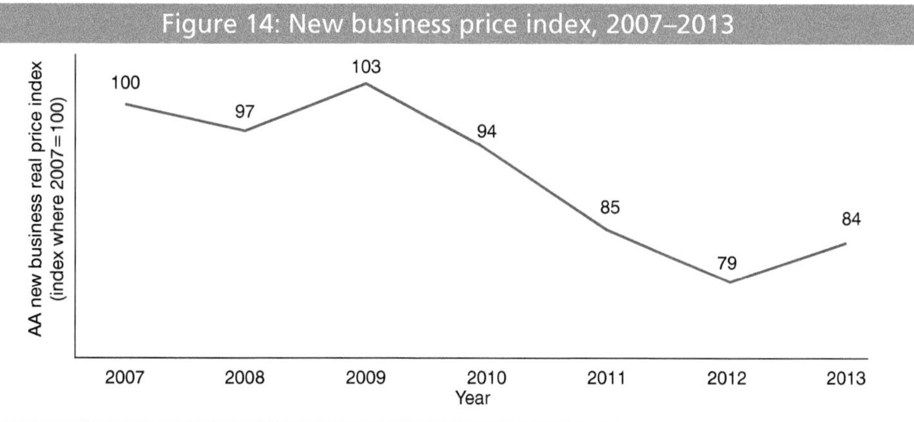

Source:AA and ONS. 'Roadside', 'Home Start' and 'Relay' vehicle price

Figure 15: Paid vs. total breakdown cover held, 2009–2014

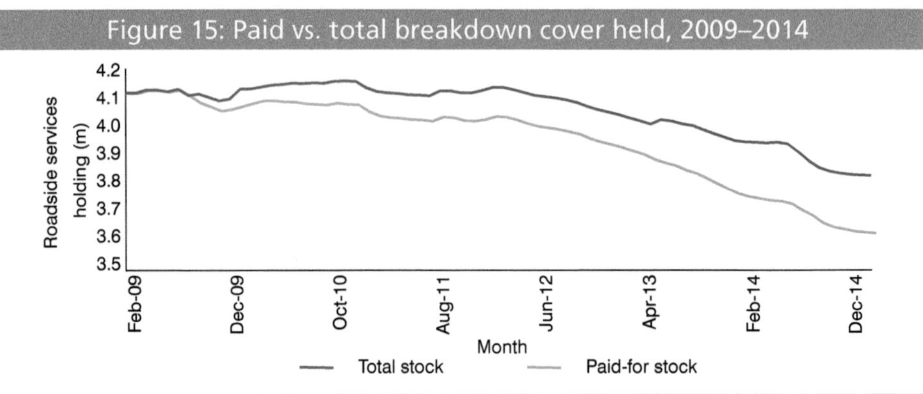

Source: AA

This, in turn, had led to a dramatic overall decay in total new business revenues for 'Roadside' (aka breakdown).

Figure 16: 'Roadside' new business revenue, 2010–2014

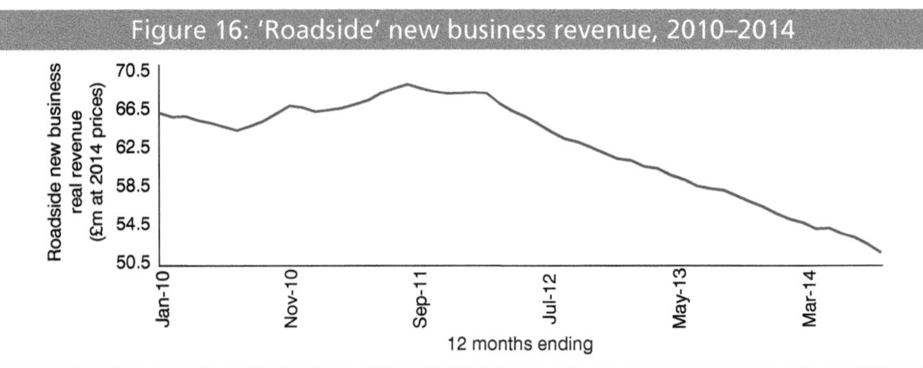

Source: AA and ONS

And if things weren't looking good for member acquisition, then membership retention wasn't looking much better.

As noted, the AA had been driving up renewal prices for more than a decade. This meant that the average renewal price was now more than double the average new joiner price, and what the marketing department had dubbed 'The AA Price Jaws' had opened wide (Figure 17).

Figure 17: Acquisition vs. renewal prices (index), 2000–2013

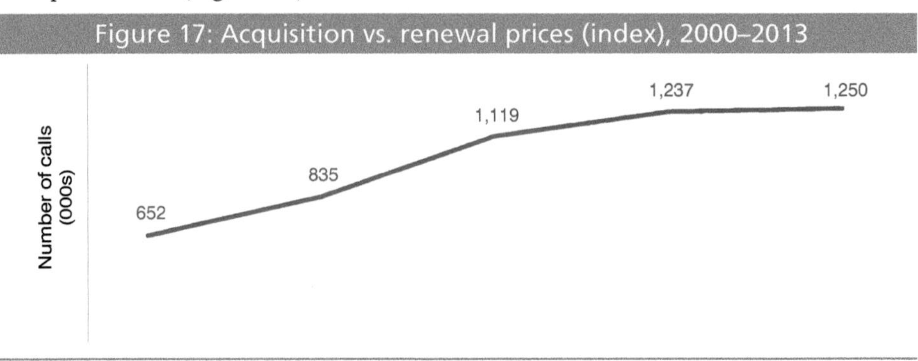

Source: AA. Option 300 ('Roadside', 'Relay' and 'Home Start'}

This had become difficult for members to stomach: calls to 'Stay AA' (the number reserved for those threatening to leave) were rising fast (Figure 18). (Indeed, in 2013 Money Saving Expert reported that the AA was the top company to haggle with.[4])

Figure 18: Calls to 'Stay AA' retention line, 2010–2014

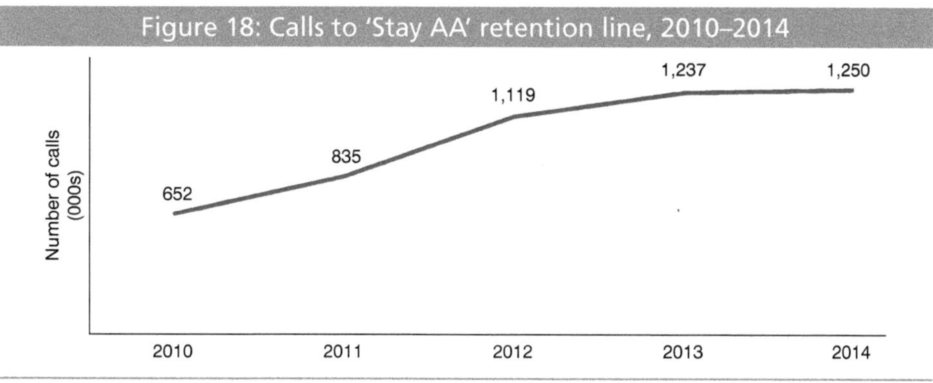

Source: AA

Consumers just couldn't see a clear justification for the gap between their (artificially low) starting price, and their (continuously rising) renewal price.

- *Most members don't experience the brand first-hand in a given year:* on average, breakdowns happen once every 2.5 years, whilst renewal happens annually.
- *Most of them hadn't seen any brand communications for years:* the only thing most members have seen from the brand were hard-selling DR comms.

As a result, demand for renewal discounts went up and the base was haemorrhaging fast for every 15 new members the brand gained, it lost 20.

This was a classic subscription-category death spiral – as experienced by categories like energy, mobile and mortgage before us (Figure 19).

Figure 19: The 'Value Trap', from AA internal strategy document, 2017

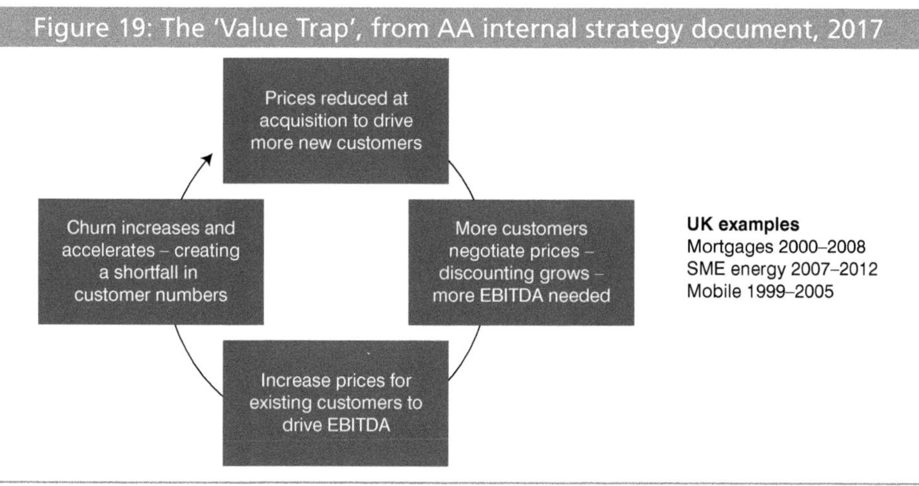

Source: AA

All of this meant that the AA's overall penetration was now in significant decline.

In fact, it was now predicted that if it continued to decline at this rate, within six years the brand's membership would reach a historic and commercially untenable low (Figure 20).

Figure 20: 'Roadside' members, projection, 1974–2020

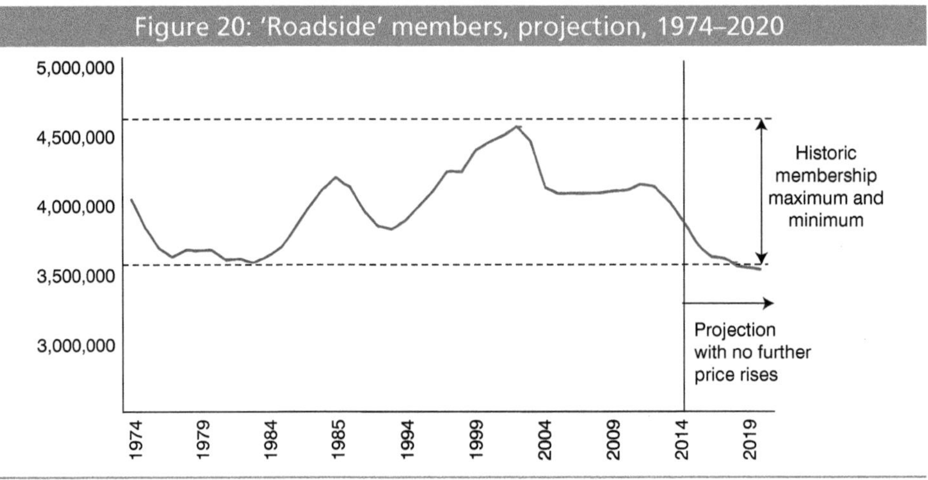

Source: AA

Our audit had revealed an enormous problem – the AA's marketing strategy was efficiently delivering short-term results, but it was also marching the brand towards a commercial precipice.[5]

To summarise:

- membership was declining at 5% YOY – and these losses would starting showing up as profit losses in around 18 months;
- we were losing 20 in every 100 members, and only replacing 15;
- stabilising this membership therefore required either a 33% increase in new members or a 25% drop in churn;
- the alternative: a slow but certain decline to zero.

Delivering either this increase in membership or reduction in churn through efficiencies alone would be unheard of – especially for a market leader in a mature category.

To turn these fortunes around, we knew we would need to instead embrace a totally different and probably quite uncomfortable new approach.

Objectives

Our objectives were clear, if challenging:

Figure 21: Marketing and communications objectives 2015–2017

1. **Deliver sustainable long-term revenue**

by

2. **Reversing the decline in membership**

by

3. **Increasing acquisition and retention (without reliance on discounting)**

by

4. **Increasing consideration and natural interest**

by

5. **Improving brand perceptions and salience**

A new approach

These objectives meant a new approach: we had to 'build not take'

For too long, value had been *extracted* from this national treasure now we had to put value back *into* it.

This meant giving up the exclusive diet of hard-selling activations, membership upselling and short-term KPIs.

Instead, we would use communications to build salience and goodwill for the brand, and so to turbo-charge all other marketing efforts and deliver better pay-back in the long-term.

The theory was nothing new we could all pretty much draw Figure 22 by heart – but the decision for the AA to abandon its focus on short-term results and, instead, follow this theory to the letter was certainly bold.

Like many before us, we had counted our brand as an exception to the rule. Maybe Byron Sharp's rule worked for FMCG, but we were a subscription business – a dominant player in a mature, low-interest segment of the insurance category, with an already huge member base.

However, in 2014, we were left with no other option.

It was time to move beyond our fixation with short-term efficiencies and instead attempt to bring a little heart to an inherently mechanical category.

Figure 22: Short-term vs. long-term effects

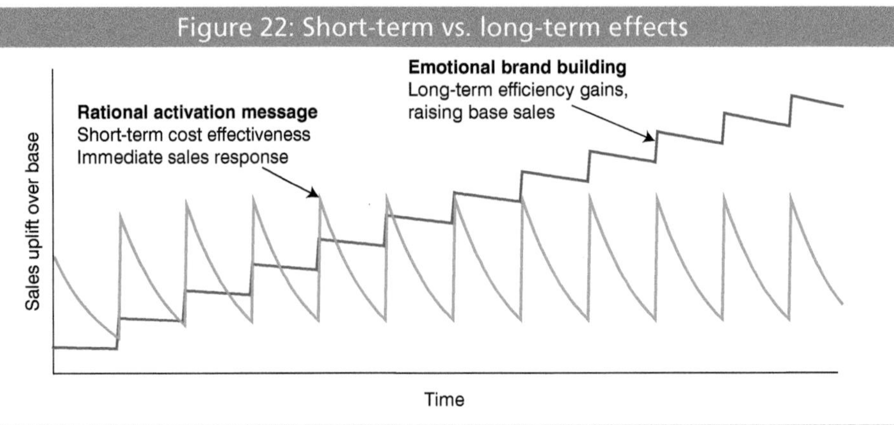

Source: Binet and Field

The strategy

To pursue this new approach, we adopted three key strategic changes.

Redefining our audience:

It had been too easy to see our 3.8m existing members as the best source of growth.

But long-term success meant broadening our focus. We thus redefined our audience: from *MEMBERS* to *MASSES*.

Redefining our media approach:

We'd reduced budgets overall, and entirely cut brand spend. Now we had to *RAISE* and *REBALANCE* this spend.

In accordance with first principles, to increase our share of market we had to *RAISE* our share of voice (Figure 23).

Consequently, by 2016, the AA had increased its marketing spend by 22% YOY.

We also had to *REBALANCE* our budget.

This didn't mean *just* focusing on emotional brand building we knew that DR was still vital for closing sales. It meant rebalancing our spend, so that our brand building worked to effectively fuel the performance of all other communications.

Again, this meant following best practice (Figure 24): spending 60% of our budget on emotional brand building and 40% on DR activations.

For the brand-building activity, we aimed to up-weight channels that could maximise fame and reach. TV was the backbone (by 2017, it took 62% of the total brand budget), with posters and radio lending further scale and frequency.

These supporting channels also allowed the campaign greater contextual relevance – with radio targeted at school runs and work commutes, and outdoor focused on key arterial roads and high traffic routes.

Figure 23: The relationship between share of voice and share of market

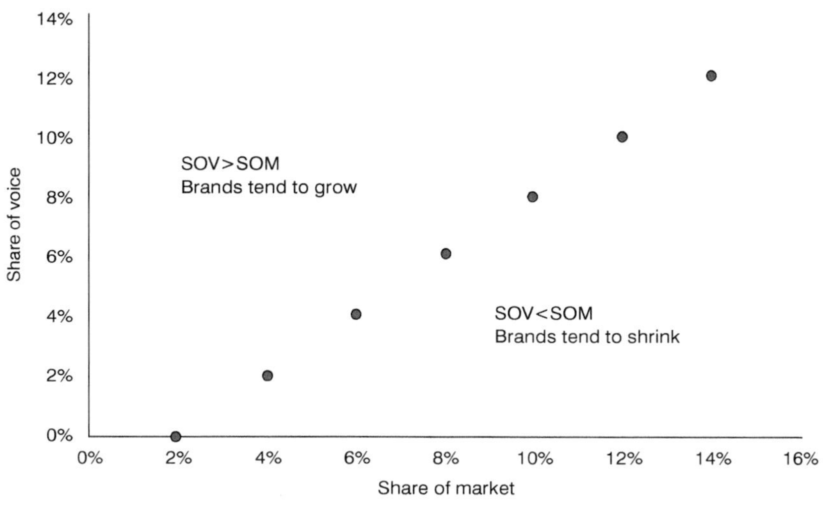

Source: Binet and Field

Figure 24: The 60:40 principle in allocating media budget

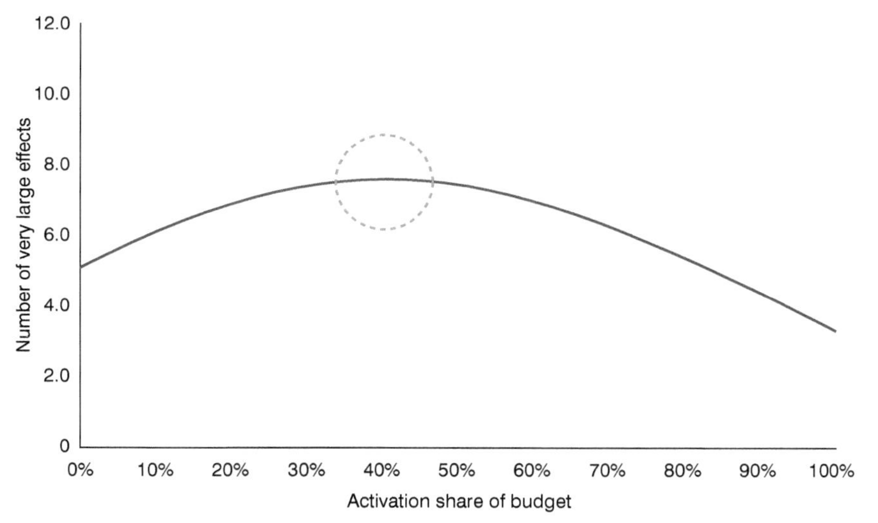

Source: Binet and Field

Redefining our messaging focus:

We'd largely stopped focusing on our core breakdown product, and instead were trying to cross-sell our auxiliary range: car and home insurance; boiler cover; second-hand car services. Reinvesting in the brand meant *REFOCUSING ON THE CORE*: the breakdown cover for which we were famous.

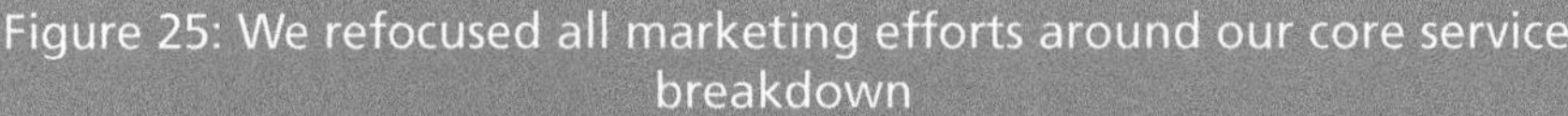

Figure 25: We refocused all marketing efforts around our core service breakdown

With a new targeting approach, a new commitment to brand building, and a new messaging strategy, we were ready to go.

Although this case focuses mainly on the effectiveness of the advertising, our plan went much further:

- The website was redesigned, with a new, streamlined ecommerce journey.
- We introduced new opt-in offers during sign-up, to increase average transaction value.
- We introduced new processes to the call centres, such as a dedicated line to retain customers phoning to leave.

(All of these effects are isolated from the advertising by our econometric model, detailed later.)

Year 1 (2015): Lessons learned

The AA was built on unparalleled technical prowess, but we'd let our pre-eminence slide. So we began by focusing on the breadth of the AA's capability. Our proposition was simple (Figure 26):

Figure 26: Our creative proposition for 2015 and 2016 campaign

No matter the situation,
the AA can get you going again

TV, radio and digital display all showed the surprising range of real-life situations in which the AA had got members going again when they'd broken down. Qualitative research suggested that, far from being abstract, our audience would imagine that 'if the AA can fix those vehicles, they can definitely fix mine!'.

Figure 27: 60-second TV stills, 2015–2016 campaign

Figure 28: 30-second TV stills, 2015–2016 campaign, 'Key Assist' execution

Figure 29: Selected MPUs, 2015

Figure 30: Selected 2015 radio

SFX: Telephone Woman: "Go past the church and then we're ... we're the second tree on the left I think ... It's an oak tree I think" Man: "Right... turn left... no, is it right?" Woman: (responding) "I've never been here before! I don't know! I don't live here!" Woman: "The last town we went through began with a 'C'" – if that helps..?" Man: "Then we carried straight on ... or did we go right?" Man: "No, I'm on the road with fields either side, so ... well there are sheep on the left hand side" V/O: "Our new app is able to find you even if you don't know where you are. We are the Automobile Association. We are the AA."	SFX: Car travelling along Woman: "I spy with my little eye something beginning with ... R?" Woman: "OK so that's four white cars, three blue ... ooh, seven red ... ooh, I didn't know red was so popular" Man: "Don't you think that cloud looks like a badger riding a unicorn?" Mum: (to kids) fighting in back "Don't fight ... please stop fighting!" SFX: Music Box Man: "Not again – please!" V/O: "With more patrols than anyone else, you won't be hanging around too long. We are the Automobile Association. We are the AA."

DR creative reflected the TV very closely – essentially it was a recut of the TV carrying a tactical message.

Figure 31: 2015 DRTV

Sadly the voiceover of our TV ad in 2015 was the subject of a successful complaint by a competitor. We changed it for 2016, but will not be basing our effectiveness case on year one results.[6]

Actually, this wasn't our only mis-step in 2015. Although we had dramatically increased our brand spend, we still relied heavily on highly targeted digital media, on which we spent £1.8m. After so many years of efficiency first, we couldn't entirely abandon it.

The result: although tracking measures started to improve, the results were relatively modest. It wasn't until 2016 – Year 2 – that our campaign really started to work hard – and it is on this period onwards that we will base our case.

Year 2 (2016): Committing to mass

We ran the same campaign idea in Year 2, albeit with a tweaked voiceover and clearer edit.

However we made big changes to the media approach, abandoning microtargeting in favour of broader reach and frequency:

- We invested more heavily in TV (from 1115 TVRs to 1,500).
- We reduced spend in targeted (and retargeted) digital activity from £1.8m to £90,000.
- We added £1.8m of outdoor spend to the plan (vs. none in 2015).

As the results will show, this optimisation of media strategy began to bear fruit.

We also introduced a new DR campaign in 2016. In 2015 we'd used brand assets to deliver superficial integration, but from 2016 we took a more nuanced approach, focusing on three priorities:

1. *Clear branding:* it was no good building the salience of our brand, if this conversion work wasn't recognised as part of it.
2. *Visual coherence:* previously, the AA's DR had felt very fragmented and confusing across different offers.
3. *Simplicity:* our other work had already taken care of the 'emotional' bit, so this work just needed to close the deal as swiftly and painlessly as possible.

Figure 32: 48-sheet poster, 2016

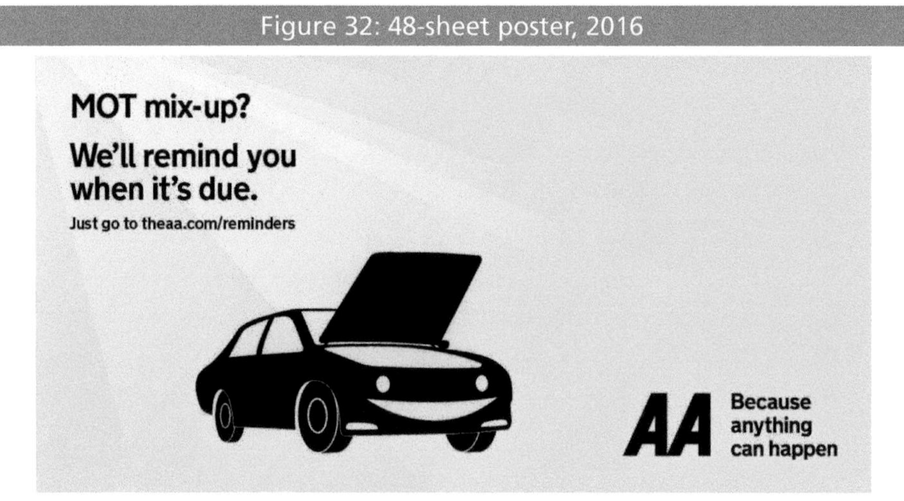

The result was an iconic suite of predominantly yellow and black executions that we consistently optimised and reissued over the following two years (Figures 33 and 34).

Figure 33: 60-second DRTV, 2016

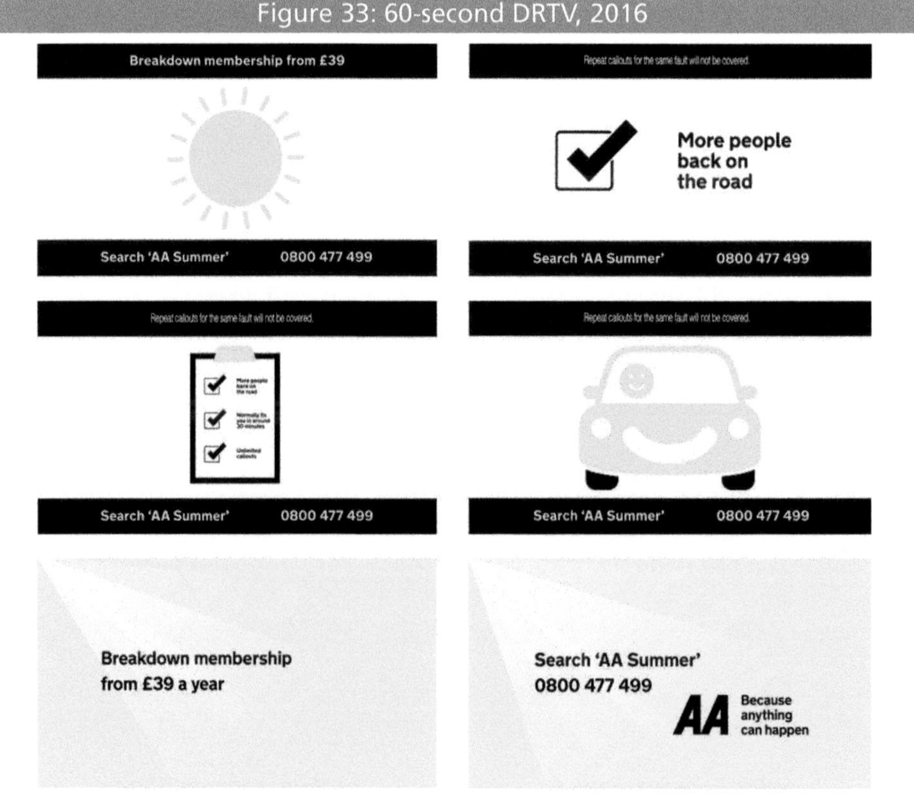

Figure 34: Example DR Press

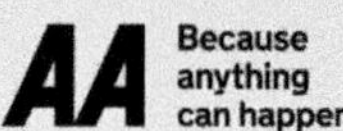

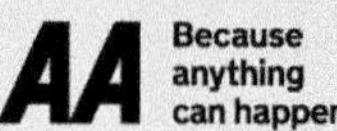

Year 3 (2017): Committing to emotion

If 2015–2016 had been about expanding our audience, 2017 was about really understanding it. During 2016, we had been working on a complete repositioning, based on a more refined understanding of our target audience.

We began by conducting a more robust piece of segmentation research to identify a 'sweet spot' audience. Segmentation isn't popular with proponents of broad mass-marketing – so why use it?

First, it went beyond members to cover all UK drivers – finding an audience that was *more mass than before*.

Working with a data scientist better known for his work understanding voter behaviour,[7] we uncovered eight segments, and focused on the 'Freedom seekers': at 24% of the driving public, they still represented 8.3m non-members and offered us the headroom we needed for growth.[8]

Second, we based the segmentation on values and beliefs, not demographics. This group already trusted the AA, but they didn't *feel* anything towards us – no surprise given our recent history. Thankfully, this tighter audience definition allowed us to find a more specific emotional insight which would still be universally relevant.

'Freedom seekers' weren't like the old archetypal AA audience – the mythical 'damsels in distress' who needed a man to rescue them. They were busy people (with a slight bias to women) simultaneously running a successful career and family, just about keeping the show on the road, and absolutely relishing every minute of the madness.

A breakdown wasn't a rescue situation. It was a schedule-shredding, plan-destroying insult to their day.

This led us to refine our brand proposition – for advertising but also for the brand more broadly (Figure 35).

Figure 35: Our evolved creative brief

From	To
No matter the situation, the AA can get you going again	The AA will do whatever it takes to keep your show on the road

This was a final big shift in strategy: from breadth of capability to the emotional benefit of our service. Or as we dubbed it, from sparkplugs to singalongs.

Instead of focusing on our capability in fixing cars, we would give our audience an emotional sample of the feeling they would get when we fixed theirs.

This also allowed us to avoid the generic, negative emotion of 'distress' and instead go entirely positive. Qualitative research had shown us that 'Freedom seekers' hated breakdowns because they disrupted the buzz of flying between their day's chaotic list of appointments, without ever missing one ... single ... beat.

We brought this insight to life in our second campaign, by using singing in the car as a metaphor for this feeling.

Advertising showed a cute baby girl's trip to the airport. Sitting in the backseat of her father's car she sings Tina Turner's 'Proud Mary' at the top of her voice and, even when her Dad's car breaks down, her show never leaves the road for a second.

Figure 36: Brand 48-sheet poster

Figure 37: 40-second TV ad

Figure 38: Product poster

Figure 39: Brand radio

Music: Proud Mary by Tina Turner I/O; With breakdown cover from The AA
We'll do whatever it takes to make sure your big wheels keep on turning...
Our mechanics usually get you going again in 30 minutes. Breakdown cover from The AA.
Because anything can happen.

And, of course, our media planning was still committed to mass reach (Figure 40):

Figure 40: 2017 media spend by channel

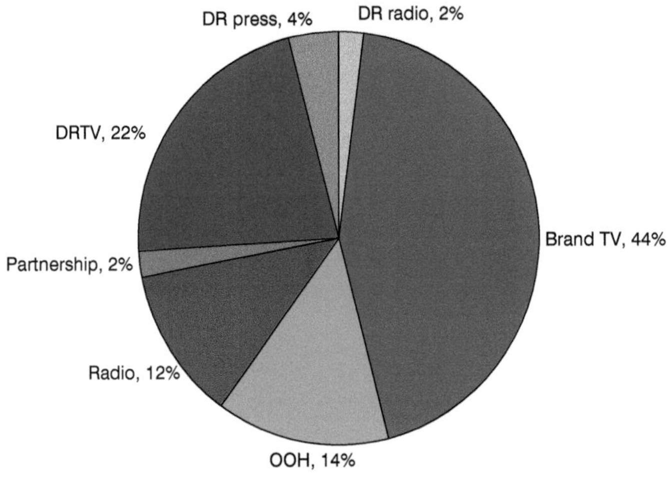

Source: AA

The results

We had persuaded the AA's board to abandon a strategy that was delivering short-term profit growth, and spend extra money doing so. Naturally all eyes were on the results.

However, thankfully, both 2016 and 2017 campaigns very quickly provided encouragement.

Here's a reminder of our objectives:

Figure 41: Marketing and communications objectives 2015–2017

1. **Deliver sustainable long-term revenue**

by

2. **Reversing the decline in membership**

by

3. **Increasing acquisition and retention (without reliance on discounting)**

by

4. **Increasing consideration and natural interest**

by

5. **Improving brand perceptions and salience**

We'll address each in turn...

Objective 1: Improving brand perceptions and salience; strengthening the brand

YouGov's BrandIndex registered significant and cumulative uplifts in advertising awareness for both campaigns (Figure 42).

Figure 42: Advertising awareness, 2016–2018

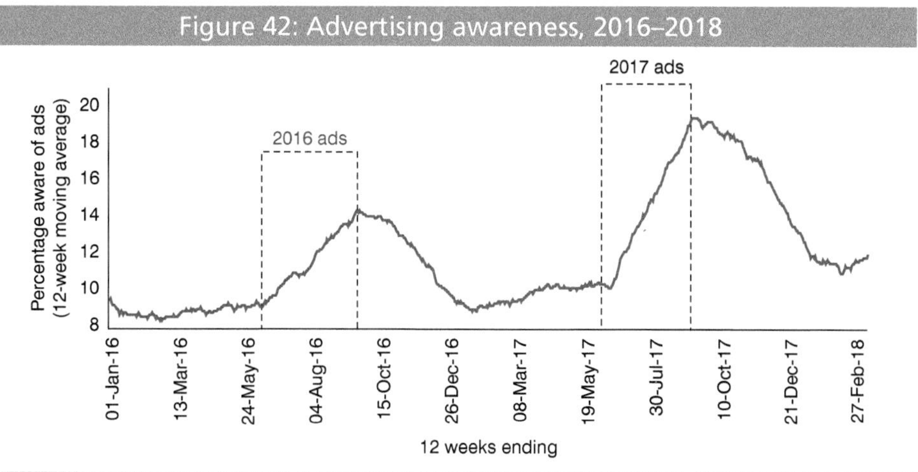

Source: YouGov

The uplift in salience in 2017 was so dramatic that YouGov even had the results picked up by the national news (Figure 43).

Figure 43: Press coverage of 2017 campaign (CityAM, 5 July 2017)

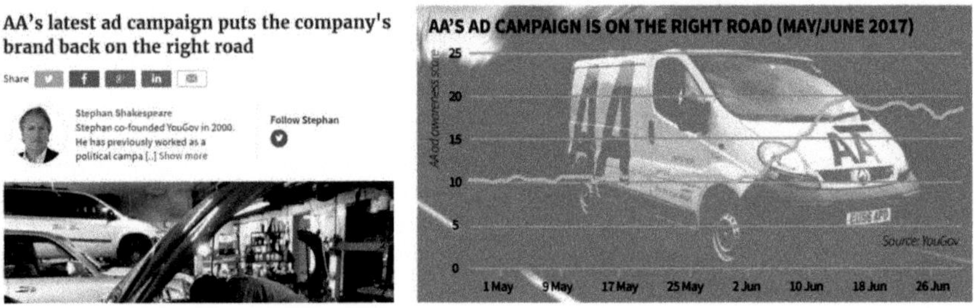

AA's latest ad campaign puts the company's brand back on the right road

Stephan Shakespeare
Stephan co-founded YouGov in 2000. He has previously worked as a political campa [...] Show more

Follow Stephan

AA'S AD CAMPAIGN IS ON THE RIGHT ROAD (MAY/JUNE 2017)

Source: YouGov

The 2017 ad in particular obviously struck a chord: YouTube search volumes suggested people liked it enough to search it out online (Figure 44).

Figure 44: Brand YouTube searches, 2015–2018

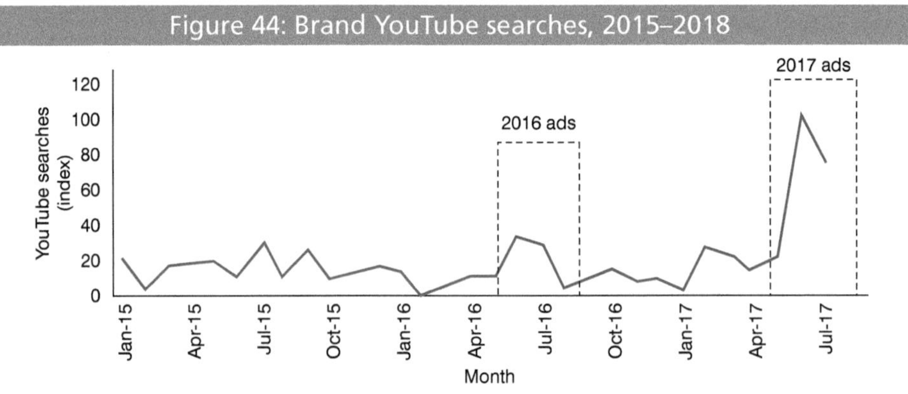

Source: Google Trends (YouTube seraches from 'the Automobile Association')

YouGov's Buzz (volume of positive sentiment[9]) and Word Of Mouth[10] metrics also further substantiated the growing positive sentiment we had started seeing around the ads (Figure 45).

Figure 45: YouGov BrandIndex 'Buzz' score, 2016–2018

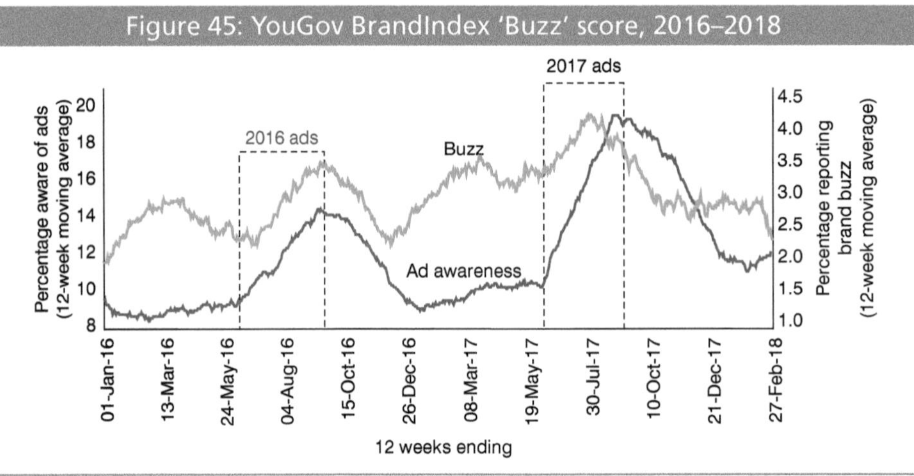

Source: YouGov

Figure 46: YouGov BrandIndex 'Word Of Mouth' score, 2016–2018

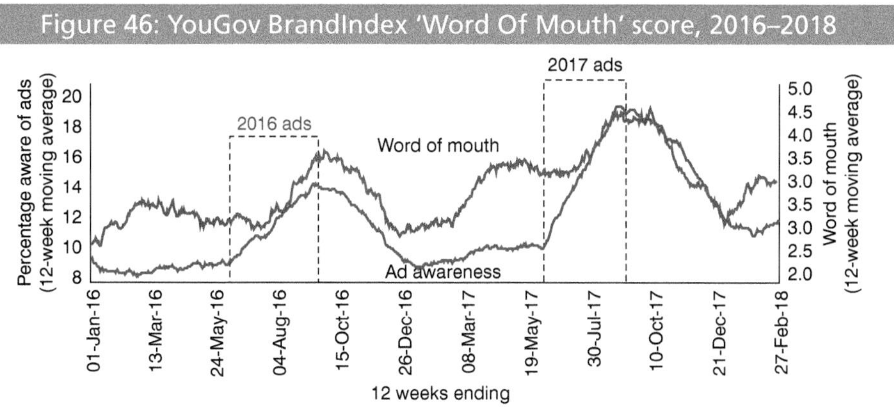

Source: YouGov

This sentiment also appeared to be sticking, with the longer-term brand attention[11] metric responding with similarly strong cumulative uplifts (Figure 47).

Figure 47: YouGov BrandIndex 'Attention' score, 2016–2018

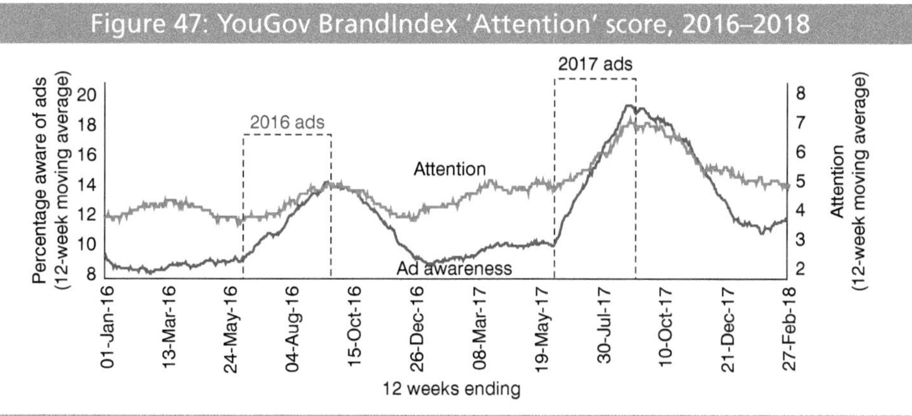

Source: YouGov

Crucially, *the advertising pushed the AA back to the forefront of the British population's mind.* The brand's spontaneous awareness had grown with each phase of our activity. (Figure 48).

Figure 48: Spontaneous awareness, pre and during campaign, 2016 and 2017

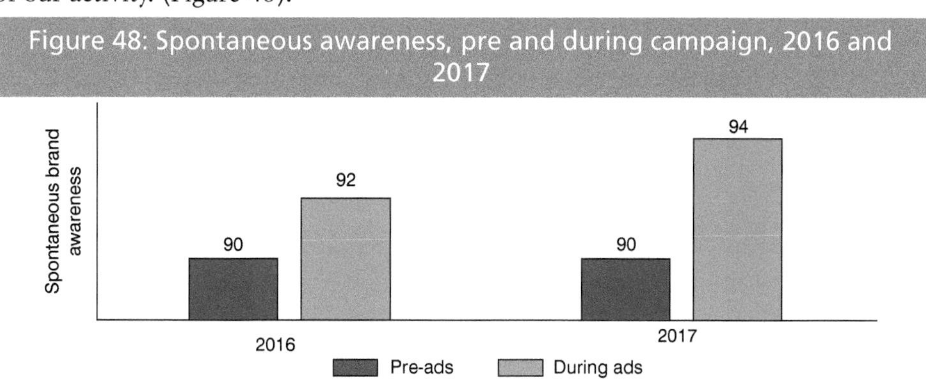

Source: AA. Pre-ads = Q2, during ads = Q3

Salience was good, but we also wanted to *improve brand perceptions, so both potential and existing members felt the AA was worth paying more for.*

YouGov reported that, both individually and in combination, these campaigns had managed to instil a newly favourable 'Impression'[12] of the brand in the public's minds. And, as we'd hoped, people also began to perceive The AA to have a higher inherent sense of quality[13] (Figures 49 and 50).

Figure 49: YouGov BrandIndex 'Impression' score, 2016–2018

2017 ads
2016 ads
Impression
Ad awareness
Percentage aware of ads (12-week moving average)
20
18
16
14
12
10
8
Impression (12-week moving average)
29
28
27
26
25
24
01-Jan-16
13-Mar-16
24-May-16
04-Aug-16
15-Oct-16
26-Dec-16
08-Mar-17
19-May-17
30-Jul-17
10-Oct-17
21-Dec-17
27-Feb-18
12 weeks ending

Source: YouGov

Figure 50: YouGov BrandIndex 'Quality' score, 2016–2018

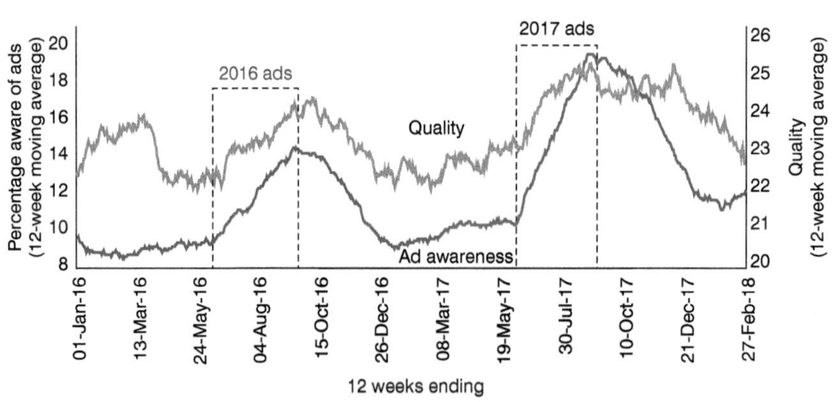

Source: YouGov

Further testimony to the brand's changing public perceptions came when we reviewed Old Street's[14] brand image tracker. Contrary to the tracking we witnessed in the months before relaunch, in 2016, we saw uplifts against every measure and in, 2017, these only increased further (Figure 51).

Figure 51: Brand image scores pre- and post-campaign, 2017

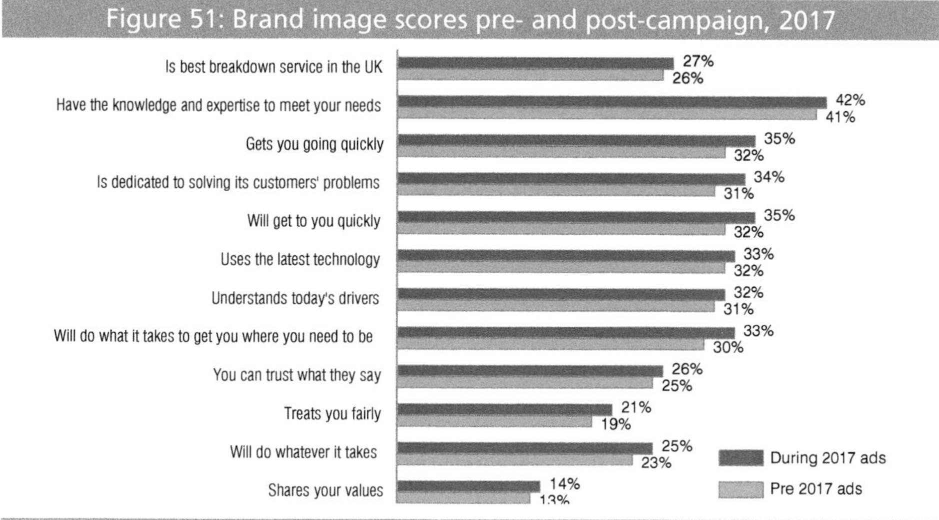

Source: Old Street Data Science. 'Thinking about breakdown suppliers, to what extent would you say that each of the following providers'. Pre-(May 2017) vs. during (July 2017). Change of supplier means there is no comparable data pre-2017.

We were also effective in our pursuit of greater emotion from 2017: System 1 (formerly Brainjuicer) reported that 'Singing baby' was the most powerfully emotive ad they had measured in two years (Figure 52)

Figure 52: System 1 star rating score, 2017

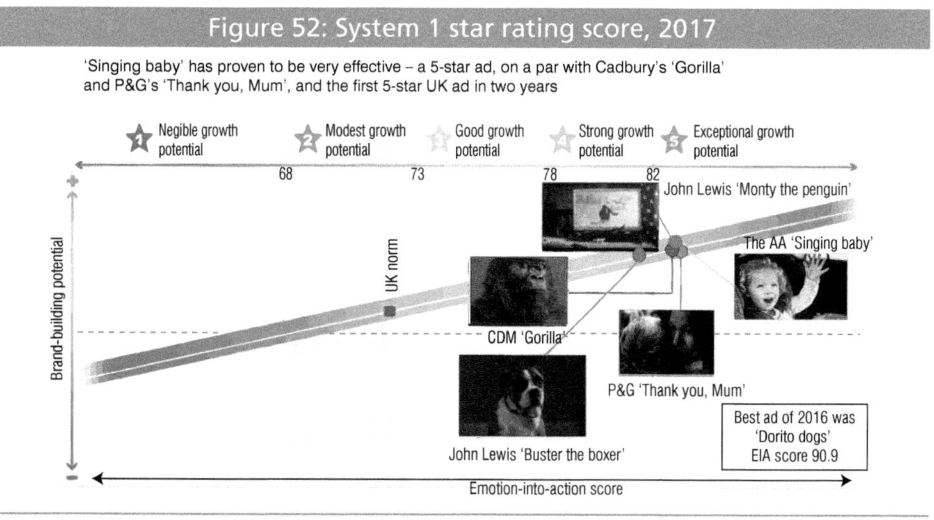

Indeed, at the time of the second campaign, some people even cared sufficiently to post bootleg copies of the song from the ad (Figure 53)!

Objective 2: Increasing consideration and natural interest

Our tracking data for the second campaign confirmed that brand consideration had risen considerably, and this was corroborated by a reversed decline in Google Search volume, sustained across both campaigns (Figures 54 and 55).

Figure 53: Song from the 2017 brand campaign for sale on Amazon

Figure 54: Purchase consideration pre- and post-campaign, 2017

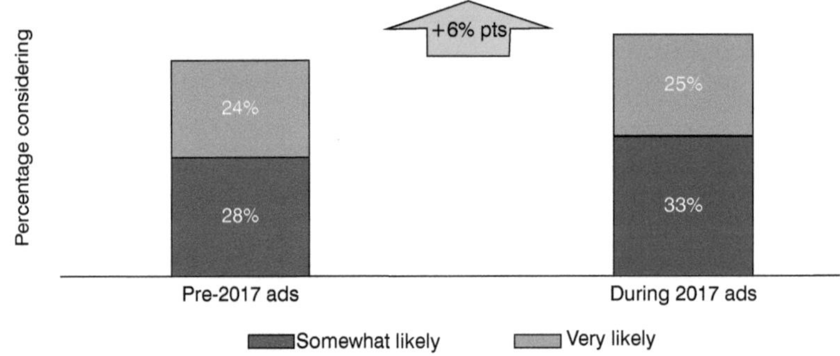

Source: Old Street Data Science. Pre- (May 2017) vs. during (July 2017).

Figure 55: Google searches for 'The AA'

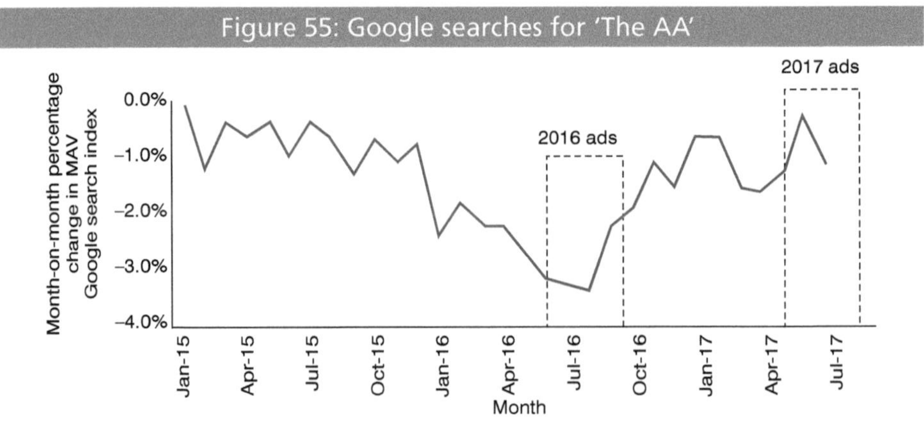

Source: Google Trends

This consideration translated into greater volumes of potential customers arriving at the AA storefront, with web traffic increasing significantly (Figure 56).

Figure 56: Visits to the AA website, 2016–2018

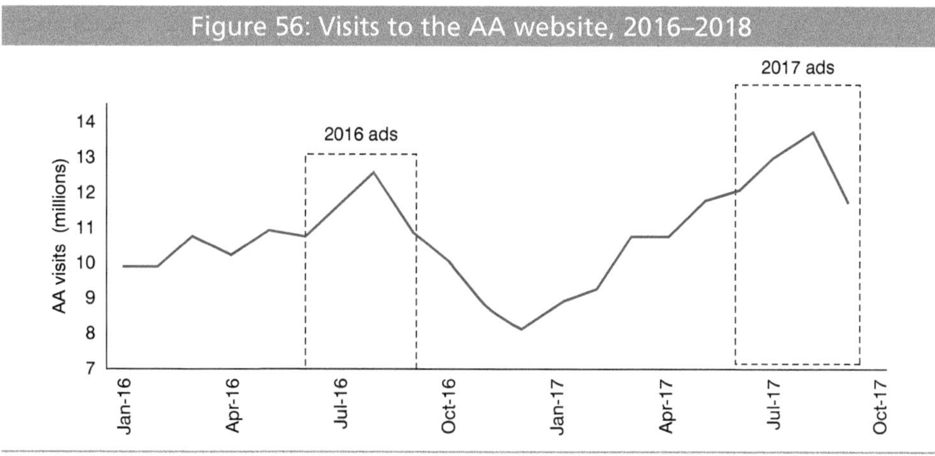

Source: AA and BARB

Objective 3: Increasing acquisition and retention (without reliance on discounting)

Interest is great – but more importantly, conversion of that traffic was higher (Figure 57).

Figure 57: Cost per acquisition as a measure of conversion efficiency, 2016–2017

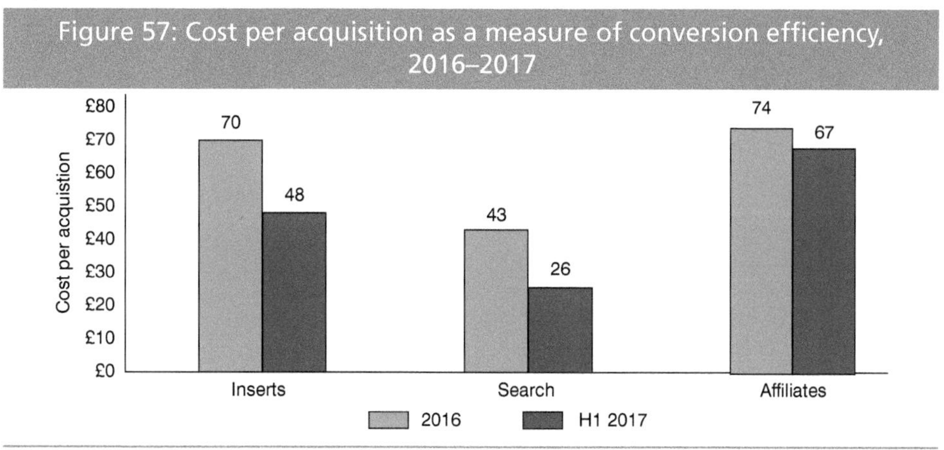

Source: AA

And the effect on acquisitions was clear (Figure 58).

Figure 58: 'Roadside' acquisitions, 2014–2017

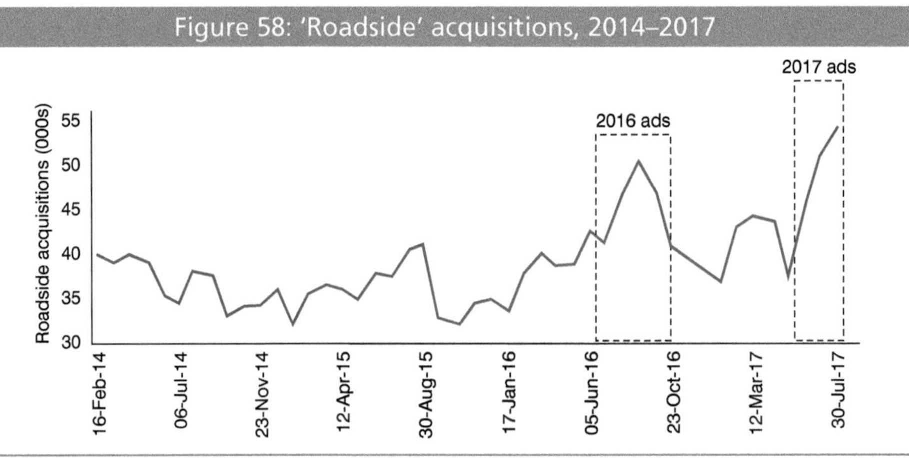

Source: AA

Our campaigns had not just slowed or steadied the brand's declining acquisition volumes – they'd totally reversed the trend (Figure 59).

Figure 59: 'Roadside' acquisitions, 2012–2017 (MAT)

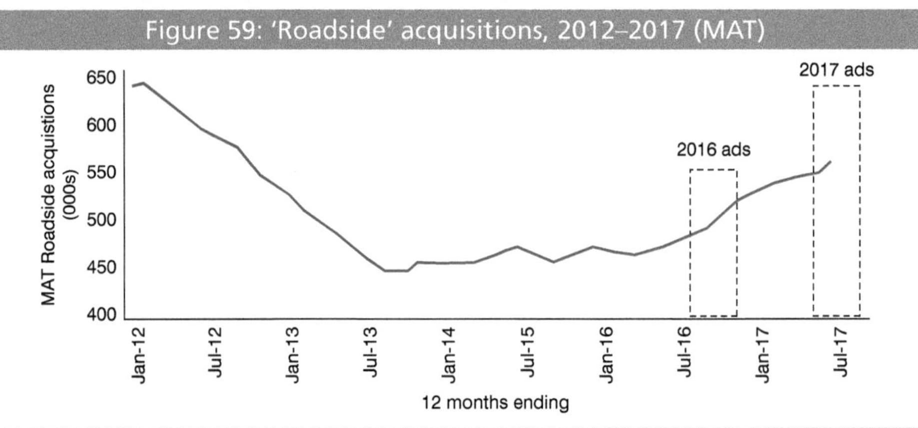

Source: AA

Usually for an IPA paper, pricing effects are discounted. Here they are part of our case: from 2016, our price index for acquisitions increased and our average promotional discount decreased – thus reducing the distance between new business and renewal prices (Figures 60 and 61).

Figure 60: Base price for 'Roadside' acquisitions (indexed)

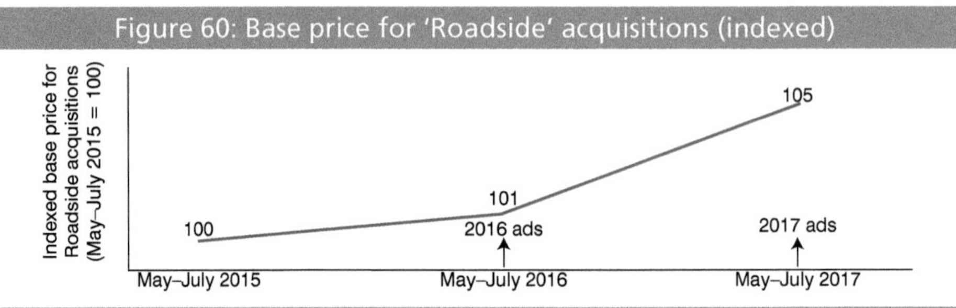

Source: AA. Base price by product weighted by sales of 'Roadside +1', 'Roadside+2' and 'Roadside+3'

Figure 61: Average promotional discount for 'Roadside' acquisitions, 2015–2017

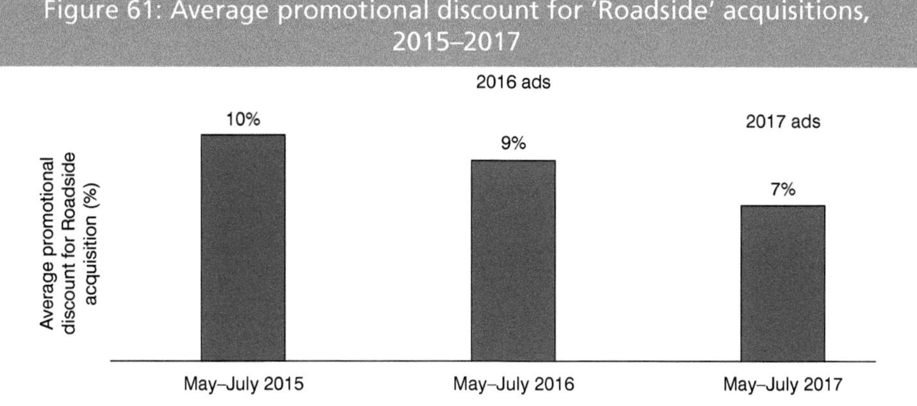

Source: AA. Discount by product weighted by sales of 'Roadside', 'Roadside+1', 'Roadside+2' and 'Roadside+3'

We had also delivered increasingly valuable acquisitions. Better brand perceptions led to more and more new joiners signing up through premium packages, generating greater revenue per recruit (Figure 62).

Figure 62: Average number of products purchased at acquisition, 2015–2017

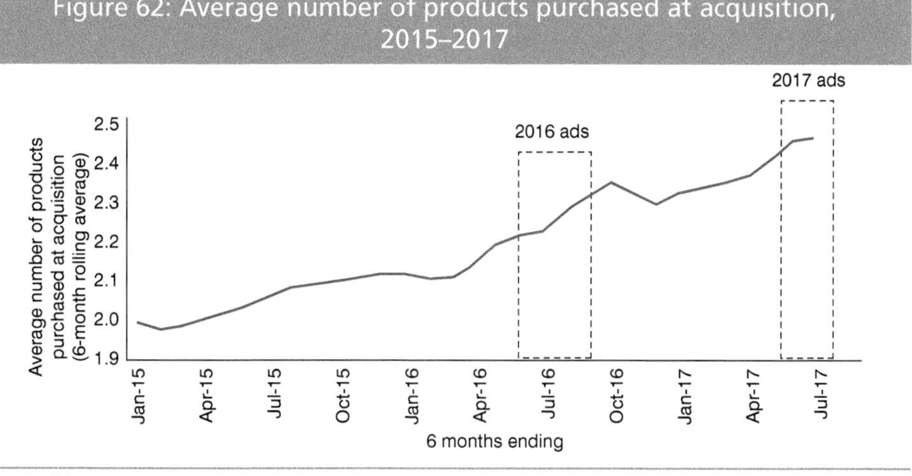

Source: AA

And of course the effect of increased acquisitions at higher prices? Acquisition revenue increased (Figure 63).

Retention

Acquisitions were only half the equation. With 3.8 million members we also needed to ensure retention stayed high.

First, the campaign strengthened the brand amongst existing customers too (Figure 64).

Figure 63: 'Roadside' acquisition revenue, 2015–2017

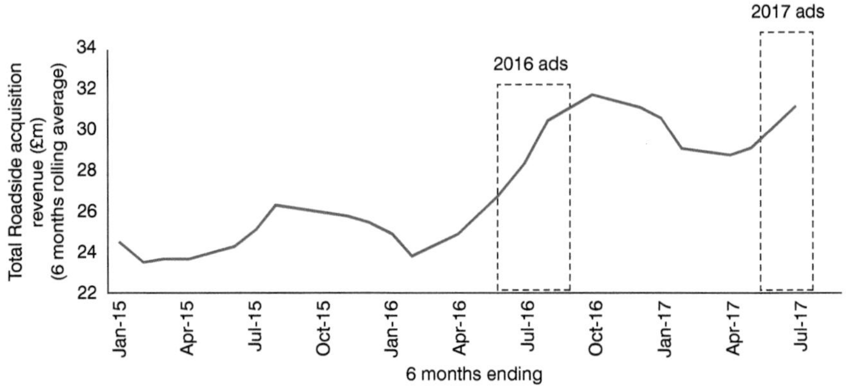

Source: AA. 'Roadside', 'Roadside+1', 'Roadside+2' and 'Roadside+3'

Figure 64: Brand image scores (existing customers), pre- and post-campaign, 2017

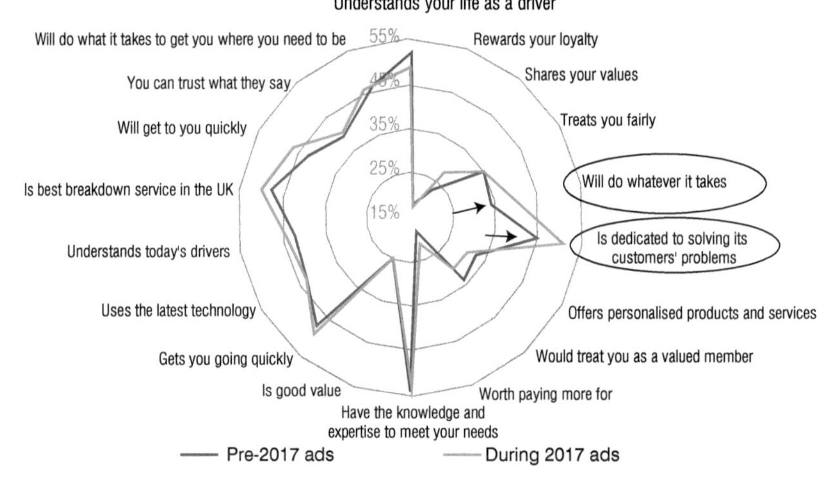

Source: Old Street Data Science

Then, response rates to member-targeted emails (including renewal communications) increased (Figures 65 and 66).

Fewer people called the 'Stay AA' line – reversing the trend of the previous years (Figure 67).

As a result, membership retention rallied to reach approximately 83% (Figure 68). McKinsey have estimated that the absolute ceiling for retention stands at 86%, due to extrinsic factors like members dying or getting married and moving onto joint cover.[15]

Figure 65: Click-through rates for membership emails, 2017

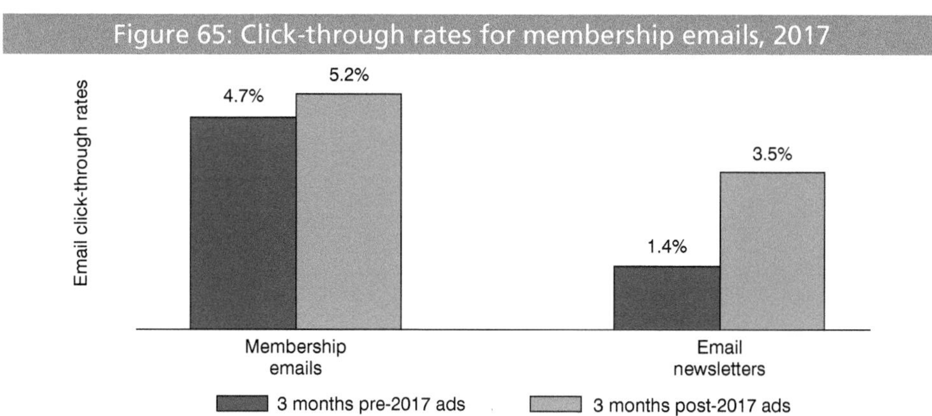

Source: AA

Figure 66: Email unsubscribe rates, 2017

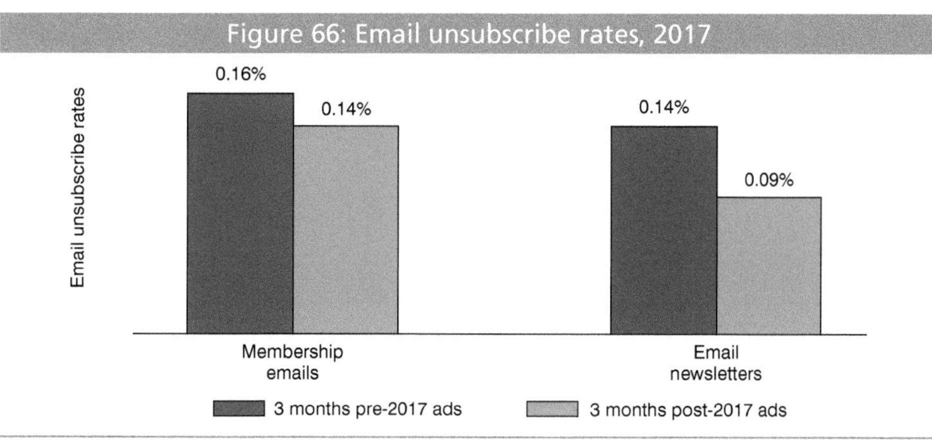

Source: AA

Figure 67: Calls to 'Stay AA' retention line, 2010–2017

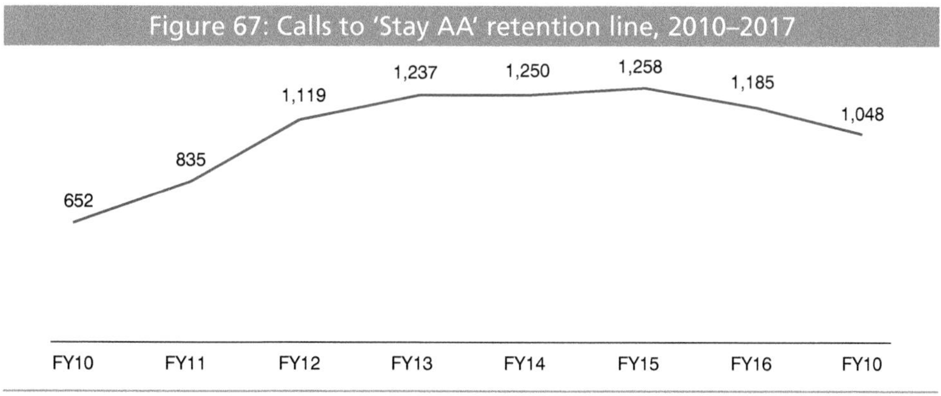

Source: AA

Figure 68: 'Roadside' retention rates, 2011–2017

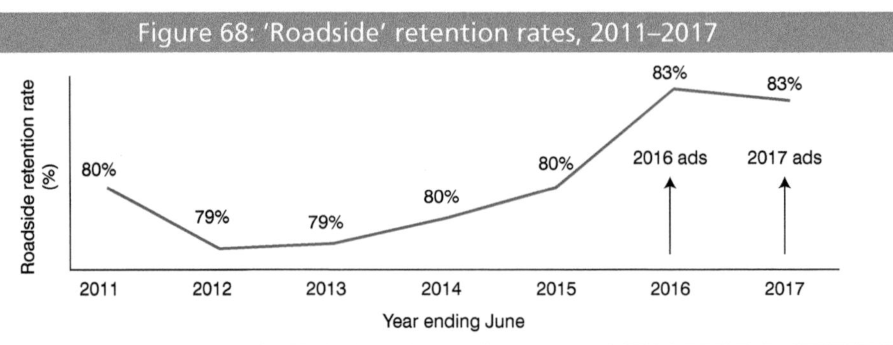

Source: AA

Objective 4: Reversing the decline in membership

The compound result of this and the brand's newly increased penetration was that the AA's deep-set penetration decline was, for the first time in a decade, fundamentally reversed (Figure 69)!

Figure 69: AA penetration, 2015–2017

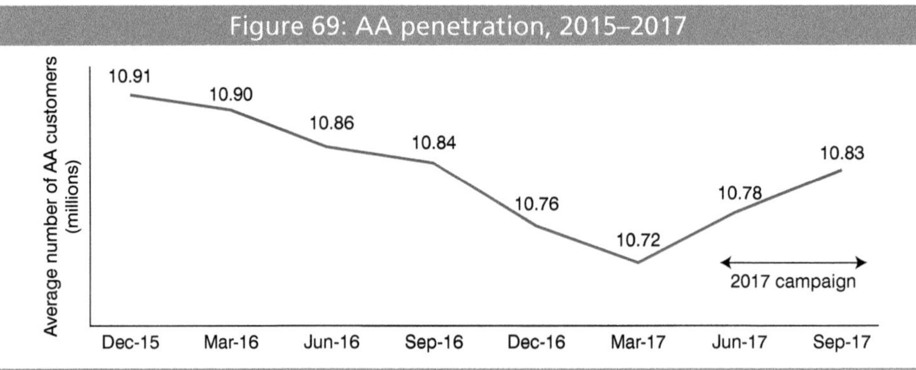

Source: TGI

And as a result, our market share returned to levels not seen since 2011 (Figure 70).

Figure 70: AA breakdown market share, 2011–2017

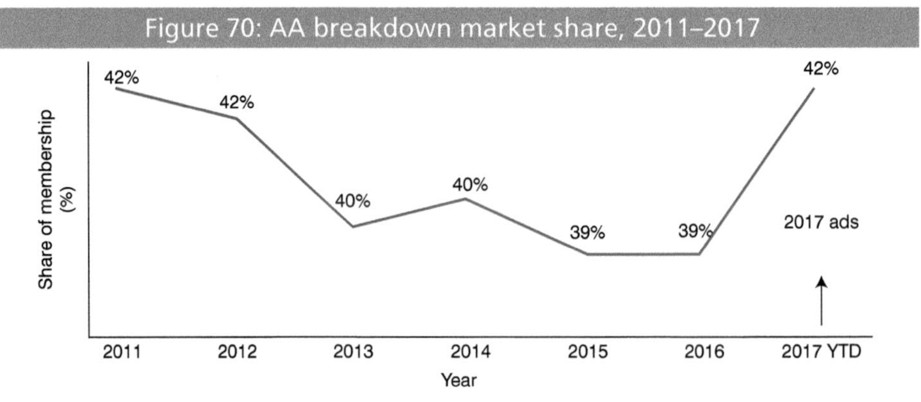

Source: AA

Objective 5: Deliver sustainable long-term revenue

As acquisition and renewals rose, at higher prices, 'Roadside' revenue increased (Figure 71).

Figure 71: 'Roadside' revenue, FY 2014–2016

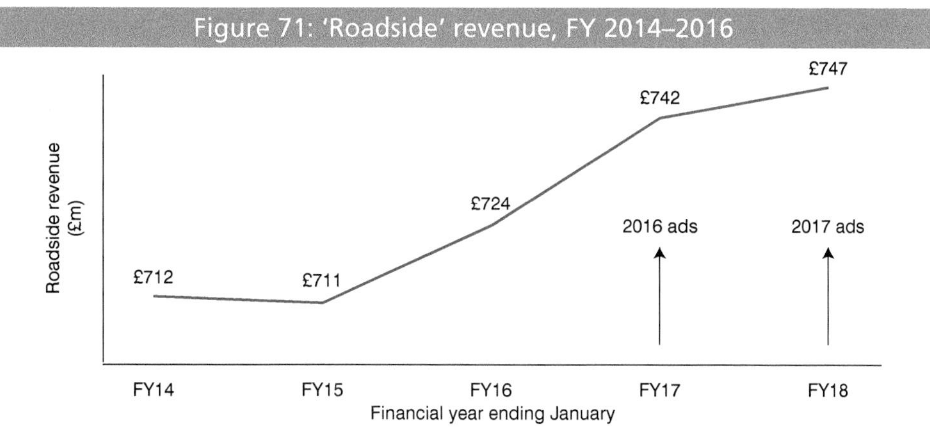

Source: AA company reports

But not only that, we also increased awareness of the other products in the portfolio (Figure 72).

Figure 72: Spontaneous awareness of other AA products, pre- and post-campaign, 2017

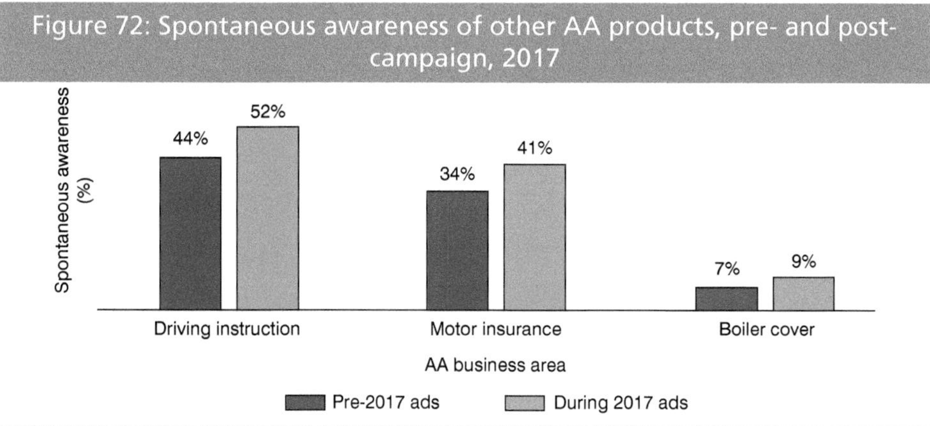

Source: Old Street Data Science. Pre (May 2017) vs. during (July 2017)

Thanks to all of these contributing factors, the AA's revenue decline was not only improved, it was totally reversed (Figure 73).

Figure 73: AA total revenue, FY2014–18

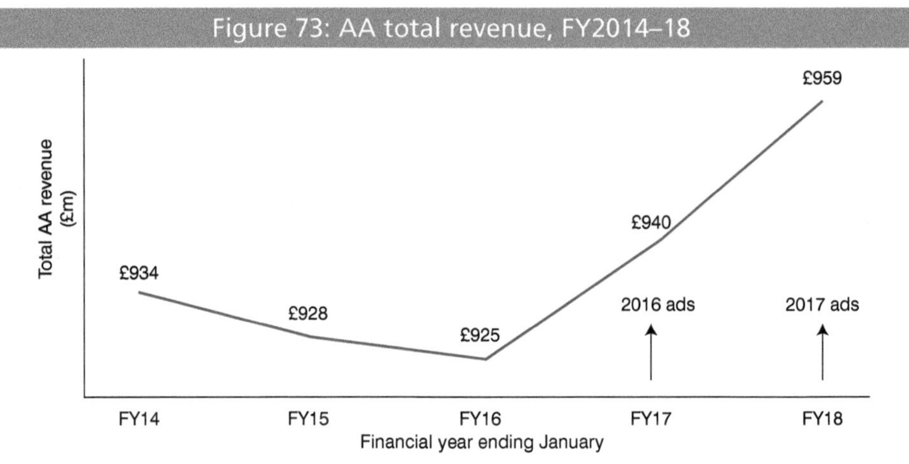

AA company reports

And although of course we know that many things affect stock price, it was heartening to see the AA's shares increase by 18% as financial year (FY) 2018 results were announced – with at least one commentator calling out the AA's achievement in growing 'new memberships in its 'Roadside' division by 7%'.[16]

Figure 74: Financial press article on recovery of AA share price, 18 April 2018

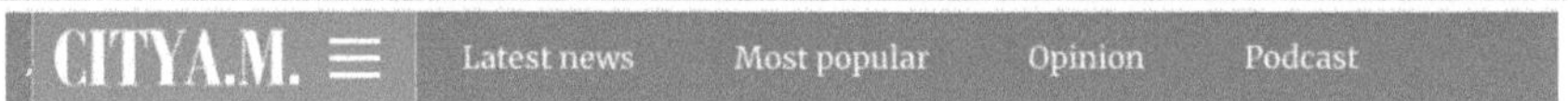

Wednesday 18 April 2018 11:38am

AA shares double in value: Markets believe breakdown giant is on the road to recovery

Share

Oliver Gill
Oliver Gill is a City A.M. reporter, you can contact him on oliver.gill@cityam.c [..] Show more

Follow Oliver

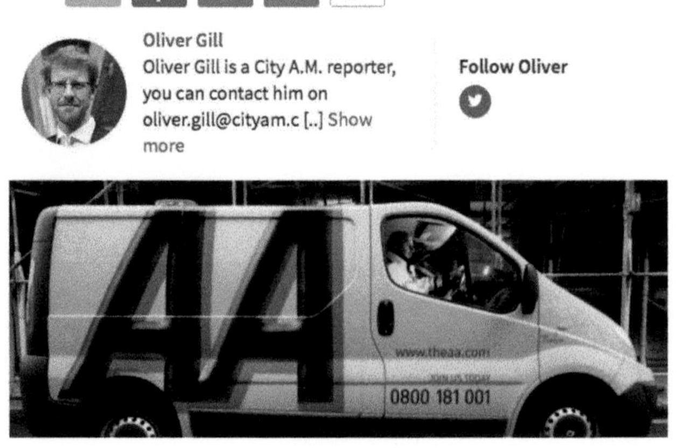

Summary of results

As we have seen, our strategy worked exactly as intended (Figure 75).

Figure 75: How our strategy worked

The ads got high awareness

They provoked a warm emotional response

They got the public and the media talking, amplifying our message

Brand salience and image improved

Consideration increased

More people started searching for and visiting AA online

'Roadside' acquisitions and renewals increased, despite firmer pricing

We reversed the decline in the membership base

The mix of products sold improved

'Roadside' revenues increased

There was a halo effect on other products and services

Total revenues hit their highest level for years

We have shown these effects grew stronger from 2016 to 2017, and we have shown that the timing of these improvements matched the timing of the advertising each year (to the very week where high-frequency data is available).

But could other factors explain this success? To answer that question, we need econometrics.

Isolating the effect of advertising

Since 2015, the AA have been using econometric modelling from consultancy Data2Decisions to measure the effect of their marketing communications. Data2Decisions' models take account of a wide range of factors that affect the AA's sales.

Figure 76 summarises the effects of the main factors affecting 'Roadside' acquisitions during the two years in question.

Market size

The results we have seen cannot be explained by an expansion of the market – as we have seen, the AA increased market share. More generally, market-wide factors such as number of cars on the road (declining) and the state of the economy only made a minor contribution during the period in question, accounting for 0.2% of growth in 2016 and 0.07% in 2017.

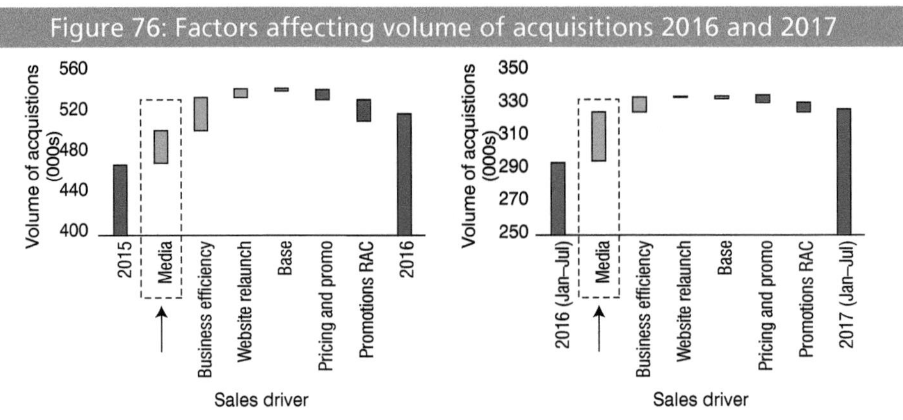

Figure 76: Factors affecting volume of acquisitions 2016 and 2017

Source: Data2Decisions modelling

Seasonality

'Roadside' sales are slightly seasonal, but this is fully accounted for in the models, and cannot explain the year-on-year growth we have seen. Where possible, we have removed seasonality from all our results charts using MATs and year-on-year comparisons.

Price and promotions

As we have discussed, prices increased during the period in question, and discounts became less generous. Econometrics confirms firmer pricing *reduced* volume during the period in question.

Competitor activity

The market did not become any less competitive. In fact, the RAC promoted their products harder, making it even tougher for us. Competitive activity is fully accounted for in the models.

Changes to the website

In May 2016, there were some improvements to the AA website, and this did increase online sales that spring. However, these changes were implemented months before the first burst of advertising, and cannot explain the sudden improvements in performance that took place when we went on air. As the Figure 76 shows, the effect on sales was modest.

Other business efficiencies

As we discussed above, advertising was part of a more general improvement in the efficiency of the AA's marketing operation. Introduced from 2014 to 2016, these changes did boost base sales, and increased the efficiency of our advertising when it went live. But they were rolled out gradually (so cannot explain the sudden sales surges we saw when we went on air) and were all in place by end 2016 (so cannot explain the big leap forward in summer 2017). They are fully accounted for in the econometrics.

Advertising

Econometrics shows that, across the whole two years in question, our advertising was the single biggest positive influence on 'Roadside' acquisitions, accounting for 18% of all sales during the modelled period (Table 1). Not only that, econometrics shows that the 2017 'Singing Baby' campaign was much more effective than its predecessor.

Table 1: The role of media in affecting sales

	Factor	Percentage of acquisitions	
1	Base	67%	Role of all other factors are accounted for in the modelling
2	Business efficiencies	9%	
3	Website	0.3%	
4	AA price/promotions	7%	
5	RAC promotions	–1%	
6	Media	18%	⇐ Role of media isolated

Source: Data2Decisions modelling

Establishing ROI

ROI from 'Roadside' acquisitions

Econometrics enables us to quantify the effect of each campaign on acquisitions (Figure 77).

Figure 77: Isolating effect of media on acquisitions

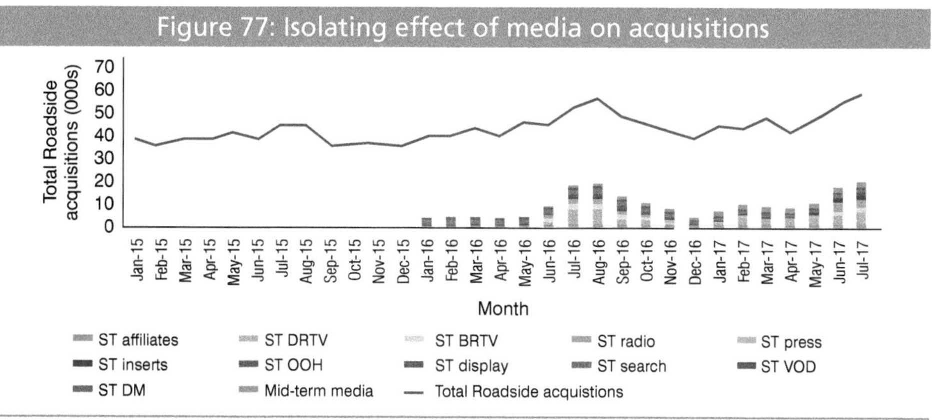

Source: Data2Decisions modelling

According to the modelling, the two campaigns had generated 194,000 extra sales by July 2017.[17] Using the AA's own estimates of customer lifetime value, we are then able to calculate return on investment (Table 2).

Table 2: Calculating the ROI

	2016	2017 (Jan–July)
Media-driven acquistions (customers)	109,8000	83.9
Medi-driven profit over lifetime of customers	£28.8m	£22.0m
Media spend	£15.0m	£9.8m
LTV profit ROI	£1.92	£2.23
LTV profit ROMI	92%	123%

Source: Data2Decisions and AA (LTV per customer)

Overall, *the campaigns paid for themselves more than twice over,* with ROI increasing by 30% as we shifted to the more emotional approach of 'Singing Baby' in 2017.

As expected, this larger pay-back effect wasn't just a result of direct sales, but also this famous campaign's more catalytic influence on all other key channels, with the ROI of DRTV and Radio also rising +36% and 49% respectively.

ROMI from other effects

We have shown that the advertising more than paid for itself from 'Roadside' acquisitions alone. But we have also shown that there were other effects – the ads increased renewal rates and promoted other products such as insurance.

In 2016, The AA commissioned Data2Decisions to measure some of these effects.[18] In line with the strategy, the largest effect was on 'Roadside' renewal rates (Figure 78).

Figure 78: Isolating the effect of media on renewal rates

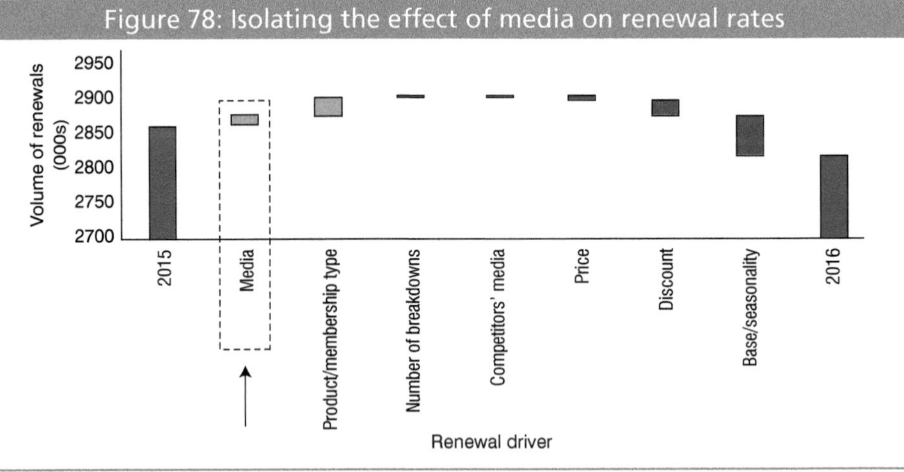

Source: Data2Decisions modelling

The econometrics also showed a smaller effect on insurance sales. Based on these 2016 results, we estimate that the total effect of advertising on sales is around 60% higher than the conservative estimate we get from 'Roadside' acquisitions alone (Table 3):

Table 3: Estimating the ROMI beyond acquisitions

Impact of 'Roadside' ads on ...	2016 ROIs indexed to 2016 acquistion revenue ROI
Acquisition	100
Acquisition + renewals	143
Acquisition + renewals + insurance halo	158

Source: Data2Decisions modelling

Furthermore, 'Roadside' media may well have an impact on B2B.[19] However, the AA FY 2017 Company Report shows that there are three times as many business members as personal members (accounting for *c.* 28% of total AA revenue). If advertising does impact B2B take up, even slightly, the additional boost to the ROMI could be very significant in terms of volume and revenue (Table 4).

Table 4: Estimating the ROMI from B2B

FY 2017	Number of 'Roadside' members	'Roadside' revenue*
Personal members	3.3m	£521m
Business customers	10.0m	£200m

Source: AA FY 2017 company reports. * revenue = number of members × average income per member

Conclusion

We all know the theory: long-term success requires mass reach and emotion.

But so often that can feel like an indulgence – especially when existing 'efficient' communications already seem to be delivering fantastic profit growth.

But appearances can be deceptive.

It's fair to say, that the AA was certainly subject to this deception.

It took a forced look at long-term metrics to discover the true commercial risks of this short-termism and, more importantly, convince the board to change its course.

The result? Within just three years, the AA completely transformed its revenue model: from artificially low acquisition prices and inflated renewal fees, to creating sustainable revenue growth through higher demand at higher prices.

We hope this serves as a timely reminder. Specifically, in 2018, as the world's business axis tilts away from commodities and increasingly towards services, we hope it provides a useful jolt for all our fellow 'subscription brands'.

From banks, telecoms, and energy companies, to the likes of Netflix, Amazon and Dollar Shave, subscription models can seem to offer a heady promise of deep-pocketed, ever-loyal customers from which to eternally draw profit.

But as we've shown, this isn't just shooting fish in a barrel it's also shooting yourself in the foot.

Milking existing customers in the short term, invariably leads to disaster in the long term.

Our marketing requires a more balanced strategy where brand building and sales-driving work in harmony to deliver sustainable profits for the years to come.

That's how we'll all keep our big wheels turnin'.

Notes

1. For readers that don't know it, the Automobile Association (AA), established in 1905, is the UK's largest provider of breakdown services and associated products.
2. Source: The AA, 2018.
3. Source: YouGov, BrandIndex.
4. https://www.moneysavingexpert.com/news/travel/2013/04/the-aa-is-the-easiest-company-to-haggle-with-in-2013
5. Based on internal AA forecast.
6. We have taken advice from the IPA on the eligibility of campaigns which have been subject to ASA rulings, and have been assured that, *provided we do not rest our effectiveness case on the executions in question, the paper is eligible*. We mention the 2015 campaign for context only. We have also included full details of the ASA adjudication as requested – but in summary, the complaint related to the wording of the TV voiceover in 2015 – which was changed for 2016 and beyond.
7. Greg Beales is a former political strategist for The Labour Party.
8. Old Street Data Science Segmentation, 2016.
9. Measured in response to the question, 'If you've heard anything about the brand in the last two weeks, through advertising, news or word of mouth, was it positive or negative?'
10. Measured in response to the question, 'Which of the following have you talked about with friends and family in the past two weeks (whether in person, online or through social media)?'
11. Measured in response to the question,'The percentage of respondents who have reported hearing anything, either positive or negative about a brand over the past two weeks'.
12. Measured in response to the question, 'Do you have a general positive or negative feeling about the brand?'
13. Measured in response to the question, 'Is it good quality or poor quality?'
14. The research agency run by the aforementioned, Greg Beales.
15. McKinsey internal strategy audit, 2017.
16. https://investomania.co.uk/2018/04/will-aa-plc-soar-higher-than-standard-chartered-plc-and-legal-general-group-plc-after-results/
17. At the time of writing, econometric evaluation was only available up to end July 2017.
18. The analysis has not been repeated recently, so only 2016 results are shown here.
19. There has been no modelling commissioned.

SECTION 3

Silver winners

SILVER

Aldi

Kevin the Carrot 2016 and 2017: How Aldi UK won Christmas with the help of a humble carrot

By Jamie Peate and Darren Hawkins, McCann Manchester; Adam Zavalis, Aldi UK

Contributing authors: Marie Koropisz and Andrew Houghton, McCann Manchester; Guy Beardsley, Universal McCann

Credited companies: McCann Manchester; Gain Theory; Shiny Red; Universal McCann; Weber Shandwick

Summary

Despite success as a discount supermarket, Aldi still had an issue at Christmas. Its core shoppers spent disproportionately more than average on making their Christmas special, but they didn't spend it all with Aldi. By creating and sticking with the Kevin the Carrot character over Christmas 2016–2017, Aldi stayed more top-of-mind for its shoppers, built an emotional connection with the brand and showcased its Christmas range. Aldi dramatically reduced its Christmas dip in market share and became the fastest-growing supermarket of Christmas 2016 and 2017.

Client comment

Adam Zavalis, Marketing Director, Aldi UK

Traditionally all retailers, including Aldi, have always looked to develop new creative work for Christmas each year. Given the importance of the Christmas period to the overall business performance of most retailers this is not that surprising. On top of this, Christmas represents a time when customers naturally become less loyal to any one store. So retailers really have to try their hardest to hang onto their customers as well as enticing new ones in. Therefore, it's not surprising that the Christmas period has become the UK 'Superbowl' when it comes to advertising.

The Christmas season now stretches all the way from the end of October to New Year, with lots of retailers that hardly advertise for the rest of the year piling into the market too. This means you need to fight even harder to get noticed, so you have to start with a bang and then have enough momentum to keep you going until the end. It's a sprint of marathon length.

We learnt that to maintain momentum you need to be integrated and agile across all channels and keep surprising and delighting your customers throughout the long Christmas season.

When we conceived Kevin in 2016 we knew we were onto something and were extremely pleased with how well he performed across all of our key metrics. However I think our really brave move was to bring him back, along with Katie and the kids in 2017. This very much went against our natural instincts which are always to come back with something new to maximise both impact and creative opportunity. Who says carrots don't help you see better!

Aldi

To read the full case study visit www.ipa.co.uk/ease or www.warc.com

Art Institute of Chicago

Van Gogh's bedrooms: The power of an immersive idea

By Clifford Schwandner and Ariel Tishgart, Leo Burnett Chicago

Contributing author: Brent Nelsen, Leo Burnett North America

Credited companies: Art Institute of Chicago; Leo Burnett Chicago; Ravenswood Studio

Summary

The Art Institute of Chicago wanted to publicise its Van Gogh exhibition and broaden the audience for art, particularly by getting more Chicago locals to visit the museum. A strategy was built on the insight that art was an immersive experience, not a series of objects to view. Digital and outdoor positioned the show as a keyhole into the artist's world, with activity culminating in a recreation of Van Gogh's painted bedroom that could be booked via Airbnb. The exhibition generated the museum's best attendance figures in 15 years, USD1.6m of long-term revenue from new memberships, and local museum visitors outnumbered tourists for the first time in 10 years.

Client comment

Katie Rahn, Executive Director of Marketing and Communications, Art Institute of Chicago

The Art Institute of Chicago is the second largest art museum in the USA and has a collection that spans the globe and encompasses 5,000 years of creativity. The museum holds the best Impressionist collection outside of Paris and TripAdvisor Travelers ranked us the top museum in the world in 2014.

And yet, our local visitation is not where we want it to be. Chicagoans are exceedingly proud of the museum, but pride doesn't always translate to a visit. So over the last six years, the Art Institute has partnered with Leo Burnett to drive attendance and make the museum more approachable and relevant to the people of Chicago ... and all on a shoestring budget.

With 'Van Gogh's bedrooms', we knew what we needed to do was go beyond the intrinsic power of a major exhibition and bring the exhibition – and the artist – to life. Leo Burnett developed the simple, galvanising insight that all of us are curious about how others live. All of us are voyeurs. And that insight led to the development of Van Gogh Airbnb, the remarkably executed installation that literally gave people the chance to step inside one of history's most famous paintings.

The results of this campaign speak for themselves, but it's difficult to overstate the excitement and buzz around the city of Chicago that this campaign engendered. But it, of course, wasn't just PR and social chatter. This exhibition brought Chicagoans to the museum in crowds we haven't seen for 15 years, fulfilling our goals, but more importantly, reaffirming their relationship with the museum and its cultural prominence in the city of Chicago.

Art Institute of Chicago

To read the full case study visit www.ipa.co.uk/ease or www.warc.com

Baileys

A radical brand turnaround story with extra sprinkles

By Katie Mackay-Sinclair and Jack Farrelly, Mother; John Thomson, Carat

Contributing authors: David Hartley, Data2Decisions; Sheila Cunningham and Kate Mudd, Diageo

Credited companies: Mother; Carat; Data2Decisions

Summary

Although a loved drinks brand, Baileys was consumed infrequently and in small amounts. Sales were declining by 8% a year. To restart growth, the 'Don't mind if I Baileys' strategy reframed Baileys as a real adult treat. Creative highlighted the versatility of Baileys as a food and drink ingredient using a channel mix including TV, programmatic, and social content. Following the activity, the number of ways people consumed Baileys grew by 30% and sales volumes increased by 11%. This case estimates there was a 54% increase in annual net profit despite lower investment.

Client comment

Sheila Cunningham, Baileys Global Head of Planning, Diageo

The last two years of the 'Don't mind if I Baileys' campaign have been full of valuable lessons for not only the Baileys team, but also the broader Diageo business, and our industry as a whole.

Our story is a reminder that the brands we shepherd needn't be forever beholden to the conventions of the categories they came from. We should be confident in future-proofing our brands through finding more dynamic category contexts to play within.

When we need to drive volume, investing all in the 'blockbuster' isn't the be all and end all. In fact, a strategy based on getting the right content in front of more of the right people at the right times can be even more effective.

We also learned that focusing upon our brands' purposes also needn't mean reverting to lofty and ephemeral causes. Instead, use purpose to drive meaningful and relevant connections with your consumers – and to do that, don't dismiss a focus on what people actually love about our brands; the products we make.

For Baileys specifically, but also Diageo as a whole, this case is a demonstration of the power of a simple strategy to galvanise an entire team and ultimately, an entire business. Something we as marketers know is fundamental to the success of today's biggest brands.

But most importantly, this is a lesson in how radically reframing our brand delivered the highest advertising ROIs of any Diageo spirits brand in any market in Europe. And that was only possible because, collectively, we never forgot the importance of always looking to learn and always striving for better.

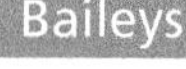

To read the full case study visit www.ipa.co.uk/ease or www.warc.com

SILVER

Barclays

Purpose pays

By Tom Roach, BBH

Contributing authors: Adam Smythe and Claire Hilton, Barclays UK

Credited company: BBH

Summary

The financial crash and banking scandals left trust in Barclays at record lows. To restore confidence and consideration, the banking group wanted to demonstrate how it helped society. Over four years, purpose-led marketing initiatives showed Barclays staff equipping different groups with digital and life skills, such as how to avoid fraud or use technology. Compared to its previous product campaigns, purpose initiatives led to 2.6 times the level of brand trust, an important driver of consideration in financial services. An estimated 460,000 financial products were sold and £153m of short-term income generated. The estimated short-term profit ROI was £2.30 for every £1 invested.

Client comment

Claire Hilton, Marketing Director, Barclays

I learnt three career-changing lessons as a result of leading our purpose-led brand campaign.

First, you have to protect a great idea no matter who is challenging you and what the gremlins might be whispering in your ear in the middle of the night. Don't allow it to be diluted – be confident, bold and ignore the naysayers.

Second, allow yourself to be vulnerable. Vulnerability allowed us to be creative and take the advertising places we have never been before. Did we know it was going to work? Absolutely not. But we believed in our strategy and we knew we could test, refine and make the work stronger as a result.

And last, challenge the norm. Do the unexpected. People expect banks to talk about mortgages, current accounts, loans but this alone doesn't drive emotional connections and the brand overall. A brand which proudly shows its role within society, communities and how it is helping individuals elevates the conversation and perceptions of it in people's minds.

How we work has completely changed. Our mantra throughout the campaign was actions not words; this means that from an insight perspective, we hardwired into the brand a relentless search for powerful insights and great examples of how people, propositions and services are demonstrating our purpose through the actions they are taking. We also held authenticity very closely to our hearts; shining a light on real people telling their own stories was at the centre of our creative expression, which was made even better when these individuals were able to pass on their own practical experiences, like a life skills lesson to millions of others.

To read the full case study visit www.ipa.co.uk/ease or www.warc.com

David Sheldrick Wildlife Trust

Hello in Elephant: Translating an endangered language to help save an endangered species

By Matthew Simms, whiteGREY

Contributing authors: Danish Chan and Chad Mackenzie, whiteGREY

Credited company: whiteGREY

Summary

Despite a decline in ivory trading, elephant populations were falling. Although there was no media budget, a way was needed to reignite concern and donations for elephant welfare. The solution was to create a unique opportunity to rebond with elephants via an app that translated human words into elephant signals. The app triggered huge media interest and social sharing, motivating people to donate. An estimated 400m media impressions were generated and donations rose by 34% versus a 10% target. Almost 4,200 new supporters were recruited and USD1.28m of incremental revenue delivered. The long-term profit ROMI was projected as £19.10 for every £1 invested.

Client comment

Rob Brandford, Executive Director, David Sheldrick Wildlife Trust

'Hello in Elephant' is an impressive piece of work. Recognised throughout the David Sheldrick Wildlife Trust as both beautiful and impactful.

Impactful: as our struggle to save elephants in Kenya and East Africa grows, so does our challenge to attract resource. We need more funds, yet it's never been more difficult to secure new supporters and donations. We're not just competing in a crowded and frankly cut-throat environmental charity space, with organisations who have vastly superior reach and resources, but with every other worthy cause that demands people's attention. This idea achieved penetration in a noisy market and generated significant impact for the organisation.

Beautiful: we try over and over to get people to feel for the cause by understanding how magnificent elephants are. Yet, outside of the limited numbers getting up close to orphan elephants at our Nursery and Reintegration Units, it's difficult for people to truly appreciate elephants. It was the beautiful fusion of creativity and technology that gave us an incredibly powerful way for the world to emotionally connect with elephants by experiencing how special they are. We gained empathy on a mass scale through this experience.

'Hello in Elephant' has given impetus to the organisation to continue to explore how we can collide creativity and technology to not only reach and engage new supporters but change how we operate and protect, rescue, raise, and release elephants back into the wild.

David Sheldrick Wildlife Trust

To read the full case study visit www.ipa.co.uk/ease or www.warc.com

Ella's Kitchen

Selling up doesn't mean selling out

By Clare Phayer, Havas London
Contributing authors: Clare Hutchinson and Nick Lee, Havas London
Credited companies: Havas London; Ella's Kitchen

Summary

With a small budget but ambitious growth targets, Ella's Kitchen needed a smarter way to get more parents to buy its baby foods and become brand fans. Using its knowledge of how weaning can be a difficult experience, it developed a strategy to recruit and support mums and dads of weaning babies. The core of the plan was an always-on model featuring an advice hub and a CRM-driven initiative of emails and other communications to encourage users to recommend the brand. The programme drew in 40% of all new UK parents of weaning babies, generating £12.6m of incremental sales, and a 10% increase in penetration.

Client comment

Jacq Ellis-Jones, 'Runs Making Friends', Ella's Kitchen

The introduction of our always on weaning programme has transformed the way we approach brand communications at Ella's Kitchen.

Parents can access relevant and engaging content at the right time for them, which means that our team can focus on driving recruitment, adopting a forward-thinking approach and ensuring the service stays genuine.

The fact that we now see 40% of all weaning parents signing up to our programme is a huge testament to its success and it continues to support the growth of the business, ensuring we maintain our number one position in the market.

Ella's Kitchen

To read the full case study visit www.ipa.co.uk/ease or www.warc.com

Heineken

A game changer: How Heineken reinvented its Champions League communications

By Ed Booty, Publicis Singapore; James Moore, Publicis Italy; Kate Hinz, Starcom

Contributing authors: Derek Muller, Tommy Cottam and Bela Zieman, Publicis Italy; Sol Ghafoor and Stuart Williams, Publicis London; Carolin Wagner, Starcom

Credited companies: Publicis Italy; Poke London; Starcom; Heineken International

Summary

Despite good awareness and brand fit of its UEFA Champions League (UCL) sponsorship, Heineken's sales growth was shrinking and penetration had stalled. Soccer fans were more likely to drink the lager when they watched matches socially than if they viewed by themselves. Featuring José Mourinho as spokesman, a new international strategy for Champions League markets motivated fans to watch with others and drink Heineken using high-impact TV and online video. Personalised reminders and content provided further inducement. Following the brand's activity, there was a 20% drop in games watched alone. Year-on-year volume growth in UCL markets grew to 13.7%, compared to declines in non-participating countries. Global brand penetration increased by 5%.

Client comment

Anuraag Trikha, Global Brand Director, Heineken

The 2016–17 season was certainly a benchmark year for Heineken and our sponsorship with UEFA Champions League. Our ambition was to become the new standard for creativity and effectiveness in a mobile first world. Early on we challenged our agencies to help us deliver experiences which would not only bring forward the Heineken POV but more importantly be relevant and enjoyable for our consumer.

Creating a narrative that consistently drives enjoyment for our consumer and for UCL fans around the world was no easy task. It meant pivoting from targeting which previously leveraged rich audience insights to targeting which was much more contextually driven which move fans from one relatable moment to the next. We even restructured our communications framework from an ecosystem which was integrated with distinct layers to one which was more responsive, always-on, real-time, and deeply data-driven.

At the end of the day, a winning strategy is nothing without winning results. We believe the volume sales growth, increase in penetration and revenue are all proof of this and to this day continue to use these insights to drive effectiveness strategies across all our platforms and sponsorships. It's because of this value to the brand that we continue to drive this into the culture of everything we do.

Heineken

To read the full case study visit www.ipa.co.uk/ease or www.warc.com

SILVER

IKEA

'The wonderful everyday'

By Kieran Bradshaw, Mother

Contributing authors: Aaron Haynes and Charlie Ebdy, Vizeum; Adam Bailey, MediaCom Business Science; Andrew Deykin, Data2Decisions

Credited companies: Mother; Vizeum

Summary

After 25 years of growth, IKEA's UK sales, penetration and footfall were all declining. It needed to gain more customers and get people to buy a broader range of its products. 'The wonderful everyday' strategy rejected seasonal or event-driven marketing for an always-on approach with more personalised copy. Media were chosen to reach consumers when they were most likely to be thinking of their homes. Penetration rose 10% and all IKEA product categories reported growth. It is estimated that £755m of incremental revenue was generated and the ROMI was calculated at £2.31 for every £1 invested.

Client comment

Laurent Tiersen, Marketing Manager, IKEA UK and Ireland

Ingvar Kamprad, IKEA's founder, said 'The feeling of having finished something is an effective sleeping pill'. At IKEA, we are never finished, always on the way, always doing and learning. So although 'The wonderful everyday' has been running for more than four years now, no two campaigns within it have ever been the same; each time we build on what we have learnt from the campaign before, and this is something we continue to do. This doesn't mean getting it right every time – we've pursued different routes that haven't always succeeded, but that doesn't mean they are dead ends, we are learning every step along the way.

But performance is only half the story, for our teams process is equally important; we have spent a lot of time working with Mother and our agencies to develop a process that is able to help us make the everyday marketing reality smoother and more effective. After all, shouldn't how we work together be as wonderful as the work we create together?

To read the full case study visit www.ipa.co.uk/ease or www.warc.com

SILVER

Nationwide Building Society

How Nationwide found its voice and the difference that made

By Gethin James, VCCP

Contributing authors: Richard Bradford, Wavemaker; Neil Holloway and Paul Hibbs, Nationwide Building Society

Credited companies: VCCP; Wavemaker London

Summary

Nationwide had a small share of the declining market in current account switchers. A shift from rational to more emotional advertising produced a temporary improvement. But it took the radical 'Voices' strategy, featuring TV poetry ads and a more individual tone across media, to set Nationwide apart from other banking brands. Following this activity, brand differentiation, trust and affinity all rose. Advertising drove an estimated 63,000 switched accounts and 242,000 new account openings. Total value created for Nationwide members was modelled at £2.66 for every £1 invested.

Client comment

Paul Hibbs, Director of Advertising and Media, Nationwide

Writing the paper has a number of positive effects that we continue to benefit from long after the paper was submitted.

First, we now have better relationships and processes in place to get hold of business performance data to the granularity required for judging marketing effectiveness. The data has often been held across various parts of the business so it proved hard to get everything we needed together in one place.

Second, in pulling together the paper, the agency now has a deeper understanding of how our specific business works. We are not a PLC seeking to maximise shareholder value but a mutual seeking to create value for our members.

And finally, the paper has been invaluable in educating our non-marketing colleagues about how our advertising works for us. Specifically, in making the hard commercial case for things that can sound soft and fluffy: emotion, image, difference and distinctiveness. The insights developed in our paper have been shared with the CEO and Executive Committee.

From here, there are a few steps we are taking to further embed effectiveness further into our culture including implementing mode detailed econometric models and integrating them more into our comms planning.

Nationwide Building Society

To read the full case study visit www.ipa.co.uk/ease or www.warc.com

Prospan

The world's first cough predictor

By Luke Brown and Angela Smith, AFFINITY
Credited company: AFFINITY

Summary

The natural children's cough remedy, Prospan, was fighting against bigger rivals to maintain its Australian sales. Its target audience – mums – was conflicted on how to deal with kids' coughs and prone to 'wait and see' before administering remedies. Using search, social and algorithms, an innovative predictor of outbreaks of colds was developed to target messages at the most opportune moments. The 'Don't ignore a cough' creative was distributed in print and activated digitally via programmatic in real-time to reach mums when coughs were likely to be increasing. Click-through on digital was 54% higher than a control group. Sales grew by 10% in six months despite an 8.5% decline in the category following one of the warmest winters on record. Market share rose by 18.5% in a half year.

Client comment

Michael Aylward, Group Marketing Manager, Flordis Australia

As marketers we're under constant pressure to do more with less, and know more about more areas of expertise, with less time. Never has this been truer for data-driven marketing. We knew we had to approach things differently and stretch ourselves to overcome a number of challenges.

We learned two valuable lessons in creating the Prospan 'Cough prediction' campaign:

1. *Qualified risks*: in order to genuinely innovative, you need to be open to new ways of thinking, thinking that may take you out of your comfort zone. The 'qualified' part is critical though. As a smaller market player we needed to know that we weren't being frivolous with our investment and just trying something different for the sake of it. Our agency partners AFFINITY, launched themselves into understanding our brand and category from every angle – including science and data. In the end this is what enabled them to pull together a truly new

approach to market. Through creating a robust test case, they were able to demonstrate that their targeting model was going to be effective with a strong level of confidence.

2. *We're better together:* the other was opening ourselves up to true partnership and learning where our own brand expertise intersected with our trusted partners' experience and expertise to propel us out of the ordinary. When brand owners work in collaboration with complementary partners and are actively open to solutions offered, then amazing outcomes can happen. It's about entering the situation with a mindset that we can all look good, so we start with an aim to not judge ideas, but to collectively make something together and 'raise the tide' to take everyone higher. Collaboration is the key to creativity and therefore innovation.

Prospan

To read the full case study visit www.ipa.co.uk/ease or www.warc.com

SILVER

Purplebricks

How Purplebricks brought 'Commisery' to the UK's estate agents

By Matt Wyatt, SNAP London
Contributing author: Mike Nicholson, General Eclectic
Credited company: SNAP London

Summary

Online estate agents had failed to disrupt the property market despite trading for almost a decade. To drive consideration and increase instructions to sell homes, the online-based Purplebricks needed to engage the mass market with its key differentiator – unlike most estate agents, it does not charge sellers' commissions. It invested in TV-led advertising empathising with people's 'Commisery' – an imagined despondency you might feel if you thought you had needlessly paid out thousands in commission. Following the campaign, consideration rose from 23% to 38%. Market share almost doubled and revenue grew by £35.1m (218%) in 2016–17. The change helped the company swing from a £4.4m loss to a £3.7m profit in one financial year.

Client comment

James Kydd, Marketing Director, Purplebricks Group

The first thing is the importance of framing. Many companies in our sector of the estate-agency market have used 'cost-saving' as a central plank of their advertising approach, but with little meaningful success in terms of building sales. In developing the 'Commisery' campaign, we too wanted to use the cost-saving benefit of not having to pay commission. By framing it in the context of 'loss aversion' we were able to give our cost-saving message greater meaning and we know that, because of this, we struck a genuine nerve. It was this insight that led to the turbo-charging of our performance, so we will never underestimate the importance of uncovering a genuine insight again!

The second key learning is that people respond more emotionally than rationally. In our previous campaigns, whilst we had recognised the strength of an emotional appeal, we had relied heavily on the rational story. With Commisery we turned this balance around and concentrated primarily on maximising the emotional pull of the ads. This included ensuring that we made everything 'look good', hence elevating the stature of the Purplebricks brand.

Lastly, we've learned that if you use television advertising in the right way, it is an incredibly powerful medium. Many people in the industry know that, at any one time, only about 8% of the adult population is 'in-market' for estate agency services. Surely therefore, by advertising on TV, we are wasting 92% of our money by talking to people who are not in-market? What we have been able to prove is that TV can yield far lower costs per instruction than many of the tightly targeted media that now exist. But only if you do it right. Commisery did it right.

Purplebricks

To read the full case study visit www.ipa.co.uk/ease or www.warc.com

SILVER

SK-II

'The marriage market takeover': How giving 'leftover women' in China a voice transformed a luxury skin care brand

By My Troedsson, Forsman & Bodenfors
Credited companies: Forsman & Bodenfors; BeOn

Summary

In China, women who are single after the age of 27 are known as 'leftover women'. Some Chinese parents post details of 'available' daughters in public 'marriage markets' to attract the parents of single sons. P&G's luxury skincare brand, SK-II, wanted to make itself more relevant to women by supporting their right to control their own destinies. It created a documentary celebrating single women and encouraging parents to respect daughters' life choices. Outdoor and activations amplified the conservation which generated huge media buzz. Following the activity, brand salience, price and market share all strengthened. Average new users per month grew by almost 100% and sales nearly doubled in a year. SK-II became Asia's number one brand in its category.

Client comment

Kylene Campos, Global Brand Director, SK-II, P&G

'Marriage market' has truly put SK-II in the map globally and in China as a brand that women can relate to on a human level and not just at a functional level. This experience has taught us that we should always remember that our consumers are human beings first and foremost, and keep this central in everything that we do. This is a higher bar indeed, and one that will help us stay relevant in today's fast changing world where consumers put value, transparency, authenticity and humanity at the centre.

To read the full case study visit www.ipa.co.uk/ease or www.warc.com

SILVER

Skittles

Breaking conventions with Pride

By David Mortimer, adam&eveDDB
Contributing author: Les Binet, adam&eveDDB
Credited companies: adam&eveDDB; MediaCom; Haygarth

Summary

UK sales of Skittles were declining. As an impulse buy, the confectionery brand needed to be top of mind and more visible in stores. To reach young adults – often light TV viewers – it sought new ways to gain salience and improve retail distribution. In partnership with Tesco, Skittles launched a new product without its famous rainbow branding, to show support for the LGBT+ community's rainbow flag and create buzz during Pride festival season. The launch generated social sharing and a total 250m impressions – 73% unpaid. In a flat market, Skittles value share rose 4.2%, with dramatic growth in Tesco stores and around Pride. Whilst decreasing in other retailers, distribution in Tesco grew 92%, opening up fresh opportunities to collaborate with the UK's biggest retailer.

Client comment

Rory Fitzherbert, Skittles Senior Brand Manager, Mars

'Give the rainbow' helped to break new ground for us as a brand. We learnt the power of working collaboratively with a retail partner, bringing them with us on the journey as we championed a cause and initiative of great importance to both businesses.

It was the first time Skittles has championed a positive cause like Pride. And with key global markets like US and Germany now picking up this support for the LGBT+ community, it has helped to deliver a global evolution of the brand. Fun and disruption was at the heart of the idea, but we were also genuine and authentic when it mattered. Whether that's the heartfelt gesture to Pride, seeking meaningful influencers or donating a proportion of profit from each pack.

The campaign has become an important case study within Mars, pioneering new ways of earning reach and driving brand growth, beyond usual channels like TV. It's also changing the way we work going forwards. Pride is now an important part of our calendar and yearly planning, offering a new opportunity to showcase our support for Pride in eye-catching ways, whilst driving desire for our limited-edition product.

The results of the campaign inspired us to bring retail and shopper insights into the planning process earlier, in the knowledge that solutions to key business challenges are just as likely to come from retailer needs as they are from consumer insights.

The campaign has also had a big impact internally. From the whole business celebrating Pride each year, to the chance for associates to join us on the float at Pride in London. Mars has also started an important partnership with Stonewall on their Diversity Champions programme – ensuring that we are supporting and celebrating diversity and inclusion everyday within the business.

Skittles

To read the full case study visit www.ipa.co.uk/ease or www.warc.com

SILVER

Sport England

'This girl can': Giving judgement the finger (and inspiring millions of women to get active)

By Vicki Holgate, Laura Pirkis and Matthew Scott, FCB Inferno

Contributing author: Nicola Willison, FCB Inferno

Credited companies: FCB Inferno; Carat; Somesuch & Co; Blue Rubicon; Kim Gehrig

Summary

In 2014, 1.79m fewer women than men were exercising regularly, and the gap was growing. Sport England's objective was to reduce this gender gap. The discovery that 'fear of judgement' was holding women back inspired a campaign (spanning TV, cinema, outdoor, digital, social, PR and influencers) that celebrated the triumph of a 'don't give a damn' attitude over society's judgement. Over two million women became more active as a direct result and the gender gap reduced from 1.79m to 1.55m. Based on incremental sports and health benefits generated, the estimated return on marketing investment was £35 for every £1 invested.

Client comment

Jennie Price, Chief Executive, Sport England

Ensuring and proving effectiveness is fundamental to any campaign, especially one for a government agency where advertising spend is unusual and subject to significant scrutiny. 'This girl can' has been highly effective in changing the behaviour of women across England. It is one of the first interventions which has a proven impact on this type of behaviour at whole population level and so has had a profound effect on our wider work.

Its effectiveness is borne from the power of insight; going beyond the obvious barriers of inconvenience, lack of time and cost to deal with a fundamental, previously unspoken issue about how women felt about their bodies in the context of sport and activity. We now place much more emphasis on emotional barriers in our wider work, and draw from a wider range of insights to ensure our interventions tackle the most fundamental issues.

Second, it has shown the importance of viewing a campaign, not as an isolated finite suite of communications, but rather as an evolving toolbox, which partners and others can use, and flexible enough to be deployed across a range of media. We have also learned that the most effective way to prove the effect of a campaign is to collect impact data in different ways, triangulating several sources and ensuring a mix of qualitative and quantitative evaluation.

Finally, whilst our intention was always to create a campaign that could live on in the hands of partners and our audience, it has taught us a powerful lesson about finding the confidence necessary to relinquish control and empower others to take ownership of a campaign. Our biggest success has been that 'This girl can' has a life independent of Sport England. Not just accepting but celebrating this is the biggest culture shift of all for our organisation.

Sport England

To read the full case study visit www.ipa.co.uk/ease or www.warc.com

SILVER

Starbucks

Starbucks and social: How Starbucks created the fourth place in coffee culture

By Matthew Philip and Rachael Lake, Manning Gottlieb OMD

Contributing authors: Faith Stevens, Annalect; Reuben Arnold and Jamie McQuary, Starbucks UK

Credited companies: Manning Gottlieb OMD; Starbucks UK

Summary

Across seven years, Starbucks UK reallocated investment from traditional media into a social strategy which evolved as consumers' social behaviour changed. Early focus on using social to communicate events and seasonal offers gave way to encouraging coffee cup imagery to be used as a creative focal point. Later, the brand saw opportunities for further growth and engagement by supporting the then nascent culture of self-expression and involving influencers. This case demonstrates how Starbucks UK has used social to deliver sustainable business growth and compares the business impact of investment in social and traditional media. Since 2010, it estimates that social generated almost £18m more for the brand than investing in traditional channels. It calculates the strategy returned almost £4 in additional profit for every £1 invested.

Client comment

Reuben Arnold, VP Brand Development and Marketing, Starbucks UK

Over the past six years social media has become an increasingly critical part of our marketing efforts and how we engage with customers. It hasn't been a magic bullet – it's been a continual learning process to understand what works for the brand and what people expect from us – moving from promotional events and building a fanbase to facilitating visual expression and involving influencers.

Looking back, it's fascinating to see how our approach has evolved, as social media and how people use it continues to change rapidly. This evolving approach has also informed our decision making along the way to shift more investment into these channels based on effectiveness insight provided by regular econometric analysis that has driven real business results along with positive brand metrics.

Looking forward we will continue to evolve our approach and gather insights to deliver effective social media activity that remains relevant to our audiences and results in a positive ROI for the business.

Starbucks

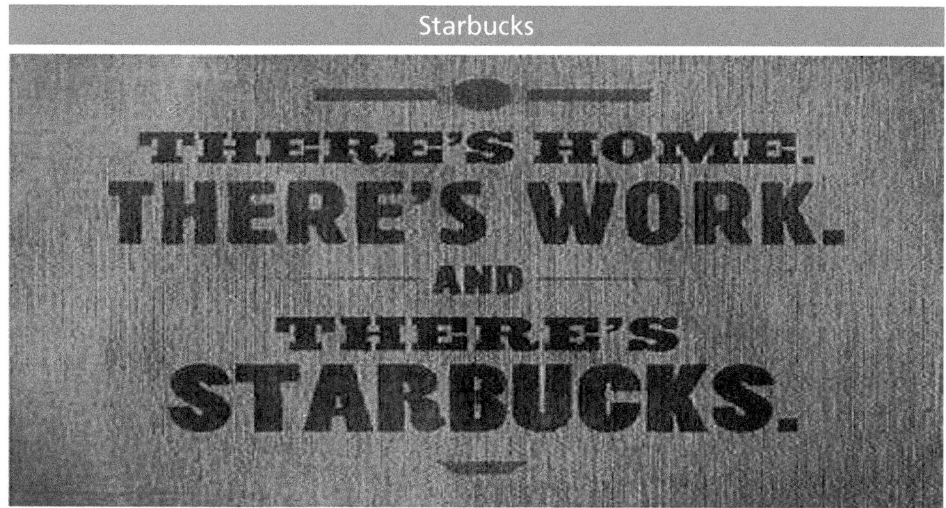

To read the full case study visit www.ipa.co.uk/ease or www.warc.com

SILVER

Virgin Media

Finding our Virginity: How fighting fact with feeling helped Virgin Media take on the might of Sky

By Ed Kurland, BBH

Contributing authors: Madeleine Young and Thomas Gwin, BBH; Bambos Neophytou, Jonathan Chapman and Stephanie Butler, Virgin Media; Elle Graham-Dixon, BBDO; Stephen Hilton, Annalect

Credited companies: BBH; Annalect; Manning Gottlieb OMD

Summary

Despite having a smaller budget, Virgin Media needed to compete better for TV and broadband customers against category leader, Sky. The role of communications was to ensure Virgin was prominent and worth a premium in consumers' minds when choosing a supplier. Over two years, TV brand and direct marketing evoked the Virgin masterbrand's rule-breaking personality to communicate the benefits of fast broadband and seamless technology more emotionally. Brand metrics improved and Virgin grew its share of net new broadband connections from 27.1% to 44.4%. Econometrics calculated that marketing drove £633m of incremental net value, based on the projected net revenues of customer acquisitions over three years.

Client comment

Bambos Neophytou, Head of Marketing Strategy, Virgin Media

Virgin has always been about emotive and disruptive storytelling, because we know that works. It's in the Virgin DNA. But to get to this point in Virgin Media's advertising, in a category riddled with competing product superiority claims (sometimes rational, sometimes not) was not quick or easy.

In some ways we were playing the category game, and not changing the rules, which is the Virgin way. Sticking to the rational claims was not allowing us to compete as effectively as we needed to, particularly against Sky.

We, with great agency support, evolved away from executing rational proposition claims to telling the world some bigger truths, through compelling, emotive and disruptive storytelling that made people feel our superiority. And as we can now prove, the emotional impact helped more people decide to choose Virgin Media.

Virgin Media

To read the full case study visit www.ipa.co.uk/ease or www.warc.com

Weetabix

A Rembrandt in the attic: Rediscovering the value of 'Have you had your Weetabix?'

By Tom Roach, BBH
Contributing authors: Tom Loughnan and Mike Campbell, Ebiquity
Credited companies: BBH; Ebiquity; Vizeum

Summary

Analysis established that the line, 'Have you had your Weetabix?', was the most powerful idea in the cereal category. But Weetabix, which was declining along with its market, hadn't used this line in years. Bringing it back in TV ads for children and adults, along with a packaging change, aimed to increase penetration and purchase frequency by making the brand more 'available' in shoppers' minds. Neuro testing showed the line was key to the ads' emotional impact. Econometrics quantified that Weetabix' marketing delivered £4.5m extra revenue in 2017 and its ROI tripled. The brand returned to growth, surpassing £150m of sales for the first time.

Client comment

Kevin Verbruggen, Head of Brand, Weetabix Food Company

Bringing back 'Have you had your Weetabix?' has made a significant, positive difference to our business: we've achieved our greatest-ever brand value; our growth has been profitable; and we have given our investors confidence in marketing's ability to deliver strong return on their investment.

As we've progressed on our journey to create our new campaign, we've learnt some lessons.

- Balancing head and heart: we have learned to make evidence-based decisions (using consumer-research methods not previously used) and balance those with creative work that captures the heart of consumers; strengthening brand recognition.
- The courage to go back: in a world where it's easier to embrace the new, it took courage for the team to return to previous campaigns, and refresh

our distinctive brand assets. The client–agency team worked together to build confidence through our businesses, that our path would lead to success.

Looking ahead, we continue our journey to change for the better:

- Patience with creating long-term consistency: as team members change, we all have a 'privileged duty' to manage the campaign, refreshing the distinctive brand assets whilst maintaining consistency. We've summarised what's worked so well; what could be even better; and developed a simple framework to brief and evaluate future work in the campaign.
- Extending the consistency: we are sharing our insights with all teams who touch the brand: other agencies within the marketing mix; other geographic markets.
- Applying the learning to our other brands: across Alpen, Ready Brek and Weetos, what other Rembrandts are in our attic? We have gained the confidence to totally change how we build our brands; to embrace distinctive brand assets; for the good of our consumers, the sanity of our agency partners, and the confidence of our investors.

Weetabix

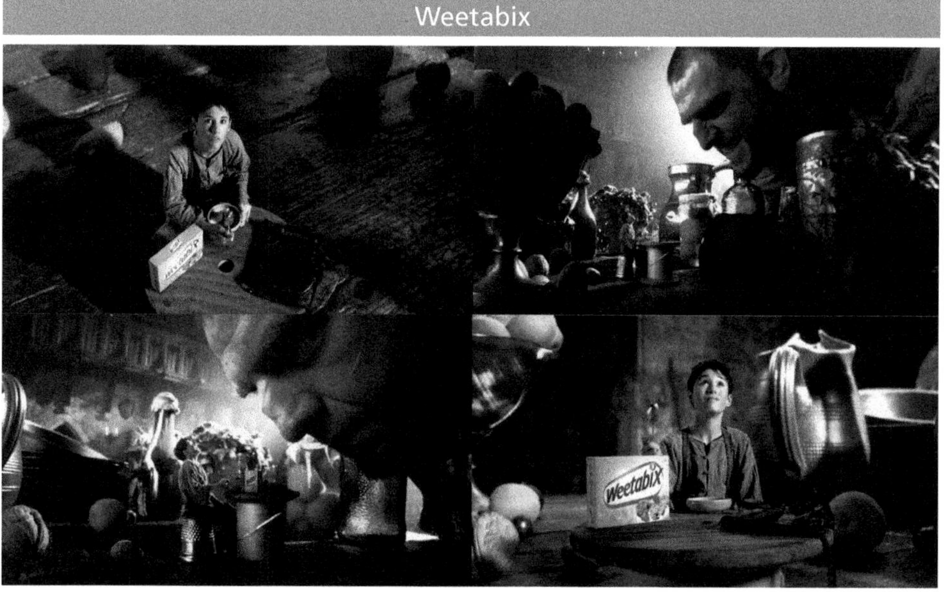

To read the full case study visit www.ipa.co.uk/ease or www.warc.com

Yorkshire Tea

Waking the sleep shoppers: A proper effective campaign for Yorkshire Tea

By Loz Horner, Lucky Generals

Contributing authors: Sam Drake, Goodstuff Communications; Emma Harries, The Nursery; Tom Loughnan, Ebiquity; Ben Newbury, Bettys & Taylors of Harrogate

Credited companies: Lucky Generals; Goodstuff Communications

Summary

Standard black tea is a habitual purchase where brand loyalty is three times the FMCG average, but in this shrinking market Yorkshire Tea needed to win consumers from other brands if it wanted to grow. The 'Where everything's done proper' strategy achieved this, waking up 'sleep shopping' tea buyers. Funny TV and online advertising featuring Yorkshire celebrities such as Sir Michael Parkinson and the Brownlees convinced consumers of Yorkshire Tea's quality. Drinkers switched and both sales and value share surged, making Yorkshire Tea Britain's second favourite tea brand. An estimated £2.81 profit was generated for every £1 invested.

Client comment

Dom Dwight, Marketing Director, Bettys & Taylors of Harrogate

The idea that Yorkshire Tea is 'A place where everything's done proper' isn't just the title of our creative campaign – it's an increasingly accurate description of our approach to measuring communications effectiveness.

Yorkshire Tea has always enjoyed strong advocacy from its loyal fans, but we've now come to recognise that in order to challenge for market leadership we need to substantially grow our customer base – and in a shrinking market that means winning over drinkers of other tea brands.

As a result, we are now tasking our agencies with generating and placing communications that can cut through the apathy of non-drinkers and communicate our quality credentials in a culturally famous way.

This in turn has influenced the way we measure success. We task our tracking partner – The Nursery – with regularly assessing whether we've engaged non-YT drinkers specifically and changed their views about the brand. Our internal analysts are now focused on the key metrics of penetration and value share, constantly examining IRI and Kantar data to make sure we are continuing to win new customers with each new burst of comms. We regularly check pricing and level of promotions to make sure we're not just buying market share temporarily but creating permanent increases in sales. And finally we conduct annual econometric analysis with Ebiquity to help us isolate the effect of communications versus all other variables.

The insights about how we can grow our brand gleaned from the 'Where everything's done proper' campaign are well understood within the business – all the way up to senior management – and will continue to help guide our decisions long beyond the lifespan of the initial creative executions.

Hopefully three or four years time we'll be back with another paper about how we have achieved our long-term goal of becoming the market leader!

Yorkshire Tea

To read the full case study visit www.ipa.co.uk/ease or www.warc.com

SECTION 4

Bronze winners

32Red

How marketing communications fuelled an online casino's hot streak

By Gerry Murray, M.i. Media

Contributing authors: Andy Brander, M.i. Media; Matt Booth, 32Red; Tony Regan, Work Research

Credited companies: M.i. Media; Cravens

Summary

Gambling business, 32Red, had an ambitious plan to double UK revenues to £100m in four years. It would involve adding more new customers in three years than it had in the previous twelve, as well as growing revenue per player. Via modelling and smart use of data, a new strategy identified high-value customers and delivered significant growth in new players through an effective mix of search, TV advertising, sports sponsorship, and content partnerships. The £100m target was reached one year early. 32Red was eventually sold for £176m, four times its valuation at the start of the growth plan.

Client comment

Matt Booth, Chief Commercial Officer, 32Red

Between 2014 and 2017, the 32Red business enjoyed exceptional growth, fuelled by our Accelerated Growth Plan (AGP). M.i. Media were central to helping formulate the plan; from modelling expected outcomes, to helping identify priority projects and then delivering an effective media strategy to bring about the aggressive targets which were required.

The impressive results delivered during this period, ultimately led to the sale of the business to Kindred in 2017. However, despite new ownership, we have not deviated from our longer-term ambition to make 32Red the number one UK casino operator and we continue to employ the same fundamentals which helped double business revenues over the previous three years. Our second Accelerated Growth Plan, is currently underway.

Given the role these channels played in our new customer acquisition growth, we continue to scale search and TV spends through M.i. Media, confident in the knowledge that our data-led approach means we have a solid grasp of when and where to find the right type of sustainable customers.

From an external perspective however, it is our continued commitment to sponsorship as an effective route to driving tangible impacts on brand growth, which is the most visible indicator of our confidence in our strategy. Our football, racing and boxing sponsorships helped see 32Red separate itself from our competitive set of casino-first operators from 2016–17 and we have now moved to widen this gap. On top of existing deals with Leeds United and Rangers, we have recently announced four new Championship front of shirt partnerships for the brand. In addition, we are beginning discussions with new partners to look at replicating the success of our Ant & Dec ITV partnership for 2019. With our new targets and plans in place, we look forward to AGP Part 2 delivering similarly impressive results.

32Red

To read the full case study visit www.ipa.co.uk/ease or www.warc.com

Aldi

Shop, Eat. Repeat. How a bold repositioning campaign restored Aldi to record growth

By Darren Hawkins and Jamie Peate, McCann Manchester

Contributing authors: Adam Zavalis, Aldi UK; Guy Beardsley, Universal McCann

Credited companies: McCann Manchester; Gain Theory; Universal McCann

Summary

Aldi's sales growth slowed from 19.3% in 2015 to 12.3% in 2016 – amounting to a £347m lost revenue opportunity. It needed shoppers to reappraise its brand and visit stores more frequently. Through the 'Everyday amazing' positioning, Aldi encouraged consumers to view its products as good enough for top-up purchases and not just a value-led big shop. The Brownlee brothers were chosen as accessible spokesmen in TV ads, online, social, in-store, and other channels. Following the activity, annual frequency of visits per customer rose from 19.1 to 19.8. Sales growth recovered to 19.1%, resulting in £1bn of incremental revenue, and 6.1% market share.

Client comment

Adam Zavalis, Marketing Director, Aldi UK

Getting more people to shop more often. It sounds simple enough, yet many lessons were learned.

Received wisdom says it's easier for a premium brand to sell more by discounting than for a value brand to add a premium. Yet we believe Aldi has shown that value brands can change their quality perception if they demonstrate the patience to change attitudes one step at a time. The key is not only to take small steps but to ensure each step is firmly consolidated before attempting the next.

We've shown that the tools of marketing continue to evolve, permitting targeting with ever-greater precision. However, identifying a behaviour these people could but currently weren't doing was the essential leap.

Creatively, the 'Everyday amazing' campaign had many strands, each tailored to work for the message and media in which they ran, yet together adding up to a cohesive whole.

This campaign proved the power of suggestion is alive and well. In targeting 'special' and 'top-up' occasions the communications presented appealing stimulus at the optimum time to elicit the desired response. We had to adapt as we listened to our customers and ensured our messaging continued to be relevant at all occasions.

Whilst Aldi may not yet be the leading player, it's already at the forefront of change in the UK grocery market. Demonstrating both agility and clarity of purpose, Aldi sticks to what it knows yet continues to question what it does, and find better ways to do so.

Not only did the campaign restore Aldi's growth rate to stellar levels, it propelled the brand to the status of a genuine contender and, in doing so, challenged the hegemony of the Big 4. In this respect, this paper should give heart to every 'David' that they can take on their industry's 'Goliaths'.

Aldi

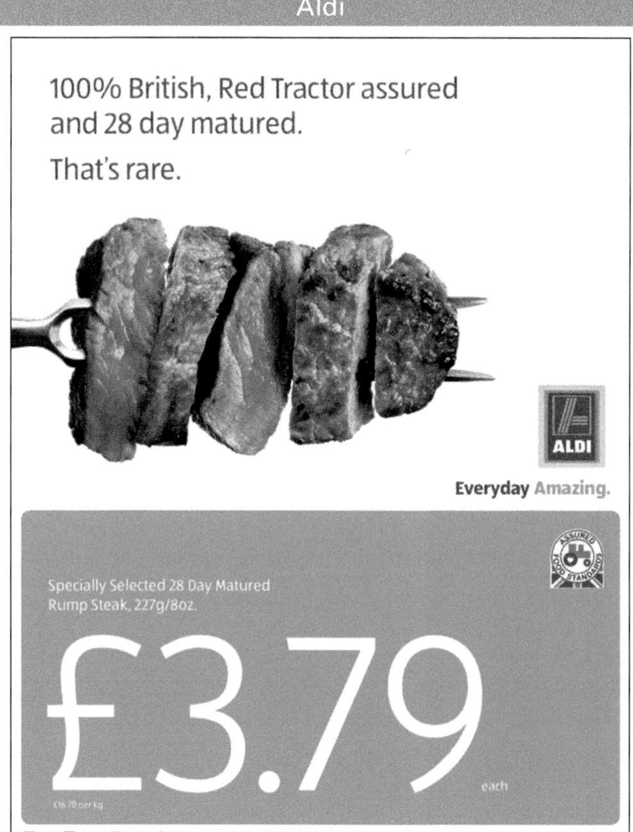

To read the full case study visit www.ipa.co.uk/ease or www.warc.com

Covonia

Rediscovering the power of Covonia

By Gemma Atkinson-Brown, Anna Donaghey and Edd Southerden, Bray Leino

Credited companies: Bray Leino; Austin Research; Dipsticks Research

Summary

The cough medicine, Covonia, had lost share to a new entrant. Without big budgets, the brand needed to gain more young customers and quickly start growing again to prevent it being dropped by retailers. Its strategy was to frame the product's strong taste as a challenge for people willing to 'fight' coughs. Provocative 'Ride the bull' creative used TV and social to build affinity with the brand's personality. Following the activity, penetration rose 12% above projection. The brand returned to market share growth. An estimated £4.45m of incremental revenue was generated and the brand's future was protected.

Client comment

Ed Round, Director of Consumer Marketing, Thornton & Ross

The 'feel the power' campaign is a proven effective creative campaign that set in motion the sequence of events that have helped to shape the future of the Covonia brand, delivering brilliant commercial creativity along the way. The research was pivotal to the success of this Covonia campaign – helping to define what was working and what wasn't and unlocked insights that changed the way we conducted many aspects of our marketing activity. The process we went through will now inform all future strategy, ensuring a clear way to measure success in everything we do.

Covonia

To read the full case study visit www.ipa.co.uk/ease or www.warc.com

BRONZE

IAG Cargo

IAG Cargo FWD.Rewards: Building strength in numbers

By Adam Blaynee and Jacob Lovewell, BBH

Contributing authors: Richard Madden and Matthew Shepherd, BBH

Credited companies: BBH; IAG Cargo

Summary

IAG Cargo was dangerously reliant on a few big global air cargo accounts. It needed to grow business from small and medium-sized enterprises (SMEs). Using audience insight into how small businesses make decisions, it developed an SME loyalty programme and a more human approach to customer relationship management. This case demonstrates that the company's loyalty scheme members spent 11% more than non-scheme customers. It estimates €14m incremental revenue was generated in 12 months on operating costs of €272,000. As a result of these changes, the gap between revenue from global accounts and SMEs was projected to halve in three years.

Client comment

Adam Chaudhri, Marketing Director, International Airlines Group

Before we started this project we were a sales-focused organisation with shoe leather delivering most of our growth by signing major global accounts (called freight forwarders).

But in order to remain a market leader and defend our share, we needed to grow our customer base. We approached BBH to assist with this. Having undertaken a detailed analysis of our customer base, we came to the conclusion that we were too focused – and dependent – on our largest customers, and we were neglecting a lucrative tier of small to medium enterprise (SME) customers.

Our challenge was clear: get SME accounts to send more cargo with us, and more frequently. The solution was clear: a loyalty programme.

In order to ensure that our work would be as effective as possible, we commissioned BBH to engage in a global primary research project, talking to over 25 SME accounts around the world. This qualitative research gave us invaluable insights that the business had never seen before – for the first time we were able to get a true feel for our customers beyond their spend and name.

Informed by the research, the resulting work of Forward.Rewards was able to refocus IAG Cargo towards customer centricity – becoming a key proof point or our new CEO's vision of customer focus.

Aside from the financial rewards our SME focus and new rewards tool has had some unexpected benefits. Our industry-leading reputation has strengthened in the minds of customers and trade press. Our sales force has been energised and invigorated, aided not only with a new service proposition to retain customers but to also better serve them thanks to the insight and data it produces.

Because of the proven effectiveness and tangible benefits of Forward.Rewards, we have commissioned BBH to produce a new loyalty programme targeting our Regional Key Account customers.

IAG Cargo

To read the full case study visit www.ipa.co.uk/ease or www.warc.com

BRONZE

National Art Pass

The art of effectiveness

By Joe Smith, MullenLowe London

Contributing authors: Jane Dorsett, MullenLowe Group; Luke Stockil, MullenLowe London

Credited companies: MullenLowe; Art Fund; the7stars

Summary

In early 2016, Art Fund was in a healthy position. Revenue had almost doubled in five years and the charity's membership had never been higher. This success changed expectations and a target of a 30% increase in new members was set. Underlying trends made this daunting. A new strategy was developed to highlight the emotions art can inspire. By adding films and podcasts to its media mix, the brand was able to tell richer stories. Following the change in approach, there was a record 44% increase in members, £12.5m of new revenue from members, and a profit return of approximately £2 for every £1 invested.

Client comment

Carolyn Young, Director of Marketing, Art Fund

This campaign has convinced us of the power of emotional advertising to influence attitudes and behaviour. We are now investing more in channels and formats that allow us to explore the emotional impact of a National Art Pass, not just its more rational features and benefits. Art Fund is committed to effectiveness and this paper is our third IPA Effectiveness paper in the past six years. We are always improving our understanding of how different parts of the marketing mix work and how we can measure their impact over time.

To read the full case study visit www.ipa.co.uk/ease or www.warc.com

Nissan Rogue

From also-ran to front-runner: How Nissan made Rogue a sales hero by making winter heroes of Canadian drivers

By Mark Tomblin, Juniper Park\TBWA
Credited company: Juniper Park\TBWA

Summary

Nissan Canada wanted its relaunched Rogue to improve on its predecessors with a dramatic and sustained rise in share of its category. It was especially important to persuade Canadians that the car performed well off-road in the country's challenging winters. The 'Winter heroes' strategy broke with automotive convention by using TV ads in the style of Hollywood superhero movies, with supporting digital and social, to distinguish the car from rival models. Between 2014 and 2017, Rogue's brand differentiation metrics strengthened. The car's category share almost doubled, with gains held over time. An estimated 64,927 extra Rogues were sold, worth nearly CAD1.9bn in incremental revenue. The net profit generated was calculated at $60.7m.

Client comment

Steve Rhind, Director, Marketing, Nissan Canada

At Nissan Canada, we have always seen creating distinctive and compelling communications as a crucial part of our marketing project – and the campaign for the new Rogue in 2014 was no different. Even so, we were very conscious that we had to make a real statement with the relaunch or risk the fast-growing crossover utility vehicle (CUV) market getting away from us.

To that end we created something not seen before – based on a uniquely Canadian take on winter as a driving environment, one that quickly resonated with people across the country and became famous well beyond its main audience of potential CUV buyers. And in the following years we built on that initial success, with direct and indirect business effects that made the period from 2014 through 2017 one of the most successful in the marque's history in Canada.

What we took from this was that advertising – brave, mould-breaking, famous advertising – can make a real difference to sales performance in the car market but that you need to truly commit to it, especially if you have well-entrenched (and well-funded) competitors, as we did. But if you do that, then you can create an almost unstoppable business momentum.

Nissan Rogue

To read the full case study visit www.ipa.co.uk/ease or www.warc.com

parodontax

Selling an oral care oxymoron: Toothpaste for gums

By Jeremy Poole, Grey London
Contributing author: Matt Gladstone, Grey London
Credited companies: Grey London; Edelman London; Geometry London; PHD

Summary

The challenge for GSK's small gum-care brand, parodontax (Corsodyl in the UK), was to convince consumers to switch from regular toothpastes to its products that also treated gum disease. Strategy developed the metaphor of a journey towards socially embarrassing disease symptoms, like bad breath and bleeding gums, unless people treated the condition early. A single creative idea was deployed internationally to maximise media spend and increase share of voice. TV ads brought impact, with other channels used to cut through with consumers in mornings or whilst travelling. Ads outperformed on awareness and likelihood to persuade disease non-treaters to buy the brand. Incremental sales of almost £50m were generated and paradontax became the world's fastest-growing multi-market toothpaste brand.

Client comment

Clare Brosnan, Global Marketing Director, GSK

When we set out to change global oral-care behaviour and step change sales for a specialist gum-care toothpaste against the tide of culture, the category and historical evidence, we were aware we faced a commercial trade-off.

On the one hand evidence from the IPA suggests we should invest every penny in boosting share of voice – the best predictor of market share. On the other hand global brand building best practice indicates there is value in adapting brand to the nuances of local culture. Yet with an increasingly complex communications landscape across more than 40 markets there is considerable cost attached.

As a small brand facing a huge challenge we made a commercial decision to trade off cultural effectiveness for global creative efficiency, in doing so freeing up extra investment for media.

But over the course of the campaign we've learnt we can have both; by unlocking a universal behavioural insight that transcends culture, we've created an approach that is both highly efficient and very effective. Our results have added to company learning about multi-market brand building and helped inform the way GSK consumer healthcare approach marketing globally.

We genuinely believe it's a model that can be applied beyond the category, providing smaller multi-market brands the ability to challenge the status quo.

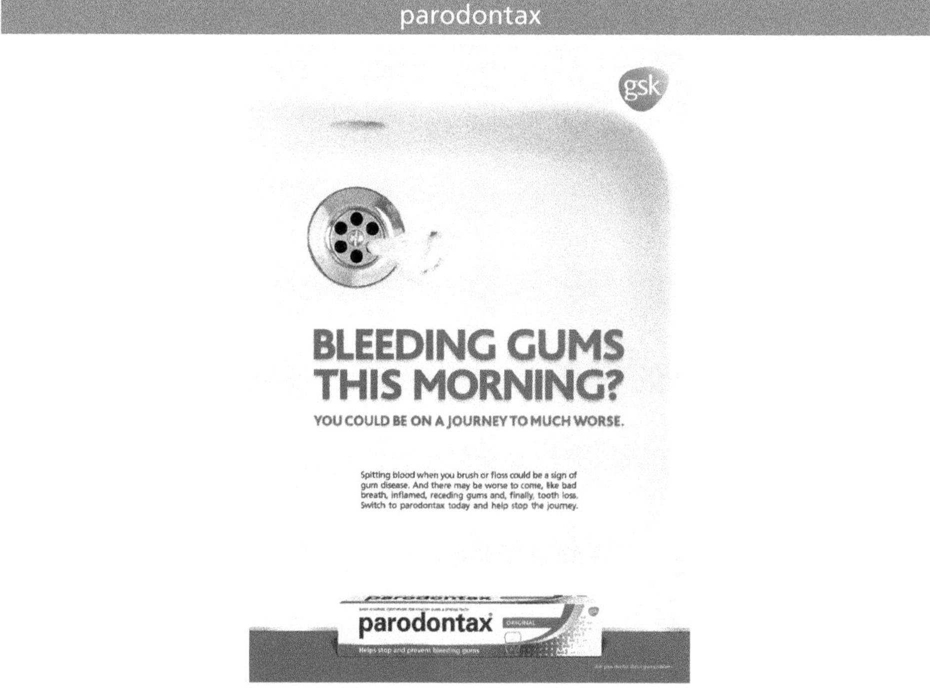

To read the full case study visit www.ipa.co.uk/ease or www.warc.com

BRONZE

Ribena

A case for the defence

By Gareth Price, J. Walter Thompson

Contributing authors: Eleanor Metcalf and Neil Godber, J. Walter Thompson

Credited company: J. Walter Thompson

Summary

Ribena was losing revenues and relevance as squash sales fell and new premium soft drinks entered the market. The brand needed to regain salience and attract new young adult buyers. It took a bold step to move away from its brand heritage to prioritise the ready-to-drink (RTD) and out-of-home drinks opportunities. Creative emphasised the experience of tasting Ribena with a quirky colour-filled world evoked via TV, outdoor, an app, social, and experiential. Awareness, relevance and taste metrics all grew. Ribena experienced 3.4% value growth despite an 11.1% decline in the RTD category. An estimated £24.1m of incremental revenue was generated and Ribena's master brand returned to growth from an 8.7% decline.

Client comment

Amie Farrell, Ribena Senior Brand Manager, Lucozade Ribena Suntory

The progress we've made – in just four years – in transforming the perception of Ribena as being a squash brand for children to being a soft drink for everyone, is outstanding. Ribena is now the market leader in the RTD category, with enviable rate of sale and distribution across our core RTD flavours.

Our commercial success is a case study for effective repositioning. RTD growth is being driven by the young adult audience that 'Ribenary' was designed to attract, and the increased perception of Ribena as a tasty, unique brand for me is everything we were hoping for when we briefed in 2014. What's more, our 'Ribenary' platform has conceived a truly distinctive multi-sensory world that we executed across the full consumer journey to gain stand out and drive conversion accordingly.

It's a world that has truly engaged our Lucozade Ribena Suntory business and our retail partners, and it's a credit to our multi-agency project team, who have worked to bring it to life in the most compelling way, across the most relevant channels, over the past few years.

Ribena

To read the full case study visit www.ipa.co.uk/ease or www.warc.com

BRONZE

Soothers

Any number of sore throats

By Katharina Vassar and Ryan O'Connell, Ogilvy Australia

Contributing authors: Toby Harrison, Hamish Hartley and Isabella Rago, Ogilvy Australia

Credited companies: Ogilvy Australia; Wavemaker Australia

Summary

Soothers – an Australian throat lozenge brand – had lost retail distribution which could translate into a projected 31% drop in market share. To stay in business, Soothers had to regain relevance quickly and reassert its place on retailers' shelves. Rather than fight in the market for cold sufferers, it repositioned as a purchase for mild, everyday sore throats. A light-hearted creative approach was delivered via channels including outdoor, digital, TV, radio, and weather apps. Following this activity, awareness and active consideration grew. Share loss was minimised from the expected 31% to 14%, and value increased in key retailers. Revenue stabilised in Year 1 and grew 20% in Year 2.

Client comment

Timothy Chung, Marketing Manager, Baking and Medicated, Nestlé Australia

This campaign has been a fantastic lesson for Nestlé and its agencies: a reminder to always keep an open mind about the future direction of a brand and its products. It's often said brands need to occasionally refresh in order to stay modern and contemporary. However such 'changes' usually involve fairly superficial alterations, like fonts, logos, art direction, creative idea, etc. Sometimes it's a little more drastic and involves a change to the brand position or strategy.

n this instance, it was major strategic business decision to change the occasion we had always played in, and the target audience we had always spoken to. It was the brand evolving, but in a completely different way than you'd normally expect, which was somewhat confronting but also exciting at the same time. With the benefit of hindsight – and success – those shifts may seem obvious or matter-of-fact now, but they were extremely significant ones at the time.

The lesson here is that when faced with extraordinary challenges, to think extraordinarily. Soothers knew it had to change if it was going to survive, and 'innovation' was the obvious answer. However, innovation doesn't always have to be product or technology led; it can simply be thinking innovatively.

The innovative thinking to explore a new occasion and new target audience enabled Soothers to fight on, and it will be a lesson we'll remember moving forward: if your product isn't as relevant to your audience or occasion anymore, don't change your product – maybe just change your audience or occasion instead!

Soothers

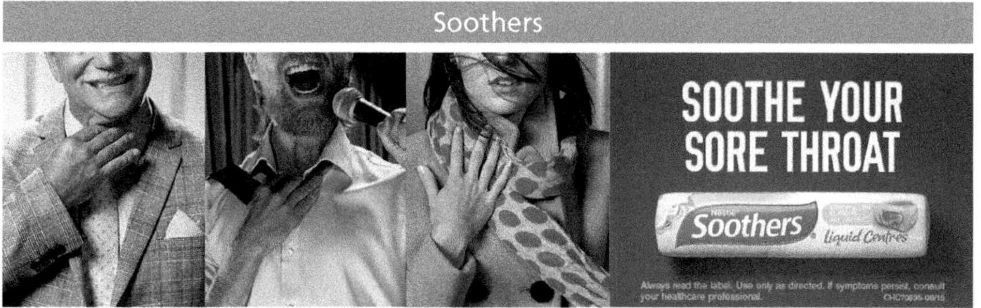

To read the full case study visit www.ipa.co.uk/ease or www.warc.com

U by Kotex

Let's move on

By Giorgia Butler and Heather Sheen, Ogilvy Australia

Contributing authors: Toby Harrison, Hamish Hartley and Isabella Rago, Ogilvy Australia

Credited company: Ogilvy Australia

Summary

With low growth for over a decade, U By Kotex, the Australian femcare brand, was under threat of deletion by retailers. By downplaying the importance of femcare brands in women's lives, U By Kotex created relevance and differentiated itself from competitors. Provocative TV ads were launched with social and online support, later amplified by outdoor. Key brand measures such as love and affinity experienced double-digit rises. An estimated AUD12.9m of incremental revenue was generated. After languishing in third position for years, the brand moved into leadership in 18 months.

Client comment

Margaret Cheung, Marketing Sector Lead, Adult and Feminine Care, Kimberly-Clark

The unprecedented response to 'Let's move on' has solidified Kimberly Clark's understanding of today's young Australian women. Having grown up in a world where they already feel empowered, young women don't want to be pandered to by brands that think they matter more than they do. We've always known the femcare category was due for a shake-up, and we've always been that brand that's willing to push boundaries. This campaign confirmed that U by Kotex is the right brand to lead the category forward.

Moving into 2018 and beyond, we've adopted a new tagline – 'Period or not, she can' – and also incorporated the "she" symbol into our logo, communications, social media and point of sale activity. In 2019 we intend to take this a step further by incorporating the 'she' symbol into our brand logo on our packaging as well. This is to show our commitment to women, placing them at the heart of our brand and everything we do.

We intend to ensure that no period, or stigma about a period, ever gets in the way of any woman's progress.

To read the full case study visit www.ipa.co.uk/ease or www.warc.com

Vype

Vype quality: A tale of two marketing models

By Donald Pirie and Florence Sharp, J. Walter Thompson
Credited company: J. Walter Thompson

Summary

The expansion of vaping brand Vype was hit by regulatory changes and negative media coverage of its category. To restart growth, the brand had to become more associated with trust and quality, whilst adding 20,000 customers. Strategy evolved from using bursts of media to build reach to always-on exposure of consumers to trust and quality messages over multiple channels. Touchpoints included pharmacies, editorial partnerships, blogs, and email. Brand metrics exceeded targets and over 33,000 net new customer additions were reported. Market share grew and Vype's retail sales increased by 18.6% in a declining sector. Short-term profit ROI was estimated at £1.04 for every £1 invested.

Client comment

Elly Criticou, Vapour Category Director, British American Tobacco

This campaign has shown us how an agile marketing and communications strategy can help maintain brand relevance in the face of challenges, and has reinforced the importance of staying true to the values of your brand in order to build deeper connections with consumers.

Vype

To read the full case study visit www.ipa.co.uk/ease or www.warc.com

How to access the IPA Effectiveness Awards Databank

The IPA Databank represents the most rigorous and comprehensive examination of marketing communications working in the marketplace, and in the world. Over the 38 years of the IPA's Effectiveness Awards competition, we have collected over 1,400 examples of best practice in advertising development and results across a wide spectrum of marketing sources and expenditures. Each example contains up to 4,000 words of text and is illustrated in full by market, research, sales and profit data.

IPA Effectiveness Awards Search Engine (EASE)

You can use the EASE search engine at www.ipa.co.uk/effectiveness/case-studies to interrogate over 1,400 detailed case studies from the IPA Databank. You can search the case studies by keywords and/or filter by any parameter from questions asked in the Effectiveness Awards Entry Questionnaire. EASE is free to use and is the first search engine on the web which allows you to do this. IPA members can also contact the Insight Centre directly where more complex searches can be commissioned and the results supplied by e-mail.

Purchasing IPA case studies

Member agencies can download case studies from www.ipa.co.uk/effectiveness/case-studies at a discounted rate of £25 per case study. Alternatively members can sign up to warc.com (see overleaf) at a beneficial IPA rate and can then download case studies as part of that subscription. Non IPA members can purchase case studies from the IPA website at £50 per copy.

Further information

For further information, please contact the Insight Centre at the IPA,
44 Belgrave Square, London SW1X 8QS
Telephone: +44 (0)20 7235 7020
Website: www.ipa.co.uk
Email: insight@ipa.co.uk

WARC.com

WARC is the official publisher of the IPA Effectiveness Awards' case histories. All IPA case studies are available at warc.com, alongside thousands of other case studies, articles and best practice guides, market intelligence and industry news and alerts, with material drawn from over 50 sources across the world.

WARC.com is relied upon by major creative and media agency networks, market research companies, media owners, multinational advertisers and business schools, to help tackle any marketing challenge.

IPA members can subscribe at a 10% discount. To find out more, request a trial at www.warc.com/demo.

www.ipa.co.uk/effectiveness

On our dedicated Awards website you can find out everything you need to know about the annual IPA Effectiveness Awards competition, including how to enter, and who's won what since 1980.

As well as viewing case study summaries and creative work, you'll also find a series of over 30 brand films from over three decades of the Awards including:

- The Economist
- Direct Line Group
- HSBC
- John Lewis
- Marmite
- Yorkshire Tea
- Cadbury Dairy Milk
- Walkers
- PG Tips

IPA Databank cases (A–Z)

* Denotes winning entries
** Denotes cases published in *Area Works* volumes 1–5
S Denotes cases published in *Scottish Advertising Works* volumes 1–4

NEW ENTRIES 2018
2018 32Red*
2018 Air Canada
2018 Aldi*
2018 Aldi*
2018 Argos
2018 Art Institute of Chicago*
2018 Audi UK*
2018 Baileys*
2018 Barclays*
2018 Bolia.com
2018 British Army*
2018 BT
2018 Budweiser
2018 Coeliac UK
2018 Covonia*
2018 David Sheldrick Wildlife Trust*
2018 DFS*
2018 Direct Line Group*
2018 Ella's Kitchen*
2018 Fleggaard
2018 Godiva
2018 Guinness*
2018 GWR
2018 Heineken*
2018 IAG Cargo*
2018 IKEA*
2018 John Lewis
2018 KFC
2018 Lidl*
2018 Lidl Ireland
2018 L'Oréal Paris True Match*
2018 Maltesers
2018 McDonald's
2018 National Art Pass*
2018 Nationwide Building Society*
2018 NCS
2018 Nissan Rogue*
2018 O_2
2018 parodontax*
2018 Philips
2018 Prospan*
2018 Pure Gym
2018 Purplebricks*
2018 Ribena*
2018 Sainsbury's
2018 SK-II*
2018 Skittles*
2018 SKODA
2018 Soothers*
2018 Sport England*
2018 Starbucks*
2018 St John Ambulance
2018 Suzuki*
2018 Tenderstem
2018 Tesco
2018 Tesco
2018 The AA*
2018 The Women's Foundation
2018 Time to Change
2018 Top Gear
2018 Translink
2018 U by Kotex*
2018 Virgin Media*
2018 Vodafone
2018 Vype*
2018 Weetabix*
2018 Wonderbly
2018 Xbox
2018 Yorkshire Tea*

NUMERICAL
2016 5 Gum
2018 32Red*
2003 55 Degrees North**
2006 100.4 smooth fm
2000 1001 Mousse*
2012 2011 Census

A
2004 AA Loans*
1982 Abbey Crunch
1990 Abbey National Building Society
1980 Abbey National Building Society Open Bondshares
1990 Aberlour Malt Whisky*
2004 Ackermans (SA)
2008 Acquisition Crime*

2006 Actimel*
2012 Admiral
1996 Adult Literacy*
2002 Aerogard Mosquito Repellent (Australia)
2016 Age UK
1999 Agri Plan Finance**
1986 AGS Home Improvements*
1988 AIDS
1994 AIDS*
1986 Air Call
2018 Air Canada
2010 Albert Bartlett Rooster Potatoes
2012 Aldi*
2018 Aldi*
2018 Aldi*
2014 Aldi UK & Ireland*
1990 Alex Lawrie Factors
1980 All Clear Shampoo*
1988 Alliance & Leicester Building Society*
1990 Alliance & Leicester Building Society*
1992 Alliance & Leicester Building Society*
1984 Alliance Building Society
2016 Allianz
1990 Allied Dunbar
1984 Allinson's Bread
1984 Alpen
1990 Alton Towers
2003 Alton Towers 'Air'**
1999 Alton Towers 'Oblivion'**
2010 Always
2012 American Golf
1990 Amnesty International*
1992 Amnesty International
2009 Ancestry.co.uk
1990 Anchor Aerosol Cream
1988 Anchor Butter
1994 Anchor Butter
2011 Anchor Squirty Cream
1986 Andrex*
1992 Andrex
1994 Andrex Ultra
1986 Anglia Building Society
1996 Anglian Water
2002 Anti-Drink Driving*
1997 Anti-Drink Driving (DoE Northern Ireland)**
2006 Anti-Drugs (Scottish Executive)
2007 Anti-Drugs (Scottish Executive)*
1990 Anti-NHS Reform Campaign (BMA)
1994 Anti-Smoking
2011 Aquafresh Kids*
2007 Aqua Optima*
2000 Archers*
2018 Argos
2006 Ariel
2018 Art Institute of Chicago*
2007 Army Cadet Force
1998 Army Recruitment*
2004 Army Recruitment*
2005 Arriva Buses*
1996 Arrol's 80
2012 Art Fund*
2016 Art Fund*
1994 Arthur's (cat food)
2005 ATS Euromaster*
1988 Audi
1990 Audi*
1998 Audi*
2006 Audi
2008 Audi*
2010 Audi*
2012 Audi*
2018 Audi UK*
1982 Austin Metro*
1980 Austin Mini*
1990 *Auto Express*
1996 Automobile Association*
2012 Aviva
2014 Aviva*
2006 Axe
2012 Axe
2016 AYGO

B

2002 B&Q
2004 B&Q
2012 B&Q
1988 Babycham
1988 Baby Fresh
1996 Bacardi Breezer
1998 Bacardi Breezer
1992 Baileys
2018 Baileys*
2002 Bakers Complete*
2005 Bakers Complete*
2006 Bakers Complete*
2005 Bank of Ireland
1988 Barbican
1990 Barbican Health & Fitness Centre
1992 Barclaycard
1996 Barclaycard*
2010 Barclaycard*
2010 Barclays*
2012 Barclays
2016 Barclays
2018 Barclays*
1998 Barclays Bank Current Account
2006 Barclays Global Investors (iShares)
2010 Barclays Wealth*
2002 Barnardo's*
2012 Barnardo's
1994 Batchelors
1998 Batchelors Supernoodles*
2005 Baxters Soup[S]
2008 BBC iplayer
2004 Beck's Bier (Australia)
2005 Belfast City

2001 Belfast Giants**
1998 Bell's Whisky
2002 Benadryl*
2006 Bendicks
2009 Benecol
1986 Benylin*
2010 Berocca*
2006 Bertolli
2007 Big Plus, The (Improving Scotland's adult literacy and numeracy)
1990 Billy Graham's Mission 89
1986 Birds Eye Alphabites*
1992 Birds Eye Country Club Cuisine
1994 Birds Eye Crispy Chicken
1982 Birds Eye Oven Crispy Cod Steaks in Batter*
1999 Birmingham, City of**
1988 Birmingham Executive Airways
2010 Bisto*
1990 Black Tower
1996 Blockbuster Video
2005 Blood Donation*
2014 Blue Dragon
1982 Blue Riband
2000 Bluewater*
2005 bmi baby
1994 BMW*
2004 BMW Films – The Hire*
1994 Boddington's*
2016 Bolia.com
2018 Bolia.com
2012 Bombay Sapphire
2008 Bonfire Night
2003 Bonjela**
1994 Book Club Associates
2012 Boots*
1998 Boots Advantage Card
1988 Boots Brand Medicines
2004 Bounty (paper towels)*
1994 Boursin
1998 Boursin
1986 Bovril
2000 Bowmore
2008 Bradesco
1986 Bradford & Bingley Building Society*
1990 Bradford & Bingley Building Society
2006 Branston Baked Beans*
1980 Braun Shavers
1982 Bread Advisory Council*
1982 Breville Toasted Sandwichmaker
2002 Britannia Building Society*
1994 British Airways*
1996 British Airways
2004 British Airways*
1984 British Airways Shuttle Service
2018 British Army*
1994 British Diabetic Association*
1980 British Film Institute*
2012 British Gas*
1994 British Gas Central Heating
1988 British Gas Flotation*
2006 British Heart Foundation* (Anti Smoking)
2009 British Heart Foundation – Watch Your Own Heart Attack*
2009 British Heart Foundation – Yoobot*
2014 British Heart Foundation – Stayin' Alive*
1988 British Nuclear Fuels
1988 British Rail Young Person's Railcard
1982 British Sugar Corporation
1980 British Turkey Federation
2005 Broadband for Scotland*S
2006 Brother
2007 Brother*
1992 BT
2008 BT
2009 BT
2010 BT
2012 BT*
2014 BT
2018 BT
2004 BT Broadband*
2005 BT Broadband (Consumer)
1994 BT Business
1996 BT Business*
2000 BT Business
1992 BT Call Waiting*
2002 BT Cellnet*
1986 BT Consumer*
2001 BT Internet (Northern Ireland)**
1999 BT Northern Ireland**
1986 BT Privatisation*
2002 BT Retail*
2007 BT Total Broadband
2010 BT Total Broadband*
1998 Bud Ice
1988 Budweiser
2002 Budweiser*
2018 Budweiser
2006 Bulldog 2004
1980 BUPA
2000 BUPA
2002 BUPA
2004 BUPA
2016 Butlins
1996 Butter Council

C
1996 Cable Television
2008 CABWISE (Transport for London)*
2008 Cadbury Dairy Milk
2010 Cadbury Dairy Milk*
2010 Cadbury Dairy Milk (India)
2012 Cadbury Dairy Milk (India)*
2008 Cadbury's Biscuits*
1994 Cadbury's Boost*
1992 Cadbury's Caramel

1984 Cadbury's Creme Eggs
1988 Cadbury's Creme Eggs
1998 Cadbury's Creme Eggs
1992 Cadbury's Crunchie
1984 Cadbury's Curly Wurly*
1980 Cadbury's Dairy Box
2004 Cadbury's Dream (SA)
1982 Cadbury's Flake
1984 Cadbury's Fudge*
1994 Cadbury's Highlights
1999 Cadbury's Jestives**
1990 Cadbury's Mini Eggs
1994 Cadbury's Roses*
1986 Cadbury's Wispa
1988 Café Hag
1996 Californian Raisins
2009 California Travel & Tourism Commission
2011 California Travel & Tourism Commission
1980 Campari*
1992 Campbell's Condensed Soup
1988 Campbell's Meatballs*
1994 Campbell's Soup
1996 Cancer Relief Macmillan Fund
2014 Cancer Research UK
2016 Cancer Research UK
1984 Canderel
2008 Capital One
1992 Caramac
1994 Car Crime Prevention
1997 Carex**
1998 Carex
2003 Carex**
2007 Carex*
2008 Carex
2010 Carling
1994 Carling Black Label
1996 Carling Black Label
1984 Carousel
1998 Carrick Jewellery
1986 Castlemaine XXXX*
2006 Cathedral City*
1992 Cellnet Callback
1988 CenterParcs
2004 Central London Congestion Charge*
1992 Central Television Licence Renewal
2010 Change4Life
2000 Channel 5
1990 Charlton Athletic Supporters Club*
1980 Cheese Information Service
1996 Cheltenham & Gloucester Building Society
1988 Chessington World of Adventures
1998 Chicago Town Pizza
2002 Chicago Town Pizza
2003 Chicago Town Pizza**
1994 Chicken Tonight
2000 Chicken Tonight Sizzle and Stir*
1992 Childhood Diseases Immunisation
2007 Child Protection on the Internet (Home Office)
1994 Child Road Safety
2004 Children's Hearings (Scottish Executive)*
2005 Children's Hearings System*
1990 Children's World
2001 Chiltern Railways (Clubman Service)**
1984 Chip Pan Fires Prevention*
1990 Choosy Catfood*
1992 Christian Aid
1998 Christian Aid*
2007 Churchill Square (Shopping Centre)
1994 CICA (Trainers)*
1992 Citroen Diesel Range
2010 Civic
1988 Clairol Nice 'n Easy
1988 Clarks Desert Boots*
1996 Classic Combination Catalogue
1994 Clerical Medical
1992 Clorets
1984 Clover
1988 Clover
2007 Coca-Cola Zero*
2018 Coeliac UK
1980 Cointreau
1998 Colgate Toothpaste*
1990 Colman's Wholegrain Mustard
2014 Colombian Ministry of Defence's Group of Humanitarian Attention to the Demobilised*
2010 Comfort Fabric Conditioner*
2010 Commonwealth Bank
2000 Confetti.co.uk*
2005 Consensia/Police Service of Northern Ireland
2000 Co-op*
1994 Cooperative Bank*
1996 Cooperative Bank
2004 Co-op Food Retail
2016 Coors Light*
1990 Copperhead Cider
2007 Cornwall Enterprise
2010 Corsodyl*
2016 Costa*
1982 Country Manor (Alcoholic Drink)
1986 Country Manor (Cakes)
2018 Covonia*
1984 Cow & Gate Babymeals*
1982 Cracottes*
2004 Cravendale (Milk)*
2000 Crime Prevention
2003 Crimestoppers Northern Ireland**
1980 Croft Original
1982 Croft Original
1990 Croft Original*
2011 CrossCountry Trains
1999 Crown Paint**

2002 Crown Paint
2003 Crown Paint**
2000 Crown Paints*
2004 Crown Paints
1990 Crown Solo*
1999 Crown Trade**
1999 Crown Wallcoverings**
1984 Cuprinol*
2014 Cuprinol*
2007 Curanail
1999 Cussons 1001 Mousse**
1986 Cyclamon*
2009 Cycling Safety*

D
2014 Dacia*
1996 Daewoo*
1982 *Daily Mail**
2002 Dairy Council (Milk)*
2000 Dairylea*
1992 Danish Bacon & Meat Council
2008 Danone Activia*
2012 Danone Activia*
1980 Danum Taps
2003 Data Protection Act
1990 Data Protection Registrar
2008 Dave*
2018 David Sheldrick Wildlife Trust*
1980 Day Nurse
1994 Daz
2006 Daz*
2008 De Beers*
1996 De Beers Diamonds*
2002 Debenhams
1980 Deep Clean*
2005 Deep River Rock – Win Big
2000 Degree
2003 Demand Broadband**
2011 Department for Transport
2012 Department for Transport*
2011 Depaul UK*
2006 Dero*
2008 Dero
1980 Dettol*
2014 Deutsche Telekom AG*
2009 Dextro Energy
2002 DfES Higher Education
2018 DFS*
2010 DH Hep (C)
1984 DHL Worldwide Carrier
2012 Digital UK*
1998 Direct Debit
2004 Direct Line*
2016 Direct Line*
2018 Direct Line Group*
1992 Direct Line Insurance*
2008 Direct Payment*
2007 Direct Payment (Department of Work and Pensions)*
2006 Disability Rights Commission
2003 District Policing Partnerships (Northern Ireland)
2016 Dixons
1990 Dog Registration
2006 Dogs Trust
2000 Domestic Abuse*
2016 Domino's
2002 Domino's Pizza*
2009 'Don't be a Cancer Chancer'*
2014 Doritos
2011 Doro Mobile Phones
2008 Dove*
2012 Dove*
2016 Dove*
2010 Dove Deodorant*
2012 Dove Hair*
2002 Dr Beckmann Rescue*
2001 Dr Beckmann Rescue Oven Cleaner**
1980 Dream Topping
1988 Drinking & Driving
1998 Drugs Education*
1994 Dunfermline Building Society
1980 Dunlop Floor Tiles
1990 Duracell Batteries
1980 Dynatron Music Suite

E
1988 E & P Loans*
2007 E4 Skins (Channel 4)*
2011 East Midlands Trains*
2004 East of England Development Agency (Broadband)*
2000 easyJet*
2014 easyJet*
2009 Eden and Blighty*
2014 EDF Energy*
1994 Edinburgh Club*
1990 Edinburgh Zoo
1980 Eggs Authority
2004 Electoral Commission (Northern Ireland)
2003 Electoral Commission/COI (DoE Northern Ireland)
1992 Electricity Privatisation
2009 Elephant Chakki Gold (ECG)
2009 Ella's Kitchen
2018 Ella's Kitchen*
1980 Ellerman Travel & Leisure
1996 Emergency Contraception
1986 EMI Virgin (records)*
1980 English Butter Marketing Company
1986 English Country Cottages
1992 Enterprise Initiative
2014 Enterprise Rent-A-Car
2003 Equality Commission of Northern Ireland
1992 Equity & Law
2007 Erskine*

2010 essential Waitrose*
1990 Eurax (Anti-Itch Cream)
2012 Europcar
1999 EuroSites (continental camping holidays)**
2004 Eurostar*
2006 Eurostar
2008 Eurostar
2016 Eurotunnel Le Shuttle*
1994 *Evening Standard* Classified Recruitment
2010 Everest*
2014 Everest*
2004 Evergood Coffee (Norway)
1984 Exbury Gardens
2014 Expedia*
2016 Extra Gum

F
2008 Fairy Liquid
2014 Fairy Liquid*
2008 Fairy Non Bio
1990 Family Credit
1998 Famous Grouse, The
2006 Famous Grouse, The*
1982 Farmer's Table Chicken
1996 Felix*
2000 Felix*
2006 Felix*
1980 Ferranti CETEC
1990 Fertilizer Manufacturers' Association
2011 Fiat*
1982 Fiat Auto UK
1980 Findus Crispy Pancakes
1988 Findus French Bread Pizza & Crispy Pancakes
1992 Findus Lasagne
1982 Fine Fare*
1984 Fine Fare
2005 Fire Authority for Northern Ireland*
2014 Fire Safety*
2016 First4Adoption*
2005 First Choice*
1996 First Choice Holidays
1998 first direct*
1992 first direct
2004 first direct
2011 first direct*
2014 first direct*
2016 first direct*
2005 First Great Western and First Great Western Link
2007 First Scotrail
2003 Fisherman's Friend**
2018 Flegaard
1992 Flowers & Plants Association
2002 Flowers & Plants Association
2003 Flymo Turbo Compact**
1994 Fona Dansk Elektrik
2014 Ford
2012 Ford C-Max
1980 Ford Fiesta
1998 Ford Galaxy*
1986 Ford Granada*
1982 Ford Model Range
2010 Forevermark*
1984 Foster's
2014 Foster's*
1995 Fox's Biscuits**
2005 Fox's Rocky*
2016 Foxtel
1998 French Connection
2000 Freschetta*
1999 Freschetta Pizzas**
2009 FRijj*
1982 Frish*
1996 Frizzell Insurance*
2002 Fruitopia
1994 Fruit-tella
2000 ft.com*
2005 Fybogel

G
1997 Gala Bingo Clubs**
1999 Gala Bingo Clubs**
2004 Garnier
2014 Garnier Ultralift*
1986 General Accident
2003 George Foreman Grills
2009 ghd*
2014 Gillette
1992 Gini (Schweppes)*
2010 Ginsters
2007 Glasgow City
1986 Glasgow's Lord Provost
1986 GLC's Anti 'Paving Bill' Campaign*
2000 Glenmorangie*S
1995 Glow-worm Boilers (Hepworth Heating)**
1996 Glow-worm Central Heating
2001 GoByCoach.com (National Express)**
2018 Godiva
1996 Gold Blend*
1984 Golden Wonder Instant Pot Snacks*
1988 Gold Spot
1980 Goodyear Grandprix
2012 Gordon's*
1984 Grant's Whisky
1988 Greene King IPA Bitter
1992 Green Giant
1990 Greenpeace
1988 Green Science
2014 Groupe Média TFO
2012 Gü*
2016 Guinness*
2018 Guinness*
1990 Guinness (Draught) in Cans
1996 *Guinness Book of Records*

2018 GWR

H
1992 Haagen-Dazs*
2009 Halifax*
2006 Halifax Bank of Scotland
1982 Halifax Building Society
1992 Halifax Building Society
1994 Halifax Building Society
2002 Halifax Building Society*
1980 Halifax Building Society Convertible Term Shares
1994 Halls Soothers*
1982 Hansa Lager
1999 Hartley's Jam**
2007 Hastings Hotels
2002 Hastings Hotels (Golfing Breaks)*
2001 Hastings Hotels (Golfing Breaks in Northern Ireland)**
2000 Health Education Board for Scotland
2012 Health Promotion Board Singapore*
2014 Health Promotion Board of Singapore
2014 Heart and Stroke Foundation of Canada*
2018 Heineken*
1994 Heineken Export
2010 Heinz*
2008 Heinz Beanz Snap Pots
1980 Heinz Coleslaw
1984 Hellman's Mayonnaise*
2016 Help to Buy
1982 Henri Winterman's Special Mild
1996 Hep30 (Building Products)
1990 Herta Frankfurters
1992 Herta Frankfurters
2008 Hewlett Packard Personal Systems Group (PSG)
2005 Hidden Treasures of Cumbria*
2005 Highlands and Islands Broadband Registration Campaign
2011 Hiscox
2007 Historic Scotland*
2006 HM Revenue & Customs (Self Assessment)*
1980 Hoechst
1992 Hofels Garlic Pearles
1984 Hofmeister*
1982 Home Protection (Products)
1984 Home Protection (Products)
2006 Homebase
2012 Homebase
1990 Honda
2004 Honda*
2016 Honda Odyssey
1986 Horlicks
1994 Horlicks
2006 Horlicks
1986 Hoverspeed
1992 Hovis
1996 Hovis
2002 Hovis*
2010 Hovis*
1990 H. Samuel
2010 HSBC*
1984 Hudson Payne & Iddiols
1996 Huggies Nappies
1994 Hush Puppies

I
2018 IAG Cargo*
2012 IBM*
1996 I Can't Believe It's Not Butter!*
2008 Iceland
1992 Iceland Frozen Foods
1980 ICI Chemicals
1984 ICI Dulux Natural Whites*
1992 IFAW*
2014 IKEA
2018 IKEA*
1998 Imodium
2001 Imperial Leather**
2002 Imperial Leather
2003 Imperial Leather**
2004 Imperial Leather*
1990 Imperial War Museum
1998 Impulse
1988 *Independent, the*
2006 ING Direct*
1998 Inland Revenue Self Assessment
2005 Inland Revenue Self Assessment*
1988 Insignia
1982 International Business Show 1981
1990 International Wool Secretariat
1992 IPA Society
2005 *Irish News, The*
2007 *Irish News, The* (Recruitment)
1992 Irn-Bru
2009 Irn-Bru
2007 Irn-Bru 32
2003 Ironbridge Gorge Museums**
1994 Israel Tourist Board
2010 It Doesn't Have to Happen
2014 ITV

J
2006 Jamie's School Dinners*
1998 Jammie Dodgers
1994 Jeep Cherokee
2001 Jeyes Bloo**
2002 Jeyes Bloo
1992 Jif
1999 JJB Super League**
1988 Job Clubs
2012 John Lewis*
2016 John Lewis*
2018 John Lewis
2016 John Lewis Insurance*
2002 John Smith's Ale

1982 John Smith's Bitter*
1994 John Smith's Bitter*
2006 Johnnie Walker
2008 Johnnie Walker*
2011 Johnnie Walker
1998 Johnson's Clean & Clear*
2011 Jungle Formula*
2010 Juvederm Ultra

K
1992 K Shoes*
1995 K Shoes (Springers)**
1992 Kaliber
1996 Kaliber
2010 Kärcher Pressure Washers*
2014 Kärcher Window Vac*
1990 Karvol
1980 Kays Catalogue
1992 Kellogg's All Bran*
1984 Kellogg's Bran Flakes*
1984 Kellogg's Coco Pops*
1994 Kellogg's Coco Pops
2000 Kellogg's Coco Pops*
1982 Kellogg's Cornflakes
1980 Kellogg's Frozen Waffles
2000 Kellogg's Nutri-Grain*
2002 Kellogg's Real Fruit Winders*
1980 Kellogg's Rice Krispies*
1982 Kellogg's Super Noodles*
2005 Kelso Racecourse
1998 Kenco
2010 Kenco
2016 Kenco*
1986 Kensington Palace*
2009 Key 103
1984 KFC
1998 KFC
2008 KFC*
2010 KFC*
2018 KFC
2000 KFC USA
1988 Kia Ora*
2014 KitKat
2004 Kiwi (SA)
1984 Kleenex Velvet
2007 Knife Crime (Police Service of Northern Ireland)
2009 Knorr*
1990 Knorr Stock Cubes*
2010 Kodak*
1988 Kodak Colour Print Film
1984 Kraft Dairylea*
1994 Kraft Dairylea
1980 Krona Margarine*
1986 Kronenbourg 1664
2006 Kwik-Fit*

L
1990 Lada
2012 Ladbrokes
2004 Lamb (Meat & Livestock Australia)*
2010 Lamb (Meat & Livestock Australia)
2005 Lancashire Short Breaks*
1990 Lanson Champagne*
2012 LateRooms.com
2005 Lay Magistrates
2014 Lay's Global
2014 Lay's US
1980 Lea & Perrin's Worcestershire Sauce
1990 Lea & Perrin's Worcestershire Sauce*
2008 Learndirect*
1992 Le Creuset
1982 Le Crunch
1988 Leeds Permanent Building Society
1988 Lego
2004 Lego Bionicle
2014 The LEGO Movie
1984 Leicester Building Society
1996 Lenor
1986 Le Piat D'or
1990 Le Piat D'or
1996 Le Shuttle
1988 Levi's 501s*
2002 Levi Strauss Engineered Jeans (Japan)
1980 Levi Strauss UK
1992 Levi Strauss UK*
2014 Lidl
2018 Lidl*
2018 Lidl Ireland
2016 Lidl UK*
2014 Lifebuoy
2005 Lift Off
2012 Lights by TENA
1990 Lil-lets*
1996 Lil-lets
1996 Lilt
1992 Limelite*
1980 Limmits
1999 Lincoln Financial Group**
2000 Lincoln Insurance
2000 Lincoln USA
1980 Lion Bar
1988 Liquorice Allsorts
1992 Liquorice Allsorts
1980 Listerine
1988 Listerine*
2004 Listerine
1998 Littlewoods Pools
2011 Liverpool ONE
1984 Lloyds Bank*
1992 Lloyds Bank
2010 Lloyds TSB*
1999 Local Enterprise Development Unit (NI)**
1990 London Buses Driver Recruitment
2009 London Business School*
1982 London Docklands
1984 London Docklands*

1990 London Philharmonic
1992 London Transport Fare Evasion
1986 London Weekend Television
2016 L'Oréal Paris Age Perfect*
2018 L'Oréal Paris True Match*
1980 Lucas Aerospace*
1996 Lucky Lottery
1980 Lucozade*
1992 Lucozade
2008 Lucozade Sport*
1988 Lurpak
2000 Lurpak*
2008 Lurpak
2014 Lux*
2012 LV=*
2002 Lynx*
2011 Lynx*
2004 Lynx Pulse*
1994 Lyon's Maid Fab
1988 Lyon's Maid Favourite Centres

M

2014 Maaza
2004 M&G
1988 Maclaren Prams
2016 Macmillan Cancer Support*
2003 Magna Science Adventure Centre**
2007 Magners Irish Cider*
1999 Magnet Kitchens**
2004 Magnum
2012 Magnum Gold?!*
2009 Make Poverty History
2006 Make Poverty History (Comic Relief)
1990 Malibu
2018 Maltesers
2006 Manchester City*
1999 Manchester City Centre**
2001 Manchester City Centre**
2002 *Manchester Evening News* (Job Section)*
2003 *Manchester Evening News* (Job Section)**
2003 ManchesterIMAX**
1982 Manger's Sugar Soap*
1988 Manpower Services Commission
2011 Marie Curie Cancer Care*
2016 M&S Food
1994 Marks & Spencer
2006 Marks & Spencer*
2004 Marks & Spencer Lingerie*
1998 Marmite*
2002 Marmite*
2008 Marmite*
2011 Marmite XO
1998 Marmoleum
1988 Marshall Cavendish Discovery
1994 Marston Pedigree*
2001 Maryland Cookies**
2006 Mastercard
2008 Mastercard
2016 Mastercard
2016 Mattessons*
2014 Mattessons Fridge Raiders*
2009 Maximuscle*
1986 Mazda*
1986 Mazola*
2008 McCain
2012 McCain
2014 McCain Ready Baked Jackets*
2011 McCain Wedges*
1996 McDonald's
1998 McDonald's
2010 McDonald's
2012 McDonald's*
2018 McDonald's
2008 McDonald's Eurosaver
2014 McDonald's Sponsorship London 2012
2014 McDonald's Virtual Coins*
1980 McDougall's Saucy Sponge
1988 Mcpherson's Paints
1990 Mcpherson's Paints
2016 McVitie's*
2000 McVitie's Jaffa Cakes
2004 McVitie's Jaffa Cakes
2010 Medicine Waste
2012 Mercedes-Benz
2014 Mercedes-Benz*
2012 Mercedes-Benz (Germany)
1992 Mercury Communications
2005 Metrication
1988 Metropolitan Police Recruitment*
2012 Metropolitan Police Service*
2003 Microbake
1988 Midland Bank
1990 Midland Bank
1992 Miele
1988 Miller Lite*
2014 MILO*
2014 MINI UK
2014 Missing People
2000 Moneyextra*
2010 Monopoly
2006 Monopoly Here & Now*
2006 More4*
1999 Morrisons**
2008 Morrisons*
2009 Morrisons*
2010 Morrisons
1988 Mortgage Corporation*
2008 Motorola*
2012 Motorola
2002 Mr Kipling*
1984 Mr Muscle
2010 MTR*
1995 Müller Fruit Corner**
1994 Multiple Sclerosis Society
2010 Munch Bunch
1996 Murphy's Irish Stout*

1992 Oxo*
1998 Oxo Lamb Cubes

P
2007 P&O Cruises
2016 P&O Cruises
2007 P&O Ferries
2014 Paddy Power
1986 Paignton Zoo
2000 Pampers South Africa*
2011 Panasonic Toughbook
2014 Pancreatic Cancer Action*
1988 Paracodol*
2018 parodontax*
1984 Paul Masson California Carafes
2005 Payment Modernisation Programme
1982 Pedal Cycle Casualties*
2014 Pedigree
1998 Penguin
1994 Peperami*
2011 PepsiCo Walkers*
1994 Pepsi Max
2016 Pepsi Max*
1986 Perrier
1990 Perrier
2000 Persil*
2006 Petits Filous
2014 Petplan
1990 PG Tips*
2000 PG Tips*
1996 Philadelphia*
1994 Philadelphia
1988 Phileas Fogg
1988 Phileas Fogg
1994 Phileas Fogg
2010 Philips
2018 Philips
1980 Philips Cooktronic
1980 Philips Video
2003 Phoenix Natural Gas
2003 Phones 4u**
1998 Physical Activity Campaign (HEB Scotland)
2009 Pilgrims Choice
2007 Pilkington Activ*
1990 Pilkington Glass
1992 Pilsner
1986 Pink Lady
1984 Pirelli
1986 Pirelli
1990 Pirelli
1996 Pirelli
1994 Pizza Hut
1996 Pizza Hut
1998 Pizza Hut*
1990 Plax
2010 Plenty
1980 Plessey Communications & DataSystems
2016 Plusnet*
1998 Polaroid*
2007 Police Community Support Officers
1994 Police Federation of England and Wales
2004 Police Officer Recruitment (Hertfordshire Constabulary)*
2002 Police Recruitment*
2002 Police Recruitment (Could You?)
2002 Police Recruitment Northern Ireland
2001 Police Service of Northern Ireland**
2007 Police Service of Northern Ireland (Recruitment)
1996 Polo Mints
1984 Polyfoam
2007 Pomegreat
1986 *Portsmouth News*
2004 Postbank (Post Office SA)
2002 Post Office*
2012 Post Office
1980 Post Office Mis-sorts
1986 Post Office Special Issue Stamps
1996 Potato Marketing Board
1998 Pot Noodle
2008 Power of One
2014 PowerPacq
2014 Premier Inn*
1984 Presto
1980 Pretty Polly*
2010 Pringles
2012 Pringles
2006 Privilege Insurance
2011 Program of Humanitarian Attention to the Demobilised*
2005 Progressive Building Society – Financial Services
2011 Promote Iceland*
2018 Prospan*
1992 Prudential
2008 Public Awareness Campaign for Helmet Wearing*
2014 Public Health England*
2018 Pure Gym
2018 Purplebricks*

Q
1984 QE2
2003 Qjump.co.uk
1988 Quaker Harvest Chewy Bars*
1982 Qualcast Concorde Lawn Mower*
2014 QualitySolicitors
1986 Quatro
1986 Quickstart
1996 Quorn Burgers

R
1982 Racal Redec Cadet
1990 Radion Automatic*
1990 Radio Rentals
1994 Radio Rentals

2008 Radley*
1980 RAF Recruitment*
1996 RAF Recruitment
2004 Rainbow (evaporated milk)*
1994 Range Rover
2014 Range Rover Sport
2000 Reading and Literacy*
1992 Real McCoys
2000 Rear Seatbelts*
1984 Red Meat Consumption
1998 Red Meat Market*
1988 Red Mountain*
1996 Reebok*
1990 Reliant Metrocabs
1994 Remegel
2010 Remember a Charity*
2012 Remember a Charity
1998 Renault
1986 Renault 5
1990 Renault 19*
1992 Renault Clio*
1996 Renault Clio*
1984 Renault Trafic & Master
2009 Resolva 24H*
2005 ResponsibleTravel.Com
2010 Retail OTP
1982 Ribena*
1996 Ribena
2018 Ribena*
2001 rightmove.co.uk**
2001 right to read (literacy charity)**
2002 Rimmel*
1986 Rimmel Cosmetics
2008 Road Safety*
2009 Road Safety
2006 Road Safety – Anti-Drink Driving (DoE Northern Ireland)
1999 Road Safety (DoE Northern Ireland)**
2003 Road Safety (DoE Northern Ireland)
2004 Road Safety (DoE Northern Ireland)*
2007 Road Safety (Republic of Ireland Road Safety Authority/DoE Northern Ireland)
2006 Road Safety – THINK! (Department of Transport)
2010 Robinsons Fruit Shoot*
1996 Rocky (Fox's Biscuits)
1988 Rolls-Royce Privatisation*
2004 Roundup
2005 Roundup Weedkiller*
1988 Rover 200
1982 Rowenta
1990 Rowntree's Fruit Gums
1992 Royal Bank of Scotland
1986 Royal College of Nursing
2002 Royal Mail
1986 Royal Mail Business Economy
1997 Royal Mint**
1990 Royal National Institute for the Deaf
1996 RSPCA
2011 Rubicon
2016 Rugby World Cup 2015
1988 Rumbelows
2012 Ryvita
2006 Ryvita Minis
2007 Ryvita Minis*

S

2004 s1jobs
1994 S4C
1988 Saab*
2004 Safer Travel at Night (GLA)*
1996 Safeway
2002 Sainsbury's* (Jamie Oliver)
2002 Sainsbury's* (Promotion)
2006 Sainsbury's
2008 Sainsbury's*
2010 Sainsbury's*
2012 Sainsbury's
2014 Sainsbury's*
2016 Sainsbury's*
2018 Sainsbury's
2008 Sainsbury's magazine
2001 Salford University**
2003 Salvation Army, the**
2014 Salvation Army, the*
1996 Samaritans
1980 Sanatogen
1986 Sanatogen
1988 Sandplate*
2016 Santander*
1986 Sapur (Carpet Cleaner)
1992 Save the Children*
2016 Save the Children*
1988 Schering Greene Science
2001 Scholl Flight Socks**
2000 scoot.com*
1980 Scotcade
2005 Scotch Beef [S]
1984 Scotch Video Cassettes
1992 Scotrail
1992 Scottish Amicable*
2008 Scottish Government: Teacher Recruitment
2005 Scottish Power*
1998 Scottish Prison Service
2005 Scruffs Hard Wear
2002 Seafish Industry Authority
2006 Seeds of Change (Masterfoods)
1980 Seiko
2010 Self Assessment*
1992 Sellafield Visitors Centre
2001 Senokot**
2002 Senokot
2005 Senokot
2016 Sensodyne*
2014 Sensodyne Pronamel*
1999 Seven Seas Cod Liver Oil**

1980 Shake 'n' Vac
1984 Shakers Cocktails*
2012 Shangri-La Hotels & Resorts*
2009 Shell
2002 Shell Optimax
1999 Shippam's Spread**
1980 Shloer*
1986 Shredded Wheat
1990 Silent Night Beds*
2005 Silent Night My First Bed*S
2009 Simple
2016 Sixt*
2018 SK-II*
2018 Skittles*
2018 SKODA
2002 Skoda*
1982 Skol
1992 Skol
2008 Sky
2012 Sky
1999 Slazenger (cricket bats)**
2009 Slendertone*
1980 Slumberdown Quilts
2016 Slurpee Flavour Fest
2016 Slurpee Xpandinator
1990 Smarties
1980 Smirnoff Vodka
1980 Smith's Monster Munch
1982 Smith's Square Crisps
1992 Smith's Tudor Specials
1992 Smoke Alarms
1994 Smoke Alarms*
2011 Smokefree North West
2012 Snickers*
2016 Snickers*
1996 So ...? (Fragrance)
2006 Sobieski (Vodka)
1986 Soft & Gentle
1996 Soldier Recruitment
1995 Solpadol**
1994 Solvent Abuse
1996 Solvite
1999 Solvite**
2000 Solvite*
1988 Sony
1992 Sony
2006 Sony BRAVIA
1992 Sony Camcorders
2006 Sony DVD Handycam
2006 Sony Ericsson K750i/W800i*
2004 Sony Ericsson T610*
2018 Soothers*
2016 SPC #MyFamilyCan
2016 SPC #SPCSunday
2014 Specsavers*
2016 Speeding (New Zealand Transport Agency)*
2016 Spies Travel*
2018 Sport England*
1996 Springers by K (Shoes)
2006 Sprite
2014 Sprite
2004 Standard Bank (SA)
2005 Standard LifeS
2009 Stanley Tools UK
2000 Star Alliance
2018 Starbucks*
1992 Stella Artois*
1996 Stella Artois*
1998 Stella Artois
2000 Stella Artois*
2002 Stella Artois*
1984 St Ivel Gold*
2018 St John Ambulance
2016 Stoptober*
2002 Strathclyde Police
1994 Strepsils*
2010 Stroke Awareness*
1990 Strongbow
2009 Strongbow
2007 Subway*
1982 Summers the Plumbers
1980 Sunblest Sunbran
1990 Supasnaps
2014 Supermalt
2000 Surf*
2010 Surf*
2018 Suzuki*
1980 Swan Vestas*
1984 SWEB Security Systems
1992 Swinton Insurance
2009 Swinton Taxi Division*
1996 Switch
1998 Switch
2003 Syndol (painkillers)**

T

2012 Ta Chong Bank*
2012 Talk Talk
1992 Tandon Computers
1990 Tango
2010 Tango
1986 TCP*
2010 TDA Teacher Recruitment*
2006 Teacher Recruitment*
2001 Teacher Training Agency**
2003 Teacher Training Agency**
1986 Teletext
2018 Tenderstem
2016 Tennent's Lager
1986 Territorial Army Recruitment
2000 Terry's Chocolate Orange*
1980 Tesco
2000 Tesco*
2002 Tesco*
2018 Tesco
2018 Tesco
2007 Tesco (Green Clubcard)

1990 Tetley Tea Bags
2018 The AA*
2010 The Army
2016 The Conservative Party*
2010 The Co-operative Food*
1992 *The Economist**
2002 *The Economist**
2011 *The Economist**
2016 *The Economist**
1982 *The Guardian*
2004 *The Guardian**
2016 *The Guardian* and *The Observer**
2010 The Happy Egg Co.
2012 The National Lottery*
2004 The Number 118 118*
2016 The Philippines
2016 The Royal British Legion*
2010 thetrainline.com*
2018 The Women's Foundation
2010 THINK!*
2016 THINK!
1984 Thomas Cook
2008 Thomas Cook
2016 Three*
1990 Tia Maria
1992 Tia Maria
2014 Tide Naturals
1990 *Times, The*
2018 Time to Change
1994 Tizer
2005 Tizer*
1980 Tjaereborg Rejser*
2010 T-Mobile*
2010 Tobacco Control*
2004 Tobacco Control (DH)*
1980 Tolly's Original
2002 Tommy's: The Baby Charity*
2018 Top Gear
1984 Torbay Tourist Board*
1986 Toshiba*
2012 TOTAL 0% Greek Yoghurt
1986 Touche Remnant Unit Trusts
1992 Tower of London
2004 Toyota Corolla
2014 Toyota Daihatsu
1996 Toyota RAV4
2008 Toyota Yaris
2018 Translink
2003 Translink CityBus
2007 Translink Metro
2003 Translink Smartlink
1982 Trans World Airlines
2016 Travel & Surf
2005 Travelocity.co.uk*
2006 Travelocity.co.uk*
1984 Tri-ac (Skincare)
2009 Tribute Ale
2008 Trident*
2007 Trident (Metropolitan Police)*
2004 Tritace
1980 Triumph Dolomite
2006 Tropicana Pure Premium*
1986 TSB*
1988 TSB*
1994 TSB
2016 TSB
2004 TUI (Germany)
1982 Turkish Delight*
1986 TV Licence Evasion*
2006 TV Licensing*
2012 TV Licensing
2014 Twix
2000 Twix Denmark

U

2018 U by Kotex*
1984 UK Canned Salmon
2016 UK Government*
1986 Umbongo Tropical Juice Drink
2003 UniBond
1999 UniBond No More Nails**
2005 UniBond Sealant Range*
2005 University of Dundee*S
1998 UPS
2003 UTV Internet
1990 Uvistat*

V

1988 Varilux lenses
1994 Vauxhall Astra
1990 Vauxhall Cavalier
1996 Vauxhall Cavalier
1999 Vauxhall Network Q**
1996 Vegetarian Society
2006 Vehicle Crime Prevention (The Home Office)*
2004 Vehicle Crime Reduction (The Home Office)
2012 Velvet Toilet Tissue*
2001 Vimto**
1986 Virgin Atlantic
2008 Virgin Atlantic*
2010 Virgin Atlantic*
2012 Virgin Atlantic*
2012 Virgin Media
2018 Virgin Media*
2004 Virgin Mobile*
2004 Virgin Mobile Australia*
2004 Virgin Trains*
2006 Virgin Trains*
2010 Virgin Trains
2012 Virgin Trains*
2014 Virgin Trains
1994 Visa
2006 Visit London
2012 VO5 Extreme Style*
1986 Vodafone
2016 Vodafone

2018 Vodafone
1998 Volkswagen*
2002 Volkswagen (Brand)*
2016 Volkswagen Commercial Vehicles UK*
2004 Volkswagen Diesel*
2006 Volkswagen Golf*
2006 Volkswagen Golf GTI Mk5*
2002 Volkswagen Passat*
2012 Volkswagen Passat
2016 Volvo Cars*
2008 V-Power
1992 VW Golf*
2016 Vype
2018 Vype*

W
1980 Waistline
2002 Waitrose*
2007 Waitrose*
2008 Waitrose*
2012 Waitrose*
2003 Wake Up To Waste (Northern Ireland)**
1992 Wales Tourist Board
2010 Walkers
2012 Walkers*
1996 Walkers Crisps*
2002 Walkers Crisps*
2016 Wall's*
1980 Wall's Cornetto
2006 Wall's Sausages
1984 Wall's Viennetta*
1996 Wall's Viennetta
1998 Wallis
1984 Walnut Whips
2003 Warburtons
1990 Warburtons Bread*
2005 Waste Awareness
1984 Websters Yorkshire Bitter
2004 Weetabix*
2007 Weetabix*
2018 Weetabix*
1988 Weight Watchers Slimming Clubs
2002 West End Quay
2005 West Midlands Hub of Museums*
1990 Westwood Tractors
2012 Which?*
1992 Whipsnade Wild Animal Park*
1980 Whitegate's Estate Agents*
2010 Wickes
1990 Wilson's Ultra Golf Balls
1988 Winalot Prime*
2010 Wispa*
2006 Women's Aid*
2018 Wonderbly
1994 Wonderbra*

X
2018 Xbox

Y
2000 Yellow Pages Norway
1980 Yeoman Pie Fillings
1980 Yorkie
1982 Yorkshire Bank
2002 Yorkshire Forward/Yorkshire Tourist Board
2012 Yorkshire Tea*
2018 Yorkshire Tea*
2008 Yorkshire Tourist Board – Make Yorkshire Yours

Z
1984 Zanussi*
1994 Zovirax

Index